# Teaching as Worship

# Teaching as Worship

## The Pentecostal Expository Sermon

JEFF McAFFEE

*Foreword by Steve Hall*
*Introduction by Mark L. Williams*

WIPF & STOCK · Eugene, Oregon

TEACHING AS WORSHIP
The Pentecostal Expository Sermon



Wipf & Stock
An Imprint of Wipf and Stock Publishers
199 W. 8th Ave., Suite 3
Eugene, OR 97401

www.wipfandstock.com

PAPERBACK ISBN: 978-1-6667-7956-1
HARDCOVER ISBN: 978-1-6667-7957-8
EBOOK ISBN: 978-1-6667-7958-5

VERSION NUMBER 05/05/26

For the Spirit-filled Bible teachers.
This book is for you.

# Contents

# Foreword

For everyone who calls on the name of the Lord will be saved. How then will they call on him in whom they have not believed? And how are they to believe in him of whom they have never heard? And how are they to hear without someone preaching?

—Rom 10:13–14 ESV

It is my subjective and objective opinion that, in this cultural moment (the first third of the second millennium), the Pentecostal Christian faith tradition generally offers the most robust evangelistic message. Primarily because it seems the current generations are not looking for a faith of information to be known and mined, but for a faith of transformation that can be felt and lived. Specifically, Pentecostal preaching, as public speaking, has the most robust evangelistic potential in this cultural moment. Our audience is not the audience of John Wesley, William Seymour, Ray Hughes, or Paul L. Walker. Therefore, our audience doesn't have ears to hear as previous audiences did. Our audience is ours and has ears acculturated to hear in a way unique to them. Pentecostal preachers in this cultural moment need to tune their minds and mouths to the ears and hearts of their hearers. For such a time as this, Dr. McAffee offers our minds and mouths a cultural tune-up.

This professional preacher tune-up is critical in this cultural moment because, as it has always been in every cultural moment since the advent of Christianity, preaching is the most important form of public speaking in the universe. Consequently, it is incumbent on the contemporary Pentecostal preacher to be the best they can be at delivering the most important message of all time.

Each year, the president of the United States delivers the State of the Union address. Yet, in the context of human history and the universe at large, presidential public speaking pales in comparison to what any Christian preacher does each Sunday. Preacher, and particularly the Pentecostal preacher, you need to level up your game.

> For we are not fighting against flesh-and-blood enemies, but against evil rulers and authorities of the unseen world, against mighty powers in this dark world, and against evil spirits in the heavenly places. (Eph 6:12 NLT)

Every time a preacher preaches, they are preaching to a seen and unseen audience. Typically, a preacher readily recognizes that the seen audience of human beings may be inspired, convicted, encouraged, educated, and loved by the preaching. However, not many preachers, even Pentecostal preachers, readily recognize that the unseen audience of devils and demons will be incited, routed, offended, revealed, and angered. This book will raise awareness of the unseen audience among each preacher who reads it. Furthermore, this book will equip them to deliver orthodox, morally conservative, and Spirit-filled punches as a knockout blow in the spiritual warfare ring of the pulpit. Dr. McAffee is a boxing trainer of sorts for the Pentecostal preacher. He will show you how to preach like a butterfly and sting like a bee, in the words of World Champion boxer Muhammad Ali.[1]

Preaching is serious work. All work of the professional ministry is eternal in nature, but the proclamation of the gospel is a distinctive feature of this unique and dangerous vocation that sets it apart from all other vocations. Heralding the good news has direct eternal consequences. What other professional public speaker can claim that? One could probably stretch nonprofessional public speaking in ministry to have a tangential effect on eternity, but preaching has the purest and most direct impact on the eternal destiny of the soul. Maybe parenting comes close to the eternal nature of preaching, but nothing has more direct and concentrated eternal influence.

Finally, listen to the weight Charles Spurgeon places on ministry in general and preaching in particular:

> He that can toy with their ministry and count it to be like a trade, or like any other profession, was never called of God. But those with a charge pressing on their heart, and a woe ringing

1. Johnston, "Muhammad Ali's Best Quotes."

> in their ear, and preaches as though they heard the cries of hell behind them, and saw their God looking down on them—oh, how that preacher begs the Lord that their hearers may not hear in vain![2]

Goodness, time to level up, preacher friends.

Stand-out features of this book are as follows:

- The organization of it. Jeff gets it right by sequencing the topics and subdividing the chapters so that the reader can easily follow and the preaching practitioner can easily reference a section of interest.
- Speaking of the practitioner, this book is written for that preacher, a practicing preacher who does the hard work of conceiving, gestating, and delivering a sermon baby each week. Although this work is rooted in high-level academia, it is accessible to the nonacademic pastor, much like any instruction manual for the layperson.
- The footnotes are particularly helpful for explaining certain words or concepts that might not be clear to a nonacademic preacher. Not that Jeff writes like an academic or in an arrogant way; it's just that when discussing the technical aspects of preaching, clear explanations of unfamiliar terms are a powerful feature of this content.
- The Pentecostal distinctive is palpable but not overpowering. There is no hint of Charismatic arrogance in Dr. McAffee's person or writing. Yet he consistently recognizes the distinctiveness of Pentecostal preaching as a genuine contrast to any other Christian faith tradition. Not better than, but distinctive; not derogatory, nuanced, not negative. Therefore, this book is perfect for any preacher, but the Pentecostal/Charismatic preacher will benefit in particular. However, any non-Pentecostal preacher will indeed hear the best teaching on the nuances of Pentecostal preaching for their own benefit.

If you believe, as I do, that professional ministry is the most important vocation on the face of the planet, and if you believe, as I also do, that preaching is the most important public speaking that can ever be done, then this is your comprehensive preaching manual. From conceiving a sermon in your heart by the Holy Spirit to gestating it with a solid intro hook, exegesis, compelling points, and a homiletical structure, Dr. McAffee gives you everything you need to deliver a healthy sermon, even

2. Hall, *Uniqueness and Danger of Ministry*, 20.

a sermon series. I'm confident you'll return to this content repeatedly and even leverage it to train other emerging Pentecostal preachers.

Godspeed,
Steve Hall, DMin
Associate Professor of Pastoral Ministry
Executive Director of the Paul L. Walker
Center for Pentecostal Preaching
Lee University, Cleveland, Tennessee

# Preface

John Jurasek is a YouTuber with nearly three million followers. He's a Zillennial food critic who critiques fast food. He's young, skinny, and comely. He's mis-dressed, awkward, and unconventional. *He eats on camera, silently*—biting, chewing, swallowing—repeatedly, for minutes at a time. There's no music, and the camera is often zoomed in. He breaks all the rules. How does he have so many followers? I'm sure everyone has their reasons. I watch out of awe and amusement, and I think he's great. But most likely, people watch him because he's *genuine*, he's not afraid to be *transparent*, and he showcases the food, *not himself.*

*Good preaching looks like this.* It comes from the space of authenticity, vulnerability, and invisibility. Sermons have little chance of success if given under false pretenses. Preachers do well when they discover their God-given individuality and celebrate the uniqueness God made them to be. This includes their personality, intellect, sense of humor, and dispositions. Congregations are excellent discerners of authenticity. If a preacher is fronting, people start looking for the back door.

Good preaching comes from a space of *vulnerability*. This is a terrifying proposition. No one wants failures and struggles on display. Yet this is a move of risk and trust that creates a bond between the preacher and the congregation. These bonds assist the congregation in the shared preaching of the sermon. They compel the congregation to help the pastor if they're struggling. They keep the congregation in sync with the sermon's rhythm and movements. The best part of vulnerability is its presence of power in the pulpit. Vulnerability does not make preachers look weak; it signals strength! (2 Cor 12:10).

*Invisibility* is a virtue in the hands of a preacher. The reality, however, is that invisibility is something many preachers struggle to effectuate. There's tremendous pressure being the center platform, with all eyes on every move. Every preacher feels the weight of this. Not wanting to look foolish in front of the congregation, preachers often put in extra effort to look good. There's a lot of grace for this, but if we're not careful, what begins as a motive to not look bad can dissolve into a motive to shine. When the preacher succumbs to the temptation to shine, they've lost touch with the reason for the worship gathering. They've forgotten that it's not about them; it's about Jesus. Good preaching is like fine dining. The experience is about the food, not the food server. For the Sunday morning church service, the focus is worship of Jesus Christ. The best sermons are those where Jesus is glorified *and the preacher is not.* The irony is inescapable.

My prayer for this text is that it reaches you from my own authenticity, vulnerability, and invisibility. My offering is not meant to make me shine; I promise you that. I offer only that which God has shown me about a unique Pentecostal approach to expository preaching that is faithful to Spirit-filled homiletics (the art and science of preaching) and Spirit-filled hermeneutics (the art and science of Scripture interpretation). It was already there. As a text, this volume is for the practitioner who, whether using it in the college classroom or at home, holds the Word of God in the highest regard and who seeks to faithfully deliver sermons where Jesus is the reason. My commitment to you is to write from a place of vulnerable authenticity and to keep what I have discovered front and center.

My credentials for writing this book are educational, professional, and experiential. Early in my marriage (and early in my faith), my wife and I were doing mission work in Southeast Asia focused on bringing the gospel to unreached people groups. During this time, I was asked to preach in our home-based missionary church, but I didn't know how. Terrified, but irresistibly drawn to the pulpit—*to the point where resistance was futile*—I began to realize how my role in the kingdom was going to involve preaching. I didn't know how to preach, but I knew God was calling me to do so.

It was also at this time that I knew I needed biblical and theological training. Kendra and I packed up our family and moved back to America, where I focused on education. I completed a master's degree in theology and, several years later, a doctorate in homiletics. One unique discovery along this journey, to my surprise, was the scarcity of scholarly and practitioner-level works on Pentecostal homiletics, which is one reason I've written this text.

## KEY TERMS

A few terms to keep in mind while working through the text: one, the term *homiletics*. If you've never heard this term before, welcome to the world behind the notes. Homiletics is the art and science of preaching. This text is a homiletical textbook. It provides a foundational understanding of the features of the world behind Pentecostal/Charismatic pulpits. When you're done reading this text, you will have a solid understanding of your role within this tradition. And you will be proud to be part of it.

As a partner to the homiletics world, you also need familiarity with the term *hermeneutics*. This term refers to the world behind biblical *interpretation*. This term is used to describe how people understand the meaning of Scripture. For example, the apostle Paul's discussion of the offices of the church in Eph 4:11, when taken in a Pentecostal interpretive framework, yields an understanding of those offices as still active in the church (as opposed to having been temporary, first-century phenomena). How do we arrive at that interpretation? The answer reveals the values, methods, and strategies within our interpretive (hermeneutical) lens. I've included a section in this text specifically dedicated to the hermeneutical framework of our movement. If you haven't yet had exposure to this world, I warn you in advance, you are going to love what you read. You're going to feel grateful to be a Pentecostal/Charismatic preacher.

Third, the term *cessationist*. This term is often used to describe our Reformed, Calvinistic brothers and sisters who hold a position that denies the Spirit's special charismatic activity in modern times. The cessationist position asserts that charismatic phenomena of the first century, such as miracles, healings, speaking in tongues, the offices of the church, and others, died out when the last apostle (John) died in approximately AD 95. The distinction is important because this particular model of expository preaching comes into sharp contrast with it, not for its own sake, but for an unavoidable and necessary comparison.

On the other side of this is the term *continuationist*. This word is typically used in Pentecostal/Charismatic circles to highlight the ongoing nature of the charismatic offices and phenomena in the church. We Pentecostals believe the offices of the church identified in Eph 4:11 (apostle, prophet, evangelist, pastor, and teacher) are still active today. We believe the miraculous spiritual gifts described in the New Testament, such as prophecy, tongues, healing, and miracles, remain active and available to the church today.

My hope for you, practitioner, as you read this book, is that you learn the art and science of developing and delivering a Pentecostal expository sermon, and that you can minister from your own authenticity, vulnerability, and invisibility. My prayer for the Pentecostal movement is for this text to serve as a primer for Pentecostal preaching, with particular emphasis on the development and delivery of a Pentecostal expository sermon.

For the professors: Please see "Appendix D—For the Professors" for insights on utilizing this text in your classroom.

# Acknowledgments

ALL THANKS TO JESUS! Thanks to Mark Williams and Steve Hall for their valuable contributions. Thanks to the Desert Nuns at Our Lady of Solitude Monastery (Poor Clares of Perpetual Adoration) for providing the sacred space for prayer, contemplation, and writing. Thanks to the supportive and understanding congregation of The Well Church for letting their pastor pursue this project. Thanks to my kids, Ethan (and Noelle), Anna (and Manny), and Ella, who fill my heart. Thanks to my wife, Kendra, who holds everything together.

# Introduction

THE PREACHING OF THE cross is foolishness to those who are perishing. Yet, God has chosen the foolish things of the world to shame the wise and the foolishness of preaching to save those who believe. The Great Commission depends on giving faithful witness to God's saving work through Jesus Christ. Whoever calls on the Name of the Lord shall be saved, but how shall they hear and believe on him without a preacher?

Never has there been a greater need for a preacher and the preached Word of God than there is today.

The world's complexity is increasing at an exponential speed. Political alliances are constantly in a state of flux. We continually hear threats of nuclear and biological terrorism and weapons of mass destruction. Violence is epidemic. Monetarily, a downturn in the global economy can devastate a nation overnight. Socially, norms once taken for granted are publicly ridiculed, and society has deteriorated to the point that, in the words of Jeremiah, "we have forgotten how to blush" (Jer 6:15; 8:12). It is an era fraught with paradigm shifts, geopolitical changes, and environmental concerns. The world longs for men and women who will effectively address the multitude of political and societal ills, but instead of statesmen, it gets politicians.

Gone are the days of the Enlightenment. Enter a world that has embraced secular humanism and moral relativism and denies the existence of absolute truth. Multiple plausibility structures are continually constructed, and the impossibility of objective interpretation is continually invoked. Power has shifted to those who control information. Truth has been regulated to technology, and beauty has been subjected to the eye of the beholder. Feelings have become synonymous with being. Philosophy has shifted to the existential; education has shifted to the skeptical; the arts have shifted to the sensual; and humanity has shifted to the transcendental, believing that he or she is his or her own god.

Ours is a world that lives in fear. Fear may be the one emotion that many in America today can identify with. They see the rising debt and the fragile economy, and they worry. They see the rising crime rate and the rampant lawlessness, and we worry. They see the drug crisis and degenerating moral values, and they worry. They see the increased secularization of society, racial divisions, homelessness, physical and sexual abuse, and we worry. They see the systematic self-destruction of the family unit, and they worry.

This ever-changing world filled with pain and fear looks to the church for hope, and instead of hope finds a church frustrated, confused, and searching for its identity. It sees some segments of the church laden with scandal while other segments continue to pursue answers to questions that no one is asking.

Perhaps the one question that continues to clamor for an answer: Is anybody listening? Does anybody really care?

It is for a time such as this and to a world such as this that you and I have been called to stand and announce, "The Spirit of the Lord is upon me, because he hath anointed me to preach the gospel to the poor; he hath sent me to heal the brokenhearted, to preach deliverance to the captives, and recovering of sight to the blind, to set at liberty them that are bruised, to preach the acceptable year of the Lord" (Luke 4:18–19 KJV).

The mission of the body of Christ is to go into all the world and preach the gospel to every person. The question is how can we faithfully and effectively communicate a first-century message to a twenty-first-century world?

In *Teaching as Worship: The Pentecostal Expository Sermon*, Dr. Jeff McAffee offers a model where the rigorous study of the Word and the radical surrender to the Holy Spirit are not competing interests but a singular act of devotion. When a minister stands to explain the biblical text, they are not merely delivering information; they are leading the congregation into a divine encounter. In this model, the "teacher" is not a lecturer, but a priest officiating at the altar of the Word.

The Pentecostal movement was birthed in a hunger for the "Full Gospel," yet in our modern pulpits, we have often neglected the office of the teacher. We have traded the slow-burn transformation of biblical exposition for the high-octane emotionalism of the moment. This book seeks to reclaim that office, arguing that true Pentecostal preaching is most powerful when it is rooted deeply in the soil of the Scriptures.

To help you navigate this journey, the author has organized this model into six progressive movements:

- Part 1: Setting the Space—Dr. McAffee begins by identifying the current crisis in our pulpits and making the case for why reclaiming the teacher's office is vital for the health of the Spirit-filled church.
- Part 2: Setting the Homiletical Foundation—We explore the internal life of the minister, focusing on the call, purpose, and unique identity of the Pentecostal sermon.
- Part 3: Setting the Hermeneutical Framework—This section bridges the gap between scientific study and Spirit-dependency, showing how the "Word on Mission" interacts with a community yielded to the Spirit.
- Part 4: Setting the Model—Here, we define what a "Pentecostal Expository Sermon" actually looks like, comparing it to traditional models and exploring its "silent infrastructure."
- Parts 5 and 6: Setting the Preparation and Setting the Delivery—The final sections provide a practical, eight-step road map. We move from the initial spark of Inspiration through the mechanics of Explanation, culminating in the Alteration—the moment when the Word confronts and transforms the hearer.

As you read these pages, my hope is that you will stop seeing "teaching" and "worship" as two separate items on a Sunday bulletin. Instead, you will begin to see your preparation as a prayer and your delivery as a sacrifice.

The goal of this book is not just to help you craft better sermons; it is to help you cultivate a pulpit where the Spirit of Truth and the Fire of Pentecost meet to change lives. When the Word is rightly divided and the Spirit is rightly invited, the pulpit becomes a place of transformation.

As you read, you will find that the model presented in these pages is more than a homiletical theory; it is a preparation for a promised outpouring. We stand at a critical juncture in church history where the hunger for the authentic, unadulterated Word of God has never been greater. Yet, the harvest is plentiful, and the laborers—those who can both "rightly divide" and "Spirit depend"—remain few.

My deepest prayer for this work is to see a new generation of women and men rise to answer the call to the Pentecostal pulpit. To the young woman sensing the fire of Jeremiah shut up in her bones: do not shrink back. To the young man wrestling with the weight of the Word: do not settle for shallow echoes.

The office of the teacher is not reserved for the elite or the academic; it is the inheritance of every servant called by God and empowered by the Holy Ghost. We need voices that refuse to choose between the library and the prayer closet—ministers who will labor over the Greek text until they sweat, then step into the pulpit and wait until they burn.

As you close this book, let it not be the end of a study, but the beginning of a consecration. May you join the ranks of those who see teaching as worship, who handle the Scriptures with trembling, and who expect the Spirit to move every time the Book is opened.

The pulpit is ready. The congregation is waiting. The Spirit is moving.

Answer the call.

Mark L. Williams, DMin
Assistant General Overseer
Church of God, Cleveland, Tennessee

# PART ONE

## Setting the Space

PART 1 OF THIS text, "Setting the Space," lays the groundwork for Pentecostal expository preaching by addressing urgent needs in our movement, reclaiming a vital biblical office, and exploring the different types of sermons. These three chapters reveal a heartfelt call to bridge biblical illiteracy, the scarcity of Spirit-filled Bible-teaching pastors in the Pentecostal movement, and an exploration of the different types of sermons.

### THE CRISIS OF BIBLICAL ILLITERACY

Expository preaching shines as a beacon amid a biblical illiteracy crisis in the Pentecostal movement, even among those who cherish the Bible. Studies like the 2025 *State of the Bible*[1] report show sharp declines in regular readers from less than five years earlier, those who engage Scripture daily, and newcomers open to faith—while indifference grows. Pentecostals face this too, historically favoring topical sermons due to fears of dryness, legalism, or stifling the Spirit, yet our exuberant worship craves the depth only sustained Word exposure brings. Without it, believers lack the joy, confidence, and transformative power Scripture promises, leaving churches as empty cisterns amid societal brokenness.

1. Fulks et al., *State of the Bible USA 2025*, x.

## RECLAIMING THE *DIDASKALOS*

Chapter 2 passionately vindicates the teacher (*didaskalos*) as a Spirit-anointed office for pulpits, not just classrooms. Rooted in Eph 4:11, Acts 13:1, and 1 Cor 12:28, this role, elevated above other "teach" terms in the New Testament (such as *katecheo* or *paideuo*), carries authority as a healer, guardian of doctrine, and post-conversion voice for discipleship. Pentecostals have embraced apostles, prophets, evangelists, and pastors, but our movement has struggled to embrace the office of teacher in the pulpit. As unique voices within the five-fold office of the church, some of the greats throughout history, like Ezra to Augustine, Aquinas, Wesley, F. J. May, and Mark Williams, bring the much-needed living water to the evangelistic seeds with doctrinal depth. The Spirit-filled Bible-teaching voices are needed in our movement.

## DIFFERENT TYPES OF SERMONS

Topical, narrative, and textual sermons serve well in specific situations, but expository preaching, with its systematic exegesis, produces text-driven sermons that equip the Spirit-filled pastor to teach the Bible in a way that avoids pulpit-driven lectures. In Pentecostal spaces, this means preparation through Spirit-inspired text selection, proclamation through elevation and explanation, and participation through confrontation, invitation, and alteration—yielding encounters in which Jesus draws near.

Pentecostal pulpits hunger for teachers who unearth Scripture's treasures, wielding them under Holy Ghost fire to heal, confront, and alter lives. As we enter the next few chapters, expect the Word to stir affections of gratitude, compassion, and courage, drawing us deeper into Christ's presence. Let's lean in together, Bibles open, hearts yielded, ready for the Spirit to move through every page ahead.

# 1

# The Need for This Book

## THE MISSING LITERACY

PENTECOSTAL CHURCHES NEED GOOD expository preaching! Several online studies reveal eyebrow-raising trends in biblical illiteracy. Though America's Christians claim to be Bible-adhering believers, very few are actually reading the Bible. The 2022 *State of the Bible Report*, published by Barna Group and the American Bible Society (ABS), revealed three alarming downward trends from the previous year that need our attention. First is a drop in the percentage of occasional Bible readers. This group is not hostile toward the Bible; they're just relatively casual about it and read it only occasionally. This percentage dropped by 11 percent from the previous year, widely considered the sharpest decline in history.[1]

The second is a decline in the percentage of people who take the Bible seriously. And this is the statistic that should concern pastors the most. These are the people who read the Bible nearly every day and let it speak to all matters of their lives. Their sales were hard hit, falling by 21 percent from the year before.[2] That means one in five people who had been anchoring their lives, their families, and society to the Bible abandoned their life-giving relationship with the Word of God!

1. Fulks et al., *State of the Bible USA 2022*, x. This group of people are identified by ABS as "Bible Users."

2. Fulks et al., *State of the Bible USA 2022*, 33. This group of people are identified by ABS as "Scripture Engaged."

Thirdly is the percentage of people who are neutral to the Bible, meaning they can take it or leave it. This is the group of people who are typically new to faith and can go either way after their initial contact. They're giving Jesus a try but a full commitment has not yet taken place. Their percentage of Bible reading decreased by 44 percent from the year before.[3] The only surveyed group of people who showed an increase, unfortunately, were those who have little to no regard for the Bible at all. These are the people who interact with the Bible once every couple of years. Their numbers increased a shocking 45 percent.[4]

In the midst of this wholesale departure of biblical interaction, and the inescapable increase of biblical illiteracy that accompanies it, floats a curious positive view of the Bible. In the article "Americans Are Fond of the Bible, Don't Actually Read It," Lifeway's senior writer Bob Smietana cites how 37 percent of Americans say the Bible is helpful today, nearly the same percent think it is life-changing, and over 50 percent say it is good for morals.[5] This is odd. Very few have a negative view of the Bible, for example, such as believing that it is outdated, harmful, or bigoted. *These percentages reflect positive beliefs about the Bible. Many Americans hold an overall positive view of the Bible, but they're not reading it.* How do we as pastors address this disconnect between the values and practices of our relationship with the Bible?

Pentecostal/Charismatics are not immune to these statistics. Many have noted the historical absence of expository preaching within our movement. One writer attributes the absence of expository preaching to dynamics such as a decline in Pentecostal colleges to emphasize the expository method, the disconnect between the dryness of expository preaching and the exuberance of Pentecostal worship, the over-emphasis and temptation of legalism normally associated with expository sermons, and a disconnect between Spirit and Word where an over-emphasis on Spirit is hindering a balanced emphasis on Word.[6]

Another Pentecostal commentator notes how too many people have experienced expository preaching done badly (we've all been there!). The last thing Pentecostal preachers want to do is put their congregation to

3. Fulks et al., *State of the Bible USA 2022*, xi. This group of people are identified by ABS as "Movable Middle."

4. Fulks et al., *State of the Bible USA 2022*, 4. This group of people are identified by ABS as "Bible Disengaged."

5. Smietana, "Americans Are Fond."

6. Gear, "Where Are the Expositors," paras. 1–4.

sleep with a painful commentary-like lecture, so most Spirit-filled pastors avoid such exposition. Secondly, he notes the frequency of Pentecostal preachers mistakenly assuming that expository sermons prevent them from dealing with contemporary issues. Thirdly, there exists an ignorance of the power of the systematic approach to teaching the Word of God that keeps most Pentecostal preachers primarily in the lane of topical preaching. And finally, a fear of over-preparation leads many Pentecostal preachers to believe that expository sermons inhibit the flow of the Holy Spirit in their preaching.[7]

Much is at risk with this growing biblical illiteracy. The Bible says God's people are destroyed by the absence of his Word (Hos 4). Without God's Word abiding in one's heart and mind, the Christian experiences of divine joy, peace, contentment, and harmony with others is greatly reduced. Inner levels of godly confidence and competencies remain low without the redeeming, reshaping, and reinvigorating Word at work in their lives.

The church is at risk of losing her power. In the midst of the church's obligation to save the lost, she's also called to disciple her converts into the depths of substantive, doctrinal preaching. When doctrinal clarity is ceded, sermons lose the guardrails that help people steer clear of the danger zones of licentiousness and hyper-charismaticism. Our societies and neighborhoods take the full brunt of the absence. Where biblical bankruptcy is shutting down the power of the gospel, the divine, transformative witness of the church must carefully avoid being counterformed into a weak, ineffective accessory to *I never knew you* Christians (Matt 7:21–23).

## THE MISSING OFFICE

Another trend working against the Pentecostal/Charismatic movement is the absence of Bible teachers in our pulpits! This has been the historical trend. Since its inception, the movement has been characterized as being anti-educational. The movement's preferred credential has always been Holy Spirit baptism, thereby qualifying anyone, regardless of education, to serve as a pastor of a local church.

A Holy Spirit–baptized pastor is, without question, the best kind of pastor to lead a Pentecostal church! However, the movement may have

7. Magruder, "Why Pentecostals Don't Preach Expository Sermons," paras. 1–7.

swung too far in this direction with its suspicions and fear-driven attitudes toward formal education. The downside is the movement's low threshold for embracing teachers on its pulpits. The rejection of the Eph 4:11 office of teacher within Pentecostal pulpits is surprising, given that the office carries the specific anointing that many would otherwise find attractive in lead pastors. Thus, one of the challenges for the Pentecostal/Charismatic movement is to recognize, embrace, and even vindicate the *didaskalos* (Greek for "teacher") in the role of lead pastor and to fully engage *all* five offices of the church in our pulpits.

This challenge first stood out to me several years ago when I noticed the scarcity of expository sermons within the Pentecostal movement. My experience was that Pentecostal pulpits were predominantly filled by talented and anointed evangelists and pastors, with sermons typically topical, and expository sermons had little to no representation. My concern wasn't the abundance of topical sermons but the brevity of expository Bible teaching in Spirit-filled worship.

Pentecostals have traditionally been a movement primarily focused on evangelism. This is a good thing! In the short time since the movement began, Pentecostal/Charismatics have gone from 0 percent of the total number of Christians in the world to 26 percent of the Christians in the world.[8] This is a faster rate of growth than the Protestants experienced in the same number of years following the Reformation.[9] We are a people infused with the sense of urgency of the Spirit and the power of the Spirit, to proclaim the name of Christ and to win souls from the darkness to the light.

But our movement has a challenge it has not been able to overcome. Our ability to *serve* has not matched our ability to save. Statistics bear this out. One study measured education levels by denomination. This study listed the Church of God (Cleveland, Tennessee) and the Assemblies of God in the bottom five, meaning that of the over thirty denominations surveyed, the two largest Pentecostal/Charismatic denominations have the least amount of education within their membership.[10] A different

8. Pew Research Center, "Global Christianity," 1.

9. Johnson, "Protestants Around the World," para. 2. Johnson reports that in the year 1600, eighty-three years after the infamous nailing of the ninety-five theses by Martin Luther (1517), Protestants represented approximately 10 percent of the Christians worldwide.

10. Murphy, "Most and Least Educated Religious Groups," para. 7. A helpful chart referencing Murphy's research is also available at Wikipedia, "Educational Attainment in the United States," under the heading "Religion."

study delivered an equally concerning statistic regarding income levels by members. In the nearly identical list of denominations surveyed, the Church of God (Cleveland, Tennessee) came in last and the Assemblies of God came in eighth.[11]

I wish these statistics were not true. What do they mean and how should they be interpreted? Here's a driving question behind the need for this text: Why are the two largest Pentecostal denominations in the world, as principals of a movement that leads the world in conversions, not able to hold on to people who are educated and make good money? The question is not the product of concern over lost resources. It's a question of concern over why these demographics leave after conversion. One paramount factor, I believe, is the lack of strong biblical and doctrinal teaching missing from our pulpits.

St. Anselm is known for his motto *faith seeks understanding*. He's right. The Pentecostal/Charismatic movement is characterized by signs, wonders, gifts, healings, and miracles. But human nature desires understanding of these phenomena. For many who are saved in our movement, when confronted with the absence of solid teaching to accompany the signs and wonders, they go to places where solid teaching can be found. It's a natural progression that flows out of who God made us to be.

In Paul's letter to the Ephesians, he identified the offices of apostle, prophet, evangelist, pastor, and teacher (4:11). Jesus gave these offices to the church for its administration. The more I considered the challenge of biblical illiteracy in the church, the more it seemed to me that the Pentecostal/Charismatic movement was overlooking an important role in its pulpits: *the office of teacher*. (More on this in the next chapter.)

The Pentecostal movement has done well in embracing the first four of these offices in its pulpits, but the office of teacher is missing. The office of teacher is well represented in our colleges and universities around the world, but not every person called to the office of teacher is called to the academy. Many are called to the local church. In a movement where evangelism is king (to our great credit!), and where our pulpits are predominantly filled by evangelists, what do teachers look like in our pulpits? How does the Bible-teaching pastor remain faithful to Pentecostal homiletics (the art and science of preaching) and hermeneutics (the art and science of biblical interpretation) while remaining true to their calling as a Spirit-filled Bible teacher? As one called to the office of teacher

11. Kosmin and Keysar, *Religion in a Free Market*, 157.

and as a pastor of a Pentecostal congregation, I have a strong interest in answering these questions.

A teacher's main tool in the pulpit is the expository sermon. Teachers live in this space of methodical explication. This is our natural, knee-jerk, instinctive starting place for sermons. We don't need to be pushed to preach expositorially; it is our desire. One of the first phrases spoken in the pulpit by teachers is "Open your Bibles to . . . ." Teachers are happy to preach topical sermons and others as well, but their God-given way of thinking, processing, storing, and delivering instruction is divinely wired for the instruction that flows from the expository structure. What does an expository sermon faithful to Pentecostal homiletics and Pentecostal hermeneutics look like? The answer to this question is the foundation of this book.

## THE MISSING MOVE

One of the key features of Pentecostal homiletics is the emphasis of the worship and exaltation of Jesus Christ in our preaching. One might be tempted to declare that exaltation is the emphasis of all preaching. *It's not.* On the contrary, for many churches, the primary purpose of the sermon is to convey information *about* Jesus. The difference between "of" and "about" is significant. One is a worship service, the other is a lecture.

Any teacher will tell you that teaching requires a subject (the teacher) and an object (the student). Content is delivered from the subject to the object, from teacher to student. What does this look like in a church service? When the preacher is *teaching*, the congregation becomes the object. They are the focus. They are the students. The main thrust of the sermon is delivering content to the congregation, where, by necessity, the sanctuary has lost its identity as a place of worship and has become a classroom. By pedagogical definition, the teaching sermon is not a sermon; it's a lecture. If the purpose of the sermon is for the congregation to learn *about* Jesus, then school is in session, not worship.

On the other hand, worship also requires an object, Jesus. Immediately, the Pentecostal minister who is called to the office of teacher, and who is teaching from the pulpit, is confronted with a challenge. If teachers teach, they need students. But if worship is the exaltation of Jesus, which is the primary purpose of the Sunday morning worship service, then how does the Pentecostal teacher in the pulpit *teach* Jesus, with the requisite object of the congregation in one hand, while doing so in the context of *worship*, with the requisite object of Jesus in the other? Can this be done simultaneously? Yes, it can! And answering this question is what this book is all about. The teaching in the Pentecostal expository sermon is never left as a stand-alone intellectual exercise.

## THE LAYOUT OF THE BOOK

This text has six parts. First, it begins by "Setting the Space" in which the need for this book exists, and a chapter dedicated to the recovery of the office of teacher in Pentecostal pulpits starts us off. The discussion of the office of teacher helps you position the act of expository teaching *as worship* that allows you to see how teaching and worship coexist together as a function of the Pentecostal worship gathering. In this section, I describe the office, provide an overview of its scriptural history and traditional handling, and outline the different types of sermons.

The next part is "Setting the Homiletical Foundation." This part presents the landscape in which the Pentecostal task of preaching comes into view. It addresses the minister's call and the primary components that make Pentecostal preaching unique: its purpose, method, and identity.

Following this is the "Setting the Hermeneutical Framework" part. This section invites practitioners into the broader world of Pentecostal Bible interpretation. Many Spirit-filled preachers are unaware of the strengths of the Pentecostal method for understanding Scripture. This section will broaden your horizons about what it means to understand the true meaning of Scripture in a genuinely unique Pentecostal approach.

In "Setting the Model," I provide my definition of expository preaching and then provide a brief work-through of its components demonstrating how the definition is faithful to Pentecostal homiletical markers and Pentecostal hermeneutical principles. I then compare my model to the leading expository models available for pastors today.

The "Setting the Preparation" part of the book brings into focus the silent, high-powered hermeneutical moves working behind the scenes during sermon proclamation that faithfully deliver bidirectional interpretation of the Word to the congregation, emphasizing how the congregation must first be interpreted by the Word before they can embrace their interpretation of the Word. This section also discusses the first two steps of the model, Inspiration and Preparation.

The final part of the book, "Setting the Delivery," sets its attention to sermon delivery. The remaining six steps of the model are described: Introduction, Explanation, Implication, Confrontation, Invitation, and Alteration. Additionally, and with the utmost respect, I address the need to tip a most sacred cow that has accidentally wandered into the pastures of Pentecostal preaching.

Reflection questions are provided at the end of each chapter. For the chapters dedicated to the model's steps, application activities are also provided.

The layout aims to equip you with an easy-to-understand approach to teaching the Bible from a Spirit-filled pulpit, fully aligned with the sermonic and interpretive characteristics important to the Pentecostal/Charismatic movement.

## REFLECTION QUESTIONS

1. Why do you think so many Americans (and Christians) maintain a favorable opinion of the Bible while rarely reading or applying it? How might this disconnect manifest in your own life, church, or community, and what practical steps could address it?
2. Have you observed a pattern of under-emphasizing the office of teacher in the pulpits in Pentecostal/Charismatic churches? What potential benefits and risks might arise from intentionally elevating Bible teachers as lead pastors?
3. Contrasting sermons *about* Jesus with sermons that lead the congregation into the worship *of* Jesus, how does this distinction challenge common assumptions about sermon purpose in Pentecostal/Charismatic contexts?
4. How might the absence of strong, systematic Bible teaching in Pentecostal pulpits contribute to issues like low education/income levels among members or the loss of converts to more teaching-oriented traditions?
5. The chapter introduces the upcoming model for a distinctly Pentecostal expository sermon that remains faithful to both Pentecostal homiletics and Pentecostal hermeneutics and the call to teach deeply. What excites you most about this approach, and what concerns or barriers do you anticipate?

# 2

# Reclaiming the Office of Teacher in the Pentecostal Pulpit

THE OFFICE OF A teacher is identified by the apostle Paul in Eph 4:11 (ESV), "And he gave the apostles, the prophets, the evangelists, the shepherds, and teachers." The office carries with it a specific anointing that begins with the call to the office, continues while the teacher is taken through a mandatory season of learning and training, and ultimately finds expression in various positions throughout the kingdom, such as in the academy, the church, the training institutes, and others. The office of teacher is an office set apart by God, through the anointing of the Holy Spirit, which serves a strategic role within the church.

It was crucial for me to include a chapter on this most important office in the church today and its significant value to the Pentecostal movement. The office of teacher stands at the intersection of Spirit and Scripture, and this chapter was written out of a concern that such a God-appointed office has been marginalized in many Pentecostal circles. The aim here is not merely to argue for another title in the church but to recover a Spirit-empowered, Christ-founded teaching office whose ministry heals, confronts, and forms the people of God in worship, doctrine, and mission. At stake is the health of Pentecostal congregations, for when the church neglects the teacher, it forfeits one of Christ's primary means of guarding the gospel, maturing believers, and sustaining a truly Pentecostal life in the Spirit. This chapter, therefore, explores the biblical, historical, and theological contours of the office of teacher so that the

Pentecostal movement might better embrace this vital office in its rightful place in the local church.

The office of the teacher is discussed in several New Testament passages. The book of Acts posits teachers in the same authoritative category as prophets of the church. "Now there were at Antioch, in the church that was there, prophets and *teachers*: Barnabas, and Simeon who was called Niger, and Lucius of Cyrene, and Manaen who had been brought up with Herod the tetrarch, and Saul" (Acts 13:1 NASB, emphasis mine). In 1 Corinthians, Paul makes a similar move by situating the office in close proximity with the offices of apostle and prophet. "And God has appointed in the church, first apostles, second prophets, third *teachers*, then miracles, then gifts of healings, helps, administrations, various kinds of tongues. All are not apostles, are they? All are not prophets, are they? All are not teachers, are they? All are not workers of miracles, are they? All do not have gifts of healings, do they? All do not speak with tongues, do they? All do not interpret, do they?" (12:28–30 NASB, emphasis mine). Those who are called into this office are endowed with an ability to understand and to explain Christian doctrines, theologies, and practices of the church, in a manner uniquely gifted for their function in the kingdom.

The Christian message is founded on the teachings of Jesus Christ. John identified Christ as *rabbi*, emphasizing Jesus' teaching ministry, at the beginning of his Gospel (1:37). Luke began the book of Acts with "all that Jesus began to do and *teach*" (Acts 1:1 NASB, emphasis mine). Jesus set the standard for the office of teacher for the church, which was then passed on to the apostles and the church. As such, the office of teacher serves a particular function within the church. The specific Greek word for this teacher is *didaskalos*. The teaching function of a *didaskalos* differs from that of other terms used in Scripture to describe teaching, such as *pedagogue* and *mathete*. As an office, the word carries a broader platform of influence. The English word *doctor* is etymologically traceable to variants of *didaskalos* (*didactorus*) and its Latin counterpart *docere*. In church history, individuals upon whom such a title had been conferred were those who had completed all courses of their matriculation and were now deemed competent to be called doctor, master, or other title of high authority to teach.

New Testament writers also utilized several different words for *teach*. A few questions need to be answered. One, when the New Testament speaks of the office of teacher, why was *didaskalos* chosen in certain situations in favor of the other New Testament words for teach? Second, what is an extensive definition of *didaskalos* and the office to which it is ascribed? Third, what is the Old Testament precursor of the office of teacher to better understand the foundation for the office in the New Testament?[1]

## "PASTOR/TEACHER" OR "PASTOR *AND* TEACHER"

There's an old debate within the church regarding the wording of Eph 4:11, "And he gave the apostles, the prophets, the evangelists, the shepherds and teachers" (ESV). Some see the apostle Paul's wording identifying five separate offices; others see only four. For the purpose of clearing the air regarding my position, I have separated teachers from the pairing, while at the same time recognizing the validity of the pairing for those who wish to keep them paired. I know this sounds like a nonanswer, but there's a reason for this. I do this not because I disagree with the Granville Sharp Rule,[2] which would keep them together, but because of the independent function of the *didaskalos* as represented throughout the New Testament.

The stand-alone value of *didaskalos* for the New Testament almost forces our hand here. There are over 150 occurrences of *didasko* in all its variants in the New Testament, as opposed to only eighteen total appearances of *poimenas* (pastor), in all of its variants. Even with the allowance for one person to be so anointed with abilities as to represent both functions at the same time, which I believe was the thrust of Paul's pairing in his letter to Ephesus, the emphasis on the office of teacher as a stand-alone cannot be overlooked.

The separate focus of *didaskalos*, distinct from *poimenas*, is evident in Sharp's argument for the rule, as observed in Titus 2:13, which states, "looking for the blessed hope and the appearing of the glory of our great God and Savior, Christ Jesus" (NASB). Here, "God" and "Savior," which are both *independent* entities of the Trinity, are applied one and the same to Christ Jesus. Paul's pairing of the two in Eph 4 does not disrupt the independence of either function within the kingdom. Another example

1. Also included in my examination of Old Testament *didaskalos* counterparts were exegesis of *yara* ("to throw, shoot, point out, instruct"), *lamad* ("to goad"), and in some cases *yada* ("to know").

2. Sharp et al., *Remarks*, 3. The rule states that when two nouns that are not proper nouns, describing a person, are connected by the word *and*, and the first noun has the article *the* while the second does not, then both nouns are referring to the same person.

is found in Paul's identical pairing of apostle and prophet earlier in the very same letter to the Ephesians, in 2:20, "having been built on the foundation of the *apostles and prophets*, Christ Jesus Himself being the cornerstone" (NASB, emphasis mine). Although paired, the offices of apostle and prophet are distinct. The individuality of the offices of pastor and teacher from Eph 4:11 are the same.

## EXAMINATION OF *TEACH* WORDS IN THE NEW TESTAMENT

In the passages just discussed, one might ask why Luke and Paul use *didaskalos* in their comments about the office of teacher[3] over against the several other words for *teach* available to them. Several Greek words are translated as *teach* in the New Testament,[4] but as it will be demonstrated in the following overview, *didaskalos* is the best. It is undergirded by authority and a function that best fit its purpose in the church.

*Didasko*: This word means to teach, direct, or admonish. It occurs ninety-seven times in the New Testament, with its meaning nearly always associated with teaching and instructing from the highest position of authority. The concept was unique to the ministry of Jesus and to the New Testament, where it entailed the didactic dissemination of information or the impartation of knowledge. It carries a distinct thrust toward teaching *Scripture* as its primary focus. Its unique component of teaching as admonition secured a prominent place in the pulpit, where teaching was infused with Spirit-empowered divine confrontation and a subsequent invitation to respond.

Thomas Aquinas, a thirteenth-century church scholar writing at the height of medieval Scholasticism, noted the *causal* nature of teaching

3. Acts 13:1; 1 Cor 12:28–30; Eph 4:11.

4. For the purposes of this examination, a variety of Bible dictionaries, concordances, and lexicons were consulted to grasp a comprehensive understanding of each word. These sources include Strong, *Strong's Exhaustive Concordance of the Bible*; R. Thomas, *New American Standard Exhaustive Concordance*; Thayer, *Thayer's Greek Lexicon*; Verbrugge, *NIV Theological Dictionary of New Testament Words*; Smith, *Smith's Bible Dictionary*; Easton, *Easton's Bible Dictionary*; and others. The New Testament words for *teach* examined are *didasko*, *katecheo*, *matheteuo*, *paideuo*, *noutheteuo*, and *paraggello*, with the exception of *paradidomai*. This word is not included because its usage is primarily focused on *betrayal* (of Jesus being handed over) with only a minor focus on instruction. Of the 120 occurrences of the word, only a handful were used in accordance with teaching, and in those cases the meaning of the word espoused a "delivery of content" as in the "delivery of a package" rather than the instruction of the same.

bound up in this word, explaining that a true teacher actively brings about knowledge in the hearer. Drawing an even richer connection, Aquinas framed teaching as a kind of spiritual healing, likening the teacher to a physician whose external work cooperates with God's deeper, interior action in the soul.[5] In his view, both physical healing and the illumination of the mind ultimately flow from God, who heals our diseases and imparts knowledge to humanity, so that learning itself becomes a participation in the healing work of the Spirit's divine light and inner restoration. In this way, Aquinas effectively identifies the *didasko* office in the church as a spiritual office of healing against the wounds associated with original sin, such as ignorance, malice, weakness, and lust.

Thirteen times *didasko* was used to describe Jesus' preaching, consistent with the typical form and style of the rabbis of his day. Jesus' teaching was revelatory, but it went beyond rabbinic methods by including personal involvement, interaction, healings, exorcisms, authority over religious figures, resurrections, and other miracles. Throughout Acts, the Pauline corpus, and the rest of the New Testament letters, teaching was often paired with the proclamation of the good news (*euangelizo*), thereby providing a rhetorical framework and appeal for the act. Paul's use of *didasko* expounded biblical principles of the faith and the skillful teaching of sound doctrine.

*Katecheo*: This Greek term means to teach orally or to sound down to the ears. In classical Greek, the primary meaning of the word connoted speaking down to people, sometimes in a proclamatory tone, other times in a teacher-to-pupil tone. This term is used to describe a public announcement made from a position of influence. In the New Testament, it carries with it the concept of systematic instruction with a focus of indoctrination through teaching. It is the word from which we derive the term *catechesis*, used in more formal contexts to denote the teaching of doctrine to children or to those new to the faith. It appears only eight times in the New Testament, with both Paul and Luke using the word four times each. However, the primary focus of *katecheo* is actually on the one receiving the instruction rather than the one giving it. This distinctive feature highlights a more passive reception of oral information rather than active instruction. Here, the focus was primarily on the pupil, with the teacher serving as the instructor.

5. Aquinas, *Summa Theologica*, 760.

*Matheteuo*: *Matheteuo* means to train disciples. This word is used only four times in the New Testament. It is used to describe the process by which a teacher *helps a disciple learn the ways of their master*. In ancient Greece, a disciple would voluntarily bind themselves to the ways, thoughts, and worldview of a master teacher. The disciple dedicated a portion of their life to the process, with the remainder devoted to passing it on to others. The journey involved following the master teacher to learn from, imitate, and indoctrinate their worldview. By nature, it implied an established master-disciple relationship that afforded the teacher a deeper, personal bond involving mutual commitment. Teaching within a *matheteu* context carried a specific impetus of making disciples. Here, the teacher was the guru.

*Paideuo*: The verb *paideuo* is teaching through discipline, training, and chastisement within a context of ontological fulfillment for the learner. It derives from the root word *pais*, meaning *child* under strict training toward maturity and the realization of full potential. The process required necessary training and discipline, including the administration of chastisement, which is the essential gist of *paideuo*. This feature of the word makes it unique within the family of New Testament words for *teach* because of the holistic discipline that often accompanied instruction, including physical discipline. Being closely related to the Greek word *pedagogue*, of the thirteen appearances in the New Testament, ten of these appearances are translated as *punish*, *chastise*, or *discipline*. One example of its use as discipline occurs in Hebrews, where we learn that God disciplines those whom he loves (Heb 12:6). The chastisement of *paideuo* becomes a kind of kindness that leads to repentance, which restores the errant learner to a posture of obedience. The process carries with it the act of forgiveness and cleansing of sin, which allows a recovery of peace between learner and teacher. It's a fatherly form of instruction that fosters a sense of belonging in the learner.

*Noutheteo*: *Noutheteo* means to reason with someone by warning them. This is a compound word in the Greek made up of *mind* and *to place*, meaning properly to place in the mind. It carries a sense of appealing to the mind through warning. It occurs eight times in the New Testament, all of which are found in Paul's writings with one exception (in which it was used in reference to Paul's teachings), with each being translated as *admonish*. By means of advice, warning, reminding, teaching, and exhorting, the learner was warned to redirect from wrong ways for behavior correction. In contrast to *didasko*, which is focused more on intellect as means of healing, *noutheteo* is focused on the development and guidance of the will and emotions. Learning within this context is seasoned with emotional stirrings that further compel the will for proper alignment with the teaching. Two of its New Testament occurrences are paired with *didasko* in the proclamation of Christ (Col 1:28 and 3:16) to form the dual thrust of instruction and admonition to produce maturity in Christ. Here the teacher is a guide.

*Parangello*: *Parangello* denotes the giving of instruction through command, order, and prescription. This is a compound word in the Greek meaning *para*, to come alongside, and *aggello*, to inform. It's used in the sense of delivering a command through the context of unmitigated authority. The essential element, then, is to place a person under obligation. Teaching here was imperative rather than merely instructive. Paul's command to Timothy to "prescribe and teach these things" in 1 Tim 4:11 was intended to orient new believers to the ways of the kingdom of God. The learning was informationally and orientationally imperative in alignment with the commands of Christ. Here, the teacher is the commander.

Based on these words, the following chart demonstrates the voice, function, and location of the different words for *teach* in the New Testament.

| Greek Word for Teach | Voice | Function | Location |
|---|---|---|---|
| *Didasko* | Doctor | Heal | Sanctuary |
| *Katecheo* | Instructor | Instruct | Classroom |
| *Matheteuo* | Guru | Impart | Path |
| *Paideuo* | Father | Chastise | Congregation |
| *Noutheteo* | Guide | Warn | Valleys |
| *Parangello* | Commander | Direct | Battlefield |

To answer the first question posed at the beginning of this chapter, why was *didaskalos* chosen over the others in the context of the office of teacher? First, *didaskalos* appears to encompass all the other words. Individually, the other words carry specific voices, functions, and locations that are unique to their purpose in the kingdom of God. However, all of these are expressed in the role of *didaskalos*. In this way, *didaskalos* functions as an overarching catch-all for the other functions of a teacher in the New Testament and is accordingly elevated above the rest in the office listings.

Second, the voice of the *didaskalos* carries the highest authority. To be recognized as a *didaskalos* meant that the person bearing the title had attained the highest levels of education and training and therefore held the highest authority. As such, those upon whom the title was conferred were naturally given the highest recognition commensurate with the authority. It is reasonable, in this context, that the best term for the church office was *didaskalos*.

Thirdly, as identified above, the overarching function of the *didaskalos* was that of healer. Empowered by the Spirit, the office of *didaskalos* held the highest secular credentials and the highest degree of Holy Spirit empowerment. In practice, the Spirit-empowered *didaskalos* led participants to learn, grow, be delivered, draw closer to God, repent, be cleansed, be changed, and be healed. It comes as no surprise that by the seventeenth century, the word *doctor* would find placement with medicine in lockstep with the word *physician*, but they were latecomers to the party. By this time, the word *doctor* had already been established in the context of healing by learning.

The *didaskalos* brought healing through the teaching, direction, and admonition of Scripture. The other terms for *teach* espoused specific functions of instruction, impartation, chastisement, warning, and direction, but *didaskalos* encompassed them all. The *didaskalos*, functioning in some ways as a spiritual doctor, was practicing, or treating, the congregation through divine proclamation of the Word. The individual moved toward healing through divine confrontation and an invitation to respond. This was their prescription. Healing took place for those who yielded to the Spirit.

Lastly, the location from which the *didaskalos* ministered was primarily the sanctuary. I use the term *sanctuary* here to denote the mode through which the *didaskalos* teaches in the context of *worship*. As such, the focus is on the occasions when the congregation has gathered to worship, and the teaching takes place accordingly. This is a key distinguishing feature of *didaskalos* over against the locations of the other words, with the instructive function of *katecheo* taking place in the classroom, the impartation of *matheteuo* along the paths of life, the chastisement of *paideuo* in congregational gathering places, the warnings of *noutheteo* in dangers of the valleys, and the commands of *parangello* in the battlefield. The *didaskalos* practiced from a position of influence that, by nature, necessitated a crowd or congregation. This feature of *didaskalos* makes sense, as it would be elevated above the other New Testament words for *teach*.

## *DIDASKALOS* IN THE NEW TESTAMENT

As to the second question at the beginning of this chapter of how the New Testament community would have understood the office of teacher, a clear job description for the office of *didaskalos* can be harvested from its usage. There are fifty-nine occurrences of the word in the New Testament, which better serve our understanding of the office today. Paul uses the word seven times in his letters. Luke uses it once in Acts. The writer of Hebrews uses it once. James uses it once. In addition to these, *didaskalos* appears in thirty-two unique stories in the Gospels.

### Gospel Story Appearances

The Gospel appearances of the word are unique in how they point to Jesus with titular respect in all but two instances. The first of these two instances appears in Luke's Gospel, in the story of Jesus as a boy in the temple. Here, *didaskalos* is used to describe the teachers with whom Jesus was speaking in the temple (Luke 2). Luke presents the contrast between the learnedness of the temple *didaskalos* against the yet-to-be-learnedness of the Christ child. The other of these two instances appears in John's Gospel, in the story of Jesus' interaction with Nicodemus. Here, Jesus declares incredulously to Nicodemus, "You're Israel's *teacher*, and you don't understand these things?" (John 3:10).

What was unique about these appearances was that they were used as a title of respect by *pre-conversion people*. In other words, this was a title of respect in which people ascribed to Jesus the highest honor they could think of in their vernacular: *didaskalos*. The totality of their appearances points to authority and respect. Those who encountered Jesus, whether followers of God or not, acknowledged his authority and showed respect for it by referring to him as *didaskalos*.

The New Testament writers, in all but two instances, refused to use the word in relation to the Jewish teachers, even though it was in widespread use at the time. The usage of the word in the New Testament bears the distinctions of authority, respect, and honor. Those who would be called to the same office in the centuries to come would enjoy the same kind of treatment upon which Christ laid the foundation. As doctors of the church, the office brought healing and life to all who received from it.

## Non-Gospel Appearances

There are ten other appearances of *didaskalos* in the New Testament from four other writers: Luke, Paul, the writer of Hebrews, and James. Throughout their appearances, the major themes of respect, honor, and authority continue to rise to the surface. Luke's use of *didaskalos*, found in Acts 13:1, identifies the office as a strategic presence of the church of Antioch and establishes it for centuries to come. Luke had several other Greek words to choose from when thinking of teacher. However, his use of *didaskalos* shows that the same honor, respect, and authority originally bestowed upon the office through Jesus Christ were also bestowed upon the church in Antioch.

Paul used *didaskalos* seven times in his letters. To the Roman believers,[6] he chided the Jewish leaders when using the word in a confrontational tone. As such, *didaskalos* was used in the context of more noble functions typically associated with true godly leadership, such as guiding, being the light, and instructing. However, the Jewish leaders were none of these things. They were feigning superiority, but it was false. His use of *didaskalos* here shows that, in Paul's mind, the word enjoyed a level of respect, honor, and ennoblement.

To the church in Corinth, Paul was teaching about the offices of the church and the spiritual gifts, two separate entities. At one point, the two topics wove together: he made comments about the church's offices, then transitioned to the gifts, and then returned to the offices.[7] By placing the office of *didaskalos* in the same company as apostles and prophets, Paul identified the *didaskalos*'s office at the same level of authority, respect, and honor ascribed to apostles and prophets. In his letter to the believers in Ephesus,[8] Paul similarly identified the offices of the church as those

6. Romans 2:20 (NIV), in context, starting in verse 17: "17 But if you bear the name 'Jew' and rely upon the law and boast in God, 18 and know his will and approve the things that are essential, being instructed out of the law, 19 and are confident that you yourself are a guide to the blind, a light to those who are in darkness, 20 *a corrector of the foolish, a teacher of the immature, having in the law the embodiment of knowledge and of the truth*, 21 you, therefore, who teach another, do you not teach yourself? You who preach that one shall not steal, do you steal?" (Emphasis mine.)

7. 1 Cor 12:28–29 (NASB), "28 And God has appointed in the church, first apostles, second prophets, third teachers, then miracles, then gifts of healings, helps, administrations, various kinds of tongues. 29 All are not apostles, are they? All are not prophets, are they? All are not teachers, are they? All are not workers of miracles, are they?"

8. Eph 4:11 (NASB), "And He gave some *as* apostles, some *as* prophets, some *as* evangelists, some *as* pastors and teachers."

given to the church by Christ through appointment, for the implantation and governance of the church. Here, he identifies apostles, prophets, evangelists, pastors, and teachers. It is the Spirit-empowered work of the apostles, prophets, and evangelists through which the local church is planted. It is through the pastors and the teachers that the local church is watered and cared for. Each office has its own anointing and giftings.[9]

Three times, Paul uses *didaskalos* in his letters to Timothy. Two of these passages are nearly identical,[10] where Paul identified himself in an elevated manner through the offices of preacher, apostle, and teacher. Again, the use of *didaskalos*, along with the terms *preacher* and *apostle*, acknowledges the superiority, authority, honor, and respect of these offices. Paul's final usage of the word is found in 2 Tim 4:3, where Paul prophesied of the day when people would no longer want to endure sound doctrine. This passage highlights the power of true doctrine being taught in the church. True doctrine must be endured because it is hard on the flesh. True doctrine reveals sickness and cuts it out. It exposes, confronts, challenges, and invites the participant to yield to the Spirit's work. For the *didaskalos*, the requirement is to teach only true doctrine.

The other two occurrences of *didaskalos* in the New Testament are found in Hebrews and James. The writer of Hebrews uses it in a scolding tone because the believers were not maturing in their faith, declaring that they should be "teachers by now" (Heb 5:12). Its usage here reveals the expectation that is upon believers to grow in their faith to a point where they not only enjoy a mature faith but also take on the voice of one who can declare sound doctrine. And though their level of faith should be so mature as to speak with doctrinal soundness, the admonishment is not allowance nor an invitation for them to enter into the office of *didaskalos*. Rather, these are the individuals whom the Scriptures invite to exhort one another in love and grace and in truth without ascension to the office of pastor or teacher.

9. John Wesley believed that the office of pastor was synonymous to the Old Testament office of priest. In his sermon "Ministerial Office" (Sermon 115), he states Jesus sent out the apostles and evangelists to start churches. The churches would then be watched over by the pastors, preachers, and teachers. The pastors were unique in that they only were sanctioned to administer the sacraments, while preachers and teachers were authorized to teach. He is unaware of any scriptural evidence that supports an evangelist administering the sacraments.

10. 1 Tim 2:7 (NASB), "For this I was appointed as a preacher and an apostle (I am telling the truth, I am not lying), as a teacher of the Gentiles in faith and truth."

And 2 Tim 1:11 (NASB), "for which I was appointed a preacher, an apostle, and a teacher."

The last occurrence of *didaskalos* in James is one of the best uses of the term in the New Testament. Here, James cautions anyone who desires to be a teacher to carefully consider their motives, warning that they will incur a stricter judgment (Jas 3:1). James is clear that teachers face greater scrutiny for their commitment to doctrinal purity, receiving a double judgment. No other warning is given in the New Testament to those who desire ministerial activity. It is a great caution for all who desire to teach that they take seriously the responsibility to which they have been called.

An interesting parallel is found when these same verses are examined in the Vulgate. Of the fifty-nine occurrences, fifty-three are translated as *magister*. This word means a *great minister*. It is often translated into English as teacher, tutor, expert, chief, head, superior, director, or master. Later, during the Middle Ages, the word was used in the context of persons being given authority to teach philosophy and the liberal arts in universities.

The remaining six occurrences of *didaskalos* in the Vulgate were translated as *doctores*. One of these was translated as such in Luke 2:46 when Jesus was interacting with the temple teachers as a young boy. Another passage occurs when Paul refers to himself as a teacher in 1 Tim 2:7. The remaining four are found in three passages that identify the office of teacher in the New Testament: Acts 13:1, Eph 4:11, and 1 Cor 12:28–29 (mentioned twice in these verses). This means that as Jerome was translating the New Testament into Latin, he made a special move when he came to the *didaskalos* passages, when those passages were associated with the office of teacher, thereby providing an elevated status of *doctores*.

## *DIDASKALOS* IN THE OLD TESTAMENT

For the final part of this chapter, we turn to our third question: how the office of the teacher might have functioned in the Old Testament. The task of such presents a challenge because the Old Testament offices of leadership were limited to prophet, priest, and king and did not include an established office of teacher. Because of this, it was no surprise that there were zero occurrences of *didaskalos* in the Septuagint (the Greek translation of the Hebrew Old Testament). There are, however, clues about how teaching occurred in each of these offices.

The prophets, for example, had a primary function as God's entrusted ambassadors, receiving and delivering the oracles of God to the

Israelites. These oracles contained messages of judgment and salvation and of events to come, among many other things. The ministry of such divine ambassadorship necessarily included teaching/instruction.

Likewise, the priests served as mediators of God's presence and were responsible for caring for the holy sites, such as the tabernacle and the temple. Their duties included sacrifices, offerings, rituals, blessings, and discernment. Similarly, their ministry carried a default function of teaching, particularly in the discernment of God's will through the usage of the Urim and Thummim and through their knowledge of the Torah in settling disputes, and would therefore include communication, teaching, and declaring of God's will, but these were not the primary function for the priesthood.

The office of the king was the same. The Israelite kings had a particularly powerful platform of influence with the people. The kings, at least those who did what was pleasing in the sight of the Lord, carried a primary function as curators of God's covenant between God and the Israelites, providing theocratic leadership where the king worshiped God, knew God, loved God, sought after God, and created laws in accordance with covenantal fidelity. Their ministry would carry a default component of teaching but was obviously not the primary thrust of their office.

The closest the Old Testament comes to *didaskalos* equivalency is the office of *scribe*. Scribes were given the name because they could read and write, not just because they were copyists. It's an important distinction. The office was identified by the Hebrew words *zakar* and *saphar* and was associated with elevated servitude and authority. Some were officials who had authority to create official documents (Jer 36:26). Others held elevated positions in the royal palace, such as ministers of finance or secretaries of state (2 Kgs 18:18; 22:3; Isa 36:3). Some were academic advisors to the king, such as Daniel.

However, the first authoritative, stand-alone, formal appearance of a *teacher* in the Old Testament is found in the scribal ministry of Ezra. According to the Bible, Ezra was a priest and a scribe (Ezra 7:12). The Hebrew word for *scribe* ascribed to Ezra is *capher*, meaning secretary. It appears only six times in the Hebrew Old Testament, all in the book of Ezra. It is a Hebrew word related to *sephar* (different from *saphar* above), meaning "books." Ezra was a keeper of the books. Specifically, he was the keeper of the Torah. As Ezra made his way into the postexilic Jerusalem, he is described as a "scribe skilled in the Law of Moses, which the LORD, the God of Israel, had given" (Ezra 7:6 NASB). He was anointed to teach the statutes of the Lord with the ability to help people understand: "They read from the book, from the law of God, translating to give the sense so that they understood the reading" (Neh 8:8 NASB). Further, he is attributed to have walked with great favor from the Lord, "because the good hand of his God was upon him. For Ezra had firmly resolved to study the Law of the LORD and to practice it, and to teach His statutes and ordinances in Israel" (Ezra 7:9–10 NASB).

Ezra was the first individual to exercise Jewish national authority outside the office of prophet, priest, or king, where the people acknowledged and accepted him as such. Through him, the office of Old Testament scribe/teacher was born. He was the progenitor of the office and function of the New Testament Jewish *scribe*, often referred to by the time of Christ as *rabbi*, a master religious teacher (though the word *rabbi* does not occur in the Old Testament). The same scribes and teachers of the law with whom Jesus sparred during his ministry are of Ezra's titular lineage. They were often described as lawyers who would argue with Christ over legal matters such as the interpretation of Scripture (Mark 9:11), tradition (Matt 15:1), purity laws (Mark 7:1–2), the Sabbath (Luke 6:7), dietary laws (Mark 2:16), and similar matters. As keepers of the law, they often served as legal counselors to the chief priests, the high priest, and the Sanhedrin. Their authority was delegated to them as interpreters of the law, not as creators of it. They were also tasked with copying the ancient texts.[11]

## OFFICE OF TEACHER AND TRADITION

In the context of faith, the word *tradition* means how the church has historically handled or interpreted Scripture. By this, we're asking what kinds of liturgical or ecclesial practices or beliefs came into existence based on the church's interpretation of the Bible. Now that a scriptural foundation for the office of teacher has been established, the next question is how the church interpreted these passages, and what kinds of practices were assigned to the office in function? In the next few paragraphs, we'll explore the major epochs of church history to examine how the office of teacher was understood in each era.

11. Achtemeier, *Harper's Bible Dictionary*, 914.

## Apostolic Era

The apostolic era roughly spans AD 50–100. Although the entire New Testament was written during this time, there were other writings considered authoritative in the church but not included in the canon. These writings are called *extra-canonical*. Many of these writings were examined to determine how the office was treated in the church's early years. What is arguably the most authoritative document among such writings is the Didache, a short book that served primarily as a manual for Christian instruction. The Didache identified the office of teacher as having equal authority to that of offices of apostle and prophet. Christians were admonished to submit to the Christ-granted authority of these offices.

The Didache is the first to identify the office of teacher as itinerant.[12] Its handling of the offices shows that, within a few decades after the resurrection and ascension of Christ, the teaching office was fully functioning and had crystallized as part of the church's ecclesial governance. Second, it revealed its connection to the nascent mission of the church, which was to teach converts to observe all Jesus had commanded the apostles (Matt 28:19–20). The office of the teacher, according to the Didache, was indispensable to the church's ontological, didactic, and missiological foundations. These observations position the office of the teacher squarely as a function of and within the pulpit ministry of the universal church, expressed in the office's roaming nature.

## Patristic Era

This era comprises roughly the years AD 100–400. This era was pivotal for the church, as it broke away from its distinct Jewishness while also adopting systematized theological and ecclesiological structures. It was also a time when the first hints of division began to arise between the Western and Eastern churches. Several writings from this era, by Ignatius, the Shepherd of Hermas, Polycarp, Justin Martyr, and the developing Catholic Church, provide insight into how the church handled the office of teacher.

Ignatius, a disciple of Polycarp (himself a disciple of John), placed the office within the duties of the *bishop* presiding over a city, a position of great authority. The Shepherd of Hermas contains several references

12. Roberts and Donaldson, *Didache*, chs. 11 and 13.

that identify the office as a key agency of authority and leadership within the church.[13] Polycarp, who was the bishop of Smyrna, a disciple of the apostle John, a contemporary of Ignatius, the teacher of Irenaeus, and executed by burning at the stake, was referred to as "*the teacher* of Asia," whose teaching ministry was so successful that he was accused of turning the Roman citizens into atheists.[14] Later, the Roman Catholic Church began to crystallize the office of teacher. Richard Osmer identifies the significance of this, saying, "The single most important development in the emergence of the teaching office was the centralization of the teaching authority of the office of bishop."[15]

## Early Medieval Era

The early medieval era comprises roughly the years AD 400–900. One of the leading theological voices during the early medieval era was Augustine. In the *City of God*, Augustine identified Paul as *the* teacher of the nations.[16] Additionally, Augustine identified the prophets as the *teachers* of piety and truth.[17] He wrote specifically about the appropriate style for teacher rhetoric, clear articulation, and quoting Cicero's chief aims of the orator: teaching, delighting, and moving; of these, teaching was the most essential.[18] For Augustine, the office of teacher was a key component of church governance and authority.[19]

13. Lightfoot, *Shepherd of Hermas* 3.5.

14. Lightfoot, *Martyrdom of Polycarp* 12.2, emphasis mine.

15. Osmer, *Teachable Spirit*, 75.

16. Augustine, *City of God* 8.9.

17. Augustine, *City of God* 18.41.

18. Augustine, *City of God*, ch. 12.

19. Augustine had much more to say over the next sixteen chapters about the office of teacher, dealing with the dynamics of the listeners, specifically how they should be moved and how they should not despise direction, praying before speaking, how it is God who makes the true teacher, using different teaching/speaking styles depending upon the occasion, ethics of the teacher living/being what they are teaching, and how it is permissible for a teacher to present to the people that which has been written by a more eloquent person than themselves.

## Late Medieval Era

This era spans roughly AD 900–1500. Anselm and Aquinas, two of the leading theological voices of the time, provide insight into how the office was understood and perceived. Anselm, though never writing directly on the office of teacher, gave certain clues in some of his writings as to his disposition regarding the office. Anselm's *Dialogues*, for example, presents theological and doctrinal information in the form of didactic interchange of questions and answers between a student and a teacher. For Anselm to use this format suggests that he held a high regard for the office of teacher as the office through which orthodox doctrine was to be generationally transmitted.

Aquinas acknowledged that the office of teacher is that which comes through direct appointment from God and upon which all requisite authority is contained. A particularly unique feature Aquinas ascribed to the office of teacher is that of healer, stating, "the teacher brings exterior help as the physician who heals: but just as the interior nature is the principal cause of the healing, so the interior light of the intellect is the principal cause of knowledge."[20] The position amplifies the teacher as healer, from whom, through the power of God's Spirit, divine truth, wisdom, and knowledge impart life to the listener's spirit, bringing healing to the wretchedness of their soul.

## Reformation Era

The Reformation era spans the entire sixteenth century. The Reformers Luther, Calvin, and Zwingli, not unsurprisingly, reacted against the Catholic Church's elevation of the office of teacher and the abuse of its authority. Luther thought the doctors of the Catholic Church, with their focus on philosophy, had become useless.[21] Calvin, a little more friendly toward the office than Luther, connected it with the divine appointment, authority, and governance of the church, and he believed the Eph 4 offices were occupied by Christ-appointed substitutes.[22] In his commentary on Galatians and Ephesians, he separated pastor-teacher, saying the two should not be confounded. "Teaching is, no doubt, the duty of all pastors; but to maintain sound doctrine requires a talent for interpreting

20. Aquinas, *Summa Theologica*, 675.

21. Luther, "Open Letter," para. 10.

22. Calvin, *Institutes* 4.3.3–5.

Scripture, and a man may be a *teacher* who is not qualified to preach."[23] As a cessationist, he went on to say that pastors and the teachers were the only offices of perpetuity through which the church would be led, as "without Pastors and Teachers there can be no government of the church."[24] Calvin saw the office of teacher as indispensable for the church.

Ulrich Zwingli, a major voice during the Reformation and the father of expository preaching, had a surprising take on the office of *didaskalos*. Scholar Daniel Timmerman notes that Zwingli considered himself to be a prophet, a rather unconventional declaration of his day.[25] Zwingli believed it was God himself who gave revelation to the teacher and that it did not need to come through human agency or office. Zwingli thus allowed for the offices of the church and acknowledged the authority contained therein, but more so than these, he relied upon the presence and graces of the Holy Spirit for true illumination of all things spiritually learned.[26]

## Post-Reformation Era

This era covers approximately the years 1600–1750. One of the major emphases of the Catholic Church in post-Reformation times was education. The Church recognized a need for capable individuals to teach the faithful. In the midst of all this, they maintained their doctrines of the infallibility of the pope and the infallibility of the teaching office of the College of Bishops.[27]

One of the leading teachers/theologians within the Swiss Reformed church during this era was Johann Heinrich Heidegger. In his commentary on the office, he noted that the responsibilities of the church's doctors were two-fold. Agreeing with Augustine, Heidegger felt that doctors of the church "powerfully informed the intellect with the teaching of truth and the refutation of falsehoods."[28] He noted other distinguishing factors of the office, namely: doctors practice a nonprescriptive ministry

23. Calvin, *Commentary on Galatians and Ephesians*, 234–35.

24. Calvin, *Commentary on Galatians and Ephesians*, 234–35.

25. Timmerman, *Heinrich Bullinger on Prophecy*, 86.

26. Timmerman, *Heinrich Bullinger on Prophecy*, 86.

27. Catholic Church, "Code of Canon Law: Book III," canon 749 §§1–2.

28. Heidegger, *Office of the Doctor*, 27; thus highlighting a powerful two-fold purpose for the office of (1) dispelling truth and (2) refuting falsehoods. This theme resounds often within academic discussions of the office of *didaskalos*.

within the church, adhering only to descriptive administrations;[29] doctors were called to handle doctrine and to train the church's catechists and exhorters[30] and carried a distinct ability to "open, uncover, and bring into view mysteries to others, so that they might also become known to them for their necessary education."[31] For Heidegger, in order to be worthy of appointment to the office, one would have the requisite faith, testing, suitability to teach, and competency in original languages and receive a terminal education in the arts and in-depth knowledge of the Scriptures.[32] Agreeing with Calvin, Heidegger believed the office of doctor was not to be permanently affixed to a local congregation but was designed to be roaming.[33]

## Modern Era

The modern era extends from AD 1750 to 1900. The works of John Wesley and Jonathan Edwards come into view. Wesley saw a clear distinction between pastors and teachers: pastors were authorized to administer the sacraments, while preachers and teachers were authorized to teach. Wesley's understanding of the office of teacher was one who had been imbued with the authority to teach Scripture and, in a manner agreeing with Calvin, though not disallowing permanent fixture to the local congregation, he nevertheless believed the office to be roaming.[34]

Jonathan Edwards spoke of the office of the teacher as being generally observed as appointed by God as "Christ's messengers (Mai. ii.7), and as representing him, and so speaking in his name, and in his stead (2 Cor. 5 v. 18, 19, 20."[35] He called out teachers as having special authority over the common exhortations and "preachings" of those noncredentialed as such. He believed that the office of teacher implied two things: one, being invested with the authority of a (New Testament)

29. Heidegger, *Office of the Doctor*, 24.

30. Heidegger, *Office of the Doctor*, 19.

31. Heidegger, *Office of the Doctor*, 29.

32. Heidegger, *Office of the Doctor*, 32.

33. Heidegger, *Office of the Doctor*, 19.

34. Wesley, "Ministerial Office," para. 18; synthesized with Wesley's comments on Eph 4:11, in "Notes on St. Paul's Epistle to the Ephesians," ch. 4, v. 11.

35. Edwards, *Works of President Edwards*, 397–98.

teacher; and two, being called to the business of a teacher, making the office the business of their life.[36]

## The Pentecostal Movement

The Pentecostal movement had much to say about the office of teacher. Donald Gee maintained the Eph 4 pastor/teacher pairing as a single role because he believed all pastors needed to be able to teach. He noted that one of the office's distinguishing features was its *post-conversion voice*. The teacher is not called to plant (evangelize) but to water.[37] He warned that some flocks are in danger from a lack of evangelistic zeal, while others are in danger from a lack of solid teaching.[38] He emphasized the necessity of a special calling and a special grace from God to occupy the office.[39] He also highlighted that teachers have the gift of discernment, which allows them to distinguish between true and false teachers.[40]

### *Pentecostal Denominational Periodicals*

Several articles were published in various denominational periodicals highlighting the movement's view on the office. The overall position held is that the office was divine in nature and indispensable for the church; the offices and spiritual gifts were connected to the power of Pentecost; that they are, and have been, in continuance, connected to church governance; and that those who occupied the office were called to work hard and take it seriously.[41]

36. Edwards, *Works of President Edwards*, 399–400.

37. Gee, *Ministry Gifts of Christ*, 66.

38. Gee, *Ministry Gifts of Christ*, 67.

39. Gee, *Ministry Gifts of Christ*, 69.

40. Gee, *Ministry Gifts of Christ*, 70.

41. These periodicals included *Apostolic Faith* (Alvin, Texas), *Apostolic Faith* (Azusa Street), *Assemblies of God Heritage*, *Assemblies of God Ministers Letter*, *Blessed Truth*, *Bridal Call*, *Bridal Call Crusader Foursquare*, *Bridal Call Foursquare*, *Bridegroom's Messenger*, *Church of God Evangel*, *Church of God General Assembly Minutes*, *COGIC (White) Roster*, *Confidence*, *Discipline (CHC)*, *El Evangelico Pentecostal*, *Foursquare Crusader*, *Foursquare Magazine*, *Gospel of the Kingdom*, *International Pentecostal Holiness Advocate*, *La Luz Apostolica*, *Latter Rain Evangel*, *Meat in Due Season*, *Minutes (CHC)*, *Minutes General Council*, *Pentecostal Evangel*, *Pentecostal Herald*, *Pentecostal Testimony*, *Popular Gospel Truth*, *Present Truth*, *Refleks*, *The Faithful Standard*, *The Pentecost*, *The Way*, *White Wing Messenger*, *Whole Truth*, *Word and Witness*, and *Wort Und*

## PUTTING IT ALL TOGETHER

Drawing on the Scripture witness of the office of teacher and the church's traditional handling of the office, several conclusions can be made. One, the office of teacher is first and foremost established by Jesus Christ. He is the *didaskalos* par excellence. The New Testament office is founded upon him as its foundation and as its model. It is Christ through whom one receives one's calling to the office. It is by his design that one so called would subsequently undergo a long season of preparation to meet the demands of, and to satisfy all the requirements of, the office. It is through Christ that one is appointed to the office at the time of perfection, according to God's plan of salvation. It is through the empowerment of his Holy Spirit that one experiences success through the office. The fulfillment of the call is acceptance of divine grace.

Two, *didaskalos* is the best term for the office of teacher, in contrast to the multiplicity of similar words used for *teach* in the New Testament. Several reasons are offered for this. First, *didaskalos* functions as an overarching catch-all for the teacher's other functions in the New Testament. The voice and function of the *didaskalos* encompassed all the voices and functions of the other words (such as *katecheo*, *matheteuo*, *paideuo*, *noutheteo*, and *parangello*). Second, the voice of the *didaskalos* carries the highest authority. This is confirmed in the Vulgate, where the *didaskalos* in Eph 4:11 is translated as *docere*, or *to teach*. Third, the office of *didaskalos* was that of a healer. In practice, the Spirit-empowered *didaskalos caused* participants to learn, grow, be delivered, draw closer to God, repent, be cleansed, be changed, and be healed. Lastly, the location from which the *didaskalos* ministered was primarily the congregation, while the others are found in the classroom, paths of life, personal/private places, valleys, and battlefields.

Three, the office is a high office. Those who are called to the office receive double judgment of their faithfulness in preparing for, and carrying out, the responsibilities enjoined thereto, and this is a distinction of which no other office of the church is so required. From this flows the invitation to embrace the office with the sobriety and gravity expected of

*Zeugnis*, and are published by Pentecostal denominations including Apostolic Faith Movement, Assemblies of God USA, Church of God (Cleveland, Tennessee), Church of God in Christ, Church of God in Christ (White), Church of God of Prophecy, Congregational Holiness Church, Independent, International Church of the Foursquare Gospel, International Pentecostal Church of Christ, International Pentecostal Holiness Church, Pentecostal Church of God, and Refleks-Publishing.

such a high calling. Upon those who are called has befallen a grace that exceeds that of the spiritual gift of teaching listed in Rom 12:7. The office is indeed undergirded and imbued with the power of the Holy Spirit, but the distinction lies in the elevation of the office to which the person has been called, and not the gift which a person has been given.

Those who may aspire ascension to the office without the call will do themselves damage, as well as others so unfortunately connected. The office is not enlivened by natural giftings of intellect, organization, charisma, or style. That the office is marked by respect, authority, honor, and ennoblement has been established through the Scriptures and through the chief theological voices throughout the ages. It is an office marked by the strategic application of God's plan for the salvation of the world. The office is a roaming office whose boundaries extend beyond those of the typical local community. It is indispensable in the economy of the kingdom of God. It is the office of the doctor within the church.

Four, the office's prerequisites require a life commitment to the call. The call is not temporary; it is permanent. The call precedes the appointment. The call precedes the preparation. One who is so called will enter a long season of preparation involving education in in-depth knowledge of Scripture with fluency/familiarity of original languages, orthodox doctrine, testing, the science of teaching, and terminal education in the arts. Those called are encouraged not to succumb to the temptation of grandstanding or to become sidetracked in matters not germane to the office.

Five, the function of the office is leadership, governance, authority, and truth. It carries with it the imperative of living above reproach. It is an office of perpetuity with no Scripture evidence to its cessation. Those who hold the office are the true doctors of the church. Empowered by the Holy Spirit, the office of *didaskalos* holds the highest secular credentials and the highest level of Holy Spirit empowerment. In practice, the Spirit-empowered *didaskalos causes* participants to learn, grow, be delivered, draw closer to God, repent, be cleansed, be changed, and be healed. Healing is manifested through the teaching, direction, and divine admonition of Scripture and true doctrine.

The *didaskalos* is the guardian/curator of the church's sacred writings, its doctrine. As such, theirs is a voice not of prescription, but of description. The office is charged with the twofold task of teaching true doctrine and refuting what is false. The *didaskalos* calls out deception. Because of the authority and authenticity of their call, the *didaskalos* has divine sensitivity and discernment against false teachers. The authority of the office beckons the church to submission. Those who do so receive the living water of Jesus Christ (Apollos was a *didaskalos* who watered that which Paul had planted). The *didaskalos* heralds a post-conversion voice suited to articulating discipleship, sanctification, transformation, and training in righteousness. Theirs is an anointing to impart truth to those whose hearts have already been surrendered to Jesus Christ. The anointing carries with it the divine ability to proclaim sacred truth. As practitioners, we impart healing through confrontation, invitation, and the impartation of grace. This is the prescription of their practice. Healing takes place for those who yield to the Spirit.

## FOR THE PENTECOSTAL MOVEMENT

The witness of Scripture and the long tradition of the church testify that the office of teacher is not a human invention but a Christ-established, Spirit-empowered vocation, grounded in Jesus as the *didaskalos* par excellence and entrusted to those whom he calls, prepares, and appoints. The office is distinguished from the general gift of teaching by its heightened authority, double judgment, and life-long, roaming (and stationary) doctor-of-the-church character, charged with healing the people of God through the proclamation of true doctrine and the refutation of what is false. Ignoring this office is a perilous endeavor. Embracing this office, however, aligns us with the divinely ordered means by which Christ shepherds his church and bolsters the very healing, discerning, truth-bearing ministry of which Pentecostal congregations ought not to be deprived.

For the Pentecostal movement, the underemphasis on this office has put us at risk of prioritizing planting without watering, relying on initial experience without sustained doctrinal and formational depth, which could directly relate to our inability to retain our educated and higher-income converts (see chapter 1). The good news is that those called into the office of teacher are wonderfully suited to further the Spirit-filled mission of the church. The office of teacher, as doctor, healer, and guardian of doctrine, integrates the full range of New Testament *teaching* functions of admonishing, discipling, chastising, warning, and commanding, into a single, congregationally located ministry that brings transformation through the Word. The opportunity for the Pentecostal movement is to recognize, test, train, and release God-called teachers into the congregation's worship life.

If the teacher is Christ's provision for the ongoing healing, sanctification, and doctrinal fidelity of his people, then the Pentecostal movement need not waste another moment relegating this office to the margins of the academy or to occasional conference platforms. Local churches need identifiable *didaskaloi* who carry both rigorous preparation and Spirit-anointed authority, whose post-conversion voice waters what evangelists and apostles have planted and leads believers into deeper discipleship, holiness, and theological stability. Embracing this office in the local church will mean creating pathways of education, discernment, and appointment; granting genuine authority to teachers; and receiving their ministry as an expression of Christ's own care for his body, so that Pentecostal worship might be not only fervent but theologically sound, deeply healed, and fully aligned with the truth.

## REFLECTION QUESTIONS

1. How does the New Testament's placement of the teacher (*didaskalos*) alongside apostles and prophets (e.g., Acts 13:1; 1 Cor 12:28; Eph 4:11) shape our understanding of the authority and function of the teaching office within the church?
2. Describe how *didaskalos* functions as an *overarching* teaching term in the New Testament. How do the other teaching words (*katecheo*, *matheteuo*, *paideuo*, *noutheteo*, *parangello*) enrich—but not replace—the office of *didaskalos*?
3. How does Jesus' teaching ministry establish the pattern and authority for the New Testament office of teacher? Why do you think the Gospels consistently present *teacher* as a title of honor conferred upon Jesus by others?
4. James warns that teachers will receive a stricter judgment (Jas 3:1). How should this warning shape both the aspirations of those who desire to teach and the discernment practices of the local church?
5. What risks does the Pentecostal movement face by marginalizing the office of teacher? What concrete steps might a local Pentecostal congregation take to recognize, train, appoint, and receive Spirit-called *didaskaloi*?

# 3

# Different Types of Sermons

The sermon in the hands of a preacher is like a golf club in the hands of a golfer. Golfers use different clubs for different situations. They use a driver on the tee box; irons are used in the fairways; and putters are used on the greens. For the preacher, different situations call for different types of sermons. The different types of sermons include the expository, topical, textual, narrative, Bible story, and sermon series. The preacher uses different styles depending on what is needed for the sermon. This chapter outlines the different kinds of sermons.

## TOPICAL SERMON

The topical sermon is probably used more than any other type of sermon format in the Pentecostal movement. It's straight, simple, clean, and to the point. The topical sermon is defined as a sermon whose focus is a *topic* or a *theme* of special interest to the pastor or the congregation. Examples of topical sermons include sermons on righteousness, love, persecution, forgiveness, mercy, or grace, etc. There are thousands of these topics within Christianity. This kind of sermon grabs one of these topics and focuses on it for the entirety of the sermon. For example, a sermon on the topic of hospitality would explore what the Bible says about hospitality and then construct a message focusing on hospitality in the home, in the workplace, and in the heart.

Once the preacher has chosen the topic of their sermon, they prepare the message through a time of study and analysis. Bible dictionaries and references are consulted and compared to arrive at the most comprehensive definition of the topic. Concordances are consulted to determine how the topic has been handled throughout Scripture. Further analysis can sometimes be conducted to determine how a particular voice in Scripture has handled the topic. This can be seen, for example, in how the topic of *work* is handled differently between Paul and James.

The preacher conducts research to discover everything the Bible says about the topic. In the process, a list of its major points is compiled. When finished, the preacher usually has more than they need for a sermon. At this point, they determine which points will be included and which points will not. This decision is based on several factors, including the needs of the preacher, the needs of the congregation, various issues with the timing, and other considerations. But one major distinction of the topical sermon is that the preacher determines the sermon's points.

The role of Scripture in a topical sermon is ancillary. This makes sense because the sermon is not about a particular Bible verse or story; it's about a Christian topic or theme. The preacher wants to discover all the Bible has to say about the topic and will ultimately reference Scripture on it, but the sermon is about the topic. It's not uncommon for topical sermons to cite as many as fifteen or twenty or more passages from the Bible.

When our church was going through a season of evangelism training, I preached a sermon entitled "Marketplace Evangelism." As I prepared the message, I went through the process just described. I began by harvesting the best biblical definition of evangelism. After this, I sought to discover all the Bible had to say about the topic. I referenced a concordance, found all the places the word was mentioned, and went through those passages. By the time I had finished, I had more material than I needed. I decided on the following points for the sermon: Marketplace evangelism is incarnational, marketplace evangelism is relational, marketplace evangelism is substantial, and marketplace evangelism is transformational. Eleven different Bible passages were substantively referenced during the sermon.

There are advantages and disadvantages to utilizing topical sermons. The advantages include flexibility to preach in alignment with issues of the day (these would include sermons about headlines, events happening in the church or community, the life of the pastor, or any other reason to preach about the topic), the freedom of the preacher to determine which points they are going to include in the sermon, and covering the topic completely through one sermon or a sermon series. Some disadvantages of topical sermons include the risk of misapplying Scripture, excessive flexibility in topic choice, which sometimes leads pastors to choose a topic for questionable reasons, and incomplete handling of the topic.

## NARRATIVE SERMON

The narrative sermon tells a story. These sermons are very popular because everybody loves a great story. The story could be fictional, personal, an actual event, or a story somebody else wrote. The sermon content is derived from the story's teaching points, with Scripture references quoted throughout. Examples of narrative sermons include the sharing of a testimony of how God moved in a powerful way in someone's life, a story of someone sharing their faith with a friend who gave their heart to Jesus, or a fictional story (consider C. S. Lewis's *Chronicles of Narnia*) that communicates biblical truths.

Preparation for narrative sermons begins with the preacher sitting with their story for a while and sifting out the teaching points. Questions are asked about how God moved, what they learned, how God revealed himself, or how they were changed because of it. Once these have been identified, the preacher is free to conduct research about these concepts and use them as the main points of the sermon.

In the process, words, concepts, truths, and principles are examined using the standard tools of sermon preparation, such as Bible dictionaries, lexicons, journals, monographs, commentaries, and concordances. Each point of the sermon is treated the same way. Explanations, descriptions, examples, and illustrations are included in the notes to best highlight the point. The preacher tells the story while working their way through the main points.

The role of Scripture in the narrative sermon is also ancillary. The main point of the sermon is to tell a story of how God moved. The truths and principles learned along the way are then bolstered by God's having already revealed them in the Bible. Scripture is brought in to support the points and to validate the claims.

A great example of a narrative sermon is when I invited our church's financial advisor to preach one Sunday. He was there on invitation to give a report at our annual church business meeting, and I thought it would be nice to ask him to preach as well. I anticipated a sermon such as "The Ten Principles for How to Manage Your Money According to the Bible," or something along these lines. Much to my surprise, he didn't talk about money. Instead, he told the story of how God has taught him to love through the lives of his two children with special needs. He recounted stories of hardship and struggle, how he learned to defend the least of these, and the authenticity of love he experienced in their unfiltered affections. We all sat and wept.

Narrative sermons have several advantages. The personal nature of the preacher's real stories creates an atmosphere of vulnerability and transparency, which in turn powerfully shapes homiletical dynamics. Narrative sermons are very popular because most people love stories. They invite the listeners to participate in the story, as storytelling often does. They allow for the illustrative delivery of truth, which is sometimes more effective than direct delivery. Some disadvantages to narrative sermons include the misinterpretation of events, proof-texting the Bible to support these kinds of unfounded interpretations, the temptation to falsify details to better enliven the story, or sloppy preparation.

## BIBLE STORY SERMON

Bible story sermons are some of the easiest sermons to preach. Everyone loves a great story, and when it's a Bible story, the lessons are already built in. The summers in Phoenix, Arizona (where I live), are very hot. This means that on any given Sunday, at least one-third of my congregation is out of town chasing the cooler weather of the mountains or the beaches. We decided early on that our summers would be a time of Bible story sermons. Our congregation loves them. We preach the popular stories, the weird stories, and the obscure stories.

The point of the Bible story sermon is to retell a Bible story as a sermon. There are different ways of going about this. One way is to read the story from the Bible in its entirety, then share the truths and principles it conveys. Another is to read a portion of the story and then share the truths and principles, and repeat until the story is delivered in its entirety. Another way is to read the beginning of the story and then recount the rest from memory while working through the points of the sermon. This approach works well with well-known, longer stories like David and Goliath, the flood, or the feeding of the five thousand, where the congregation can fill in any missing information not covered directly in the sermon.

Preparation for Bible story sermons begins by sitting with the story and reading through a few times. Questions are asked to identify the five Ws (who, what, when, where, and how/why), the context and setting, the truths and principles, and why God chose to include this story in Scripture. What are the lessons we learn? What does the story reveal about God or any other theological categories? Research comes next to bolster understanding and to illuminate all angles of the story. After this, the preacher is ready to refine the sermon's main points so they can tell the story and preach them simultaneously.

Scripture leads the way in Bible story sermons, and this is its primary function in this kind of sermon. The main points of the sermon are derived from the story and depend on it. There are no points of the sermon that are not found directly within the story. The sermon is the story. It is also common for other passages of Scripture to appear in Bible story sermons, which further illustrate the points being made.

There are hundreds of stories in the Bible. One example of a Bible story sermon is Jesus healing the Gerasene demoniac in Mark. I've preached this sermon, and when I prepared for it, I sat with the story for a few hours. I had a long list of observations worthy of pulpit enunciation. But the longer I sat with it, I discovered several revealing principles about Jesus. I shortened the list to seven and made them the points of the sermon: Jesus is not afraid to go to dark places, Jesus has power over demons, Jesus cares for demonized people, Jesus has the power to restore the unrestorable, Jesus is offensive to the spiritually undiscerned, Jesus expects his followers to be testifiers, and Jesus won't stay where he's not wanted.

After my introduction, I read the story to the congregation in its entirety. The story is only twenty verses long, so I was able to read it in one reading. After this, I went through my list of seven principles we learn about Jesus. Each point along the way emphasized a different portion of the story. By the time we were finished, the congregation had heard a multi-angled sermonized retelling of the story.

The advantages of Bible story sermons include the increase of biblical literacy among the congregation, providing greater familiarity with Bible stories, allowing the Bible to speak for itself, and the popularity of storytelling. The only disadvantage of this kind of sermon is for the preacher who struggles in telling stories.

## SERMON SERIES

A sermon series is a collection of sermons that run consecutively for a determined period that focus on the same topic or run through a particular book of the Bible. Sermon series are good for the congregation and should be part of the preacher's regular diet of sermons throughout the year. The length of the series can vary, but too few sermons won't feel like a series, and too many might grow stale for the congregation. Six or eight sermons are about right for a series. For longer books, the pastor can preach for six or eight weeks, then take a few weeks off before continuing.

Each sermon in a sermon series does not have to maintain the same format as the others. A six-week series through the book of Ephesians, for example, could include topical, expository, or textual sermons. Each sermon follows its own preparation method. One of the primary tasks in preparation is to outline the entire series. If the series is a topical one on faith and politics, for example, the pastor would want to identify all the sermons they plan to preach in the series and create an outline for each. This assures the preacher that they can cover everything in the series.

Examples of sermon series include amazing men or women of the Bible, angels, armor of God, tithing, walking by the Spirit, Ruth, Esther, Obadiah, etc. The advantages of a sermon series are the regularity and predictability for the congregation, less contextual research for the preacher, and always knowing what your next sermon will be. Some disadvantages include the series being too short or too long or the congregation or the pastor growing weary of it.

## EXPOSITORY SERMON

The expository sermon is the primary pulpit tool for the teaching pastor. It involves a methodical, systematic exegesis of the passage, which is then presented to the congregation in a clear, coherent manner. The preacher exposes the truths and principles contained in the verse's words, phrases, nuances, and hidden messages. A comprehensive presentation on the context, history, author, audience, purpose for writing, etc., is included. It stands above all other types of sermons as the teaching sermon, scoring highly on educational measures.

Preparation for the expository sermon involves a commitment to thorough exegesis, the process of discovering all that can be derived from the passage. Passages are brief in expository sermons, usually limited only to a couple of verses or a single pericope (a single unit of thought). Words and phrases are studied in their original languages to solidify accurate definitions. Syntax and grammar are analyzed to reveal original inspiration. Observations are made to identify relationships among the various components of the passage. Cross-references are examined to see how certain words have been used in other places in Scripture. Commentaries and other resources are researched to see how others have interpreted the passage. A clear, unifying idea or concept emerges as the main idea of the sermon as it takes shape.

The Scripture passages stand front and center in the expository sermon. The preacher carries with them no preconceived agenda other than to discover what can be taken away from the passage. This is not an exercise in proof-texting. They are not searching for what the passage might say about a certain topic that the preacher has in mind. They let the text speak for itself. The text is researched and analyzed as it is. Various translations are placed side by side to note differences in interpretation. Literal translations are compared with paraphrastic translations.

The points of the sermon are derived from the text. This stands in contrast to the topical sermon, where the points are determined by the preacher. The expository approach requires the preacher to approach the text with no agenda other than to discover what can be removed and to faithfully deliver that content to the congregation. The main idea of the sermon is determined by the text. The main points of the sermon are similarly determined. The preacher need not worry about what to preach because once the passage has been chosen, the content flows from it rather than the preacher bringing an agenda to it.

The expository sermon is nonoccasional, meaning it does not sit at the mercy of any holiday or occasion that would normally require a certain topic to be preached. Christmas and Easter are two such occasions. Expository preaching does not allow any occasion to dictate what is being preached because the content of the sermon is determined by the text.

Expository sermons are like sermonized Bible studies. The passages being studied are carefully and systematically analyzed. Words and phrases are defined. Concepts are described and explained. Truths and principles are waved as banners for all to see. Upon completion, congregants walk away with solid exposure to the passage and a woven familiarity with it. When asked what their pastor preached on, they respond with the reference. "My pastor preached on Micah 6:8 today."

An example of an expository sermon might be John 14:6 (NASB), "Jesus said to him, 'I am the way, and the truth, and the life; no one comes to the Father except through Me.'" The exegete would quickly note the teaching points for this sermon: Jesus is the way, Jesus is the truth, Jesus is the life, and Jesus is the only way to God. In preparation for this sermon, the preacher would thoroughly and carefully exegete the passage and search out the definitions of words such as way, truth, and life. They would examine the passage's context and determine why Jesus made this statement. They would research the other ways people in his day falsely claimed to be acceptable paths to God, for example. They would segue into some of the ways people today falsely claim as acceptable paths to God, such as being a good person or believing that God is real. They would do this for all the points of the sermon and arrive at the pulpit with notes in hand, ready to teach their findings.

There are several advantages to the expository approach. Biblical literacy rises for the congregation. Solid teaching about doctrine and theology abounds. The Bible becomes approachable, less intimidating in the hands of a skilled exegete. Expository sermons are enjoyable when done correctly. Some disadvantages include the risk of boring, dry messages. When done wrong, expository sermons can sound like the preacher is reading from an encyclopedia. Not many people want to sit and listen to that. They can be too academic. Sometimes, preachers load the sermon with theological jargon and concepts that go over the heads of the congregation. These kinds of scenarios leave the congregation with little understanding and feeling dumb.

In chapter 13, I offer a definition of expository preaching that is faithful to the unique distinctives of Pentecostal preaching and to the unique markers of how Pentecostals interpret the Bible. I follow this up in chapter 14 with a comparison of this definition against other well-known definitions for expository preaching.

## TEXTUAL SERMON

The textual sermon combines the topical and expository sermons. It is a popular method used by many preachers. It employs several of the preparation requirements for the expository sermon while allowing more freedom in the preacher's delivery. The congregation experiences a depth of teaching counterbalanced with fresh commentary and insights from the preacher. When people are asked what their pastor preached on, they respond with both content and reference, "My pastor preached on how we're supposed to be the salt and light to the world from Matthew 5." Both topic and text shine through, and both are carried away by the congregation.

It's called textual because its foundation is the text, but its content is allowed to drift into topical lanes. Here, the preacher will begin with a verse that they have subjected to the exegetical methods described above but will also allow for exploration of themes and concepts related to the text, but not in the text, to find expression in the sermon. An example of this can be seen in a sermon I once preached on 2 Cor 4:16–18 (NASB):

> Therefore we do not lose heart, but though our outer person is decaying, yet our inner person is being renewed day by day. For our momentary, light affliction is producing for us an eternal weight of glory far beyond all comparison, while we look not at the things which are seen, but at the things which are not seen; for the things which are seen are temporal, but the things which are not seen are eternal.

For one of the points of the sermon, I took Paul's declaration of not losing heart and turned it into an imperative for the congregation to not give up. Paul did not tell the believers in Corinth not to give up in these verses, but it was an easy and appropriate theme to incorporate into the sermon.

Another example can be found in a sermon I preached on Gal 6:7–10, where Paul warns us not to be deceived because God cannot be mocked and that we reap what we sow. As I studied these passages, ultimately, the Lord led me to preach a message with these points: God cannot be mocked; you reap what you sow; you reap where you sow; you reap in a different season; and you reap more than you sow. The last two of those points were not addressed in the text but were incorporated into the sermon I titled "The Reaping Principle."

In the textual sermon, Scripture functions as its anchor and foundation. The sermon begins with the passage. The passage is subjected to the normal best practices of exegesis. The points of the passage are directly related to the passage, even if not clearly articulated in the passage. The content is limited to that which is directly related to the text.

The textual sermon offers advantages that allow the preacher to preach biblically while also having the freedom to include related content that is not exegetically derived. It allows the congregation to experience sound biblical teaching, balanced with commentary, content, and insight from the preacher. It allows the preacher to explore the application of truths and principles to other areas of life, giving the Word personal points of entry for the congregation. The disadvantages of this approach are that inexperienced preachers can see and preach on connections that aren't there. Forays in these areas can be confusing to the congregation.

In the end, every sermon type is a tool in the preacher's hand, with each one designed to serve the particular agenda of the Spirit. No single approach stands above the others in every circumstance. The expository sermon grounds the congregation in the authority of Scripture; the textual sermon blends structure with flexibility; the topical sermon brings relevance to current issues; the narrative and Bible story sermons awaken the imagination and reach the heart through the power of story; and the sermon series provides consistency and depth over time. The wise preacher knows not only how to craft each type but how to discern which one the moment requires.

Selecting the right sermon type involves both pastoral sensitivity and theological integrity. The preacher must listen closely to the Spirit, to the congregation, and to the cultural moment, allowing those voices to inform which homiletical form will carry the message most faithfully. What unites these various methods is not their structure but their purpose: to proclaim Christ and edify his people. When used rightly, each sermon type becomes a unique vessel for divine truth, serving the preacher's mission to communicate the Word of God in ways that are both clear and compelling.

## REFLECTION QUESTIONS

1. Compare and contrast the role of the preacher's agenda in topical versus expository sermons. How does the shift in authority between the preacher and the text affect the final message delivered?
2. Given the risk of misapplication of Scripture in topical preaching, what specific safeguards or hermeneutical tools should a preacher employ to ensure they remain biblically faithful while addressing contemporary social headlines?

3. Why is the expository sermon categorized as the "primary pulpit tool for the teaching pastor"? Explain how the process of systematic exegesis contributes to the high educational value of this style.
4. Evaluate the textual sermon as a middle ground between topical and expository styles. How does this hybrid approach provide the preacher with flexibility while still maintaining a strong anchor in the biblical text?
5. Select two sermon types from the chapter and describe a specific congregational need for each. How does a preacher's "pastoral sensitivity" determine which homiletical tool is most appropriate for a given Sunday?

# PART TWO

## Setting the Homiletical Foundation

One key insight I've gained over the years is how homiletics students need a broad-based understanding of the Pentecostal movement's homiletical tradition. Many of my students have been surprised to learn about the unique features of our homiletical landscape, especially when they are contrasted with cessationist preaching models (see the definition for this term in the preface). Most are pleased with their discovery that Pentecostal preaching is an altogether different kind of proclamation of the Word. The chapters of this section introduce you to the rich contours of Pentecostal preaching.

What follows is a primer, a concise guide meant to introduce you to the major voices and recurring themes that have shaped Pentecostal preaching over the past century. The insights in this chapter are drawn from an extensive survey of practitioners and scholars who have charted the path for Pentecostal homiletics. While academic in origin, the purpose of this summary is pastoral and practical: to give you a foundational grasp of how Pentecostal preachers have historically understood the purpose, method, and identity of Spirit-empowered proclamation.

Because the published literature on this subject is limited, the material presented here distills the significant contributions of classic leaders such as Guy P. Duffield, Ray H. Hughes, and Charles T. Crabtree, as well as modern voices such as Aldwin Ragoonath, John Lombard, and Mark L. Williams (with Lee Roy Martin). Their writings, along with select academic reflections edited by Martin, help us see that Pentecostal homiletics cannot simply be categorized as a sub-category of broader evangelical patterns. It must be discerned within the context of a movement whose preaching flows from the dynamic experience of the Spirit. (For a complete list of the key Pentecostal preaching resources that shaped this section, including full citations for the works by Duffield, Hughes, Ragoonath, Crabtree, Williams, and Martin, see appendix A at the back of this book.)

My aim in this section is not merely to summarize these voices, but to guide you toward understanding what it means to preach Pentecostally, to proclaim the living Word in the power of the Holy Spirit, with the expectation that the same Spirit who inspired the text also animates the preaching event. Whether you are a student preparing for ministry or a lay pastor serving your congregation, this chapter will help you recognize the distinct theological and practical commitments that make Pentecostal preaching Spirit-empowered proclamation.

Is there anything different about a Pentecostal sermon? If so, what are the unique markers of Pentecostal preaching that distinguish it from cessationist preaching? Is there something other than *stereotypical theatrics* that makes Pentecostal preaching unique? Is there anything about our preaching that could easily identify it as Pentecostal? The answer to these questions is yes. The Pentecostal sermon is different than all the rest. It enjoys a place of special character. When you're done reading these chapters, you're going to feel proud to be part of the Pentecostal/Charismatic movement.

# 4

# The Minister's Call

THE MINISTER'S CALL STANDS as the bedrock of authentic Pentecostal preaching, an undeniable divine summons that presupposes the Spirit-filled homiletical journey. Far more than a personal ambition or vocational choice, the call originates in the Spirit's inner stirring, a percolation that crystallizes through stories, timelines, and transformative encounters. Whether the preacher experiences a Damascus Road flash like Paul's, a lifelong series of formative events, or even the rare kind of clarity from birth, the call stands as a divine prerequisite for pulpit ministry.

Pentecostal ministry calls us to discern true calling in the midst of real struggles. People chasing platforms of influence, inner healing they imagine will accompany the office, or theological education as a means of functioning as a preacher often crash because they never received a call. Only the authentically called have the staying power indispensable to pulpit ministry. The minister's call delivers a divine survivability that holds them through doubts, job hunts, and runaway moments. The call frees the minister to be fully themselves, that is, their God-given personality, smarts, humor, passions, even brokenness, ditching fake imitation that kills anointing so our true eternal self can shine bright in Jesus.

This chapter walks through how the call really feels from those early God-moments that get you wondering, to the defining encounters that seal it, helping preachers test their sense of calling against Scripture and their own story. Grasping this foundation keeps us from copying others and unlocks Spirit-filled preaching that flows from God's choice, not our own effort, where our weaknesses become the very place his power shines and every limp reminds us of his grace.

## THE UNDENIABILITY OF THE CALL

One of the more sensitive aspects of ministerial leadership are the occasions when I've had to help someone seeking the pulpit who has *not* been authentically called by the Spirit. Some people are attracted to ministry for ulterior motives. These might include, for example, someone needing greater access to the health and healing they know the church offers. Others seek the platform because they desire the power associated with the pastoral influence. And still others may be simply confused about their direction in life. I've often wondered, given the high frequency of pastoral demise, whether those who have abandoned their posts were ever truly called to the ministry. Only God knows.

How does one know if they are undeniably, incontestably called in the ministry? Typically, when preachers are asked this question, they tell a story. There's always a good story that characterizes the call's undeniability. This usually involves several definite points on a timeline of stories and circumstances that made it clear to them. Usually, the call begins with an inner stirring, or percolation, from the Holy Spirit, signaling that God is calling them into full-time ministry. This may still involve part-time work in other capacities, but it does not take away from the call to full-time ministry.

It's rare, but sometimes preachers report being called from birth. Such individuals find themselves behind a microphone at very early ages. Preachers can have their own Damascus Road experience, where God dramatically interrupts their lives to show them how much they must suffer for the kingdom of God, as Paul was prophetically informed by Ananias (Acts 9:16). Other times, the call can unfold over a long series of events throughout a person's life that ultimately lead them to a place where they know they are called. This can include being asked to speak at events or lead Bible studies or finding themselves providing comfort in a crisis to those in need, and others. Regardless of the circumstances God uses to bring the individual to the point of certainty, one thing remains constant in every preacher's story of their call: a deep inner sense from the Holy Spirit that God is setting them aside for this very important full-time work.

The call gives birth to an all-in level of commitment. Some individuals enjoy preaching when called upon. There are others who pursue service within the church that involves occasional preaching. But for the preacher who has been called, the response to the call is an all-or-nothing affirmation. Though the preacher might, out of necessity, be bivocational, this does not diminish the all-in commitment to the call. The nature of the call requires that level of commitment. The invitation to the preacher is like Jesus' invitation to his disciples: to leave everything and follow him.

For the called, there is nothing else to which they could dedicate their life other than the pulpit ministry of the church. Try as they may, even in times of frustration, the call is inescapable. Preachers who carry the call live in a constant state of tension between enjoying the greatest level of vocational satisfaction every time they preach, on the one hand, and the fumbling and stumbling of carrying the burden of the call, on the other. The burden of the call is part of God's design. The call ministry is never meant to be a burden that the preacher can carry on their own. God does this on purpose. If the preacher could carry the weight of the call on their own, then they would never need the Lord.

Moses gives us one of the best examples of this dynamic. Moses grew up in levels of opulence that transcend imagination. He was so rich that it took forty years for him to be ready for the call. This was all part of God's design. By the time Moses encountered God in the burning bush, he was a murderer on the lam, married to a foreign woman, tending somebody else's sheep, living as a nomad out in the wilderness, and he had a stutter.

By all outward appearances, Moses was the least qualified person to lead the greatest story of redemption in world history. He was not a general. He did not command a great army. He was not famous. He was not loved by the masses. He was not a skilled orator. The divine irony in all this points to God's brilliance and the nature of the call. Moses was perfectly qualified to lead the exodus because God knew Moses would have to rely upon him every step of the way.

Those called to preach are invited to carry the burden of Moses. God says to the preacher, "I'm calling you to serve me, and to speak for me, and my grace is such that I will make sure that you cannot do this without me." For the preacher, this means the call is often fraught with doubt and insecurity and with innumerable attempts to leave the ministry and do something else. Moses experienced this throughout his ministry. The Scriptures record several stories of Moses arguing with God and threatening to quit. Moses is not unique in this dynamic. Every person whom God has called in the Scriptures has suffered through the burden of the call. And yet, ironically, the call carries a compulsion to continue. The preacher says time and again how they cannot imagine doing anything else in the world other than being a full-time preacher.

## MARKS OF THE CALL

The call to preach delivers certain manifest characteristics. First, a passion for the Word of God and for the opportunity to proclaim it is evident. Passion finds expression in words, beliefs, and behaviors. When asked about the Word or about preaching, the called ones speak with enthusiasm, depth, and intensity.

A willingness to serve is another marker of the calling. Stephen and Philip were two men whom God used in powerful and profound ways in the book of Acts. Stephen was the church's first martyr. He was killed because of the eloquence and passion with which he spoke about the gospel. The Bible says he was full of wisdom and power (Acts 6). Philip was similarly described. The Holy Spirit sent Philip to Samaria, where he spoke with authority, performed signs and wonders, cast out demons, and led an Ethiopian eunuch to the Lord.

What's unique about both Stephen and Philip is that they began their ministries by serving tables. There were part of the seven men, of good repute, full of the Spirit and of wisdom, chosen to serve food to the widows of the church. They were not put off by the small start. Those called to preach are not offended when asked to serve tables. Service is the starting place of ministry.

Humility is a mark of the call. The presence of humility is not merely the absence of arrogance. There are many people in the church who lack arrogance, but that does not mean they walk in the call and the requisite humility that accompanies it. Humility is also not merely the presence of a low self-worth. On the contrary, humility embraces a high evaluation of self-worth, all the while knowing that that high self-worth comes from the deep assurance that they belong to God, and that the ministerial utility of that high self-worth is made manifest only through one's weaknesses.

Those who carry the call also carry a desire to learn. This makes sense. One of the beautiful ironies of the call is how God typically calls us into areas where we have little-to-no natural ability. God does this on purpose. It keeps us humble. Moses was called to be one of the greatest orators of all time, but he had a stutter. He was no natural orator. Preachers who are called carry a Moses-like dependency upon God. With that dependency comes a lifelong desire for learning. Called preachers are students of their trade.

The call is marked by an unmistakable fear of the Lord. Some called to preach may have Peter-like tendencies that get them in trouble (speak before thinking, act without planning, threaten to call down judgment on critics, etc.), but that doesn't mean they are without a deep, committed acknowledgment of God being sovereign in their life and a healthy fear, reverence, and awe of his authority. The call is marked by such obedience.

Called preachers typically walk with a limp. That is to say, they bear the marks of having wrestled with God. Like Jacob, who, in Gen 32, wrestled with God and lived, he carried with him a lifetime effect of the encounter. The limp is evidence of God's grace. God's grace comes and says to the preacher, "I know you can't do this. I've heard your protest. I know there's a side of you that's filled with fears, doubts, and a desire not do this. But that's why I chose you; it's why I can trust you. This limp is my reminder to you about how much you need me."

Moses walked with a limp. He wrestled with God. He didn't want the job of leading Israel out of captivity. Same with Paul. The Bible says Paul asked God to remove a thorn from his flesh three times (2 Cor 12:8–9) only to hear God tell him, "No, my grace is sufficient for you, for my power is made perfect in weakness." Called preachers are easily criticized. Like Peter, their faults are on full display.

The final mark to be considered is the call's love/hate nature. Only those with the call understand this dynamic. Called preachers testify that they will probably preach until the moment they die. They say things like, "They'll have to pick me up from behind the pulpit." They cannot fathom a life without access to a microphone. Yet those same preachers will also testify of the numerous times they were tempted to leave full-time ministry because their fears, doubts, and failures.

Many called preachers, in fact most of them, are protected from the trappings of worldly success in their ministry. Paul was the greatest post-ascension preacher in the New Testament, yet he never knew his impact. All he knew about was a bunch of small, struggling house churches he left behind scattered around Europe and Palestine. What this means for the called preacher is that their ministry is marked by a passionate love for preaching, carried through the limps of fears, doubts, and failures.

But this is the nature of the call. Passion, humility, a willingness to serve, an insatiable desire to learn and grow, and a fear of the Lord, all packaged in a person who loves to preach but is scarred from the constant battles of ministry.

## CALL TO AUTHENTICITY

The minister's call is a call to authenticity. As one who has taught college homiletics for many years, I've seen too many ministers preach in ways that are inauthentic to who God created them to be. It's hard to watch. It's painful, actually. It's one thing to appreciate, and even somewhat emulate, the approach of a favorite preacher, but it's another thing to flat out copy them or to be someone God never intended us to be.

A few features come into view when we discuss the preacher's call to authenticity. The first is personality. God gives personalities when he knits us together in our mother's womb (Ps 139). They come through divine assignment. As such, our personalities are given to us for a reason. Personalities don't change over time. The personality that you were born with is the same personality that you will die with and that you will carry with you into eternity.

If we fast-forward a few thousand years into the future, what kind of person would I meet if I bumped into you in heaven? What version of you is the eternal version? What will you look like when all the encumbrances of sin and all the layers of masking are removed, and you are able to rejoice in the truest expression of who God created you to be? One thing I know for certain is that I will see your God-given personality shining, unfettered and without inhibition, in the brilliance of Christ!

Every called preacher needs to know their personality type. Your personality is a gift from God! If you haven't already done so, take a test and make a commitment to minister only within the individuality God has given you. If your personality is primarily introverted, you're doing yourself and others a disservice if you try to minister through forced extroversion. The opposite is also true.

The second is the preacher's intellect. Some preachers have a scholarly intellect, while others are average. If you're one of the brighter ones, congratulations, you're part of a rare, upper echelon of leaders that will serve the church handsomely. If not, and if you're a Spirit-filled Bible teacher, there may exist a temptation to feign intellectualism higher than what was gifted you. Avoid this temptation. You're in the majority, and you're perfect just the way you are.

I remember a time in my life when I was trying to be intellectually greater than who God created me to be. This was back when I started my master's degree. Looking back, I can see quite clearly what happened. Being immersed in the world of scholasticism had awoken within me a greater desire for education. And if you don't mind the transparency, this desire, coupled with some of the depths of brokenness I was experiencing at the time, created what I thought was a pathway to better self-acceptance for me. The thought was that maybe I could respect myself more if others saw me as smart. There was nothing wrong with this desire. In fact, I later realized this desire was divine in origin, and that one day it would find fruition, *but not until I could learn how to exist authentically*, according to the personality and intellect God gave me.

Maybe you were a person blessed with a simpler, more beautiful form of intellectualism. That's perfectly fine. I've seen God use ministers at all levels and in powerful ways. Are you ready for some good news? Spirit anointing is never presupposed by high intellectualism. It is, however, presupposed by authenticity. Can you embrace the level of intellectualism God has given you? Until that day comes, you will not flow in the anointing of the Holy Spirit, and you will wonder why your sermons and worship services are struggling.

Thirdly is one's sense of humor. Are you a person with the natural gift of gab? Can you make people laugh without even trying? If so, may I encourage you to flow in the sense of humor God has given you? Maybe you have a dry, dark sense of humor. That's perfectly fine. I celebrate with you in your God-given sense of humor. Embrace it. Preach from it. Be authentic.

I've gone through the embarrassing seasons of trying to be funny in the pulpit. I naively thought that sermons had to be entertaining. I was wrong. Sermons do not need to be entertaining. They need to flow from the preacher's authenticity. Your congregation will hang on your every word when you are preaching authentically from who God made you to be. For some, that means the congregation will frequently erupt in laughter. For others, it means the congregation will enjoy well-positioned, light-hearted comments, perfectly and appropriately placed throughout the sermon. Either way, the invitation for the preacher is to be authentic.

Before we leave this point of authenticity, let me finish with a few comments regarding your passions and your brokenness. I've come to enjoy a few themes in my life that are fueled with great passion. These are life themes of divine origin, interwoven into all facets of my ministry. A few of these include authentic relationality with Jesus Christ, preaching/teaching against false teachings in the church, and suffering for the kingdom.

God gave these passions to me. I did not contrive them myself. What are yours? If you're not certain, there are a couple of questions you can ask yourself. One, what are the themes/areas that you keep going back to in your thinking, conversation, writing, preaching, etc.? Are you seeing a pattern developing? Second, ask yourself about the things that make you mad. I used to get hot under the collar when I saw Christian leaders with high levels of influence abusing their authority with false teachings. It became clear to me that this was a passion. This is from the Lord, and it's a big part of my ministry. I need to be true to this passion. What about you? What are yours?

When it comes to brokenness, an entire book could be written about preaching from the cracks of our earthen vessels. Let me ask you this: What was the last crisis you experienced? What did you learn about God while you were walking through that valley of the shadow of death? How many sermons did you preach from it? Did you know that every crisis is an opportunity to learn something about God and for your faith to grow? Can you think of any better preaching material than this? If there were ever a space where the minister can preach with passion, conviction, experiential knowledge, and the invitation for your congregation to be changed because of it, this is it.

## THE CALL IS EXPERIENTIAL

The minister's call is experiential. Typically, the call begins with a season of precursory, lead-up experiences that prompt the preacher to think, ponder, and wonder whether God is doing something in their life that might point to a more full-time engagement in ministry. The story of Moses gives us a great picture of this phenomenon. Moses grew up in the house of Pharaoh, where he experienced riches and opulence that transcend imagination. It's possible that his wealth blinded him to the struggles and plight of everyday people.

Yet, one day, something stirred him to go check on the welfare of his enslaved, oppressed, and mistreated Hebrew brothers. Upon witnessing an Egyptian soldier abusing one of his Hebrew brothers, and after making sure no one was looking, Moses took matters into his own hands and killed the Egyptian and buried his body in the sand (Exod 2). What was it that stirred this level of concern within him? Something was happening. God was moving on Moses. The call was beginning to materialize in his life.

Upon hearing that Pharaoh sought to kill him for his deed, Moses fled to the desert, where he encountered another such moment of divine intervention that would ultimately become the bedrock of his ministry. In this story, Moses was sitting at a well when some young women showed up to draw water for their father's flock. Next on the scene, shepherds appeared who began to abuse the young women. Once again, at the sight of helpless people being abused, the call that was percolating inside Moses began to materialize. He intervened and rescued the young women from danger. This was another precursor experience in which God gave Moses a foretaste of his call. The father was so impressed that he gave Moses one of his daughters in marriage, and they had a son. These two stories occurred before Moses received his call in the burning bush event.

For most preachers, the call begins with stories like this, designed to prompt them to think, ponder, and wonder whether God is doing something in their lives. They begin to experience events where the hand of God is at work. My call experience was no exception. In the years leading up, several events occurred in which elements of the supernatural manifested, prompting me to walk away in reflection. These were moments like Mary experienced in the first few chapters of Luke, where elements of the supernatural caused her to "ponder these things in her heart."

It begins with divine confrontation. Called preachers can always tell the story of when they received their call. There's a defining point in the timeline of their life. When asked, they'll describe it in great detail. They tell you about the time of day, what they were doing at the moment, where they were, and the effect it had upon them. Usually, it's a stopping moment, the kind that makes them pause to process what they had just experienced.

I was working in the room service department at a resort when the call came. It was daytime. I was outside. I was on my way to deliver some food to a room. I had been sensing the call to full-time ministry for several months, spending much time contemplating, wondering, and praying. The moment was a flash. I knew it was from the Lord. I wish I could tell you I was met by the incarnate Jesus Christ or by some high-ranking angel dispatched to deliver the news, but it was much simpler than that. For me, it was a moment of supernatural inspiration. It was a divine download of wisdom.

Part of my contemplation was figuring out what life would look like and how I would support my family if I were to make the move. The Holy Spirit, in a flash of wisdom, downloaded the plan for how everything would work out. I discerned the moment was more than just a good idea. I knew it was from the Lord. The Lord later confirmed it as such when I told my wife about it, and she agreed. The call begins with such moments of divine encounter. The moment confirms what the Holy Spirit had been stirring in the months leading up to it.

## THE CALL IS THE SECRET TO MINISTERIAL SURVIVABILITY

If you're like my wife, you love a good puzzle. And if you're lucky, you have her same tenacity and stubbornness to never quit until the puzzle is finished. Her method is always the same. She starts with the border, and if she gets stuck on a missing piece, she doesn't give up until she finds it. She knows the piece is there; she just needs to keep searching until she finds it. It's the guarantee that all the pieces are there that fuels her tenacity in searching for the missing piece.

The minister's call is like the guarantee that all the pieces of the puzzle are there. The call comes and deposits a divine survivability that carries us through seasons where we would otherwise be tempted to give up. Sometimes we find ourselves stuck and struggling to find the missing piece. The call comes in to remind us during such times that God has a plan and all the pieces are in his hands.

In a different light, the call not only affords divine survivability but also safeguards us with compulsory preservability. If you're like me, there have been a few seasons where the struggles of ministry have gotten the best of you. You lost sight of the call. And what happens during seasons like this? We try to leave. We update our resumes. We apply for secular positions. We look for parachurch positions. We even create profiles on job search websites.

God has a lot of grace for this. But what do we learn in the process? We learn that, like Jonah, when God calls us, there's only one answer: yes.

We discover some key truths that are discoverable only in such seasons. One is that God calls us to that which is greater than our natural ability. Of course ministry is going to be challenging. If someone told you otherwise, they told you wrong. If we could do it in our own natural abilities, we would never need to exercise faith in God. This is a kind of lesson that isn't learned in books; it's learned through the struggles of ministry. And two, the call preserves us. It keeps us. It doesn't let us go. Like Jonah, even if we try to leave our efforts are in vain if God has determined to use us. The call is like heavenly handcuffs. I have found it to be consistently true: every time I have tried to leave, the Lord hasn't let me go. I made it through all those seasons and collected all the lessons the Lord intended for me to learn along the way, and can now minister in and through a peace that transcends understanding. This is good news. The call protects us, preserves us, and develops us. One of the best features of the call is its ability to comfort us.

## REFLECTION QUESTIONS

1. Reflecting on Moses' call, discuss the nature of divine calling, and what lessons can preachers learn from his example about dependence on God's grace?
2. Why is authenticity emphasized as essential in preaching, and what are the dangers of trying to imitate others instead of embracing one's unique, God-given personality and style?
3. How can personal brokenness and crises be transformed into powerful preaching moments? What does the chapter suggest about the connection between suffering and spiritual growth in ministry?
4. Why is self-awareness, including understanding one's personality, intellect, and passions, crucial to fulfilling the ministerial call authentically, and how can this awareness enhance effective preaching?
5. How does the minister's call act as a safeguard for ministerial survivability, and what lessons about obedience, perseverance, and reliance on God can preachers draw from Jonah's and Moses' experiences?

# 5

# Purpose of Pentecostal Preaching

## EXALTATION OF THE RESURRECTED JESUS CHRIST

The primary purpose of Pentecostal preaching is the exaltation of the resurrected Jesus Christ. Let the reader lean into this and read it a thousand times. This exaltation occurs not merely through doctrinal affirmation but through a Spirit-empowered proclamation that reveals Christ as living and active among his people. Pentecostal preaching invites hearers to encounter the risen Lord, not as a historical figure confined to the past, but as the present, risen Christ who saves, heals, and fills believers with his Spirit. In this way, the sermon becomes an event of divine encounter, where Christ is both proclaimed and experienced.

Pentecostal sermons continue to rally around this exaltation. Duffield emphasized this in his work, stating that Pentecostal preachers are called to preach Jesus, with the exaltation of Christ as the paramount function of the sermon, aligning with John 15:26, where the Holy Spirit glorifies Jesus. His assertion makes sense. On the night that Jesus was betrayed, he sat with his disciples in the upper room, shared a meal with them, and then things got serious. Jesus declared to them in no uncertain terms that tonight would be their last night together. The Bible indicates that the disciples' hearts were troubled (John 14:1). To comfort them, Jesus promised to send his Spirit to be with them so that they would never be alone. Jesus provided several details about the coming of his Spirit in John 14–17.

One of those details speaks to the unique purpose of Pentecostal preaching: the exhortation of the risen Christ. In John 15:26–27 (ESV), Jesus says, "But when the Helper comes, whom I will send to you from the Father, the Spirit of truth, who proceeds from the Father, he will *bear witness* about me. And you also will bear witness, because you have been with me from the beginning" (emphasis mine). *The Spirit of Christ bears witness to the person and ministry of Christ.* Pentecostal sermons, delivered by preachers filled with the Spirit of Christ, come back to the same resounding chorus of exalting the name of Jesus Christ. Pentecostals preach Jesus because the Spirit is exalting Jesus' name.

These exaltations are filled with admiration for the risen Christ. The sermon is a key component of Pentecostal ecclesiology. It's an act of worship. Many people often mistake worship for music, but the sermon is an integral part of worship. It is the exaltation of Christ. The exhilaration of the sermon's presentation is in lockstep with the preacher's admiration-filled heart. It's easy for worship to flow out of the Pentecostal sermon because of how Jesus saved the preacher. The preacher isn't there to report information about Jesus; they're there to proclaim what he's done and why he's worthy of our worship.

A holy reverence is wrapped up in this exaltation. The Pentecostal sermon is not the place for casual familiarity with God. God is sovereign. His Son was crucified. He has risen. It's a common mistake for preachers to load their sermons with layers of informality and conviviality. These are certainly acceptable in splashes throughout the sermon, but they are a disservice to the pastor and the congregation when Jesus is treated with irreverent familiarity. Jesus is love, but he's not our buddy. Pentecostal preachers don't treat Jesus with such contempt because the Spirit of Christ, with whom they are filled, would not allow it. He is venerated in the highest expressible terms.

The agape love of Christ is conveyed in Pentecostal sermons. Agape love is filled with grace and truth. Jesus is the only one who can reconcile these two components, which are fundamentally at odds with one another. Grace communicates that Jesus sees sin, but his love remains untarnished. His grace says, "I know about your sin, but my grace is bigger; for those who will come to me, I will forgive, cleanse, and restore to right relationship with God." Truth comes to interrupt, interject, and intercept. It comes to cut, pierce, and penetrate. It calls sin, sin. Only the Spirit of Christ can unite these together in the same unifying sentiment. Preachers without the anointing will try to preach grace but come off as permissive. Conversely, they try to preach truth but come off as legalistic. Only the Spirit can bring the authoritative balance between grace and truth in the same thrust.

The praise of Christ goes hand in hand with Pentecostal preaching. Pentecostal preachers are often heard saying, "Someone in this house give him praise!" There's much reason to praise his name. He has risen, given hope, restored, and forgiven. He has given sight, made the lost found, and brought the dead to life. Jesus' ministry was marked by signs and wonders. The signs pointed. The wonders captivated. Most who were on the receiving end of them shouted with praise and sought to leave their lives and follow him immediately. When the Spirit of Christ is moving, preachers and congregants are praising. Praise is indispensable in the exaltation of Christ.

Exaltation flows out of hearts overflowing with gratitude. Steve Land, a premier Pentecostal theologian, describes gratitude as a posture of worship (thanks and praise). He says, "Gratitude is evoked through the remembering what God has done in Christ to atone for our sins, what God has done to call one out of the world of lost souls, what God is doing to keep and to protect, and what God will do to bring in the kingdom . . . One shows gratitude through verbal and physical acts of thanksgiving."[1] Pentecostal preaching is gracious preaching. From the pulpit to the pew, the name of Christ is exalted in the thanks and praise that pour from hearts filled with gratitude.

The deity of Christ is affirmed in his exaltation. He is not just a prophet or a wise man. He is not just a martyr. He is the living Son of God, eternally begotten before the beginning of time. He is the Son of Man prophesied of in Daniel and declared by himself throughout his ministry. He is God in the flesh. He is 100 percent God and 100 percent man at the same time, with both natures fully intact in one being. To exalt the name of Christ is to affirm that he is God. Only God can forgive sin. The Pentecostal preacher, fully forgiven, exults in and exalts the name of Jesus in their preaching.

Some Pentecostal preachers get overcome by emotion as they preach. I personally know many who do. When asked about their experience, they report strong feelings of adoration toward Jesus for the grace they've received and for the grace being experienced as his Word is proclaimed. Many Pentecostal preachers testify that such experiences

1. Land, *Pentecostal Spirituality*, 140.

occur even as they prepare their messages. Hearts filled with the Spirit are hearts filled with adoration toward Jesus.

## EVANGELISTIC COMPULSION

Another primary purpose of the Pentecostal sermon is evangelism. Evangelism is a distinct privilege to which the church has been called. Its primary function is to save souls. Its primary location is the marketplace. But what does evangelism look like inside the sanctuary, the location of worship? What does evangelism look like in sermonic form? The Greek word *euangelizo* means to preach or proclaim the good news. The good news is that Christ died according to Scripture, was buried, and was raised from the dead according to Scripture (1 Cor 15:1–3). The exaltation of the risen Christ is evangelism in sermon form. By virtue of the exaltation, Pentecostal sermons are evangelistic.

Adding to this are other dynamics with Pentecostal spirituality that characterize our movement as evangelistic. These include the fulfillment of the Great Commission, the reality of hell, and the urgency of the times. In what is known as the Great Commission, moments before Jesus ascended into heaven, he formally passed the baton of his ministry over to his disciples (Matt 28). The disciples were told to wait in Jerusalem until they had received the promise. The promise was the sending of his Spirit, which he had declared to them in detail during the Last Supper.

That promise was fulfilled in the Pentecost event recorded in Acts 2. The same shaking and fire that occurred in the giving of the law on Mt. Sinai was manifest again in the upper room in the giving of the Spirit. A new covenant had begun. And the same Spirit that empowered the signs and wonders of Jesus' ministry was now empowering the disciples' ministry. The fulfillment of the Great Commission is a natural outworking of what it means to be baptized in the Holy Spirit.

The reality of hell is a powerful incentive for Pentecostal preaching. Not that avoiding hell is more important than pursuing heaven, but Spirit-filled Pentecostal preachers are fueled with a passion for Jesus that produces a compulsory pursuit of the lost. This dynamic is presupposed by a soteriology (a theology of salvation) that acknowledges that Good News is good only in contrast to the bad news. The bad news is hell is real, and those whose names are not recorded in the Lamb's book of life will be bound there for eternity.

Hell is described in the Bible on many occasions. It is a place of utter darkness and a torturous heat that burns but does not consume, unquenchable pain and suffering, aloneness and isolation, immaterialness, and no hope for an end. The Bible says that God would have it that no one should perish (2 Pet 3:9). His compassionate love for humanity compelled him to send his Son to die for us. The Spirit of God, who is the fullness of God, seeks to draw all hearts unto God.

Compassion for the lost is defined by Steve Land as the "implantation of God's own nature and love into a fallen race . . . sustained by Christ . . . which moves on the believer to respond according to the pattern of Christ."[2] It moves with urgency, pity, and longing for the lost.[3] It is that which keeps one separate from the world, yet at the same time moves one toward those who are lost. Where gratitude gives birth to testimony, compassion gives birth to mission.[4]

The evangelistic foundation of Pentecostal preaching is also fueled by the urgency of the times. The Pentecostal movement has historically been characterized by its eschatological fervency. Harvey Cox discusses this, describing Pentecostalism's return to *primal hope*, the kind of hope that can only come from the Spirit who knows the end and how everything works for good for those who are in Christ Jesus.[5] The Holy Spirit stirs within the believer a hunger and zeal for the second coming of Christ and the new creation that accompanies his return. The hope of a kingdom of peace where Jesus rules from his eternal throne injects a yearning and a stirring for its fruition.

Historically, the Pentecostal movement has been held together by this unifying expectation. Worship gatherings were characterized by this fervency. The movement believed they were living in the days of the latter-day rain. Along with this was the expectation that the Holy Spirit was creating a pure and spotless church, ushering in the last days. A renewal of the kinds of activities seen in the book of Acts was being experienced. This was eschatological (connected with the last days) and marked by passionate anticipation of Christ's soon return. Sermons were propelled within this framework of anticipation. An evangelistic zeal stirred the communities of faith to bring as many people as possible into the faith. The signs and wonders taking place in the gatherings added to the outreach.

2. Land, *Pentecostal Spirituality*, 141–43.
3. Land, *Pentecostal Spirituality*, 144.
4. Land, *Pentecostal Spirituality*, 148–49.
5. Cox, *Fire from Heaven*, 102.

Sermonic evangelism within the Pentecostal movement was unique in that it not only contained the gospel message, which, according to Paul, is the power of God unto salvation (Rom 1), but was also undergirded by love and by the power of the Holy Spirit. The preaching of the gospel message centered on the two themes of the shed blood of Christ and the empty tomb. That's the gospel message. Even today, over 140 years after the movement began, worship gatherings continue to be shaken by the preaching of these two core themes.

The love of God is an indispensable feature of evangelism. It's the love of God that moves the lost into repentance. Paul talked about this when he said God's kindness leads to repentance (Rom 2). This is an unsurprising expectation of Spirit-filled preaching. The love of God, which sees sin and calls it out as such, says it has come to embrace, forgive, cleanse, and restore the sinner. And, of course, one of the key characteristics of Pentecostal preaching is the empowerment of the Holy Spirit.

## Broadening the Scope of Worship-Service Evangelism

This brings an important distinguishing feature of sanctuary-driven evangelism to light. It's one that broadens the scope of evangelism to a more universal, all-encompassing effect. Evangelistic compulsion applies to all hearers in the room, not just the lost. Evangelistic zeal, foundational to the Pentecostal preaching, extends beyond the initial call for salvation. If it's true that the primary purpose of the Sunday morning worship service is the exaltation of Christ (it is; see the first sentence of this chapter), then that changes how evangelism functions within the worship service. Evangelism draws not just the unsaved soul. Its reach envelops the mature believers as well.

I think a good image of this is the updraft dynamics of a raging fire. Pentecostal preaching that exalts Jesus Christ ignites a divine updraft, much like the roaring column of air that fuels a raging wildfire. Just as flames at the base of the fire create a vacuum that draws the surrounding atmosphere upward into its consuming heat, so the sermon's Christ-exalting focus generates a spiritual vortex at its core. In a wildfire, the intense heat lowers air pressure at ground level, drawing in cooler air from all directions to feed the blaze. This dynamic updraft sustains and fuels the fire's power, pulling everything within reach into its transformative fury. Pentecostal preaching is like this. It lifts the resurrected Christ high—his glory, authority, and resurrection power—creating a spiritual updraft that draws the congregation into worship of Christ.

The immediate effect radiates outward, creating a universal evangelistic pull that sweeps every listener toward Jesus. *No one remains untouched*; the atmosphere of the sermon bends toward the exalted Son, compelling souls into his presence whether they resist or yield. This thrust transcends human technique, operating as a supernatural conviction born from Christ's elevation alone.

Pentecostal preaching shines the light of Truth into all pockets of darkness. The Bible says that for every follower of Christ, there remains a constant warfare between the desires of their sinful nature and the desires of their spiritual nature (Rom 6–7). The apostle Paul wrote famously, "Wretched man that I am! Who will deliver me from this body of death?" (Rom 7:24 ESV). For the believer who's been a follower of Christ for fifty years, there's still room to surrender more of their sinful nature to Jesus. For the new believer, there's plenty of space to say yes. The evangelistic thrust, therefore, is not, and should not, be aimed solely at the conversion of unbelievers, but is broad and all-encompassing and is a natural by-product of the updraft of the Spirit in the worship of Jesus.

## Absence of Discipleship and Application

Of equal importance is what is *not included* in Spirit-filled sermons: discipleship and application. When we think of the term *discipleship*, certain words come to mind, such as *catechism*, *teaching*, *mentoring*, *training*, and related concepts. Most cessationist preaching holds these concepts firmly in hand in the pulpit—an emphasis I believe is mislocated. Pentecostal preaching is different. The purpose of our Sunday morning gatherings is the exaltation of Jesus Christ, an entirely different point of emphasis. And though Pentecostal preaching can be rich in teaching, the teaching exists only in the context of the exaltation. As such, the learning that takes place is a by-product of the worship experience, not its point. (Chapter 24 has a full discussion of these dynamics. Feel free to skip ahead if needed.)

When we think of the word *application*, our minds go to lists, how-tos, and sermonic takeaways designed to help the believer apply the Word to their life. Again, while a conviction revered in cessationist preaching, Pentecostal preaching takes place with a different point of view. This is not to say that Pentecostal sermons do not contain application, but that application is more properly situated in the context of discipleship, not in the sermon. Pentecostal sermons have been traditionally characterized, and continue to be so, by the unapologetic, unabashed, and unashamed worship and exaltation of the name of the risen Christ. Because of this, the inclusion of application within Pentecostal sermons deserves special care when it appears.

As one who is called to the office of teacher, this has been a delicate issue for me. One of the reasons I wrote this text was to share what I discovered in the homiletical and hermeneutical structures within the Pentecostal movement that allow teaching to be included in the sermons while at the same time remaining faithful to our ways. One of the truths I discovered is that the application is a feature that often works *against* the aim of the worship and exaltation of Jesus. This will be expounded upon in chapters 19–20.

## DIVINE ENCOUNTER

Pentecostal preaching finds its heartbeat in a genuine encounter with the exalted Christ. This principle was a unifying thread piercing through diverse homiletical voices surveyed in my research. All of our great homileticians (Duffield, Hughes, Williams, Martin, Lombard, and others) hone in on this feature of the Spirit-filled worship gathering. Their works reveal encounter not as peripheral but as the gravitational core, drawing congregations into divine presence where the exaltation of Christ gives birth to conviction, worship, and Spirit-wrought change.

Of all the reasons for Christians to gather as a genuine community of faith, encounters with Jesus are the moments that bring about radical transformation in believers' lives. The Bible is filled with such stories in both the Old Testament and the New Testament. From Abraham, Isaac, and Jacob, to Joseph, Moses, the prophets, priests, and kings, to the disciples, Paul, and the many people on the receiving end of Jesus' ministry, they've all had divine transformative encounters.

One thing we've learned from these biblical stories and from our own experiences is that one moment with Jesus can change a person forever. The Pentecostal movement is unique in its expectation that such encounters will take place in our worship gatherings. We expect God to move. We want the Word to speak. We long for the Holy Spirit to touch. It makes our preaching alive with anticipation.

These encounters are personal. Every person on the receiving end of Jesus' ministry was known by him, seen by him, and touched by him in a personal way. They were touched in a personal, nongeneric way. Jesus didn't just speak a generic blessing over them or encourage them to be godlier. There was more to his ministry than that. He knew the people he encountered. Andrew was taken aback as Jesus said he had seen him under the fig tree. The Samaritan woman at the well could hardly believe that Jesus knew she had had five previous husbands. Pentecostal preaching has these kinds of encounters in hand.

The movement of the Holy Spirit in Pentecostal gatherings is powerful and transformational. We believe the writer of Hebrews when he said the Word of God was alive and active and sharper than a double-edged sword (4:12). What does this mean in the hands of a Spirit-filled preacher? It means the preacher expects and anticipates the Word to personally intersect, interrupt, interact, and confront. Thy know deep down that that Word, if faithfully delivered, will cut, pierce, and penetrate straight into the hearts, bodies, and souls of those gathered for its proclamation.

For those gathered, worship becomes transformational, that which transcends change. A caterpillar can move to a different place in the forest or decide to eat from a different plant; that's change. Transformation takes place when it becomes a butterfly. Natures are changed when touched by Jesus. The Gerasene demoniac was found sitting, clothed, and in his right mind after Jesus touched him. Instead of wanting to live in the caves within the tombs, he wanted to follow after Jesus and live with his traveling entourage. Sinful desire becomes the object of righteous disdain. Where there was once an absence of desire for holiness is replaced with a hunger for righteousness.

Encounters with Jesus are revelational and revolutionary. The Bible tells us that after the feeding of the five thousand, Jesus instructed his disciples to get into a boat to cross to the other side of the lake. Those disciples obeyed, and they were in the center of God's will. Fear gripped them as the storm enveloped their boat. In the middle of the night, Jesus appeared to them walking on the water, with the very danger that had been threatening their lives squarely under his feet. The moment was revelational. The disciples were experiencing Jesus in a way that they had not yet experienced.

Such encounters with Jesus are revolutionary. They overthrow fleshly natures and help people become more like Jesus. They become the incubators of Holy Spirit zeal and passion that revolutionize complacency with courage, or indifference with compassion. These are the moments when believers move from people who are happy to be a Christian to people who cannot stay silent about being a Christian. Using spiritual gifts, love for others, and willingness to reach out to the lost become the norm. Pentecostal preachers enjoy witnessing such revolutionary encounters with their congregations.

One thing Pentecostal pastors need to watch out for is the temptation to create such dynamics on their own. These are the times when they experience a quenching of the Spirit rather than an outpouring. It highlights the difference between the pastor's role of curator and creator. The encounter belongs to the Spirit. The signs and wonders belong to him. The personalness belongs to him. As curators, we have a role in protecting the space but not creating the encounter.

## REFLECTION QUESTIONS

1. How does the Pentecostal emphasis on exalting the resurrected Christ shape the tone, structure, and expectations of the sermon, and in what ways does this differ from preaching traditions that prioritize teaching, explanation, or doctrinal instruction?
2. The chapter argues that Pentecostal preaching is an act of worship rather than primarily a teaching moment. How does this distinction affect the preacher's responsibilities, the sermon preparation, and the congregation's expectations during the worship gathering?
3. The chapter describes evangelistic preaching as creating a "spiritual updraft" that draws all hearers toward Christ. How might this metaphor help explain the universal appeal and transformative potential of Christ-centered proclamation?
4. Why are discipleship and application are better suited to contexts outside the sermon, and how might this perspective challenge common assumptions about what preaching is supposed to accomplish in the local church?
5. What does the chapter suggest about the preacher's role as a curator rather than a creator of divine encounters, and how might this understanding protect both the integrity of the worship gathering and the authenticity of spiritual transformation?

# 6

# Method Behind the Pentecostal Approach

PENTECOSTAL PREACHING SHINES IN its interplay of Spirit-led purpose and method, where the exalted Christ draws hearers into transformative encounters. This chapter unveils the heartbeat of homiletics that pulses through the Wesleyan-Pentecostal tradition, starting with Jesus-centric proclamation, scriptural fidelity, and Holy Spirit empowerment. Far from emotional excess or intellectual dryness, the Pentecostal method balances rigorous study with real-time flow of the Holy Spirit, ensuring sermons pierce souls as the living Word, ignite the affections, and draw people to the altar.

*Method* is the often-unseen architecture beneath every sermon, shaping how a preacher moves from the moment of inspiration to the heat of proclamation. In this sense, method is more than technique; it is an identifiable pattern of habits, convictions, and practices, working behind the scenes, that carry a sermon from the heart of God, through the heart of the preacher, to the hearts of God's people. In a movement where spontaneity, flow, and responsiveness to the Spirit are highly valued, our methodology is the means through which the Spirit moves with clarity, consistency, and power.

Our attention to method answers the "how" question of Pentecostal preaching. If purpose explains why sermons exist and identity clarifies the makeup of the Pentecostal sermon, method names how the preacher actually goes about receiving, forming, and delivering the message entrusted by God. For Pentecostals, this involves a distinctive blend of rigorous study, fervent prayer, Spirit-dependent interpretation, and Spirit-sensitive flow during delivery. Method, in this sense, is not a substitute for anointing; it is the outworking of the anointing. It is the Spirit-shaped discipline that allows anointed preaching to be faithful to Scripture, clear to listeners, and responsive to what God is doing in the room.

Pentecostal homiletical method is, therefore, deeply theological. It arises from convictions about Scripture as living, verbally inspired, and Christocentric; about the Spirit as the one who both inspired the text and illumines the preacher; and about the altar as a place of emptying and filling. Understanding method also protects Pentecostal preaching from the two common pitfalls of sloppy emotionalism and distant intellectualism. On one side, neglecting the method can lead to sermons that rely on volume, charisma, or momentary passion rather than on the steady power of the Word and the Spirit. On the other, leaning on hyper-intellectualism can yield sermons that are technically sound but spiritually dead . . . messages that parse the text accurately yet miss the Spirit's agenda for the congregation. The Spirit-filled methodology combines doctrinal depth with Spirit-led responsiveness, allowing the preacher to move with passion and authenticity.

This chapter, then, will explore the method behind the Pentecostal approach as a Spirit-formed patter. Method will be examined in terms of a Jesus-centric focus, Scripture fidelity, and Spirit guidance. By naming and clarifying this method, Pentecostal preachers can stand resolutely in the midst of their call.

## JESUS-CENTRIC PROCLAMATION

One key distinction of Pentecostal preaching is its Jesus-centric focus. As discussed in chapter 5, the principal purpose of Pentecostal preaching is the exaltation of the risen Jesus Christ. Purpose is driving the method here. I often challenge my students to survey how many times their Pentecostal pastor mentions the name of Jesus in their sermons. Many are amazed at how often the name of Jesus is lifted up. This should come as no surprise. Jesus promised us that the Spirit would testify about him (John 15). The method is tied to the sermon's primary purpose.

The altar experience is exclusive to the Pentecostal movement. Though charismatics have embraced this to a great degree, it remains a distinct characteristic that originated in the movement's early days. This is an integral part of the methodology. Preachers tailor their sermons with the altar specifically in mind. They ask questions like, "How will this point assist the congregation in altar sacrifice?" These are important questions in the methodology. One moment with Jesus can transform a person for the rest of their life. Encounters with Jesus are divinely responsive.

As the Word is being proclaimed, the Spirit is at work convicting, encouraging, confronting, and stirring the congregation. The altar is the place of response, of emptying and filling. Jesus has already given the invitation for the heavy laden to come to him to find rest. The altar is the place of emptying the soul of the heavy burdens of life. It is the place where emptiness becomes the catalyst for receiving rest. Pentecostal churches serve their members well when regular, devoted times and spaces are provided for the people of God to bring their sacrifices.

The invitation is from Christ and, therefore, is fulfilled only at the altar, where the laying down of sacrifice frees the believer to embrace the true life found only in Christ. The believer arrives at the altar with a self-offering, a living sacrifice. The Holy Spirit–inspired move opens the person's spirit to receiving divine life. The surrender empties the believer of self-directed strategies for deliverance. It is the emptying of pride and reliance upon self. With Jesus as the model, it is the humble emptying of self in every conceivable way, arriving at the altar wanting only Jesus.

The emptying then sets the stage for the divine impartation of what the Spirit is calling the believer to receive. Self-emptying is replaced with the infilling of eschatological hope and glory. The darkness of emptiness is driven away by the approaching infilling of light. God's glory comes to inject the divine purpose in place of self-deception. The infilling then equips the believer for kingdom service.

Being Jesus-centric means the methodology perfectly straddles the distance between intellectualism and experience. A common critique of the Pentecostal movement is that it relies too heavily on emotionalism. We don't need to be surprised by the charge. It comes with the territory. Though some weak and inexperienced preachers seek to manipulate such emotions, they eventually grow out of it. Regardless of the poor reflection, as a movement, we need to embrace better training to avoid such occurrences. If one were to call out the movement for such occurrences, I say, "Guilty as charged." However, it must be noted, in the spirit of tit-for-tat, that as quick as our cessationist brothers and sisters are to point out the foul, they carry their own oversights. If the Pentecostal movement is guilty of over-emotionalism, the cessationists are guilty of over-intellectualization.

I have much compassion for our cessationist brothers and sisters who don't allow for emotional responses to genuine encounters with Jesus. In my estimation, they're missing out. It's like going to a party with no singing, or a football game with no cheering, or a dance with no dancing. Much of the Bible is written in language meant to evoke emotion. If God wrote it with such intent, then why wouldn't his children respond accordingly? Why wouldn't we shout in moments of deliverance, healing, and revelation? Why wouldn't we mourn in moments of conviction, confrontation, and repentance? If we can be demonstrative at other occasions, we can more so shout in our worship of the risen Christ.

In the end, we're left with a commitment to balance and order. Balance is the preferred approach. As many have seen, too much, unfettered emotionalism lends itself to sloppy worship. Order is the Spirit's method. First Corinthians 14 provides the structure. What's at risk is a quenching of the Spirit as people savor the experience more than the Savior. Balance is found in the proclamation of sound doctrine, theological insights, and solid Bible teaching.

## SCRIPTURAL FIDELITY

One area in which the Pentecostal movement finds agreement with our cessationist brothers and sisters is with our high view of Scripture. We embrace a conservative view that holds doctrinal commitments of inerrancy and infallibility squarely in hand. *Inerrancy* is a word that is used to describe how Scripture does not hold, affirm, or defend anything untruthful. There is nothing in the Bible that can be pointed to as being false. There are no contradictions, heresy, or false conceptions about reality.

The term *infallibility* is understood within the context of the verbal inspiration of Scripture. Verbal inspiration is the belief that the Holy Spirit inspired the writers of Scripture and that every thought contained within Scripture is holy. As such, the writers, under the divine superintendence of the Holy Spirit, were guaranteed freedom from the possibility of error as the Scriptures were compiled. That means the Bible is not only free from error, it is free from the possibility of error.

Pentecostals acknowledge the christological nature of Scripture. The Word is Christ. John begins his Gospel with the claim, "In the beginning was the Word, and the Word was with God, and the Word was God" (1:1 ESV). This view believes that all of Scripture is recapitulated in Christ. The history of Israel finds its summation in Christ. The Law and the Prophets find their fulfillment in Christ. The priesthood finds its ultimate expression in Christ where Jesus is not only the high priest but also the sacrificial Lamb. All the Old Testament feasts and festivals are all grounded in Christ. The Old Testament office of king is completed in Christ as the King of kings. And, of course, all of the New Testament speaks to Christ.

Scripture is spiritually discerned. The Bible is arguably the finest piece of literature ever written, and it continues to be the number one best seller of any book in history. And, though the Bible enjoys such lofty literary credentials, its content is not discerned through conventional means of understanding. Those with high levels of intellectualism have no advantage here. Its stories and truths are up for intellectual mastery, but that does not equate with spiritual discernment.

Paul addresses this dynamic in 1 Corinthians, where he says, "The natural person does not accept the things of the Spirit of God, for they are folly to him, and he is not able to understand them because they are spiritually discerned" (2:14 ESV). Jesus acknowledged this dynamic in John 5 while sparring with the Pharisees, "You search the Scriptures because you think that in them you have eternal life; and it is they that bear witness about me, yet you refuse to come to me that you may have life" (5:39–40 ESV). This is seen in universities where religion is studied objectively and the content of Scripture is mastered by scholars, not as the living Word of God, but as the sacred writings of the Christian religion. Scripture is authored by the Spirit. The same Spirit who inspired the writers of Scripture is the same Spirit who illumines the readers.

The Bible is the *inscripturated* Word of God. God's special revelation of himself, through the person of Jesus Christ as testified to in Scripture, is closed, as far as the process of canonization is concerned. No more books will be added to the Bible; no books will be removed. Yet the Word remains alive and active and is still experienced in personal ways. As continuationists, Pentecostals believe that the Spirit of God who spoke through the prophets is still alive and speaking today. We expect the eternal Word to continue to speak to us through words of wisdom and knowledge, prophecies, insightful prayers from others, through the proclamation of the Word, and in koinonia conversations. The Bible is a compilation of a complete, verbally inspired, inscripturated, special revelation of Jesus Christ. But the Word is eternal, alive, and active and still speaks. It is never in contradiction to Scripture. It is always in alignment with Scripture.

When we say the Bible is revelation, we refer to the unique way Scripture reveals God and to the special plan God has for all of humanity to be restored to right relationship with him. After creation, all was good between humanity and God. After the fall, humanity was in serious trouble and needed reconciliation with God. God's plan for restoration is revealed through Scripture. The story of how God revealed himself to Abraham is the story of God revealing himself to humanity. God is real. Abraham's belief in God was reckoned to him as righteousness.

The revelation continued through Isaac, Jacob, Joseph, Moses, the prophets, the priestly system, the kings, and the poets. All the Old Testament stories of God's interactions with the chosen people of Israel are about God revealing to humanity that he is real and that he has provided a plan for humanity to be reconciled to him. The same is true of the New Testament stories of Christ. The entire Old Testament finds its fulfillment in Christ. Everything points to him. The Bible is the special revelation of God and God's plan to send his Son to provide reconciliation to all who want it.

Scripture is alive. As a movement, Pentecostals are the only faith tradition that understands the living nature of the Word in pneumatological terms (from the Greek word *pneuma*, which is where we get the word *Spirit*). The same Spirit who illuminated the writer is the same Spirit who illumines the reader. It's the same Spirit who enlivens the proclaimed Word as a sword to cut, pierce, and penetrate into the hearts of the congregation. Only the Holy Spirit can do this.

The Spirit-driven Word is a double-edged sword. In the same thrust of its proclamation comes conviction of sin on one side of the sword, with forgiveness, cleansing, and renewal on the other. The Holy Spirit is the only One who can pull this off. It is in such moments of divine enlivening that we realize we are not studying the Word; it is studying us. We are not holding the Word; it is holding us. We are not mastering the Word; it is mastering us. The Bible is not merely a collection of sacred, axiomatic propositions held by adherents to the Christian religion; it's a living Word that meets us personally, in real time, in our context.

The Bible is the power of God unto salvation. Paul makes this fact clear. His assertion in the opening comments of Romans reads, "For I am not ashamed of the gospel of Christ: for it is the power of God unto salvation" (1:16 KJV). What does this mean? It means that the revelation of the gospel found in Scripture is the most powerful force at the Pentecostal preacher's disposal. This is not a surprise. We already have a high view of Scripture. People make decisions for Christ not because of impressive oratory, the power of influence or rhetoric, or the preacher's reasoned presentation of evidence or proof. Decisions for Christ are made when the gospel is being proclaimed.

A good example of this is found in the story of Philip and the Ethiopian eunuch in Acts. Philip was directed by the Spirit to help the eunuch understand some Bible verses he was reading on his way back from worshiping in Jerusalem. The Bible says Philip explained the passages he was reading and then told him the good news about Jesus. The eunuch became a believer right there on the spot and was immediately baptized. Pentecostal preachers understand the power of God unto salvation; it's in the Holy Spirit–empowered proclamation of the gospel message.

## SPIRIT GUIDANCE

Pentecostal preaching stands out as one of the most vibrant and transformative practices in the Christian church today. At its heart, this methodology revolves around the Holy Spirit's active, moment-by-moment guidance, turning every sermon into a living encounter with God. Unlike cessationist approaches, Pentecostal preaching isn't just about delivering information—it's about partnering with the Spirit to exalt Jesus, convict hearts, and lead people into life-changing response.

From choosing the sermon topic to kneeling at the altar, the Spirit leads the preacher every step, making the pulpit a sacred space where heaven touches earth. This isn't theory; it's the heartbeat of countless Spirit-filled gatherings where ordinary words become swords of the Spirit, piercing souls and igniting revivalistic fervor.

### The Spirit's Whisper in Topic Selection

Every great Pentecostal sermon begins with the Holy Spirit planting a seed. Often, this begins with a divine nudge, a burning burden, or a clear impression that won't let go. For me, it usually consists of one word or phrase from which the Lord invites me to come to him for the content. Divine inspiration is not random brainstorming or chasing trends; it's the same Spirit who inspired the Bible writers now speaking fresh words for today's needs. Jesus promised in John 15:26 that the Spirit would testify about him, and Pentecostal preachers lean into that promise, letting topics/passage selection emerge from prayerful listening rather than personal agendas.

The preacher asks practical questions: What's stirring in the congregation's hearts? Is God highlighting a passage through personal devotions, a prophetic word, or congregational conversations? High expectations fuel this process. Pentecostals don't just hope for a good sermon; they anticipate God moving mightily, delivering souls, healing bodies, and filling hearts with fresh fire. Without this Spirit-led start, preparation feels forced, like pushing a car uphill. But when the topic flows from divine inspiration, the preacher arrives at the pulpit *locked in*, ready for what God has prepared.

Consider, for example, a pastor sensing unrest in the church. While praying over the congregation's needs, the Spirit drops Acts 27 into their heart. Paul's storm-tossed ship comes into view. Within their sanctified imagination, a phrase is heard in their spirit's ear, "Trust me in the storm." Sermons tailored this way exalt Jesus as the ultimate Deliverer, setting the stage for altar encounters where burdens lift and faith rises. This guidance ensures preaching isn't preacher-centered but Jesus-exalting, the hallmark of Pentecostal methodology. (More on this in chapter 16.)

## Preparation: A Holy Conversation with God

Sermon preparation in Pentecostal preaching feels like a divine dance where study meets prayer, intellect bows to illumination, and the preacher's heart gets searched first. Four key movements mark Pentecostal sermon preparation: adoration, observation, interrogation, and interpretation (described in chapter 17). Beginning with curating the right heart space (the preacher's version of the singer warming up by singing scales), the preacher then spends quality time with the text and makes simple, nonacademic observations, then moves into a more formal interrogation of the text, and ultimately arrives at the destination of interpreting the text for what it is. As the preacher digs into Scripture, the living Word

(Heb 4:12) digs back, exposing hidden sins or fresh revelations. The preacher is not just studying God; God is studying them. The Spirit, the same One who breathed the text, now illumines it, turning preparation into personal transformation.

Time in the Word is time in the Spirit. Pastors recount seeing depression lift, strongholds break, and visions clarify during sermon preparation. Questions flow: "How's the Spirit moving in our church? What trajectory is God setting?" All of this is characterized by the high expectations within the Spirit-filled Pentecostal community. Spirit-filled preachers believe in miracles, not just insights. Without such expectation, sermons become not-very-impressive words; with it, they carry heaven's weight.

Spirit-interpretation takes sermon preparation to deeper spaces. Well beyond rational exegesis, Pentecostals embrace pneumatic discernment (1 Cor 2:13–14). The Spirit bridges writer and preacher, unveiling Jesus in every text. Pharisees scoured Scripture but missed Christ (John 5:39–40); not so for the Spirit-led preacher, who sees Old Testament shadows fulfilled in him. The preacher's notes are there but are often utilized rather minimally. The goal is Spirit-spontaneity. By the end of preparation, the preacher is "tight and ready," locked into the Spirit's agenda, and poised for God's move. (More on this in chapter 17.)

## Delivery: Where Anointing Meets the People

Sermon delivery is held within the simplicity, beauty, and flow of the Holy Spirit. The Spirit anoints the sermon's delivery, empowering the preacher to preach with power. Passion flows from pastoral authenticity. The persuasive nature of the Word, soliciting and receiving response from the congregation, takes hold of the encounter. Just as the Word interpreted the preacher during preparation, it is now interpreting the congregation, preparing it for the altar. Courage replaces fear; passion rises and falls; whispers draw in, shouts awaken.

Congregants feel it. Affections shift from worldly cravings to holy longings (Ezek 36:26–27). Gratitude swells, compassion stirs, courage rises. No manipulation is needed here. Genuine anointing moves inescapably. Acceptance gives birth to transformation; resistance gives birth to growing conviction. Pastors who are in the flow discern the spiritual tides.

Watching carefully, with a shepherd's heart, they are constantly analyzing, "How does this lead to the altar?" (More on this in chapters 19–23.)

## Altar: The Climax of Spirit-Led Surrender

Pentecostal services crescendo at the altar. Sermons aren't complete without it; preachers craft points asking, "How will this get people there?" The altar empties then fills: self-surrender precedes divine infilling. This is the place where Jesus has invited the weary to unload the burdens of pride, strategies, sin (Matt 11:28), making room for his righteousness. One Jesus-moment here can transform a life forever.

The preacher leads through spiritual intuition. The altar becomes a place of laying on of hands, discerning of needs, prayer, sacrifice, and divine impartation. High expectation undergirds the encounter. No formulas, just faith. Churches thrive by providing these spaces weekly, where souls empty and overflow for kingdom service. (More on this in chapter 23).

## REFLECTION QUESTIONS

1. How does the Pentecostal emphasis on Jesus-centric proclamation shape the preacher's approach to sermon preparation and delivery, and why is this focus vital for transformative encounters in the congregation?
2. How does the understanding of Scripture as verbally inspired, inerrant, and Christocentric influence the Pentecostal preacher's interpretation and proclamation of biblical texts?
3. Consider the dynamic between self-emptying and divine infilling at the altar. How do these theological concepts function practically within Pentecostal worship and preaching methodology?
4. Why is the altar experience considered a distinctive and integral element of Pentecostal preaching, and how does it serve as the climax of the Spirit-led sermon?
5. How does Pentecostal preaching's expectation of miracles and divine encounters during sermons affect the preacher's attitude and preparation compared to more traditional homiletical approaches?

# 7

# Identity of the Pentecostal Sermon

WHAT MAKES A SERMON unmistakably Pentecostal? What gives it distinguishable differences from other preaching? In the chapters leading up to this one, we've explored the foundational traits of Pentecostal preaching: its fierce Jesus-centeredness, where every word lifts high the risen Christ; the high view of Scripture as a living, breathing sword that pierces the heart; the centrality of the altar call as the service's beating heart; and the balance of deep emotion with solid doctrine. These are the DNA of Spirit-filled preaching. We've seen how Pentecostal preachers prepare not in isolation, but through divine guidance from the Holy Spirit, allowing him to shape the message from start to finish. And we've marveled at how this preaching demands response, turning listeners into responders who encounter Jesus in real time.

In addition to the other characteristics of Pentecostal preaching discussed thus far, this chapter dives into two defining pillars that reveal the identity of the Pentecostal sermon: Holy Spirit anointing and prophetic grounding. These aren't abstract ideas for theologians; they're practical realities every Spirit-filled preacher and lay pastor can grasp and experience.

## HOLY SPIRIT ANOINTING

How do we know when a sermon is anointed by the Holy Spirit? There are several features to look at. First, a sermon is anointed when it is accompanied by the Holy Spirit's resurrection power. This is the power of life over death. It's the power of deliverance over bondage, of healing over sickness, of commanding demons to flee, and the power of grace and truth over condemnation of deception.

The same Spirit phenomena that accompanied Christ during his ministry is present in the Spirit-anointed sermon. The church does not need to be surprised by this. As Christ passed the baton to the church on Pentecost Sunday, the Spirit anointing that accompanied Christ during his ministry was transferred to the church to empower it to complete the mission to which it had been entrusted. The same Spirit phenomena witnessed in the ministry of Christ were now to be experienced in the church.

These phenomena include the authoritative posture from which Jesus taught, the healing of the sick, the deliverance of people from strongholds, the expulsion of demons from the demonized, the resurrection of the dead, the dominion over nature, and the duality of grace and truth, which only the Spirit of God can effect.

## Power

Holy Spirit–anointed preaching is presupposed by Jesus-centricity. Jesus declared that one of the Holy Spirit's primary functions would be to *testify about him* (John 15:26). The first principle of Spirit-anointed sermons is that their starting place is the exaltation of the risen Jesus Christ. This is one of the unique characteristics of Pentecostal homiletical methodology. The fire of the Spirit burns brightest when Jesus is being exalted. When the Spirit is moving, he is testifying about Jesus. He is testifying that he is the fulfillment of Old Testament prophecy. He is testifying about his supernatural birth, his life, his ministry of signs and wonders, his suffering and crucifixion, his resurrection, his ascension, and his promise to come again. He is testifying about his incommunicable attributes like his eternality, his equality with God, his transcendence and his immanence, his self-sufficiency, and his omnipotence, omniscience, and omnipresence.

One of the first things people think of when it comes to Spirit anointing is power. Luke tells us that Jesus promised to send his Spirit, who would come upon them in power, and that the result of such imbuing would be their transformation into witnesses (Acts 1:8). Spirit anointing is an anointing of power. The power of Spirit baptism is transformative.

Jesus did not tell the disciples they would witness; he told them they would *be* witnesses.

Spirit-baptized preachers affirm, in the simplest terms, that this transformative power is the Holy Spirit's presence. The presence is transformative, finding its purpose in empowering the individual to witness to Jesus. The presence brings a defining courage, a love-filled courage, that eliminates the fears that would normally inhibit the preacher from testifying.

The power is not a gift given to the preacher to evoke on demand. It is the omnipotent presence of the Holy Spirit. The anointing is not something the preacher *has*. It's the opposite. *The Spirit has the preacher.* Here's a super simple illustration I often use when teaching this principle: Spirit-baptized Pentecostal preachers are like cucumbers. Once a cucumber is baptized into the vinegar solution, it undergoes a transformation. The cucumber has not changed; it has undergone a transformation into something altogether new. From that moment forward, no matter how the pickle is being utilized, it is infused with the effects of its baptism. Preachers don't possess the power of Spirit anointing in the sense that it can be switched on or off at will. The anointing possesses them.

## Passion

*Passion* is a word often associated with Holy Spirit anointing. Passion is a normal human experience. Passion is experienced when someone's favorite sports team is winning, as shouts, cheers, and fist-pumps fill the room. It's experienced at concerts, as hands wave, voices rise, and people jump with enthusiasm. It's experienced in moments of sadness in fallen tears and moans and wails of despair. Passions are presupposed by triggers, some kind of event that elicits the response. Passion is also experienced as a natural outworking of Spirit empowerment.

Passion manifests within each preacher's personality. It matters not whether the preacher is choleric, sanguine, melancholy, or phlegmatic (to use ancient personality trait labels). Passion shines through. Some preachers are by personality somewhat reserved and introspective (like me). This does not hamper the manifestation of passion. I've seen too many preachers like this who, when the anointing drops, become quite passionate in their delivery. Passion has nothing to do with animation, volume, antics, rapid speech, or flair. The same goes for the preachers who are more outgoing and extroverted. Passion is more demonstrative in such individuals, but it is in sync with their personalities.

As the Spirit moves the preacher, the congregation responds. Divine alignment is taking place in these moments of Spirit passion. The response is inescapable. Congregants have a choice: either accept the stirring of the Spirit or reject it. Acceptance means Spirit accommodations are being imparted that continue to impact the individual. Transformation is taking place. The righteousness of God is being interwoven into the person. Minds are being transformed. Hearts are being changed. Wills are reoriented out of the mind and into alignment with the person's spirit.

Spirit-filled preachers are often accused of exploiting or manipulating passion during their preaching. It's true. Some do. Such preachers need more training and development. Cheap and cowardly attempts at manipulation are unnecessary for those anointed with the Holy Spirit. For those who are, no apologies are needed for the passion that occurs when preaching. No apologies are needed when the congregation responds in kind. If humanity can become passionate in response to base things, even more so can we become passionate in matters of the Spirit.

## Persuasion

Jesus told the story of the tax collector praying next to a Pharisee. The tax collector, who had fallen under conviction, was filled with sorrow as he beat his chest and could not even look up to heaven. He begged God to forgive his sins (Luke 18). Conviction is the progenitor of holy sorrow. There's no better place for that kind of passion to be displayed than in the context of worship. Luke tells the story of the man born lame and his healing by Peter and John. His response? He went walking and leaping and praising God (Acts 3). Healings give birth to demonstrative praise. The worship service is the appropriate place to express such praise. No apologies necessary.

Spirit-filled preaching always demands a response. In everyday life, for those who walk by the Spirit, the Spirit guides and leads. Luke tells us about the first church council, which discussed what demands ought to be placed on new gentile converts (Acts 15). The matter was settled when they said, "It seemed good to the Holy Spirit and us . . . ." Paul recounts how the Spirit prevented him from going to Bithynia (Acts 16). These instances of guiding and leading demand a response. Will we follow or will we go our own way?

The move of the Spirit is no different in the context of worship. Worship brings hearts of adoration to God as the congregation declares its love for him. It is within such openness, vulnerability, and transparency that the Spirit probes and searches the hearts and minds. He exposes sin as the congregation is brought into the light. Secrets buried for decades are brought to remembrance. Conviction is at work here. Only the Holy Spirit can pull this off. Unanointed, preacherly attempts come off as too permissive or too legalistic. Only the Spirit can expose sin and, at the same time, embrace and draw the believer closer to God. It demands a response.

The Spirit stirs and compels longings for holiness into the believer. These are the moments of divine opportunity. The Spirit of God is "knocking on the doors of our hearts," inviting us to receive the gift of God's righteousness. It demands a response. We see this in Ezek 36:27 (ESV), "And I will put my Spirit within you, and *cause* you to walk in my statutes and be careful to obey my rules" (emphasis mine). In addition, Paul notes that righteousness comes from God and is not manufactured by the believer (Rom 3:22; Phil 3:9). How does the believer become righteous? Through the work of the Spirit.

The Spirit stirs up longings for righteousness in the context of worship. Yearnings and groanings, too deep for words, take captive the hearts of the congregation. They want to be more holy. They want to be better Christians. For those who say yes, the righteousness of God is imparted into their hearts. *Impartation* is a special word; it implies a sacred interwovenness of God's holiness into the very core of what it means to be human. It's ontologically transformational. It's a divine realignment of the individual becoming more like God. The congregation, caught up in the agenda of the Spirit, suspended in divine undoing, must make a choice. Will they accept this move of the Spirit and respond affirmatively, or will they reject it? Either way, they leave changed.

## Affections

The affections are the deep desires, longings, and cravings of the soul. They become transformed, as a work of the Holy Spirit, away from the desires for sinfulness to desires for holiness. The believer's drive and attractions undergo a divine metamorphosis, becoming a thirst for godliness. Religious affections include gratitude, hope, desire, godly fear, contrition, zeal, courage, empathy, etc.

Affections can be easily misunderstood. Religious affections are not mere feelings or emotions. Feelings and emotions are, by nature, unreliable and indiscriminate. Jonathan Edwards, one of the premier preachers during the Great Awakening of the eighteenth century, says, "The affections are no other than the more vigorous and sensible exercises of the inclination and will of the soul."[1] The soul is that which constitutes a person's mind, will, emotions, personality, intellect, dispositions, sense of humor, etc., the *intangible* parts of what it means to be human. The soul is the point of origin for the affections.

Affections differ from emotions in three distinct ways. First, affections have no triggers. Emotions are triggered by events, thoughts, activities, and other factors that give rise to positive or negative feelings. Think of the last time you got a case of the giggles at an inappropriate time. This could have been hearing a story about a grandfather getting hit by a golf cart and ending up in the ICU while trying not to laugh at the sheer shock of the mental image, your aunt singing too loudly and off-key at a funeral, or noticing how the pastor looked exactly like Yoda mid-service. Laughter has triggers. The same is true of tears and other emotions. Affections, however, are better understood as holy and passionate *dispositions* that are not dependent upon triggers.

Second, emotions are unreliable. This makes sense because human understanding is imperfect. Emotions flow whether we have the right perspective on the information or not. A misinterpreted comment can trigger positive or negative emotions. Third, emotions are involuntary. Their manifestations appear without our permission and without the direction of our will. In contrast, the affections manifest outside the direction of human will.

Steve Land conducted much research in this space. He noted how Wesley placed the affections at the very center of what it means to be a Christian. For Wesley, the love of God and neighbor was the heart of true religion, without which one was not a Christian.[2] Land placed the seat of the affections in the heart, out of which they flow as the integrative center of the mind, will, and emotions. As such, says Land, "the affections are more than mere feelings."[3]

1. Edwards, *Treatise on Religious Affections* 1.1, para. 1.

2. Land, *Pentecostal Spirituality*, 128.

3. Land, *Pentecostal Spirituality*, 128.

Land described the affections as objective, relational, and dispositional. They are objective in that they take an object and that God is both the source and the object of affect. They are rational because they require an ongoing expression with God, the church, and the world. They are dispositional in that the affections are abiding dispositions which dispose the person toward God and neighbor in ways appropriate to their source and goal in God.[4]

Why do the affections matter in relation to Spirit empowerment? The affections matter because they are the proof of the divine transformation taking place within the believer. For the skeptic, they are the evidence. It's the kind of transformation that can happen only through the power and presence of the Holy Spirit. Thus, Spirit-empowered passion is the evidence of God's weaving his righteousness into transformed minds, hearts, and wills. Far from manipulation or emotional triggers, authentic Spirit empowerment demands no apology. If people can erupt in fervor over uncontrolled triggers, how much more should worship ignite unbridled passion for the eternal Savior?

## Compulsion

Pentecostal sermons are compulsory in essence. What does this mean? It means Spirit-anointed sermons go beyond information-based presentations about Jesus. Rather, they usher the congregation into authentic worship encounters *of* Jesus. Furthermore, Spirit-anointed sermons are not characterized by the absence of intellectualism, but rather by its transcendence. The sermon is not just about Jesus; it's an invitation to join in the worship of Jesus. And though Spirit-anointed sermons contain features of didacticism, intellectually stimulating content, and practicality, these are not the driving force, nor are they the reason for the sermon.

The compulsory nature of the Spirit anointing is at work in the Pentecostal sermon. As the Word goes out, the Bible tells us that the Word of God never returns void (Isa 55:11). The Word of God is alive and active and sharper than a double-edged sword (Heb 4:12). As the Word goes out, it demands a response, and when it comes back, it carries the response.

The compulsory nature of the Word solicits our response. It compels us to act on how the Spirit is moving. And so the question for the

4. Land, *Pentecostal Spirituality*, 130–31.

congregation is "How are we going to respond?" Is our answer "Yes, Lord have your way," or "No, we're not ready for this yet"? The compulsory nature of the sermon forces a response and, with it, an accompanying move either toward Jesus or away from him. God's Word never returns void.

## Flow

Pentecostal sermons are carried by the thoughts, actions, words, and movements of the Spirit. The preacher, caught up in the flow, finds themselves in lockstep. Sermon flow is characterized by noteworthy features. First, flow allows the preacher to trust their instinct as comments and teaching points move beyond what may have been prepared in their notes. Flow allows a break from note-dependency and from what may have been set forth for memorization, allowing the preacher to pull from a deep well of knowledge while under the superintendence of the Spirit.

Secondly, flow liberates the preacher from pretense. Cast aside are the robes of religiosity, style, expectation, or emulation. Abandoned is any compulsion to fulfill an agenda. Flow releases us from the need to impress others. Thirdly, flow accentuates God-given identity. Bound up in this is the preacher's personality, intellect, sense of humor, passions, proclivities, and many other traits God has woven into us when he formed us in the womb. The flow of the anointing does not automatically dictate a certain demonstrative style or stereotypical mannerisms. Flow is inseparable from identity. In the same way that Scripture was written in and through the unique identity of its authors (consider the precision of Luke and the passion of Paul) under the superintendence of the Holy Spirit, so the preacher similarly flows under the Spirit anointing to accentuate their unique, God-given identity.

Is the preacher melancholic or phlegmatic? The anointing is carried within their God-given disposition. Are they of average intelligence? Then the anointing is not stifled when they embrace and celebrate the perfect level of intelligence given to them by God. Do they have an edgy sense of humor? The anointing flourishes in their ability to release that sense of humor in the sermon.

## PROPHETIC GROUNDING

Pentecostal preaching has never been merely about filling a time slot in the worship service. It has always carried a sense of holy urgency, a felt awareness that something is at stake when the people of God gather around the proclaimed Word. Pentecostals instinctively know that when a preacher steps to the pulpit, more is happening than the exchange of ideas or the conveying of religious information. A transaction is taking place between heaven and earth, and the sermon becomes one of the primary ways the Spirit of God meets the people of God in real time.

At the heart of this understanding is the conviction that Pentecostal preaching is prophetic. By prophetic, this does not mean merely predictive or sensational, but that the sermon is a Spirit-breathed word spoken into the concrete circumstances of a particular people at a particular moment. The preacher does not simply speak about God; they speak *from* God, having been summoned, shaped, and sent by the Spirit to bear witness to Jesus in the midst of the congregation. In this way, the Pentecostal sermon participates in the long, biblical stream of prophetic ministry through which God confronts, comforts, corrects, and calls God's people.

This prophetic quality gives Pentecostal preaching its unique weight and texture. It explains why Pentecostal preachers speak of a "burden" to preach, why they wrestle and "pray through" for a word, and why the pulpit is treated as a sacred trust rather than a mere platform. The sermon is not viewed as a religious talk that happens to follow the music set; it is understood as an event in which the living Word, Jesus Christ, encounters the gathered church through the written Word, in the power of the Holy Spirit. When preaching is approached in this way, it becomes more than exhortation. It becomes participation in God's mission.

In what follows, the prophetic grounding of Pentecostal preaching will be explored. The discussion will move through several key dimensions drawn from the biblical portrait of the prophets and applied to the Pentecostal pulpit: the divine call of the preacher, the reality of an entrusted message, the demand for faithful delivery, the living and active nature of the Word, the freshness and timeliness of the sermon, and the contextual sensitivity of Spirit-anointed proclamation. Each of these aspects helps to clarify why Pentecostal preaching is, at its core, prophetic preaching and how this shapes the identity of the Pentecostal sermon.

## Called

Every prophetic ministry in Scripture begins with a call. Before a prophet ever uttered "Thus says the Lord," there was a moment when God interrupted an ordinary life and laid a holy claim on a human soul. Ezekiel was torn out of the ordinariness of his life through grand visions. The Word of the Lord called Jeremiah in his youth. The throne room opened to Isaiah before he ever pronounced a single "woe." Moses received his calling as a man already advanced in years as he turned aside to gaze at a burning bush (Exod 3:1–4). Samuel was just a young boy when he heard the voice of God calling him to be a prophet (1 Sam 3:4–14). Hosea's call was through God's message for him to marry a prostitute and to have children with her (Hos 1:2–3).

Calling, then, is not a sentimental feeling about ministry or a piqued interest in spiritual things. Calling is the decisive act of God by which God summons a person, marks them as God's own, and sets them apart for the lifelong task of bearing God's Word to God's people. In this way, the call of the Pentecostal preacher stands in direct continuity with the call of the Old Testament prophets.

The calling of the Pentecostal preacher is not incidental to Pentecostal ministry; it is foundational. Before there is a sermon, before there is a congregation, before there is even a pulpit to stand behind, there is a summons from God. This has always been the pattern. The prophets of Israel did not volunteer for their assignments, nor did they inherit their offices through bloodline or institutional appointment. They were interrupted by God, seized by a word not their own, and thrust into a vocation they could neither manufacture nor escape.

The same holds true for those who stand in the Pentecostal pulpit today. A genuine call from God is the bedrock upon which everything else is built. Without it, the preacher is merely a speaker. With it, the preacher becomes a vessel through whom the Spirit moves with purpose and authority. Understanding the nature of this call with its divine origin, its personal particularity, and its binding force sets the foundation for grasping why Pentecostal preaching carries the weight that it does.

Recall the importance of the divine nature of the call from chapter 4. First, it legitimizes the preacher's placement in the local church. The preacher does not stand in the pulpit on the strength of a résumé, a personality, or a personal dream, but on the ground of God's decision. They are there not because of the exercise of their own will but by the exercise of God's will. This gives both the preacher and the congregation confidence that something more than human ambition is at work when the Word is proclaimed.

Second, the divine call locks the preacher into place. The call is inescapable. It may be resisted, run from, or buried for a season under fear or distraction, but it will not disappear. The prophet Jonah knew this dynamic quite well. His attempt to run from God's call landed him in the belly of a whale. The inescapability of the call becomes an anchor in seasons of criticism, discouragement, or apparent fruitlessness, when any rational person might be tempted to walk away, but the called preacher cannot.

Third, the divine call carries with it the empowerment of the Holy Spirit. God never calls without also providing the grace needed to fulfill the assignment. The same Spirit who summons the preacher also equips the preacher, illuminating the Scriptures in study, granting boldness in delivery, and making the preached Word effective in the hearts of the hearers. The legitimacy, perseverance, and power of Pentecostal preaching all derive from this divine call.

## Entrusted

The prophetic nature of Pentecostal preaching centers the sermon's delivery as the fulfillment of a task entrusted with a divinely given message. Preaching on a particular verse or topic is not a fanciful idea or something that made good sense in a staff meeting. Choosing sermon topics is a sacred task of obedient listening, searching, and sitting with the Lord. Many Pentecostal preachers talk about "praying through" to receive from the Lord what they should preach on next Sunday. Sermon topics in this vein are received through sacred inspiration. They are divine in origin.

A more detailed discussion of this appears in chapter 16, where we examine sermon inspiration. There, we will examine the various ways the preacher receives divine inspiration for their sermon topic. The concept of the sermon being entrusted to the preacher is important because it helps safeguard the preacher against preaching a sermon devoid of the anointing of the Holy Spirit.

## Faithfully Delivered

Third, the prophetic nature of Pentecostal preaching is evident in the preacher's faithful delivery. A good example of faithful delivery is the work of an ambassador. These individuals are selected by a head of state as people who can be trusted. Their task is to deliver an official message to another head of state. The ambassador does not craft their own messages. They do not alter the message given to them. Their task is to simply receive the message and to faithfully deliver it. Such is the task of the Pentecostal preacher. Sermon topics are delivered to the preacher under divine inspiration from the Spirit of God. Our task is to deliver.

When preachers start with this as a point of reference, they can never go wrong. They can never go wrong because the message is Spirit-inspired. By the time the preacher gets the microphone, they are ready to deliver the message that they have become theologically burdened to deliver. The delivery of the sermon is the delivery of the life-giving Word from the Lord.

## Alive

Fourth, the Word of God is alive and active. Its kerygmatic proclamation is nothing short of delivering a living message, personal to the recipient, that demands a response to heaven. The essence of this is seen in two key Bible verses: Heb 4:12 and Isa 55:11. The writer of Hebrews describes the Word of God as alive and active and sharper than a double-edged sword (4:12). Understanding the Word as alive and active means that it is a living entity. The apostle John refers to the Word as existing in the beginning, with God, and as God. This, of course, refers to Jesus as the Word.

The concept is breathtaking. The preacher faithfully delivers the Word as the living, breathing presence of Christ. The presence of the Word is an active presence. The Greek word for *active* is *energes*, from which we get the English word *energy*. It is used only three times in the New Testament, where it carries the connotation of efficiency, effectiveness, power, and productivity. It means the Word is at work, affecting results.

The image of the double-edged sword brings together the grace and truth of Jesus from John 1:17. Grace and truth are never divorced from one another. Truth brings forth the indictment of sin to us who stand guilty before the Lord. Grace brings forth the forgiveness that comes only from Jesus. The thrust of the double-edged sword of grace and truth can only be accomplished by the Spirit of Christ as the Word goes forth in the sermon. When preachers attempt to accomplish without the Spirit's anointing, they come off as either too permissive or too legalistic.

The prophet Isaiah informs us that when the Word goes out from God, it returns to him having accomplished its purpose (Isa 55:10–11). Isaiah uses the rain as a metaphor to describe how it comes down from heaven to water the earth, "making it bring forth and sprout, giving seed to the sower and bread to the eater" (ESV). God's Word goes out from the preacher as the living water bringing forth life within the congregants, providing both bread and seed for future bread.

The Word never returns void. The Word, as an alive and active presence of Christ, goes forth from the preacher and demands a response. Each person has two choices in the moment: one, either come into submission under the Word, or two, reject the Word and stand in judgment against it. First, the recipient stands in the light of grace and truth. They see themselves within this light, having been thrust by the double-edged sword of truth and grace, and are at the same time confronted and forgiven. For the second, the recipient stands in the darkness of deception. They see themselves within this deception, having avoided the thrust of the double-edged sword, and are at the same time free from indictment and in no need of forgiveness. Either way, they are changed. God's Word, alive and active, accomplished its purpose.

## Fresh and Timely

Next, the Word is always fresh. It doesn't matter if the preacher is delivering a message they have already delivered dozens of times, because, as an ambassador, if God has birthed the message within the preacher, it is a fresh word. God's Word is timely. The Spirit of Christ is never out of time. The Word is always in season.

The Word never misses the point. As that which is alive and active, God's Word is delivered from God to the church for a specific purpose. God always has an agenda. And as his Word is being preached, his purposes are being accomplished. As the Spirit of Christ moves during the sermon, some are being taken to the woodshed, some to the mountain top, and some to the cool stream.

And since God's Word is personal, each person engages with it in ways unique to their life circumstances. The same message, alive and active, has its effect. The same principles in the Word speak both grace and truth, both corporately and personally.

## Contextual

Additionally, because the preacher is endowed and imbued with the power of the Holy Spirit's anointing and the Spirit's power, the sermons remain in lockstep and in perfect context with the times. The Old Testament prophets were the theological commentators of their times. Sent in by God when Israel had fallen into violation of the covenantal law, their task was to confront the people with commentary on their violation.

The Old Testament prophets spoke to specific circumstances in which Israel found herself. The prophetic nature of today's Pentecostal preaching calls the preacher to do the same. The times of the church, the needs of the congregation, the times of what's going on in the city or the neighborhood in which the church is located, and the current affairs of what is happening in the state or around the world . . . all these come into prophetic view with the preacher.

## REFLECTION QUESTIONS

1. Reflecting on the concept of "power" in the Holy Spirit anointing, in what ways does this power transform the preacher's delivery and the congregation's experience, extending beyond mere human ability or charisma?
2. "Passion" in an anointed sermon is distinct from mere emotional triggers. How do you differentiate authentic Spirit-empowered passion from manipulative emotional appeals within a worship context?
3. Discuss the persuasive nature of Spirit-anointed preaching. How does it demand a response from listeners that goes beyond intellectual assent, leading to tangible transformation and spiritual growth?
4. Evaluate the idea that "affections" are soul-deep cravings reshaped toward godliness, distinct from fleeting emotions. How might a Pentecostal sermon cultivate such deep-seated affections within individuals?

5. The Word of God is described as "alive and active." How does this understanding, particularly in the context of grace and truth, shape the delivery and expected impact of a Pentecostal sermon?

# PART THREE

## Setting the Hermeneutical Framework

I HAVE HAD THE privilege of preaching in several countries. Sometimes these sermons require a translator. This is the person who is fluent in the target language and in my language. The greater the translator's fluency, the better their ability to convey the exact meaning of my message.

Translation is more than word replacement. Every language carries nuance, expressions, and figurative language. Because of this, translators need intimate knowledge of such grammatical quirks. As a preacher, you are the translator between Scripture and the congregation. You need intimate knowledge of the quirks of Scripture. The greater the level of fluency in your ability to grasp all the theological grammar of the text, the greater your ability to faithfully translate its meaning to the congregation.

From where does this fluency come? First, it comes through dedicated study and the sacrifice of spending much time in the Word every day. One of my homiletics professors, Dr. John Lombard, a foundational, scholarly voice of the Pentecostal homiletical world, was once asked how he had acquired so much knowledge of the Bible. His response, "Oh, about twenty years' worth of studying 'bout five hours a day, five days a week." I wondered at the time if he was exaggerating. It's been twenty years since I first heard his comment, and I've come to learn he wasn't.

Second, this kind of fluency comes from embracing the principles of biblical interpretation that are both globally ecumenically accepted and those embraced within the Pentecostal/Charismatic community. This chapter brings these principles into view. The purpose of including this chapter is twofold. One, to provide you with an introductory foundation to the principles. And two, to lay the groundwork of understanding for the interpretive moves that take place while you're preaching.

The technical word used for biblical interpretation is *hermeneutics*. The word simply refers to the principles and methods involved in biblical interpretation. The process is part art, part science, and part Spirit. Second Timothy 2:15 instructs preachers to pursue biblical interpretation: "Do your best to present yourself to God as one approved, a worker who has no need to be ashamed, rightly handling the Word of truth" (ESV). The chapters in this section break up the world of Pentecostal hermeneutics in an accessible, easy-to-understand format. Chapter 8 focuses on the old stand-by categories of scientific approaches for interpreting the Bible. These scientific approaches (also called the higher criticisms) are the primary tools our cessationist friends use for biblical interpretation. They have value in the interpretive world but are best held at arm's length by Pentecostals because of their resistance to Spirit illumination as part of the interpretive journey.

As for the history behind these methods, they were birthed out of the Enlightenment and have progressed and expanded since. It's important for every Pentecostal/Charismatic preacher to have a basic knowledge of them in order to embrace their usefulness in their own sermon preparation. Their inclusion in this text is intended to be pastoral, with a distinct emphasis on accessibility. Because of this, my descriptions are general and first-level, on purpose. For those seeking a fuller, more concise exploration of these concepts, hermeneutics classes are their next step.

The next few chapters examine what biblical interpretation looks like within a Pentecostal paradigm. This is an entirely different approach than that taken by our cessationist friends. Here, interpretation is found in the intersection of Spirit, Word, and and the preacher's community. Pentecostal preachers need a solid grasp of what this world looks like. Along the way, you will be introduced to the major theological voices that have brought into view a clear-cut understanding of the dynamics involved in this intersection. My approach here is to distill the heart of their scholarly contributions and compile everything into neat, cohesive components that make sense for the Pentecostal preacher.

# 8

# The Scientific Approaches

"All Scripture is breathed out by God and profitable for teaching, for reproof, for correction, and for training in righteousness, that the man of God may be complete, equipped for every good work" (2 Tim 3:16–17 ESV). This passage speaks to the verbal inspiration of the Bible, which Pentecostals understand as Scripture's insulation against error, contradiction, or falsification. It is part of the Pentecostal/Charismatic foundation that holds that the only authority needed in the Christian life is the Word of God alone. It is a bedrock principle of Pentecostal hermeneutics that the same Spirit who inspired the writer is also the Spirit who illuminates the reader.

The Pentecostal approach to hermeneutics holds this principle firmly in its grasp. Our unique approach to biblical interpretation, a scripturally faithful model balanced within a Spirit-Word-Community triad, stands as a restorative breath of fresh air, free from the scientific methodologies that emerged from, and as a result of, the antagonism of the eighteenth- to nineteenth-centuries Enlightenment era. The scientific methods for understanding the meaning of Scripture addressed more synthetic, overarching questions: who wrote the book, when, with what sources, and in what historical setting, going beyond the text's wording to its literary and historical origins.

Although not explicitly cessationist, these methods presuppose a *nonsupernatural* approach to Scripture, effectively sidelining the Spirit's active role. That is to say, the basic approach for interpreting Scripture found within these models bears little to no reliance upon the Spirit other than marginal references that function more obligatorily than they do structurally. These have also been historically referred to as the *higher criticisms*. The phrase *higher criticism* arose to distinguish a newer kind of historical-literary study of Scripture from earlier "lower" or textual criticism, which focused mainly on copying errors among ancient manuscripts and on restoring the wording of the text. These models offered information about the world behind the text but often did so under rationalist assumptions that were antagonistic to traditional biblical faith and the supernatural undergirding from which the church finds its grounding.

The world of scientific approaches is broad, with several areas of specialization existing within. For the sake of what I want to accomplish in our brief, pastoral, nonacademic discussion, I have grouped these specializations into three overarching approaches: the author-centered approach, the text-centered approach, and the reader-centered approach. Each of these approaches emphasizes discovering the meaning of Scripture by focusing on the author's world, the world behind the text, or the reader. There are many other areas of specialization within the discipline of hermeneutics beyond those I have discussed here. But these are offered as representative of the major voices within each category. If you prefer a more thorough, systematic examination of these, please sign up for a hermeneutics class near you.

Why should this be important for the Spirit-filled reader? A Pentecostal/Charismatic preacher benefits from understanding these methodologies because they remain the dominant framework in much of modern biblical scholarship. Academic commentaries, theological textbooks, and even translations often operate from assumptions shaped by them. Without a basic grasp of these interpretive systems, the Pentecostal preacher risks misunderstanding or misapplying academic resources, or worse, allowing rationalistic presuppositions to influence their theology and preaching. Awareness enables discernment. When a preacher knows the origins, motivations, and limitations of these methods, they can engage the scholarly conversation without compromising their Spirit-empowered hermeneutic.

Moreover, understanding higher criticism equips the Pentecostal preacher to pastor and teach within an intellectually honest faith. Today, congregants encounter popular documentaries, podcasts, and online content that challenge the Bible's authority by employing precisely these critical methods. A preacher equipped with knowledge of how Enlightenment rationalism approached Scripture—divorced from divine inspiration—can better articulate why the Pentecostal view restores Scripture's theological and spiritual integrity. This preparedness strengthens both proclamation and apologetic, allowing the preacher to shepherd a biblically literate congregation in an age of skepticism.

Finally, studying the history and structure of these critical models reminds Pentecostal interpreters of what is lost when interpretation is stripped of the Spirit. It clarifies that Pentecostal hermeneutics is not anti-intellectual but reintegrative, bringing back together the experiential, revelatory, and communal aspects that Enlightenment rationalism has disassembled. Understanding higher criticism, then, becomes an exercise in theological maturity: learning the grammar of the opposition in order to articulate, with greater depth, the wisdom of the Spirit-led approach. A preacher who knows why these methods failed to capture Scripture's living voice can more confidently proclaim that voice with conviction and power.

Armed with this foundational understanding of higher criticism's historical and methodological contours, Pentecostal preachers can embrace them, when appropriate, for what they are. These author-centered, text-centered, and reader-centered approaches represent the Enlightenment's unenlightened quest for meaning, each sidelining the Spirit's illuminating role. As we examine them, the superiority of our Spirit-Word-Community triad discussed in the following chapters emerges ever more clearly, restoring Scripture's transformative power for preaching and ministry.

## AUTHOR-CENTERED APPROACH (APPROACHES FOCUSED ON THE AUTHOR AND HISTORICAL CONTEXT)

The author-centered approach has a focal point: it holds that the best approach to sound interpretation is to focus on the text's author. By nature, it looks for the meaning of the text *outside* of the text. More specifically, research is focused on the author, their world, and their thoughts. Research about the author includes searching all biblical references to the author and extra-biblical references (if they exist).

For example, when reading Jude, an author-centered approach to interpreting his epistle would involve researching every instance in which his name appears in the Bible. One would find rather quickly that he was identified as one of the brothers of Jesus (Mark 6:3); as one of

Jesus' brothers he was also the brother of James (same James who wrote the epistle); he identified himself as a bond-servant (Jude 1:1); along with his brothers he did not originally believe in the Messiahship of Christ (John 7:3–5); he was one of the family members waiting outside as Jesus taught because they were worried that Jesus was mentally unstable (Mark 3:21); and by means of his epistle we know he was a leader in the church, which means at some point he had had a major conversion.

The author-centered approach to biblical interpretation enquires the extent to which these things inform us about the content of his epistle. Taking these facts into consideration, what kinds of concerns could have occupied Jude's mind? What kinds of emphases would normally be associated with someone coming from this background? From here, research moves into the realms of authorial context. What was life like for those living in ancient Palestine? What struggles would Jude have experienced religiously, socially, economically, etc.? Research would now pivot to the examination of cultural distinctives, existential concerns, etc.

This approach also examines the sources used during composition. It was customary during this time for literary works to be composed alongside other works, with their content incorporated and in tension with existing oral tradition stories. During biblical times, incorporating someone else's material was not considered plagiarism; it was considered a compliment.

For example, a reading of Luke's Gospel reveals his reliance on other sources (Luke 1:1). We know Luke had Mark's Gospel on the table as he wrote because about 50 percent of Luke is made up of nearly all of Mark. And approximately 25 percent of Luke is identical with Matthew. Most scholars agree that they most likely shared a common source for this material, identified as Q (from the German word *quell*, meaning "source").

Special attention is given to understanding why certain sources were used by the author rather than others. *Sources* represent the other writings in circulation at the time of composition. Was there a theological reason the author prioritized one source over the others? Does the answer to these kinds of questions reveal anything about the author? If so, what is the impact of that revelation in terms of how we understand the meaning of their text?

The author-centered approach holds that the text is a window into the historical world it describes. It carries the attempt to reconstruct the story behind the text's composition. There are two major schools of interpretation within the author-centered approach: historical-grammatical criticism and redaction criticism, where the term *criticism* is used in an inquisitive sense. Each of these is briefly examined below.

## Historical-Grammatical Criticism

Historical criticism examines the text's historical context. It is the most commonly relied-upon scientific approach used by Pentecostal preachers. Klein, Blomberg, and Hubbard Jr., in their widely acclaimed text, *Introduction to Biblical Interpretation*, identify three reasons why understanding the historical background of the Bible is important: perspective, mindset, and contextualization. To the first, perspective, they assert the strategic value in gaining the perspective of the author and recipient behind the writing in order to see the text through their eyes, thereby providing meaning otherwise not available at the surface level.[1] The second reason, mindset, addresses mental attitude or inclination of the author and recipient, thereby revealing the intended emotional impact imbedded within the text, and thereby revealing affective meaning of the text.[2] Their third reason, contextualization, emphasizes how the text speaks to today's audience, conveying the need for understanding the text's historical (original) meaning before understanding meaning for today.[3] Several components of the text's historicity come into view. First is the identity of the author. What is known about them? What is their name? What is known about their family? Where were they born? What is known about their salvation history? Were they married or did they have children? What do we know about their life? And what kinds of emphases do they embrace in their writings?

This approach seeks the specific reason the text was written. What was its intent? What was the reason for the writing of the text? A good example of this is found in John's Gospel, where he tells the reader the exact intent for his writing the text (John 20:30–31). Other intents are not so easily discerned and require some digging. Paul's epistles are good examples of this kind of phenomenon, where we must dig to find verses like 1 Cor 5:1, "It is actually reported that there is sexual immorality among you" (ESV). We know from this statement that Paul had received information about the current state of affairs in the church and intended to write to them about it.

1. Klein et al., *Introduction to Biblical Interpretation*, 229.
2. Klein et al., *Introduction to Biblical Interpretation*, 230.
3. Klein et al., *Introduction to Biblical Interpretation*, 231.

The question being asked is, *why* did the author write this text? Was it in response to reports received about current conditions? Was it meant to encourage believers during persecution? Was it to faithfully record the story of Jesus? Historical criticism holds that the text's real meaning cannot be discovered without first discerning the author's intent. Discovering this involves examining the text's historical context. What was the city in which it was written? Who was the audience? What was the year of its composition? What were the circumstances of the writer? Were they in duress? Were they rich or poor? Similarly, what was the audience's condition? Were they suffering through tribulations? Were they in need of a warning or a scolding? Where is the writing situated in the history of salvation? All of these queries aim to reveal both the author's original intentional meaning and the audience's original reception meaning.

Historical-grammatical criticism, as a scientific methodology, delivers information about the world behind the historical setting of the text's composition. It seeks the author's intent within the historical and grammatical context. The approach holds that when one discovers the text's historical and grammatical context, one discovers its meaning. The technique delivers factual information but does not require Spirit reliance. The Pentecostal preacher, when seeking understanding of the text, holds this in mind when leaning on historical-grammatical criticism. The process may deliver information that stands up to every angle of scrutiny but may still be far from the Spirit's intent for its composition.

## Redaction Criticism

Redaction criticism seeks to discover the theological emphases of the author and the community in which the author resides. When a document is redacted, it has been edited. Either the author or someone other than the author has reviewed the text with the intent to remove or add content. The edits have been made in accordance with the objectives or agenda they carry. What was their reason for the edits? Discover their agenda, and you've discovered the true interpretation of the text, so the redaction critic claims.

Redaction criticism seeks to understand how writers and editors chose, edited, and altered texts. Norman Perrin, one of redaction criticism's earliest scholars, wrote a text about the discipline. In the opening pages, he describes the process as being "concerned with studying the theological motivation of an author as this is revealed in the collection, arrangement, editing, and modification of traditional material, and in the composition of new material or the creation of new forms within the traditions of Christianity."[4] A good representative case in point is the Gospel of Mark. Tradition holds that after Mark abandoned Paul and Barnabas during Paul's first missionary journey (Acts 13), he later joined Peter as his assistant, translator, and recorder. According to early church tradition (as recorded by Papias), Mark based his Gospel on Peter's preaching. Though this remains a subject of scholarly debate, many believe that Mark's Gospel is a collection of Peter's sermons and teaching material. A redaction critic enquires about the theology behind Mark's arrangement of this material. With everything Mark had at his disposal, what were the reasons behind his choosing some stories over others, and what was the significance of their arrangement?

Editing a story involves combining certain details and portions of the story. Other details have been expanded. In many cases, other features of the story have been omitted. And in some cases, the setting may be changed to better highlight other features of the story. The redaction critic analyzes all these components, seeking what is both obvious and nuanced in order to uncover the editor's agenda.

Redaction critics also look for certain motifs present within the document. The "I Am" statements in John, for example, are examined to reveal the motive behind their inclusion. They look at Matthew's heavy use of Old Testament proof texts in his Gospel. The precision and detail associated with Luke's Gospel is taken into consideration. And they study Mark's standout emphasis on Jesus' insistence that people keep his messianic identity secret.

Redaction criticism, then, has the potential to be a valuable, though limited, conversation partner for the Spirit-filled preacher. By paying attention to how a Gospel writer selected, arranged, and emphasized certain episodes or themes, for example, the preacher has potential for gaining a deeper sense of each book's pastoral burden and theological heartbeat.

## TEXT-CENTERED APPROACH (APPROACHES FOCUSED ON THE TEXT ITSELF AS LITERATURE)

The next focal point is the text-centered approach. Within this approach, the key to interpretation is found in the text itself. Moving away from the

4. Perrin, *What Is Redaction Criticism?*, 1.

concept of discovering meaning in the author or the author's intentions, the goal here is to examine the world the text creates, with particular emphasis on the Bible's literary beauty and unity, and with particular disregard for the historical context in which the text was composed. The approach seeks to divorce the text from the author as a free-standing entity whose words and grammatical conventions speak for themselves.

A close analysis is undertaken of the text's words, grammar, syntax, rhetoric, figurative language, and forms. Foundational to this approach is a commitment to the text's objectivity. Any information about the author is held in secondary or tertiary consideration. For example, a reading of Paul's instructions for spiritual warfare in Eph 6 need not include any consideration of the fact that Paul was in chains as he wrote these words and that a few feet away from him was most likely a Roman centurion in full garb. The meaning of the text is found solely in the grammar.

The text is an end in itself as opposed to being a window of discovery about the author or the times/circumstances in which the text was composed. There are three major schools of interpretation within the text-centered approach: narrative criticism, literary criticism, and textual criticism.

## Narrative Criticism

Narrative criticism approaches the Bible as a cohesive literary narrative, examining how the text's final form functions as a story to convey meaning. Rather than probing the historical author or original audience, this twentieth-century method surveys the *narrative's big picture*—its plot, characters, and setting—allowing the story to speak through its own internal dynamics. Focusing specifically on story dynamics, interpretation emerges from how these elements interact: the plot's rising tension and climax, the development of protagonists and foils, and the symbolic role of time, place, and circumstance.

One of the premier texts on narrative criticism is Mark Allen Powell's *What Is Narrative Criticism?* Powell identifies two aspects of narrative: story and discourse. He says, "Story refers to the content of the narrative, what it is about. A story consists of such elements as events, characters, and settings, and the interaction of these elements comprises what we call the plot. Discourse refers to the rhetoric of the narrative, how the story is told. Stories concerning the same basic events, characters, and settings can be told in ways that produce very different narratives. The four Gospels provide excellent examples of this."[5]

Key questions guide the narrative critic: What drives the plot forward? How do complications resolve? Who are the characters? Are they flat or round, reliable or unreliable narrators? How do their actions and dialogues reveal deeper truths? Where and when does the story unfold, and how does the setting shape the reader's experience? For instance, in the parable of the prodigal son (Luke 15), the distant country evokes alienation, the father's embrace signals restoration, and the elder brother's resentment heightens the climax of grace. Narrative criticism thus uncovers the text's rhetorical power, emphasizing how the story invites readers into its world.

This refined focus equips Pentecostal preachers to appreciate the Bible's artistry as a Spirit-crafted narrative that draws hearers into divine drama. Handled with discernment, alongside the Spirit-filled approach (examined in the next chapters), narrative insights have the potential to enrich preaching by illuminating the text's inherent power to transform.

## Literary Criticism

The literary criticism approach broadens the horizons from its close relative of narrative criticism. Literary criticism delves further into vocabulary, grammar, syntax, and genre. Vocabulary is examined to discover how words are handled by the author. An example of this can be found in John's use of the word *word* in John 1:1, "In the beginning was the Word, and the Word was with God, and the Word was God" (ESV). John was writing in Greek in a world still transitioning to the Roman Empire. John's audience was still very much steeped within Hellenistic thought and culture. As such, they would have immediately been tempted to connect John's use of *word* with Plato's use of the same word, where Plato proposed *word* as a supernatural personage of logic or reason that created and governed all existence.

The object of analysis is the text as literature in a wide sense (not the text as a stand-alone story, as with narrative analysis). Grammatical constructions are interrogated to discover the meaning of the text. What is the tense of the text? Is the author writing in the future tense or the past tense? Are there any idiomatic expressions present? Are there

5. Powell, *What Is Narrative Criticism?*, 23.

any emotional tones that need to be discerned? What was the setting or mood? Verbs, nouns, adjectives, and all the other grammatical components are studied to ferret out meaning. The process involves appraising the text in its original languages of Hebrew, Aramaic, or Greek.

The syntax of the text is considered. Syntax is the way words are integrated to form phrases, clauses, or sentences. The process begins broadly, then works its way deeper into specific, detailed analysis. The first step of syntactical analysis begins with determining the genre of the text (prophecy, law, gospel, history, etc.), then the dominant sections of the text (for example, tracking the geographical shiftings between Galilee and Jerusalem in the Gospels), followed by smaller units of thought (pericope), and finally, examining words themselves. When one discovers the shaping of the words, they have delved deep into the author's mind and thus gained a better understanding of the text's meaning, according to the theory behind this approach.

Grant R. Osborne's text *The Hermeneutical Spiral* contains a chapter devoted to the features of literary criticism, which invite the preacher to seek greater insights of Hebrew and Greek language development, attention to verbs and verb tenses, nouns and noun cases, prepositions, particles, and clauses. For the Pentecostal preacher, literary criticism provides potential insight into the rhetorical artistry of the author. Such a revelation holds genuine fascination. Its handling requires the gloves of Pentecostal shrewdness. Reducing the living Word to aesthetic analysis risks conceding Spirit interpretation to clinical methodology.

## READER-CENTERED APPROACH (APPROACHES FOCUSED ON THE READER'S RESPONSE)

The reader-centered approach, a postmodern development of the twentieth and twenty-first centuries, shifts the focus to the *reader's role* in interpretation. Rather than asking, "What did the text mean?" it asks, "How did the people interpret it?" regardless of the author's intent. It probes the *history of effect*, how interpretations by specific groups, in particular times and places, have shaped cultures and actions. Humanist skeptics, for instance, dismiss Scripture's reliability by highlighting resolvable Gospel discrepancies, while nineteenth-century slaveholders misused Noah's curse on Ham's descendants (Gen 9) or New Testament prescriptions—originally addressing indentured servitude—to justify racial bondage.

At a personal level, reader-centered methods prioritize the question, "What is the text saying to *me*?" Spanning from early medieval times, this pivot was a reaction against corrupt church leadership's stubborn stronghold on biblical interpretation. The Catholic Church was the biggest culprit in this, where Scripture was read only in Latin (regardless of the vernacular of the local church), and the priests were the only ones allowed to read and understand the Bible. The rising suspicion continued to fester through the Enlightenment's rejection of objective truth, all the way through to postmodernity's embrace of subjective expressionism.

## Reader-Response Criticism

Powell's text *What Is Narrative Criticism?* (previously mentioned) provides a good primer in this area. Powell states, "Reader-response critics study the dynamics of the reading process in order to discover how readers perceive literature and on what bases they produce or create meaning for any given work."[6] Powell goes on to highlight the various theories within the discipline, offering insights into particularities and nuance.[7] Additionally, the approach asks the reader, "What is your response to the text?" The true meaning of the text is found in the collaboration between the writer, the reader, and the text. The dangerous subjectivity embedded in these approaches yields a recreation of the text with each new reading. These sentiments carried over into biblical interpretation. For example, Paul's discussion of how he can do all things through Christ who strengthens him (Phil 4:13) could be interpreted by some more as performative (I can win this soccer game) rather than perseverance (I can survive this persecution).

The text serves as the evocative agent that elicits a response from the reader based on the reader's experiences, thoughts, feelings, pre-analytical dispositions, worldview, inclinations, and prejudices. The text bears no allegiance to any notion of original authorial or Spirit intent. The text is ontologically neutral, carrying no objective meaning. Its meaning is subjective.

For the Pentecostal preacher, this approach to biblical interpretation stirs more than casual interest. On the one hand, if it's true that Scripture is alive and active (Heb 4:12), then the personal reaction from

6. Powell, *What Is Narrative Criticism?*, 16.

7. Powell, *What Is Narrative Criticism?*, 16–18.

the hearer must be given voice. On the other hand, such a voice needs the safeguarding of a Spirit-filled community. In the end, the Pentecostal preacher fares well when they interact with the reader-centered insights as secondary diagnostics, at best, with extreme caution standing guard against misinterpretation. Hearers' biases lend too much occasion for the Word distortion, risking the domestication of Scripture's objective anchor with endless reinterpretation. Only the Spirit-Word-Community triad restores Spirit authority, ensuring proclamation pierces the heart rather than mirroring the hearer.

## CONCLUSION: THE RESPECT OF AN UNINSPIRED SCIENCE

Pentecostal preachers must approach the higher criticisms as useful when handled with respect, but dangerous when wielded without intent. Tools such as historical criticism, redaction criticism, and literary analysis are not inherently enemies of faith. In their proper place, they can clarify context, reveal purpose, and enrich exegesis. Yet when employed without prayerful reliance on the Holy Spirit, they tempt the preacher to transform living revelation into lifeless data. Preaching born of mere analysis seldom stirs repentance or faith. It may inform the mind but leaves the heart untouched.

The danger of these methods lies not in their questions but in their assumptions. The higher criticisms arose from a worldview deeply antagonistic to the miraculous, supernatural, and transcendent origins of Scripture's composition. The scholars of the Enlightenment era meant well—they sought order, clarity, and historical grounding. But they often did so by removing the very element that makes the Bible "alive and active" (Heb 4:12), the very breath of the Spirit. When Scripture is treated as a specimen for scientific observation rather than the living voice of God, the preacher risks exchanging real-life transformation for information.

Every Pentecostal preacher must guard against the temptation. It's easy to become enamored with the precision of the scholarly technique and thus slowly concede genuine encounter. The biblical text itself, in the hands of a Pentecostal/Charismatic preacher, is not fodder for intellectual analysis; it is the sacred fire meant to ignite conviction and transformation through the Spirit's anointing. If the Author is sidelined, the preacher begins to sound more like a lecturer than a herald.

Our task, then, is not to abandon the tools of study but to utilize them in the context of sanctified preparation. A Spirit-filled hermeneutic does not reject scholarly inquiry; it redeems it. The holy Word is studied diligently, but always on a bent knee. We analyze grammar and historical background, but only so the living voice of Scripture can be heard more clearly. We consult ancient sources, linguistic data, and academic commentaries, but we never forget that the Author still speaks, and is ultimately the main Object of inquiry.

## REFLECTION QUESTIONS

1. Considering the risks of reader-response criticism that treats meaning as entirely subjective, how might participating in a Spirit-filled community guard against personal biases distorting the objective authority of Scripture?
2. In your own preaching or teaching, how do you currently balance diligent historical and literary study with prayerful dependence on the Holy Spirit to hear the living voice of God in the text?
3. What practical steps could you take in your devotional life to ensure that scholarly methods remain servants to the Spirit rather than becoming the primary lens through which you interpret Scripture?
4. How does the historical tendency of higher criticism to exclude supernatural explanations challenge your understanding of the Bible's inspiration and transformative power in everyday Christian life?
5. Imagine explaining to a skeptical friend why you believe a Spirit-led hermeneutic restores the Bible's vitality in a way that Enlightenment-based methods cannot. What key convictions would you emphasize in that conversation?

# 9

# The Spirit-Filled Approach

THE SPIRIT-FILLED APPROACH TO biblical interpretation takes on different dimensions from those just discussed. Rather than relying on scientific methodologies, the Pentecostal/Charismatic method acknowledges the continuing role of the Holy Spirit and community in understanding the Word. This chapter visualizes the landscape that shapes the Pentecostal movement's interpretive approach. It, along with chapters 10–12, is drawn from the works of many of the premier Pentecostal scholars in hermeneutics. These include Ken Archer, Craig S. Keener, Chris Green, Jackie David Johns, Cheryl Bridges-Johns, Amos Yong, Rickie D. Moore, and John Christopher Thomas. *These people are the experts.* The Pentecostal/Charismatic community owes them a debt of gratitude. My heart for this chapter was to analyze their works and to present a synthesis of the interpretive world they have brought to life for the Spirit-filled community.

I've attempted to craft this chapter so that it does not read or feel like an academic treatise but rather provides the shortest possible pathway to insights and understanding of how we make sense out of Scripture, which will hopefully better ground the Pentecostal/Charismatic Bible-teaching preacher on the platform to which they have been called. By necessity, our interaction with our scholars requires proper attribution. To the best of my ability, I have presented their research in the most reader-friendly manner. For those interested in a fuller exploration of these conversations, please reference appendix B.

## EXPERIENCES

From its very beginning, the Pentecostal movement has been marked by Spirit phenomena such as speaking in tongues, divine healing, miracles, power-filled preaching, and similar manifestations. God was moving in a way that was fresh for the times. This was not to say that God had since ceased to move this way, as the cessationists make claims. Instead, the early leaders of the movement understood it as the fulfillment of the Old Testament's "latter rain" motif.

The latter rain motif appears in passages that promise God's blessings, providing not only the spring rains needed at the beginning of the harvest but also the heavier, more robust latter rains of the fall. The early pioneers of the movement interpreted the fresh outpouring of the Spirit as a fulfillment of these passages. They saw the Acts 2 outpouring of the Holy Spirit as the early rains and the late nineteenth-century outpouring of the Spirit as the latter rains. Some key passages supporting the latter rain motif include Zech 10:1, Deut 11:14, Joel 2:23, Jer 5:24, and Jas 5:7–8.

## WORLDVIEW

The worldview of the early Pentecostals was *full gospel*. Paul wrote the believers in Rome that the signs and wonders and the empowerment of the Spirit that accompanied his preaching had *fully proclaimed* the gospel (Rom 15:19). The presence of healings, prophetic utterances, miracles, and the like, that accompanied Paul and the other disciples, and that were *also* accompanying the preaching and ministry activities of the early Pentecostal movement, were signs of God's presence.

What does this worldview mean in terms of how Pentecostals go about interpreting the Bible? No one has traced the context of our unique approach to biblical interpretation better than Ken Archer. Please see the annotated bibliographic entry in appendix B for more information on Ken's watershed text, *Pentecostal Hermeneutic* (2009). Several key distinguishing features of a Pentecostal worldview are identified in Archer's research on the early days of the movement. For example, Archer notes how the early Pentecostals were concerned more about heartfelt conversion than orthodox belief,[1] and how they were similarly more

1. Archer, *Pentecostal Hermeneutic*, 16.

concerned with faithful living than proving the existence of God based on philosophical arguments.[2] Pentecostals sought to demonstrate God's existence rather than merely talk about it. This means that identifying the characteristic markers of a Pentecostal hermeneutic indicates that Bible interpretation was more missional than academic.

## REBELLIOUS RESTORATIONIST ATTITUDE

One of the Enlightenment's overarching values was the embrace of higher criticism as a means of interpreting the Bible. The Enlightenment was the era in which science became dominant, and a deistic approach to knowing God became the favored approach to religion. Deism, among its many characteristics, embraced an understanding of God grounded in natural theology and a wholesale rejection of the supernatural phenomena of Scripture. It valued reason over revelation and was founded on a bedrock antagonistic suspicion of the supernatural aspects of Scripture. Scripture was valued more for its moral teachings than the supernatural witness that the God who created the heavens and earth was breaking in to make himself salvifically known and available.

The higher criticisms, as discussed earlier, employed measurable, testable methods to study works of literary antiquity. When these techniques were applied to the holy writings of Christianity, they did not allow adequate consideration of the supernatural or miraculous. One of the challenges of this approach was the obvious absence of any reliance upon the Holy Spirit involved in interpretation. With the rejection of the supernatural in the original stories came, by default, the accompanying rejection of the supernatural in the act of interpretation. The same Spirit who was rejected in the narrative was likewise rejected in the illumination.

By the time of the Pentecostal movement's birth, the church was ready for the restoration of wonder and awe in its biblical interpretation. As the early leaders of the Pentecostal movement assumed leadership, they were, in part, driven by what Archer describes as a rebellious reaction against the over-intellectualism that had taken hold of biblical interpretation methods. Archer characterizes the nascent stage of the movement as paramodern (as opposed to premodern or antimodern)[3]

2. Archer, *Pentecostal Hermeneutic*, 87.

3. Archer, *Pentecostal Hermeneutic*, 38, 45.

and countercultural.[4] Reacting against the dry, often inaccessible, and unrelatable interpretations proffered by scientific models, the Pentecostal movement sought to restore the simple, rich, and powerful interpretation that comes from allowing the Author of Scripture to interpret Scripture.

## VOICES OF TRADITION

The Pentecostal tradition owes many of its theological distinctives to the voices of John Wesley and the Higher Life movement. Ken Archer highlights these historical connections with superb clarity. Without going too deeply into the history, a few comments on sanctification and experience can be made here that help us understand the theological trajectory to which we are connected.

Sanctification, as a distinct, measurable event in the timeline of the salvation journey, is a unique characteristic of the Pentecostal economy of salvation. Both John Wesley and the theology that emerged from the Higher Life movement (from the Keswick meetings in mid-nineteenth-century England) embraced a kind of Christianity that sought this higher plane of spiritual existence. Each having its own distinctives, both produced extensive writings about the concept of sanctification (a concept that Wesley understood as Christian perfectionism). The concept highlighted the Spirit's activity in the mortification of the flesh while also imparting and cultivating the Christian graces that create within the believer a desire for, and a presence of, holiness. It is believed that these can be enjoyed by believers in their fullest expression.

Sanctification involves loving God with all one's heart, soul, mind, and strength, and loving one's neighbor as oneself. It is characterized by a pure intention to do God's will, a deep sense of humility, and an unwavering faith. The doctrine was not about moral perfection in human terms but about a complete and ongoing transformation by the Holy Spirit, enabling believers to live lives of holiness and love. This emphasis on growth in grace and the possibility of achieving a mature Christian character was central to the movement's teaching and remains a distinctive feature of Pentecostalism.

Before Wesley, experience as a stand-alone component of theological reflection or inquiry carried little value. The standard approach for theological composition embraced Scripture, tradition, and reason.

4. Archer, *Pentecostal Hermeneutic*, 24.

Experience was too subjective and therefore carried too much room for error. Wesley was balanced in his insistence on including experience. Scripture remained the primary source. Experience was added as confirmation of scripturally grounded truths, particularly those concerning the economy of salvation.

## METHODOLOGICAL FOUNDATION

The guardrails of today's Pentecostal hermeneutical highway are affixed firmly to the posts of those who have gone before us. Archer describes how the early days of the movement adhered to an inductive approach to interpreting the Bible, combined with common sense, and were intentionally free of higher-critical methodologies.

The overall approach embraced by the early leaders had two simple principles. The first relied upon observations of the text. Observations were conducted responsibly, acknowledging reliance on the Holy Spirit in the process. And second, these observations, in the context of reasonable Spirit-guided consideration, yielded suppositions, truths, and principles that were firmly grounded in Scripture and in line with the overall thrust of God's revelation.

Common sense realism, according to Archer, was part of the overall interpretive approach, which held that the "mind can perceive what is actually there because the object contains the property that produces the sensation in the mind."[5] For the early leaders of the movement, the inductive approach combined with Common Sense Realism together produced a "confidence that one could discover the facts of Scripture as easily as one could discover the facts of science."[6] For our movement, this delivered a solid, reliable biblical interpretation.

Archer describes how the distinct method for approaching Scripture was Jesus-centric and praxis-driven and involved simple inductive observation combined with sound analysis and synthesis. The approach typically involved a concordance in which word studies could be conducted that were intense, comprehensive, and capable of producing a biblical doctrinal position. When needed, efforts extended to higher criticism, particularly the historical-grammatical method, but only when the plain meaning

5. Archer, *Pentecostal Hermeneutic*, 51.

6. Archer, *Pentecostal Hermeneutic*, 52.

was not possible through induction and common sense. Additionally, the original languages were studied only in similar contexts.

The approach called for a complete biblical consideration of a word or concept, which was then harmonized into a defensible and appropriate position. As a movement that held the highest respect for Scripture, this pre-critical approach enabled a partnership with the Holy Spirit that safeguarded the search for truth found in God's revealed, inscripturated Word.

## THE NONNEGOTIABLES

Describing a Pentecostal hermeneutic requires that certain nonnegotiables be on the table. Nonnegotiables are the must-haves in place when making a decision. For example, when my wife and I are discussing possible places for a family weekend getaway, I always ask about the nonnegotiables. She says things such as "I need some peace and quiet" or "I need the beach." To that, I usually add something like, "I need a golf course," or "We need a place that accepts dogs." Once we have our list of nonnegotiables, we're ready to start looking for our perfect destination.

When piecing together a hermeneutical strategy for the Pentecostal movement, several nonnegotiables must be brought into view. These include discussions of the self, a Spirit framework for knowledge, Spirit-groundedness for refinement and experience, the role of the Holy Spirit, the role of Scripture, and the role of community. As we proceed with a brief discussion of these nonnegotiables, our conversations with the Pentecostal movement's leading hermeneutics scholars continue.

## THE PREACHER'S IDENTITY AS SPIRIT-FILLED CO-AGENT

### Active Participant in the Biblical Narrative

When the preacher's identity is brought into the discussion, it is done so with special consideration of *location*. A leading question here is, "What is the best positioning and the best point of view for accurate biblical interpretation?" For example, one of the best ways to enjoy a professional baseball game is sitting right behind home plate about twenty rows back (an expensive, rare treat for me). Every pitch comes straight up the middle. The ball flight of every hit is followed with ease.

The starting point for interpretive location is always that of a *direct participant in the biblical narrative.* Archer highlights this dynamic when he states, "Interpreters see themselves as participants in the same drama as the Bible."[7] And with this, the voice of our next scholar of Pentecostal hermeneutics comes to the table here, Craig Keener. See appendix B for bibliographic access to Craig's work *Spirit Hermeneutics* (2016). Keener's on the same page with Archer here: "All Christians should read Scripture as people who are living in the biblical experience—not in terms of ancient culture, but as people living by the same Spirit who guided God's people in Scripture."[8]

Active immersion into the narrative is the starting place of the self in the act of biblical interpretation. Engagement with the Word is intentional, immersive, and participatory. When engaging narrative books of the Bible, for example, the preacher learns to rise and fall with the plot's undulations. The plight of the characters becomes the interpreter's plight. The interpreter becomes part of the scene in the same way that the moviegoer laughs, cries, or startles while watching their favorite movie. Keener says it like this,

> If we really hear God's heart in Scripture, we will read Scripture differently. A rascal will read Paul's claims to be the least, because of Paul's past persecution of Christians, as clever, mock humility (1 Cor 15:9; Eph 3:8; 1 Tim 1:15); conversely, someone who has deeply experienced grace will identify with the gratitude such a claim expresses (cf. 2 Sam 16:10–12; Luke 7:44–47; 18:10–14). Those of us who experienced anger from authority figures early in our lives may recoil at expressions of God's anger in Scripture; but the larger narratives that encase these expressions usually make clear how slow to anger God is, despite how people provoked him and resisted.[9]

An additional component that comes into view regarding the preacher's identity is their attention to the ongoing story of God's activity in the lives of his people. God revealed himself through the Old Testament stories of calling, rescuing, delivering, and positioning his chosen people, Israel. God revealed himself in the special revelation of Jesus Christ in the New Testament. God's revelation has not ceased. It continues through Word gifts such as knowledge, wisdom, prophecy, teaching,

7. Archer, *Pentecostal Hermeneutic*, 194.

8. Keener, *Spirit Hermeneutics*, 5.

9. Keener, *Spirit Hermeneutics*, 42.

and preaching, etc. God's revelation also continues through his interactions with those who belong to him. The interpreter sees themselves as an ongoing participant in salvation history. The God of the Bible is the God of today. This location, as a participant in salvation history, changes the exegete's perspective. The spectator becomes a prize witness.

## Timeless Participation

Past, present, and future become fused in the act of interpretation. Past narratives become present narratives. Past truth becomes timeless truth. Present interaction with the Almighty becomes part of God's ongoing story of redemptive history. My story becomes part of the biblical story. Keener writes, "In the global Pentecostal approach to Scripture, the supernatural God of the Bible is the God of the present, real world. The line between salvation history in the biblical narrative and continuing salvation history today is thin, so that readers approach the text as a model for life and ideally expect God to continue to act as he acted in Scripture."[10]

Add to this the present participation in future glory, and interpretive clarity comes into full view. One way I illustrate this principle to my students and parishioners is by asking them what kind of person they will be in heaven. I'll ask, "Let's fast forward ten thousand years and we bump into each other in eternity. What kind of person will I meet?" The follow-up question is easily anticipated for the preacher: "What's holding you back from being that person today?" When applied to the interpreter, this positioning oneself in the future fullness of glory is an intentional interpretive move that makes the full liveliness of the Word visible. Salvation history has eternity in sight. Keener says, "Jesus not only announced the coming kingdom; his signs were a foretaste of the fullness of that kingdom."[11]

## Follower of Christ

This next point may seem somewhat elementary, but it cannot be overstated. This point positions the preacher as a *true follower of Christ*. At this point, we invite our next expert guest to the hermeneutics table: Chris E. W. Green. Chris advances a distinctly Pentecostal approach to

10. Keener, *Spirit Hermeneutics*, 28.

11. Keener, *Spirit Hermeneutics*, 50.

hermeneutics by framing biblical interpretation as a spiritual vocation oriented toward holiness rather than merely an academic task. Green's text *Sanctifying Interpretation* (2015) highlights the importance of this in his discussion of how interpretation has an ontological component of a Jesus-centric identity.[12] Jesus comforted his disciples upon learning of his departure at the last supper by informing them that he would send something better than being with them in person: himself in Spirit, leading, guiding, and comforting them. This makes logical sense. It also demonstrates that, without the transformative ministry of his Spirit, which provides illumination, our attempts to understand his Words are left to our intellectual imagination.

The Pentecostal interpreter is one who has the Spirit of Christ within them, empowering the interpreter to read Scripture from a distinctly Christ-centered perspective. Keener chimes in here and says it like this, "Ultimately, a 'Pentecostal' approach is an apology for reading Christian texts in a specifically Christian way, rather than the way we sometimes read those texts in the academy."[13] No amount of education or training in higher criticism can replace being an authentic follower of Jesus Christ. There are too many PhD professors who treat Christian writings as ancient religious literature rather than the living Word—and who know the content of Scripture perhaps at levels no regular believer could ever imagine—but still do so as an academic venture rather than as active participants. It's possible to know the content of Scripture without ever having met its Author. Jesus will say to many on that day, "Depart from me; I never knew you" (Matt 7:23).

## Baggage in Hand

Every preacher arrives at the pulpit with their own particular point of view, shaped by years of experience. Some of the colors of this view are antagonistic, some Pollyanna. That is to say, no interpreter ever engages the Word free from prejudice. No interpreter is free from the baggage of the past. Prejudice is forever part of the interpretive equation. This is a common trait of hermeneutical considerations. Keener talks about this in more than one place in his text, stating, "Pre-understanding shapes

12. Green, *Sanctifying Interpretation*, 109.

13. Keener, *Spirit Hermeneutics*, 11.

how we come to the text,"[14] and, "The assumptions we bring to the text help determine the meaning that we supply to textual indeterminacies."[15] Here's an example: Many of those called into ministry come from broken backgrounds (this is true of most biblical characters as well). If the interpreter was raised in a context of rejection, there will inevitably be an ongoing struggle to identify with the gospel's love and acceptance. The love of the Father will remain somewhat elusive, always in view through salvific experience, but unavoidably filtered through the scarred lenses of past rejections.

By God's design, that tint of prejudice will always be part of the lenses of the interpreter. Paul knew this from his own experiences. God told us through Paul that he puts his treasure in earthen vessels (2 Cor 4:7). He uses the cracks in our brokenness to reveal the splendor and brilliance of his glory. These become part of the interpretive journey. Keener references this dynamic. For the one called to preach, the task is simple in principle: Know the baggage of the past and understand the prejudice it brings to the interpretive encounter. This awareness safeguards against faulty, prejudicial interpretation.

## Charismatic Phenomena as Normalized Phenomena

I think one of the most important components of self-location is the normalization of the charismatic life. The Spirit-filled interpreter carries an expectation of charismatic experience. The cadence is not specialized, spaced, or driven by surprise. It's anticipated. The presence of Spirit inbreaking is part of the normalized Christian life. Keener says it beautifully, "If God poured out the Spirit on the day of Pentecost, then much of what we envision as 'revival' is simply part of the normal Christian life."[16]

If this is true, then the interpretive act transforms us into agents of co-witness of the Spirit's activity in salvation history. David isn't just writing poetry. The Spirit of God is actually with him as he kills a bear, slays a giant, and leads his sheep through valleys of danger. A reading of Acts 2 is not an empowerment of the early church for a momentary season of church history. It's a permanent, continuing empowerment of God's people through his Spirit for all generations to follow.

14. Keener, *Spirit Hermeneutics*, 40.

15. Keener, *Spirit Hermeneutics*, 123.

16. Keener, *Spirit Hermeneutics*, 53.

## SPIRIT FRAMEWORK FOR KNOWLEDGE

Next, we turn to a somewhat philosophical component of the Spirit-filled approach, which focuses on the concept of truth and on how the Pentecostal preacher accesses, apprehends, and processes it. A Spirit framework for knowledge is nonnegotiable because the interpreter, safely positioned within this framework, understands knowledge as having *God as its sole source*. The philosophical word for this is *epistemology*. It's similar to one's worldview but different in that epistemology asks questions such as what knowledge is, how we know what we know, the different ways of acquiring knowledge (reason, experience, divine, etc.), and the limitations of knowledge. A person's worldview is a broader, comprehensive concept referring to the structure of beliefs, values, and assumptions that filter how they perceive and process reality. One's epistemology, combined with their worldview, then becomes the pre-analytical driving force, functioning behind the scenes, that guides, compels, and orients the will.

Here's an example of the difference between the two. Sarah is a scientist. Sarah's epistemology holds that the scientific method is the best way to gain knowledge. She might use a telescope and astronomical data to study the stars and planets. Based on her epistemology, Sarah has a worldview that believes the universe had a *big bang* point of origin and humanity has evolved through evolution.

On the other hand, Michael is a new-ager whose epistemology holds that knowledge is perceived through the soul's connection with nature and the mother universe. Based on his epistemology, Michael holds a worldview that sees the universe as alive and believes humanity can connect with it through nonreligious spiritual methodologies.

The Spirit-filled preacher, seeking to understand God's revelation in Scripture, holds that all knowledge derives from God, as God is the creator of all things. The pursuit of knowledge, then, is a distinctly spirit-driven endeavor that is dependent upon God's Spirit for true understanding. A Pentecostal epistemology is a vast topic. In our discussion, we will address a few key points. These include experience and Scripture.

The discussion of a Pentecostal epistemology is, of course, pneumatically driven. We now welcome the scholarly voices of Jackie Johns and Cheryl Bridges-Johns, married scholars, who bring this to the forefront in their landmark article articulating a Pentecostal methodology for group Bible study. (See appendix B, "Yielding to the Spirit: A Pentecostal Approach to Group Bible Study," 1992). The Johnses remind us that the

Spirit is the one who *causes* knowledge.[17] The Spirit reveals truth (John 14:26, 1 Cor 2:10–14). The Spirit provides interpretation of knowledge (1 Cor 2:13). The Spirit communicates the words of Jesus (John 14:26, rather than the speaker's words), indicating that knowledge can sometimes transcend mere cerebral content.[18] The Spirit serves as an impetus for knowing the mind of God.[19] And they show us how the Spirit stands at the center of communion with God and experiential knowledge of God.[20] The Johnses' article is a classic. If you haven't done so already, download this article to your library. Ingest it in its entirety.

## Spirit-Dependent Experience

When held to the standards of higher criticism, the interpreter's *experience* is an unconventional starting point that typically leaves scholars somewhat unsettled. The admitted challenge with experience is its given potential to steer the preacher into faulty interpretation. The concern is not unreasonable. And with this dynamic on the table, we welcome the voice of our next scholar, Amos Yong. A name who's probably already in your library, Yong is extensively published and is a leading hermeneutical voice in our tradition. Yong's text *Spirit-Word-Community* (2002) offers a comprehensive theological hermeneutic rooted in pneumatology and the doctrine of the Trinity (see appendix B for more information). Yong dismisses the experiential concern, noting that the Spirit himself is the ontological prerequisite for human experience.[21] What he means is that, if it's true that humanity is made in God's image, as spirit, then the very possibility of the existence of humans is dependent upon the Spirit of God. His argument makes sense.

Adding to this is the Johnses' discussion of experience in the context of *yada*, a Hebrew term denoting knowledge of God. In the Old Testament, intellectual knowledge of God was a by-product of experiential knowledge. Knowing God meant having an experience of God, which made the encounter both personal and divine.[22] They go on to say that

17. Johns and Bridges-Johns, "Yielding to the Spirit," 114.
18. Johns and Bridges-Johns, "Yielding to the Spirit," 115.
19. Johns and Bridges-Johns, "Yielding to the Spirit," 115.
20. Johns and Bridges-Johns, "Yielding to the Spirit," 116.
21. Yong, *Spirit-Word-Community*, 228.
22. Yong, *Spirit-Word-Community*, 112.

experience is the encounter through which the Spirit imparts knowledge of the Divine.[23]

Not one to leave his chair unattended, enter Rickie Moore into our discussion. Moore is a highly respected voice in theological conversations. Moore's article "A Pentecostal Approach to Scripture" (2013; see appendix B), articulates a Pentecostal approach to Scripture that emphasizes encounter, testimony, and the active presence of God in reading the biblical text. Moore explains that, because of the high level of intimacy involved in such experiences, the same word is used to describe the kind of knowledge that occurs within marriage.[24]

Two closing characteristics of the *yada* experience are noteworthy. First, according to the Johnses, experiential knowledge of God is *kerygmatic* in nature, meaning that the experience always demands a response. The response, in the form of obedience, serves as the divine venue for the individual's transformation. Second, experiences with God demand submission to God's will and a precise focus on knowing God (rather than rote conformity).[25]

## Spirit Reading of Scripture

Moving to a different angle of the Spirit experience with Scripture, we now look at what it means to read Scripture through the Spirit. Craig Keener has done great work on reading the Bible pneumatically. He argues that Scripture is integral to knowledge and that the only effective approach to reading Scripture requires a faith-filled posture, centered on Jesus, and dependent on the Holy Spirit. Keener acknowledges that Scripture is the starting place for God's revelation.[26] This is evident in how God is revealed in his dealings with the Israelites in the Old Testament and in the special revelation of Jesus Christ in the New Testament. Keener focuses on self, Jesus, faith, and the Spirit. And the importance of this revelation lies not only in the accessibility of God but also in the apprehension of knowledge itself.

Keener notes that faith is essential to reading Scripture as a means of Christian grounding knowledge. It's not the content of Scripture that

23. Yong, *Spirit-Word-Community*, 114.

24. Moore, "Pentecostal Approach to Scripture," 12.

25. Johns and Bridges-Johns, "Yielding to the Spirit," 112–13.

26. Keener, *Spirit Hermeneutics*, 173.

delivers knowledge (which can be mastered by any individual regardless of their salvific standing). It is the transformational component of the encounter. Keener states, "Scripture read as a *fuller, thoroughly believing reading* is how one reads as a believer,"[27] and "faith is an act of sharing the mind of Christ."[28]

Furthering his case is Keener's assertion that the centrality of Jesus is experienced through a Spirit-reading. All Scripture points to Jesus. This pointing encompasses all the features of the Old Testament, including the stories, the prophets' messages, the establishment of the sacrificial system and the priesthood, the governorship of Israel's kings, the feasts and festivals, and the rituals. And of course, the New Testament points to Jesus, including the Gospels, Epistles, and apocalyptic material (from both Testaments). The Bible's message, in its entirety, presents Christ as the only possible means by which a person can be made right with God.[29]

Keener reminds us that the overall message of Scripture is out of reach for those who engage Scripture without the Spirit.[30] I think his point here is germane. The Holy Spirit is the starting place for interacting with Scripture. Knowledge of revelation is more a spiritual endeavor than an intellectual one because the Spirit bears witness with our spirit and provides the expected layer of conviction.[31] And though the meanings of the words found in Scripture may be comprehensible to any person, aided or unaided by the Spirit, true understanding remains unapprehensive unless the author of Scripture communicates to the reader the essential truth intended in its original composition. So the Spirit who inspired the writer is the same Spirit who illumines the reader. Keener puts it like this,

> Nonbelievers and even anti-believers can contribute valuable insights about the grammar, history and even literary characteristics of Scripture. By definition, however, they do not understand Scripture in the fullest personal sense that Scripture invites, because such understanding includes embracing its truth (by virtue of which one is no longer an unbeliever), not simply explaining the grammar.[32]

27. Keener, *Spirit Hermeneutics*, 173, emphasis mine.
28. Keener, *Spirit Hermeneutics*, 162.
29. Keener, *Spirit Hermeneutics*, 174.
30. Keener, *Spirit Hermeneutics*, 182.
31. Keener, *Spirit Hermeneutics*, 176.
32. Keener, *Spirit Hermeneutics*, 164.

## THE BRIGHT, SHINING LIGHT OF EXPERIENCE

The presence of experience is significant to a Pentecostal approach to biblical interpretation. A person's experiences provide the colors and the contours of how they interact with reality. The dynamic is quite powerful. For example, someone who has experienced divine healing has a unique perspective on Scripture passages that speak to this kind of deliverance. They think about it differently. They speak about it matter-of-factly. They preach about it confidently.

The experiences of the Spirit's movement in the preacher's life deposit life-long presuppositions. They change the way we perceive reality. They bestow a knowledge of God that transcends the bounds of intellectualism and is often unattainable through standard methods of higher criticism. Archer argues that interpreting Scripture outside experience is an illusion and thereby connects experience to a framework of discipleship and Christian formation.[33] The value of this is immeasurable. Moore agrees, and he argues that such experience is indispensable for understanding Scripture.[34]

Keener sees the same thing. He notes the power of experiences with the Spirit as an active member of the interpretive journey. He says our experiences shape how the text (or any communication) affects us.[35] Early in our marriage, my wife, Kendra, fell down some stairs. The biggest impact of the fall was the healthy respect she developed for stairways. Now she approaches stairways with a little extra caution. Her experience of falling shaped her understanding of the inherent dangers within a simple set of stairs. The invitation for the Pentecostal interpreter is to carry a healthy awareness of the experiences that have left behind presuppositions that affect how we engage Scripture.

Experiences are never divorced from the interpretive journey. With this truism, however, comes the indispensable need for warning. Experience needs caution. Inasmuch as experience is crucial for interpretation, it is best held in the proper balance with the primary authority of Scripture leading the way. Keener provides a warning by bringing John Wesley into the conversation, "The interplay between experience and Scripture involves a sort of hermeneutical circle, but, as with Wesley's incorporation of reason, tradition, and experience, Scripture must remain

33. Archer, *Pentecostal Hermeneutic*, 98–99.

34. Moore, "Pentecostal Approach to Scripture," 12.

35. Keener, *Spirit Hermeneutics*, 30.

paramount."[36] Those who stand in opposition to experience are not wrong to point out the subjective dangers it entails. The primacy of Scripture, however, provides the guardrails for legitimizing divine experiences. The axiom is simple: the kinds of experiences that find no scriptural referent have no place in exegesis.

Chris Thomas's voice now joins the conversation. Thomas's article "Women, Pentecostals and the Bible: An Experiment in Pentecostal Hermeneutics" (1994; see appendix B for full bibliographic information) brings this dynamic fully into view. Focusing on the first meeting of the New Testament church leadership, recorded in Acts 15, he shows both the importance of experience and its place within Scripture. As the author, Luke, tells the story, the early church leaders were called to discuss the church's response to the massive influx of gentile believers resulting from Paul and Barnabas's efforts in Antioch and abroad. The question at hand was deciding whether the new gentile converts needed to be circumcised and follow all of Moses' laws and customs.

The story begins with Paul and Barnabas reporting the exciting experiences of how the Spirit was moving among the gentiles. Peter chimed in, reminding of the Spirit's movement at the house of Cornelius (Acts 10). The timeline location of the testimonies is important here. The church's attempt to seek direction began with their experiences of how the Spirit was moving among the gentiles *first*. It was with such experiences in hand that they then moved to searching the Scripture for guidance. Thomas accentuates this positioning, noting how the normal approach involves moving first from the text, then to context. However, on this occasion, the interpreters moved from their context to the biblical text.[37] The result was that the current experiences of the Holy Spirit (gentile conversions) helped them understand the light of Old Testament Scripture. Their interpretation of Scripture and the council's ensuing decisions changed the trajectory of the New Testament church. By the conclusion of the council, the church had shed its shackles as a distinct sect within Judaism and had emerged as the fulfillment of God's missional agency, through which the Spirit would draw all men unto him.

36. Keener, *Spirit Hermeneutics*, 121.

37. J. Thomas, "Women, Pentecostals and the Bible," 50.

## Praxis

The companion of experience within a Pentecostal hermeneutic is praxis. The idea of praxis is basically putting one's ideas into action or taking what one learns in theory and applying it to the real world. It encompasses a dialectical dance between practice and reflection that continually gives rise to new revelatory insights. It is, according to the Johnses, the merging of thought with doing in the sense of interaction with society.[38] Moore says, "We Pentecostals see an inseparable interplay between knowledge and lived experience, where knowing about God and directly experiencing God perpetually inform and depend upon one another."[39]

Here's an example of what praxis looks like in the everyday life of a preacher: Pastor William is passionate about the Bible's teachings on helping the less fortunate. In one of his sermons, he preached on the parable of the good Samaritan, emphasizing the importance of compassion and action. As a follow-up, Pastor William put his passion into action by organizing a volunteer soup kitchen at the church. This provides a tangible way for him and his congregation to put into practice what the Bible teaches about helping those in need.

The experiences at the soup kitchen provide Pastor William with valuable insight into the plight of the disadvantaged that transcends academic knowledge. For Pastor William, the issues of homelessness have become personal. The names and stories have become intertwined with his own. His self-image is now held within this context. The experiences have deposited a layer of insight into how he engages the Word and the world. Compassion and action are more than outreach ideas. They have become interwoven into the fabric of his being. The story of the good Samaritan has changed. Pastor William is no longer a spectator to a narrative account; he has become part of the story.

Within a Pentecostal hermeneutic, praxis is the vehicle through which the aspects of our experiences emerge as objects for theological reflection.[40] Embracing this dynamic requires moving beyond the rigors of the higher criticism, which has historically separated theory and practice. The move allows, according to the Johnses, seeing them as "twin moments of the same activity that are united dialectically."[41]

38. Johns and Bridges-Johns, "Yielding to the Spirit," 120.

39. Moore, "Pentecostal Approach to Scripture," 12.

40. Yong, *Spirit-Word-Community*, 247.

41. Johns and Bridges-Johns, "Yielding to the Spirit," 120.

The relationship between praxis and a Pentecostal approach to biblical interpretation is rooted in the Spirit-fueled creation of meaning. Interpretation within this understanding is that which is produced, revealed, and illumined by the Spirit's leading and creating hand. Archer described the "creation of meaning" as the result of a dialectic transaction between the reader's contribution (their experiences in the Spirit) and living presence of the Word.[42]

With this survey of the Pentecostal landscape of biblical interpretation in hand, we can now turn our attention to the three features of the Pentecostal approach: Spirit, Word, and community.

## REFLECTION QUESTIONS

1. In what ways does locating oneself as an active participant in the biblical narrative challenge detached or purely academic readings of Scripture, and how might this participatory posture shape preaching, discipleship, and pastoral decision-making?
2. How does the Pentecostal emphasis on experience function as both a source of interpretive insight and a potential liability, and what safeguards help ensure that experience remains accountable to Scripture rather than replacing it?
3. What does it mean to describe the Pentecostal hermeneutic as missional rather than primarily academic, and how does this orientation affect the goals, methods, and outcomes of biblical interpretation within ministry contexts?
4. How does the concept of "rebellious restorationism" help explain the Pentecostal movement's historical resistance to Enlightenment-driven interpretive models, while still engaging reason, common sense, and disciplined study of Scripture?
5. How does reading Scripture through a Christ-centered and Spirit-dependent lens shape the interpreter's expectations regarding divine action, transformation, and continuity between biblical events and contemporary Christian life?

42. Archer, *Pentecostal Hermeneutic*, 173.

# 10

# Spirit Dependency

We now shift our attention to the primary focus of a Pentecostal approach to biblical interpretation: the interwoven relationship among Spirit, Word, and community. These three form a kind of trinity, in which each has a unique, stand-alone presence yet functions interrelatedly as a cohesive unit. The interpretive journey unfolds at this intersection. The Word stands as the divine, ancient, sacred object, in which the interpreter seeks both original and modern understanding. The Spirit, as the author of the ancient text's original composition, stands as the interpreter's only hope of divine illumination of the endeavor. The community stands as the interpreter's shaper, guide, and protector of the interpretive act.

As we direct our attention to the first leg of this triad, Spirit dependency, we invite the familiar scholarly voices from the last chapter back to the table. As some of the foremost voices in Pentecostal hermeneutics, they bring to life the hermeneutic framework within which biblical interpretation occurs. Welcome back Ken Archer, Craig S. Keener, Chris Green, Amos Yong, Rickie D. Moore, and John Christopher Thomas.

Spirit dependency is where Pentecostal homiletics ceases to be a theory on a page and starts breathing. Before exegesis turns into an outline and the outline turns into a sermon, the preacher must decide a fundamental question: Will this message ultimately rest on my skill or on the Spirit's presence? Everything in this chapter assumes the latter. Pentecostal preaching is not simply good communication with a few Spirit phenomena sprinkled in. It is a proclamation that leans its full weight on the Spirit who inspired the Word, who now indwells the church, and who confronts both preacher and congregation in real time.

This is why the Spirit-Word-Community triad is more than a clever diagram. Any preacher can do word studies, chart verb tenses, and analyze narrative trajectories. But such methodologies do not guarantee understanding. They can still miss the point by a mile. The Spirit, however, refuses to be reduced to a footnote in our method or a perfunctory prayer at the start of sermon prep. The same Spirit who superintended the Word during our study is now superintending our imagination, our delivery, and our altar calls.

Undergraduate preachers-in-training especially need this reminder. The more tools you gain, such as Greek, commentaries, higher criticism (cautiously engaged), and rhetorical prowess, the easier it is for revelation to slip away in the fog of information. Spirit dependency is not interested in discarding interpretive tools; it simply refuses to idolize them. It insists that every grammatical insight, every historical detail, and every narrative observation be held under the searching gaze of the Spirit who guides, illuminates, bridges horizons, and relentlessly exalts Jesus. In the paragraphs that follow, you're going to discover that Spirit dependency is not an optional Pentecostal *flavoring*; it is the atmosphere in which true interpretation happens, the posture without which even our best sermons risk being well-crafted lectures that heaven never authorized.

Yong approaches the role of the Spirit with great respect. He says the Spirit *breaks into the interpreter*.[1] This carries a modern-day prophetic feel in the same way the Spirit broke into the Old Testament prophets with messages for the Israelites. He says interpretation is more of a spiritual experience and is not simply a cognitive affair.[2] He echoes my longstanding argument in biblical interpretation that the Holy Spirit guided the entire process of canonization from start to finish, including any redactions, marginal insertions, and edits, as well as any other developments along the way.[3]

Archer tells us the primary task of interpretation is asking, "What is the Spirit saying through the Word and community?"[4] God has chosen to work alongside human agency in the inscripturated revelation of himself. The Spirit who inspired the writer is the same Spirit who brings

1. Yong, *Spirit-Word-Community*, 222.
2. Yong, *Spirit-Word-Community*, 238.
3. Yong, *Spirit-Word-Community*, 235.
4. Archer, *Pentecostal Hermeneutic*, 252.

understanding to the reader. Meaning begins with this question. The Spirit's interpretive role is seen as guide, illuminator, bridge builder, and exalter of Jesus Christ.

## GUIDE

As a guide, the Spirit shows us how to maneuver through God's Word with direction and purpose. The Spirit points the way in what would otherwise be a journey of confusion or intellectual emptiness. Yong acknowledges this dynamic, noting that any approach attempting to apprehend the ineffability (incomprehensibility) of the Transcendent is error-laden.[5] Keener points out that the role of Spirit as guide is not a dismissal of the old, textual approach for interpretation, but it simply submits to the Spirit's leading and affirms application, which is sought via the Spirit's continued guidance.[6]

Chris Thomas noted, going back to the Acts 15 narrative of the first church council, the Spirit heavily influenced even the selection of Scriptures used in their attempt to understand the movement of the Spirit among the gentiles.[7] In this way, the Spirit was leading the church to God's revelation that spoke directly to their situation. And this kind of guiding and leading continues to this day.[8] Preachers who walk in the Spirit walk in the confidence of knowing the Spirit is at work, leading and guiding them in their sermon preparation. Thomas wrote that the letter sent by the church leaders included the comment "It seemed good to the Holy Spirit and to us," indicating that the process of interpretation was guided by the same Spirit who inspired the original Scripture.[9]

One aspect of the Spirit's guidance often overlooked is the kerygmatic demands placed upon *the preacher*. The Bible is alive and active and sharper than a double-edged sword (Heb 4:12). God's Word never returns to him void (Isa 55:11). What happens in the process of sermon preparation when the interpreter is taken by God's Word? They succumb to its demand for response. A sanctifying tempering takes place. Keener saw this in Paul's

5. Yong, *Spirit-Word-Community*, 227.
6. Keener, *Spirit Hermeneutics*, 117.
7. J. Thomas, "Women, Pentecostals and the Bible," 50.
8. J. Thomas, "Women, Pentecostals and the Bible," 45.
9. J. Thomas, "Women, Pentecostals and the Bible," 45.

writings, commenting, "Paul expects that the full message of the Spirit can be embraced fully only by those conditioned by the Spirit."[10]

The Spirit's guidance in the interpretive act shapes us. Green tells us to expect this. He says, "'When we read the way the words run,' we do so in expectation that the Spirit will 'shape our imaginations in a manner that forces us to read the world Scripturally rather than vice versa.'"[11] The dynamic is historically anchored in the Pentecost event of Acts 2. Keener writes in the introduction to his text, "my objective here is to help to articulate how the experience of the Spirit that empowered the church on the day of Pentecost can and should dynamically shape our reading of Scripture."[12] He goes on to say, "When we truly hear the Spirit's message in the text, we commit to it. It becomes heart work and not simply homework."[13]

During interpretation, the Spirit acts as an active guide, showing the preacher the way to understanding. The Spirit-filled preacher trusts this guidance. With no concern for second-guessing on the table, the preacher can follow the Spirit's leading into understanding.

## ILLUMINATION AND BEYOND

Our starting point for the Spirit's role in illumination acknowledges how any person has the capacity to understand the intellectual content of Scripture. But the task of biblical interpretation transcends this simple task. The mission is not deciphering the meaning of the words on the pages but hearing the heart of the Author who wrote it. When trying to understand meaning, it's better to go the Author than to go science. The heart of God found in his revealed Word is available only to those who hear it directly from his lips.

For example, if I wanted to understand the lyrics of a song, I could employ one of several interpretive approaches to lyric interpretation, or I could ask the songwriter directly. Although most artists would appreciate unique interpretations, if one really wanted to discover the truth behind their lyrics—what they meant when they wrote them, the inspiration and

10. Keener, *Spirit Hermeneutics*, 161.

11. Green, *Sanctifying Interpretation*, 154, quoting Stanley Hauerwas, *Working with Words: On Learning to Speak Christian* (2011), 108.

12. Keener, *Spirit Hermeneutics*, 8.

13. Keener, *Spirit Hermeneutics*, 258.

circumstances behind the work, and what the lyrics actually mean—one would need to hear it from the artist themself.

The Holy Spirit is the author of Scripture, and we have full access to him. He is the preacher's only hope of Scripture comprehension. The process is called illumination, and it transcends traditional academic understanding. Archer states that the Spirit is the one who brings divine illumination.[14] Keener underscores the active, continuing presence of the Spirit's work in the interpretive process. He says, "Christians in general agree that the Spirit who acted in inspiration remains active in providing understanding."[15]

The invitation for the preacher is to embrace this divine dependence upon the Holy Spirit in the act of interpretation. The challenge is great for those who are gifted with high levels of intellectualism, where the temptation to lean on one's own understanding puts them at great peril of missing the point altogether. The dependency makes sense.

Yong raises two points that help our understanding of this dynamic. First, he discusses the need for Spirit dependency in our wrestling with the tension between a God who both has revealed himself in his Word and yet remains unknowable.[16] One of the warnings I give my theology students is that the process of theological enquiry always involves the presence of humility, because any attempt to posit a factual claim about God must always be accompanied by the understanding that we are finite beings with fractional knowledge, at best, all of which stems from a mind that is still connected with a flesh nature. Secondly, he illustrates how our horizon is ever shifting, so we're moving while trying to apprehend that which is never in clear view to begin with.[17]

But this gets better. The relationship between Spirit and interpreter extends even beyond illuminative comprehension of the text. Chris Thomas says, "Such explicit dependence upon the Spirit in the interpretive process clearly goes far beyond the rather tame claims regarding 'illumination' which many conservatives (and Pentecostals) have often made regarding the Spirit's role in interpretation."[18] He goes on to say, "in this paradigm the Holy Spirit's role in interrelation is not reduced to some vague talk of illumination, but creates the context for interpretation

14. Archer, *Pentecostal Hermeneutic*, 195.

15. Keener, *Spirit Hermeneutics*, 250.

16. Yong, *Spirit-Word-Community*, 240.

17. Yong, *Spirit-Word-Community*, 231.

18. J. Thomas, "Women, Pentecostals and the Bible," 49.

through his actions and, as a result, guides the church in the determination of which texts are most relevant in a particular situation and clarifies how they might best be approached."[19]

## BRIDGE BUILDER

A common theme in hermeneutic discussions is the gap that separates the interpreter and the text, created by differences in culture, language, location, time, contextual insights, customs, and practices. This is often seen, for example, in Paul's frequent imperative for believers to greet one another with a holy kiss (Rom 16:16; 1 Cor 16:20; 2 Cor 13:12; 1 Thess 5:26; or "kiss of love," 1 Pet 5:14). Is this a command for all believers today? Or is there something we're missing in our interpretation? There's obviously more to the story in these commands. With minimal effort, we would discover that the kiss in question was a standard form of greeting during New Testament times. It was social rather than romantic. And we would discern the importance of the word *holy*.

The Holy Spirit is the one who bridges understanding between original and contemporary horizons while keeping both horizons intact. The tension between them is necessary. Keener has an important point here,

> Exegesis in the usual sense focuses on the text's original horizon; reader-oriented approaches focus on the present horizons. The former without the latter is informative but requires the life-giving breath of the Spirit to transform us. Exclusive attention to a present horizon without attention to the original one can lead to overwriting the original, inspired meaning with an unrelated one. If the goal is merely fusing horizons, insufficient objective distance remains to hear the text as something other than mirroring one's thoughts.[20]

A surprising and divine reversal of interpretation occurs in Spirit-led interpretation. The interpreter finds that as they study the Word of God, God is studying them. Keener catches on to this. He notes that the reader must also be engaged by the text, in that both horizons must be maintained, and that connecting the two horizons without obliterating them is often considered the role of hermeneutics.[21]

19. J. Thomas, "Women, Pentecostals and the Bible," 55.

20. Keener, *Spirit Hermeneutics*, 258.

21. Keener, *Spirit Hermeneutics*, 258.

Yong addresses this through his discussion of the interpreter's divine imagination, drawing on moments of sanctified reflection on the text. He says, "Imagination is that which bridges the gap between the self and the other and is therefore dependent upon Spirit intercession."[22] Yong uses the word *slippage* to describe that which occurs in the gap between original authorial intent and what the interpreter takes the current meaning to be.[23] What's at risk here is the preacher's loss of grip for accurate interpretation if the Spirit is not leading the interaction.

## EXALTER OF JESUS CHRIST

Central to the ministry of the Holy Spirit is the exaltation of Jesus Christ. Keener says, "The Spirit came to reveal and exalt the person of Jesus Christ."[24] Jesus makes this point clear. A great story unfolds in John's Gospel in the upper room with Jesus and his disciples on the night he was betrayed. Many people know the foot-washing and communion scenes in this story, which occupy only a small portion of the narrative. One of the more powerful components of this story, spanning chapters 14–17, is Jesus' words as he seeks to comfort his disciples, who are obviously worried about how they will get along with him.

In the opening words of chapter 14, Jesus says, "Let not your hearts be troubled" (ESV). In the following discourse, Jesus explains to his disciples that it was better for him to go because he would send them his Spirit. He was in essence saying it's better for you to have my Spirit *in* you than it is for you to have my physical presence near you. Yong emphasizes the Spirit being the very Spirit of Christ. Though different theological persons, they are one and the same. The Spirit of Christ is he who gives us the mind of Christ.[25]

Jesus' words of comfort to his disciples provide the church with a fundamental foundation for the ministry of the Holy Spirit. In his warnings of the coming persecutions, Jesus said of the Spirit, "But when the Helper comes, whom I will send to you from the Father, the Spirit of truth, who proceeds from the Father, he will bear witness about me" (John 15:26 ESV). One of the key aspects of the ministry of the Holy Spirit is how he witnesses about Jesus. The Spirit exalts the name of Jesus.

22. Yong, *Spirit-Word-Community*, 224.

23. Yong, *Spirit-Word-Community*, 234.

24. Keener, *Spirit Hermeneutics*, 237.

25. Yong, *Spirit-Word-Community*, 257.

This is evident in Spirit-anointed preaching, where the name of Christ is repeatedly lifted up.

## CONCLUSION

Bringing all this together, Spirit dependency means that the preacher never stands alone with a Bible and a blank page; the preacher stands within a living conversation among Spirit, Word, and community. In this chapter, the Spirit has emerged as guide, leading us into and through the text; as illuminator, opening not just the meaning of words but the heart of God behind them; as bridge builder, holding together both the ancient and contemporary horizons without collapsing either; and as relentless exalter of Jesus, ensuring that all faithful interpretation bends toward the glory of Christ. When these roles are taken seriously, sermon preparation becomes less about research and more about the preacher being read, searched, and reshaped by the very Word we hope to proclaim.

For the Spirit-filled preacher, this is both wonderfully freeing and intensely sobering. It is freeing because the pressure to be brilliant gives way to the call to be surrendered. The Spirit, not the preacher, shoulders the interpretive weight. It is sobering because Spirit dependency is not a mood or a last-minute prayer; it is a disciplined, ongoing posture that brings exegesis, community discernment, and personal holiness under the Spirit's steady hand. Ultimately, a Spirit-dependent homiletic is not caged in cold rationalism without fire, nor is it enthusiasm without grounding. It insists that the same Spirit who inspired the text now guides the church in understanding and proclaiming it, so that sermons do not merely inform minds but awaken a people to the living Christ.

## REFLECTION QUESTIONS

1. How does viewing the Spirit, Word, and community as an interdependent triad reshape your understanding of what faithful biblical interpretation looks like in both personal study and public proclamation?
2. Describe a time when your encounter with Scripture became more than academic insight and felt like divine illumination. What does this experience reveal about the Spirit's active role in understanding God's Word?

3. Reflect on the idea that the Spirit not only helps us read the text but also uses Scripture to "read" us. What implications does this have for the preacher's spiritual formation and integrity?
4. Considering the Spirit's role as guide, how might intentional practices of prayer, discernment, and community accountability keep your interpretive process aligned with divine direction?
5. Why is it vital for preachers to remember that the Spirit's ultimate goal in interpretation is the exaltation of Jesus Christ, and how can this focus recalibrate the motives behind preaching?

# 11

# Word on Mission

ISN'T IT GREAT KNOWING that the Word is active, penetrating, and initiating? The Bible is not a passive object in the hands of a clever communicator; it is the living, speaking, Spirit-breathed Word that goes out from God and never returns to him empty. It creates, confronts, comforts, and commissions. In other words, Scripture does not merely *inform* the church's mission; the Word carries its own mission and graciously sweeps the preacher and the congregation up into it.

The intent of this chapter is to follow the trajectory of the mission of God's lively Word. The same Bible that stands as the collection of our holy writings also stands in the pulpit as an active agent, forming Christ in us, interpreting us, and sending us outward into God's world. The task is not to tame the text into three neat points but to approach it with reverence, faith, and just enough humility to admit that the Bible is far better at reading us than we are at reading it. Along the way, we get to enjoy the company of some trusted guides. So, pull your chair back up to the table as Ken Archer, Craig S. Keener, Chris Green, Jackie David Johns and Cheryl Bridges-Johns (the Johnses), Amos Yong, Rickie D. Moore, and John Christopher Thomas rejoin the conversation, helping us see how this Word, in the hands of the Spirit and within the life of the community, is always on the move, always on mission, and always a step ahead of the preacher who dares to proclaim it.

Coming to the second leg of the intersection between Spirit, Word, and community stands the holy Word of God. Our approach to the Scriptures must always be taken with the greatest of sacred appreciation for the encounter.[1] The illuminative work of the Spirit yields "new understandings," according to Archer, but will never be in violation of Scripture.[2]

Scripture is spoken, living, and written. The Bible is God's speech that reveals his identity and provides a clear pathway for humanity to be reconciled to him. As such, the Bible serves as the "one revelation that virtually all Christians agree on as the 'canon,' or measuring stick, for all other claims to revelation," says Keener.[3] Our discussion of Scripture examines its definition, our orthodox posture of engagement, and its function.

## DEFINING SCRIPTURE

Scripture is the eternal Word of God. It carries the highest authority. The Johnses highlight how Scripture is not simply words *about* God, nor is it words *from* God (implying distance), but that Scripture is the Word of God and that God is always present with his word.[4] The Bible is alive and active; it never returns to God void (indicating the mission of the Word). The Johnses say rather poignantly, "It is an objective, historical reality which cannot properly be understood outside of the bounds of reason. Yet it is a personal, subjective Word carried by the Holy Spirit. Out of the text flows the infinite presence of God, which addresses the finite limitations of humanity."[5]

Chris Thomas shares this view. He notes that within a Pentecostal hermeneutic, Scripture does not function in a static fashion but in a more dynamic manner that invites the preacher to approach the text in a manner that transcends mere cognition.[6] Yong concurs, "Sometimes language does not suffice for adequate expression of that which has been encountered."[7]

Pentecostals hold a high view of Scripture. We embrace its inerrancy and infallibility. The word *inerrant* means that the Bible is free from error. There are no contradictions, inconsistencies, falsities, mistakes, or

1. Johns and Bridges-Johns, "Yielding to the Spirit," 118.
2. Archer, *Pentecostal Hermeneutic*, 251.
3. Keener, *Spirit Hermeneutics*, 111.
4. Johns and Bridges-Johns, "Yielding to the Spirit," 118.
5. Johns and Bridges-Johns, "Yielding to the Spirit," 130.
6. J. Thomas, "Women, Pentecostals and the Bible," 55.
7. Yong, *Spirit-Word-Community*, 252.

lies contained within it. The term *infallible* elevates this concept, asserting that the Word cannot be wrong. This means that if someone were to allege an inconsistency, contradiction, or error was found in the Bible, *they* would be wrong, not the Bible.

The Bible is verbally inspired. This concept holds that the exact words of the Bible were inspired by the Spirit, not merely its overall message. Preachers who believe in verbal inspiration take the original wording seriously and rely heavily on original-language dictionaries (Hebrew, Greek, and Aramaic) during sermon preparation.

Scripture is christological, meaning that the whole of Scripture is a testimony to Jesus. Everything in the Old Testament points to Christ: the giving of the law, the sacrificial system, the priestly system, the messages of the prophets, the narratives, and the apocalyptic content all point to Jesus. And of course, the entire content of the New Testament points to Jesus. The revelation of Scripture is God's testimony of who he is and the plan of salvation found only in Jesus Christ for the reconciliation of humanity to a right relationship with God.

The Bible is spiritually discerned. The apostle Paul wrote about this in his first letter to the Corinthians. His comments were a direct confrontation to the claimed wisdom of the Greeks. It was a harsh affront to the world's curators of wisdom. Paul emphasized how the natural person cannot understand the truths of the Bible because they are spiritually discerned (1 Cor 2:10–16).

The Word of God is creative. It was by the very words of God that all things were brought into creation. It is by the same words found in the Bible that one finds the power of God to create out of nothing everything needed for life. The proclaimed Word of God, in the context of a Spirit-filled worship, has the power to change lives. It has the power to draw people into repentance. It has the ability to create the context through which truth can penetrate even the hardest of hearts. It is always accompanied by the very presence of God.

The Bible is the truth. For Christians, this claim of Scripture is bedrock in the economy of salvation. The Bible sets the foundation for reality. God, as the author of all creation, has revealed himself through Scripture. Since all of creation owes its existence to its creator, the words of the creator hold as the starting place for all truth. When the preacher is asked, "What's your opinion on abortion?" he responds with, "The Bible says every life is a miracle from the giver of life, and therefore God is the only one who can take it" (see Ps 139:13–16; Job 33:4; Gen 30:22).

## ENGAGING SCRIPTURE

If Scripture is all we claim it to be, then the next question is how one ought to approach Scripture. Is there a certain preferable mindset or posture? More specifically, in light of our discussion up to this point, what is a well-defined, faithful, Pentecostal point of view to interacting with Scripture? Several factors are at play here.

### Reverence

This first is reverence. And though this is not unique to a specifically Pentecostal point of view, it is nonetheless a nonnegotiable in our structure. Since the original composition of Scripture was under divine verbal inspiration of the Holy Spirit, the interpreter is invited to acknowledge the divine authority of the Word and to place themselves in subjection to its teachings. When the preacher aligns themselves with this maxim, it empowers them to approach the Word with the requisite totality of respect.

With this respect comes a willful suspension of disbelief and doubt. Keener discusses this concept in detail. Suspending disbelief is not blind allegiance, similar to stubbornly holding on to one's belief in Santa Claus or the Tooth Fairy. Rather, one suspends disbelief and doubt in the context of embracing the holy writings of a worldview to which we have committed ourselves.[8] The practical outworking of this is demonstrated by the preacher's commitment to truthfully acknowledge a problematic passage in Scripture while concurrently acknowledging Scripture's authority and reliability. The mindset delivers a suspension of disbelief that invites the preacher to press in for deeper understanding. The tension is divine in nature, and its resolution is delivered by the Spirit.

Green affirms that the Old Testament and New Testament are one word, inspired by the Holy Spirit, and in need of the Spirit's illumination for proper interpretation.[9] The teachings of the Bible apply to all situations in life. The preacher knows this. The Spirit who authored Scripture shows the preacher its usefulness to all of life's circumstances. The Johnses remind us how the "Paraclete will bring the words of Jesus to bear in a meaningful way on all the situations of life."[10]

8. Keener, *Spirit Hermeneutics*, 200–202.

9. Green, *Sanctifying Interpretation*, 117–18.

10. Johns and Bridges-Johns, "Yielding to the Spirit," 129.

Reverence means also that the exegete approaches the Word in context and in truth. Keener chimes in here, emphasizing that a contextual reading of Scripture must align with how God provided it[11] and also honoring the shape in which it was given.[12] Ancient contextual meaning matters, according to Keener, because it serves as the "anchor and arbiter for claims to interpret the text today."[13] Scripture must be read in its immediate context that allows the interpreter to embrace the text with the same set of givens its original audience would have embraced. What would have been the original audience's assumptions? What were the parts that required no explanation? Reading the Bible in context is a necessary countermeasure to reader-centered approaches to interpretation that risk denying authorial intent and original audience phenomena. The task of biblical interpretation brings both horizons fully into view.

## Reading the Bible as Truth

Engaging the Bible as truth may seem elementary, but the point warrants significant attention. Reading Scripture as truth transcends intellectual acquiescence. Reading the Word as truth demands a faithful response. I like where Keener took this: "Indeed, Scripture invites us to arrange our thoughts around and devote our entire life in light of its message,"[14] and "affirming God's Word as truth means submitting our lives to it more than it means the sorts of issues that Christian scholars sometimes divide over."[15]

Green underscores this dynamic. In his discussion of a *sanctified reading* of Scripture, Green proposes a posture of engaging the Bible that begins with a saturation-driven approach. The mission here is communal and individual immersion into the Word. This dynamic provokes the "imaginative and affective sensitivities needed to read Scripture sanctifyingly."[16] Secondly, Green details a *rereading* of Scripture that acknowledges the rich voices of tradition that have gone before us as well as the significance of how Scripture is both objective and subjective at

11. Keener, *Spirit Hermeneutics*, 112.
12. Keener, *Spirit Hermeneutics*, 117.
13. Keener, *Spirit Hermeneutics*, 119.
14. Keener, *Spirit Hermeneutics*, 187.
15. Keener, *Spirit Hermeneutics*, 189.
16. Green, *Sanctifying Interpretation*, 142.

the same time, via the Spirit.[17] What he means by this is that reading Scripture sanctifyingly is a faith-filled reading that allows us to embrace both the objectifiable witness of the original Spirit's intent and composition, while at the same time hearing the Spirit's voice in how Scripture is being applied to circumstances and experiences of today. The emphasis of both horizons is held in tension as the voice of the Spirit is heard only through faith in the Bible as truth.

## Reading in the Spirit

Building off of my comments from chapter 9's discussion of Spirit dependency and Spirit reading of Scripture, we now add the dimension of reading Scripture in the Spirit. This has two distinctives that must be part of our understanding. First, according to Keener, is reading Scripture from the vantage point of Pentecost.[18] The place where Keener takes us here is important. The outpouring of the Spirit in the Acts 2 narrative forever changed the contours and the landscape of what it means to belong to God. In the Old Testament, the Spirit was poured out episodically on individuals, in times when supernatural assistance was needed to fulfill a God-ordained mission. The stories of Othniel (Judg 3), Gideon (Judg 6–8), Samson (Judg 14–15), King Saul (1 Sam 10), and King David (1 Sam 16) highlight this phenomenon.

But God declared through his prophet Amos that a day would come when he would no longer pour out his Spirit on a particular individual to accomplish a specific task, but would pour out his Spirit on all his people (Joel 2) to accomplish the eschatological task of all people belonging to God. This would be a day when the Spirit would be poured out not just on the judges and prophets but on sons and daughters, old men and young men, and even on the male and female servants. God's people observed the fulfillment of this prophecy on the day of Pentecost, as described in Acts 2.

Second, Keener says a Spirit-baptized reading of Scripture involves reading the Word missionally. It means reading from a posture of humility, with complete dependence on God's Spirit. It means reading the Bible with an anticipation of realized eschatology and from a continuationist

17. Green, *Sanctifying Interpretation*, 147–48.

18. Keener, *Spirit Hermeneutics*, 39.

perspective. When read in the Spirit, one's view of Scripture is undergirded with a *last days* point of view.[19]

Reading in the Spirit also involves a faithful reading of Scripture. Green handles this well. He says we have to let the Spirit rescue us from distorted images of God that appear from a nonfaithful reading.[20] Here, Green acknowledges the dangerous reality of reading Scripture for what one wants to see (proof-texting) rather than allowing the Spirit to illuminate what was actually said.

Reading Scripture in the Spirit is a supremely christological privilege. If I were pressed to answer the question "What is the primary ministry of the Holy Spirit?" I would point to the unfettered, unashamed, unabashed mission of the Holy Spirit to exalt the name and person of Jesus Christ. This claim makes sense both scripturally (see John 15:26; John 16:13–14; 1 Cor 12:3; and Acts 2:32–33, for example, not to discount all the other components of the Spirit's "job description") and logically. What other preeminent purpose could the Spirit fulfill than to point all of a broken and depraved humanity toward the only one who can make us right with God? Keener says, "Ultimately, for a Christian, christological reading and personal reading cannot be incompatible."[21] When read in the Spirit, all of Scripture points to Jesus. Archer also emphasizes this, "Scripture must be read as a witness to the gospel of Jesus Christ."[22] And Green says we must read "Scripture in light of the good news of Christ's victory over sin and death and the promise of New Creation."[23]

Arguably, one of the strongest features of a Spirit reading of Scripture is reading the Word with expectation. As continuationists, Pentecostals believe the Spirit phenomena that occurred during the first-century church never ceased with the death of the last apostle (John, AD 95). The upshot of this Pentecostal approach to reading the Bible in the Spirit is the expectation that the Spirit moves today in the same way he has moved all throughout the witness of Scripture. Keener brings this sharply into view. He notes, "The genius of the traditional Pentecostal hermeneutic was to live in the biblical worldview, expecting God to act."[24] Keener invites us to engage the Word with as much knowledge as possible and to enter the

19. Keener, *Spirit Hermeneutics*, 39.

20. Green, *Sanctifying Interpretation*, 128.

21. Keener, *Spirit Hermeneutics*, 260.

22. Archer, *Pentecostal Hermeneutic*, 247.

23. Green, *Sanctifying Interpretation*, 130.

24. Keener, *Spirit Hermeneutics*, 199.

narrative of the scriptural world with the suspension of disbelief, cultural alienation, and other forms of distancing, and to expect to meet the living God therein.[25]

The story of the Bible becomes our story today. The Johnses, in their Pentecostal approach to small group Bible study, highlight this reality. Making the story of the Bible our story immerses the reader into the *mindset* of Scripture. They say that a Spirit reading of the Word "Presupposes that the reader is in living contact with the same realities about which the author in the Sacred Text is speaking."[26] The takeaway is that a Spirit hermeneutic regards the stories and experiences of the church as indispensable to interpretation.

Continuing, Yong helps us understand how Scripture mediates the Word of God rather than simply circumscribing it.[27] The Word, as that which is alive and active and does not return to God void, is an ongoing story of God's redemptive acts in history. As active participants, we see ourselves as part of that story. God is still moving. The Spirit is still at work. Yong also draws in an extraordinary and exclusively Pentecostal understanding of the Bible. He notes how the Bible is the "inscripturated Word" of God and how it stands only fractionally against the totality of Word as a concept.[28] As a continuationist movement, Pentecostals embrace the continued presence of God's Word in the form of words of knowledge, words of wisdom, and words of prophecy. The Spirit of God still speaks. His Word is alive and present. And with the authority of the Bible established, these continued words will never stand in violation of his inscripturated Word.

## Respect for Higher Criticisms

In closing out this section, it is worth our attention to incline our ear to Keener's appeal for an appropriate respect for higher criticism. I agree with the emphasis. The respect is fitting, especially when the methods are understood for what they are and are valued to the extent to which they deliver insights about Scripture that would otherwise not be attainable. Keener writes, "Determining what the biblical writers were

25. Keener, *Spirit Hermeneutics*, 200.

26. Johns and Bridges-Johns, "Yielding to the Spirit," 128.

27. Yong, *Spirit-Word-Community*, 262. That is, explaining it.

28. Yong, *Spirit-Word-Community*, 260.

communicating in their original historical setting may not seem flashy like some revival phenomena, but it is foundational to a sound Pentecostal hermeneutic."[29] Keener articulates the balance well. He goes on to say that a Spirit reading of Scripture may be more than simply traditional exegesis, but it should also not be less than traditional exegesis.[30]

## FUNCTION OF SCRIPTURE

With a sound, Pentecostal definition of Scripture in one hand, and a robust profile of how Pentecostals handle Scripture in the other, we can now turn our attention to a Pentecostal understanding of the purpose and function of Scripture. To that end, we will be focusing on the formational and transformational power of Scripture, its interpretive prowess, and missional preparation.

### Scripture as Formational and Transformational

Green gives us much to work with regarding Scripture's formative and transformative presence within the Christian community. He highlights, for example, a prophetic element of Scripture that overthrows false conceptions of God. In the same way that the Old Testament prophets appeared on the scene to interrupt and disrupt the Jews in their pursuit of sinful activity, so Scripture comes in to interrupt us in the same way. As idolatrous and false conceptions about God are exposed, the light of truth takes root to form within us right conceptions about God.[31]

I appreciate Green's portrayal of Scripture as contradicting us to fully align us with it.[32] This provides a new layer to the Pentecostal interpretation of the Word as being alive and active, and sharper than a double-edged sword (Heb 4:12). The Bible shapes us to better reflect the image and likeness of Christ. This is particularly seen in the shaping of the sharing of the fellowship of the sufferings of Christ. Green writes, "Scripture forms Christ's sufferings within us and thereby forms virtues of humility, patience, etc."[33]

29. Keener, *Spirit Hermeneutics*, 114.
30. Keener, *Spirit Hermeneutics*, 116.
31. Green, *Sanctifying Interpretation*, 129.
32. Green, *Sanctifying Interpretation*, 134.
33. Green, *Sanctifying Interpretation*, 126–27.

## Scripture as Interpreter

I had the privilege of studying under Dr. Hollis Gause (PhD, Emory University) while completing my master's degree. Gause is considered one of the founding fathers of the Pentecostal scholastic movement. As a forerunner, Gause helped blaze a trail of scholarship examining the distinctive features of the Pentecostal movement, bringing it into mainstream academic dialogue. I'll never forget the lecture when he described that when a person studies the Bible, they're not studying God; God is studying them.

Scripture interprets us. The preacher might think they're studying God, but a Pentecostal approach to sitting with Scripture embraces the notion that we are the ones being handled and not the other way around. The Johnses said it like this, "Our approach is to bring our life to the text so that the Word of God might interpret us. The key element in understanding the text is the power of the Holy Spirit to work in spite of and even through our subjective nature."[34] Yong takes this to its logical conclusion by emphasizing the indispensability of divine self-reflection in the interpretive process.[35]

If you're reading this book as a preacher, you've probably experienced this phenomenon many times. In preparation for a sermon, teaching, devotion, etc., or even during a simple devotion, you've encountered the in-breaking of the Spirit as you sat with the Word. It always catches me when I least expect it and forces me into a posture of contemplative, divine self-examination. These are moments of scriptural formation, when the same Spirit who inspired the Word now brings the kind of transformative illumination that only the Spirit can bring.

Scripture carries a preparatory function for mission. Green draws our attention to this feature, arguing for a deeper understanding that embodies the Word in a manner that transcends revelation.[36] Within this paradigm, Scripture is the manual through which a believer is prepared for the universal mission of the church. It contains foundational teachings, examples and models, strategies and principles, and encouragement and inspiration. It provides the necessary knowledge, skills, and motivation for believers to realize the church's mission.

34. Johns and Bridges-Johns, "Yielding to the Spirit," 128.

35. Yong, *Spirit-Word-Community*, 245.

36. Green, *Sanctifying Interpretation*, 110.

This is further underscored by the Scripture's role as a standard-setter for the church. Thomas says, "The experiences of the church must be measured against the biblical text and, in that light, practices or views for which there is no biblical support would be deemed illegitimate."[37] In this regard, Scripture serves as the barometer for orthodox experience. This is an invaluable component of a Pentecostal understanding of Scripture's function. The Bible serves as the safeguard against unorthodox subjectivism. The Bible is the source of truth, a benchmark for beliefs, a guide for practices, and the church's moral compass.

## Genres

Scripture plays an important role in hermeneutical constructions across the various genres in which it has been composed. Genre is a category used to classify creative works based on shared characteristics. These characteristics can include style, form, and content. Genres help us organize and make connections between works that share similarities and carry expectations about what will be experienced in our encounter.

Each genre has its own set of interpretive rules. For example, it's easy to see how one would handle the reading of the Gospels differently than how they would handle their reading of apocalyptic material. And though a full and appropriate presentation of these genres can be found in biblical interpretation textbooks, a brief identification of biblical genres includes the following categories:

Law—Instructions and precepts of God given to us through Moses that serve as the primary foundation for the Pentateuch (Genesis, Exodus, Leviticus, Numbers, and Deuteronomy).

Narrative—Recounts God's actions throughout history, including accounts of creation, the Israelites' journey to the promised land, and the lives of prophets and kings through story.

Wisdom Literature: Collections of wise sayings and theological reflection, including Proverbs, Job, and Ecclesiastes.

Poetry—Psalms, Song of Solomon, Lamentations, and much of the content of the prophets, uses figurative language and evocative imagery to express a wide range of emotions and ideas.

37. J. Thomas, "Women, Pentecostals and the Bible," 55.

Prophecy—Messages from God delivered through prophets, which include warnings of judgment or calling for repentance, and offering hope for the future.

Gospel—The four Gospels (Matthew, Mark, Luke, and John) recount the life, ministry, death, and resurrection of Jesus Christ.

Epistle—A letter written by an apostle or early church leader to a church or individual, addressing matters of doctrine, ethics, and Christian practice.

Apocalyptic: Revelation, Daniel, Ezekiel, and portions of other books that employ symbolic language and imagery to depict the end times and God's ultimate triumph over evil.

## FINAL WORD ON THE WORD

The final word on the Word is that the Word never stops speaking. By the time the preacher opens the Bible on Sunday morning, the Spirit has already been at work stirring hearts, raising questions, and preparing the congregation. The sermon is never the starting point of the Word's mission. It's simply one more stop along its Spirit-driven journey. The preacher is not tasked to set the Word in motion; we are merely blessed to be caught up in its divine agenda.

Scripture is less a tool in the preacher's hand and more an updraft in which the preacher is caught up. The Spirit-filled preacher stands before this Word with humility and gratitude. With holy awe, we wonder that the same Word that spoke galaxies into existence is now speaking to us and through us. That's enough to make even the most seasoned preacher tremble knowing that God still chooses to speak through ordinary clay.

This chapter has drawn us back to the mystery that the Bible is not a dusty museum relic. It doesn't need our polish or rhetorical cleverness to do its work. The Word itself is living, breathing, and relentlessly missional. It forms Christ in us. It calls us into community. It sends us into the world. In this light, preaching becomes less about showing off what we've discovered and more about joining what God is already doing. The Pentecostal preacher, especially, stands in the grand tradition of those who expect that the same Spirit who inspired Scripture is still speaking today. We read with reverence, we listen with expectation, and then, with trembling joy, we proclaim with boldness. The Spirit still breathes through the Word to bring life to dry bones and light to weary hearts.

The Word on mission reminds us that God's story didn't end with Revelation's final "Amen." The same Spirit who hovered over the waters in Genesis still hovers over pulpits, prayer groups, and humble kitchen tables where Scripture is opened. The story continues, and we get to take part in it. That's the thrilling, humbling, and sometimes humorous truth of preaching—the very act is both an act of faith and an act of surrender. So let the preacher take courage. The Word is sharper than our clever outlines, deeper than our illustrations, and stronger than our limitations. It leaps off the pulpit not to display our eloquence but to accomplish God's purpose.

## REFLECTION QUESTIONS

1. How does the concept of Scripture as "active agent" rather than passive object challenge your current approach to sermon preparation? In what practical ways might you need to shift from mastering the text to being mastered by it?
2. Reflect on a time when you experienced Scripture interpreting you rather than you interpreting Scripture. What did that encounter reveal about your understanding of God, yourself, or your calling as a preacher?
3. What does it mean practically to "suspend disbelief" when encountering difficult or problematic passages in Scripture? How is this different from ignoring intellectual honesty, and how might this posture deepen rather than diminish rigorous biblical interpretation?
4. Evaluate your own reading practices: Do you approach Scripture primarily from a pre-Pentecost or post-Pentecost perspective? How might reading from the vantage point of Acts 2 transform your interpretation of Old Testament narratives or New Testament imperatives?
5. Consider the relationship between Scripture's inscripturated Word and the Spirit's continued speaking through words of knowledge, wisdom, and prophecy. How do you discern authentic Spirit speech while maintaining Scripture's ultimate authority in your preaching ministry?

# 12

# Communal Conditioning

Our segue into the final leg of the Spirit-Word-Community triad begins with the acknowledgment that preachers do not arrive at the text alone. Every preacher is accompanied by the communities in which they have been raised, to which they have dedicated seasons of their lives, and from which they are currently immersed. Pentecostal interpretation is never simply one person with an open Bible and a cup of coffee. It is the living overflow of a Spirit-formed people, with their stories, testimonies, songs, and scars all quietly standing in the room while the preacher studies. In that sense, this chapter is not introducing community to interpretation so much as naming what has always been true, but that the Spirit-filled people of God, as a worshiping community, shape how we hear the Word of God.

Throughout these chapters, several conversation partners have helped us see this more clearly, and it is worth bringing them back to our discussion right at the outset. Keener starts us off by reminding us that understanding Scripture blossoms within a believing community. This pushes against any notion that "me and my Bible" is sufficient for faithful exegesis. Thomas agrees, refusing to have the church be relegated to a passive audience, describing it instead as a crucible in which the Spirit actively forges testimony, examines interpretations, and refines what the community will ultimately embrace as faithful. Archer then steps in to give Pentecostals a kind of family photo, tracing how our community identity, narrative tradition, and charismatic experiences have shaped our reading of Scripture from the very beginning.

These are not merely abstract scholarly opinions; they are descriptive of what Pentecostal/Charismatic preachers actually live. Anyone who has tried to prepare a sermon in a Spirit-filled church knows this instinctively. The text sounds different when you read it with the Spirit's moving from last Sunday still echoing in your memory. Community is not background noise. It is the environment in which interpretation flourishes. To preach as a Pentecostal is to embrace the Spirit-filled community in which you exist and from which you have come.

Bringing these scholarly voices back into focus helps frame the chapter's journey. As the chapter unfolds, we will explore the identity of the Pentecostal community, the identity of the reader shaped by that community, the ways our shared narrative tradition configures what seems "rational," and how the community safeguards interpretation from both wild subjectivism and icy objectivism. In other words, you are about to discover that your preaching is more communal than you may have realized, and that this is very good news for anyone who wants to hear the Spirit's voice in the Spirit's Word.

## IDENTITY OF THE COMMUNITY

Biblical interpretation is an act that is dependent upon one's community. While individual study is crucial, Keener argues that true understanding blossoms within a believing community.[1] According to Thomas, this community is not merely a passive audience. Rather, it serves as the crucible in which the Holy Spirit acts, fostering "testimony" of God's work. Here, interpretations are offered, assessed, and ultimately accepted or rejected, leading to a richer and more nuanced understanding of the divine message.[2] This chapter explores community as the context for interpretation, the identity of the Pentecostal community, the identity of the reader, and how the community safeguards against unorthodox, individualized interpretation.

So who is this Pentecostal community? How are we defined as a group? What are the markers that make us unique within the body of Christ? Ken Archer has provided some of the best research into answering this question. Through his examination of the movement's early

1. Keener, *Spirit Hermeneutics*, 277.

2. J. Thomas, "Women, Pentecostals and the Bible," 55.

writings and historical accounts from both friends and foes, he has identified a clear definition of who we are as a community.

As a people of the Spirit, the community provides the basic structure of the Pentecostal narrative, says Archer.[3] The structure, in turn, provides the validity of the interpretation. He says, "The Pentecostal interpretation of Scripture was validated by Scripture and by the presence of the miraculous that accompanied the movement."[4] All of this was done, especially biblical interpretation, with the book of Acts as a motif and a model fully in view.[5]

## The Latter Rain Motif

Ken Archer provides the best historical tracing of the Pentecostal movement's self-understanding as the realization of the latter rain motif referenced in Scripture. The early leaders of the Pentecostal movement interpreted the outpouring of the Holy Spirit as a fulfillment of the latter rain motif found in the Old Testament. The people of the Spirit were the people of fulfillment of this promise.[6] The motif emphasizes that the initial outpouring of the Holy Spirit in Acts 2 was the "showers of spring" and the outpouring of the modern Pentecostal movement was the "rains of autumn." The early Pentecostal leaders associated the outpouring as that which would precede the second coming of Christ (which then provided the backdrop to the eschatological fervency inherent within the community).[7]

The time of drought between the Acts 2 outpouring and the Pentecostal outpouring was caused by the great apostasy of the Roman Catholic Church during the Middle Ages. The motif provided a coherent explanation for the restoration and resurgence of the charismatic gifts and served to bring the true church to perfection and unity while empowering individual Christians with supernatural power to witness.[8]

3. Archer, *Pentecostal Hermeneutic*, 136.
4. Archer, *Pentecostal Hermeneutic*, 154.
5. Archer, *Pentecostal Hermeneutic*, 156.
6. Archer, *Pentecostal Hermeneutic*, 137.
7. Archer, *Pentecostal Hermeneutic*, 138.
8. Archer, *Pentecostal Hermeneutic*, 138, 139, 148.

## Primitivistic Impulse

Archer spotlights a *primitive impulse* within the Pentecostal community. His terminology is helpful here. The Acts 2 empowerment of the Spirit was understood as the faith once (and always) delivered to the saints. The primitive church was meant by God to be the permanent and perpetual church, with no cessation of the Spirit's gifts or activities. It was the apostasy of the church during the Patristic period, and afterward, that caused the lessening of miracles and charismatic phenomena.[9]

## Unique Characteristics of the Pentecostal Community

Archer highlights several key distinctives of the Pentecostal community's authentic identity. He notes how Pentecostals are people of the margins (that we inherited from the black spirituality and Catholic spirituality). Of course, Spirit baptism was unique to the Pentecostal movement. Pentecostals embrace the event as a distinct component of our economy of salvation. We are a people of supernatural manifestations. These charismatic phenomena are a regular part of the worship experience and of community interactions.

The Pentecostal community is a distinctly eschatological community. With the understanding of the latter rain motif firmly in hand, we connect the outpouring of the Spirit as that which the Old Testament foretells, that which accompanies and precedes the imminent second coming of Christ, and as the empowerment of the church for bold witness.

The apostle Paul ministered from this reality, "I will not venture to speak of anything except what Christ has accomplished through me in leading the Gentiles to obey God by what I have said and done—by the power of signs and wonders, through the power of the Spirit of God. So from Jerusalem all the way around to Illyricum, I have fully proclaimed the gospel of Christ" (Rom 15:18–19 NIV). The phrase *full gospel* refers to preaching the gospel through the signs and wonders of the Spirit. Paul had academic, theological, and intellectual credentials that far exceeded those of many of his day. The point he was making was that his preaching did not rely on any of these credentials and was dependent solely on the presence of the Holy Spirit.

9. Archer, *Pentecostal Hermeneutic*, 151–53.

The Pentecostal community is revivalistic in that we are called "to re-live the Apostolic experiences that are related in the New Testament."[10] The concept of revival here is embraced as an awakening to what was meant to be characteristic of the church all along: the faith once delivered to the saints was a faith filled with the permanent and perpetual charisms of the Spirit. Along these lines, Archer discusses how the Pentecostal community is also restorationist.[11] More than a nuance, the notion of restorationism is that the Pentecostal community understands itself as the church being restored to the pure days of the church before she was stained by the Catholic apostasies and Enlightenment-driven hyper-intellectualism.

The Pentecostal community is characterized by the infusion of charismatic activity.[12] The functioning of the gifts is expected. The focus is not on the gifts themselves, but on the Spirit who gives them and is embraced as their source and empowerment. Understood in this way, the Pentecostal community speaks of the gifts not so much in terms of possession but as indwelling. One does not *have* a certain gift; they have the Spirit, who is the source of all gifts.

What's more, the Christian community's immersion in the fullness of the Spirit identifies it as the normative Christian life. Scripturally anchored supernaturalism is part of the fabric of what it means to belong to Christ. His Spirit within us characterizes the community as a continuation of the church in Acts. Archer understands the identity of the Pentecostal community as the foundation for understanding the true meaning of Scripture, both in ancient and present terms. The Pentecostal community, as the closest representation of Christ this side of eternity, and infused with the very Spirit of Christ, becomes the context of interpreting the Spirit's voice within the Spirit's Word.[13]

## CONTEXT FOR INTERPRETATION

One of the bedrock principles for biblical interpretation is the discovery of context. Every passage in the Bible was given within a certain context, and an accurate interpretation of that passage is dependent upon

10. Archer, *Pentecostal Hermeneutic*, 175.
11. Archer, *Pentecostal Hermeneutic*, 175.
12. Archer, *Pentecostal Hermeneutic*, 176.
13. Archer, *Pentecostal Hermeneutic*, 177.

the preacher's ability to properly flesh out the circumstances present at the time of composition. These include, but are not limited to, authorial setting (identity, date, place, location, circumstances, occasion, etc.), audience setting (same considerations), language, customs, beliefs, traditions, practices, and others.

Passages taken out of context deliver faulty interpretation. For example, consider how Paul's declaration of confidence in Phil 4:13 ("I can do all things through Christ who strengthens me") changes when his circumstances come to light. Some are surprised to learn that Paul was imprisoned as he wrote this passage. His faith declaration was not intended to be fuel for someone to win their weekend soccer match against a stronger team. It was a declaration of trust in Christ in the most severe of persecutive circumstances.

The preacher's context is also a factor in biblical interpretation. Archer addresses this concept. He notes that interpretation never occurs in a neutral vacuum but always takes place within the contextual horizon of the reading community.[14] The preacher is never divorced from the context in which they exist and from which they have been mutually shaped. In a Christian setting, the community provides the context for hearing the Spirit's voice, which includes a variety of Spirit manifestation (testimonies, charismatic gifts, preaching, teaching, witnessing, and prayer).[15]

Community in the realm of the Spirit serves purposes far beyond social satisfaction, says Keener.[16] This is true. When Jesus spoke of community, he did so with the disclaimer that when any two or more are gathered in his name, he would be in their midst (Matt 18:19–20). The *in his name* part of the equation changes the nature of the community. The Johnses identify communities as those held together through covenantal bonds.[17] Green identifies the community as a worshiping community and highlights how essential this is to the Spirit's moving and shaping in the interpretive act. He discusses worship within the community as a frame of reference for reading Scripture in that it develops within the individual believer a kind of inner sense of God's ways which, in turn, helps guide the believer in the interpretive journey.[18]

14. Archer, *Pentecostal Hermeneutic*, 173.
15. Archer, *Pentecostal Hermeneutic*, 248.
16. Keener, *Spirit Hermeneutics*, 278.
17. Johns and Bridges-Johns, "Yielding to the Spirit," 116.
18. Green, *Sanctifying Interpretation*, 150.

The Spirit moves in the context of community. Thomas points out the Spirit's direction during the Acts 15 council, noting that the decision handed down by the leadership was first discussed in a communal setting. The leadership made the final decision, but not before processing it with guidance from the Holy Spirit and the Christian community.[19] The community was Spirit-committed. The stories of Stephen's appointment for service and the sending out of Paul and Barnabas reveal this truth. In Acts 6, Stephen was chosen after the apostles instructed the church to select seven men full of the Holy Spirit to oversee the food ministry. Additionally, it was through the laying on of hands by the community that Paul and Barnabas were sent out in Acts 13.

The Spirit is the shaper of understanding. I recently had a conversation with one of my daughters about a problem she was having. I quickly discerned that her perspective on the issue was flawed. I came alongside her and shared a few insights for her consideration. She later told my wife that the conversation was a big help for her as she found a resolution. I was the "shaper of understanding" for her in our conversation. Yong discusses this fathering of the Spirit. He shows how the Spirit is the shaper of interpretation and how this works interrelationally in the community.

Yong outlines three unique ways in which the Spirit accomplishes this shaping. First, he notes the function of tongues within the community. Drawing on the early days of the Pentecostal movement, he notes how the early Pentecostal believers saw tongues as a unique marker of their identity as people of the Spirit and how it served as a sign that they were people of God and that the Spirit of God was in their midst, which included, among many phenomena, the shaping of interpretation. Second, he discusses the significance of Acts as a motif for interpreting the community. He draws out the implications of the Lukan depiction of the Spirit's movement upon, within, and throughout the Christian community after the Pentecost event in Acts 2. The early leaders of the Pentecostal movement connected their experiences of Spirit baptism to the Acts narrative as the norm for the Christian life. And third, the Acts 2 narrative was seen as an inverse of the language confusion of Babel. The universal impartation of "one language" of the Spirit was a sign that the Spirit of God was tabernacling among his people, leading and guiding them into all truth.[20]

19. J. Thomas, "Women, Pentecostals and the Bible," 49.

20. Yong, *Spirit-Word-Community*, 282–95.

## IDENTITY OF THE READER

What's not uncommon in the realm of interpretation is how the identity of the interpreter is, by and large, a product of the community in which they are located. My children know they belong to the McAffee family. It's a part of their identity that they proudly embrace. The McAffee family carries certain characteristics that all members share. These include our Christian identity, baptism in the Holy Spirit, being Bible-believing Jesus followers, a love for family game night, and the need for thick skin amid constant good-natured teasing.

The Pentecostal movement, as a Spirit-filled community, has members who reflect the identity of the whole. This means that, at the individual level, the same identifiable markers of the community (see above) are present in each person. Each person becomes an extension of the community and is fully part of the whole.[21] Adding to this, Yong declares, "This means that my listening to what the Spirit is saying includes my being open to being transformed by what is said, and not just myself, but all those who claim to be of the Spirit of God and are claimed by that same Spirit."[22]

### Mutual Conditioning

It's true that every person, at any given moment, is a product of the communities to which they have belonged. The values, beliefs, traditions, and practices of those communities have left their indelible marks upon the fabric of their identity. The wise preacher knows this maxim well. They know their interactions with Scripture are never divorced from the coloration of their interpretive lenses. The implications of this are for every preacher to carry a sober understanding of these colorations to protect themselves against undue prejudice in the interpretive journey.

There's a difference between influence and prejudice. The former is welcomed while the latter is to be avoided. If influence serves as the lens of perception and interpretation, then prejudice is the coloration, or the smudge, that prevents us from perceiving and interpreting clearly. So the presence of prejudice is mutually inclusive with the presence of faulty interpretation.

21. Archer, *Pentecostal Hermeneutic*, 225.

22. Yong, *Spirit-Word-Community*, 255.

This is good news for the Pentecostal preacher fully immersed within the Pentecostal tradition and Pentecostal community. They have been historically conditioned, which compels them to participate in the interpretive journey not with an intellectually bankrupt blank slate but as an individual illuminated in, by, and through the same Spirit who inspired the original text.[23]

Since the interpreter's identity is influenced by the community's identity, the reverse is also true: the community's identity is conditioned by the interpreter's. This is a kind of reverse or mutual conditioning. Yong states, "Community identity is embedded in the stories that are shaped by the community's members."[24] The practical outworking of this is evident in how individuals' charismatic experiences shape the community's charismatic ethos. There's a divine, cyclical affirmation of the Spirit's presence, activity, and mission. So the shared charismatic experiences are part of the economy of biblical interpretation.

The Johnses add to this, saying, "Knowledge therefore in the community of the Spirit is both a desire to know and to be known."[25] As a stand-alone entity, knowledge is first a Spirit-led communal endeavor, and biblical interpretation takes place within the same communal construct. God's answer to every person's desire to be in right relationship with others is the very means by which he reveals an illuminative understanding of his Word.

## Narrative Tradition in Community

The term *narrative tradition* refers to identity-shaping stories that circulate within the community. By stories, I do not mean the campfire stories of being chased by a bear while hiking in the forest. I mean the ones that define who we are as a faith movement. For example, part of the Pentecostal narrative tradition is that we are a people who see ourselves as restorationists to the charisms, power, and witness of the first-century believers.

Archer shows how the narrative tradition of the Pentecostal movement helps shape the interpreter's identity in four key areas. The first of these is moral reasoning.[26] The Pentecostal movement has close ties

23. Archer, *Pentecostal Hermeneutic*, 129.

24. Yong, *Spirit-Word-Community*, 277.

25. Johns and Bridges-Johns, "Yielding to the Spirit," 116.

26. Archer, *Pentecostal Hermeneutic*, 132.

with our fellow holiness and fundamentalist movements. The high moral compass within these traditions is also in ours. Secondly is the interpreter's point of view. Archer shows how one's point of view is crafted by the community in which the hermeneutics belongs.[27] Third and fourth are rationality and experience. Archer says, "Therefore rationality is not individualistic or entirely subjective, but is dependent upon the narrative tradition of the community in which the interpreter exists."[28] His point here is epistemological. Knowledge, rationality, and logic are defined by the community's values.

For example, when a person encounters the divine, they've experienced an otherworldly event that transcends the normal, rationally accessible contours of reality. Everything is clean within these contours. But everything changes in the experiences of the Spirit. As one who transcends natural reality, the Spirit is more than real; he's hyper-real. During the encounter, the meeting ground of supernatural experience becomes the location where logic is birthed into a higher realm. The experiences of the Pentecostal community have changed our definition of rationality.

## SAFEGUARDING OF INTERPRETATION

One of the standard critiques against the Pentecostal movement is its loose grip on subjective experiences of the divine. As a movement that embraces the theological richness of divine encounter, we are also at constant risk of misinterpreting these encounters. More so, we exist in the sometimes murky waters of *nondivine* encounters being mistakenly interpreted as having been a genuine move of the Spirit. The critique is not without warrant. There have been too many embarrassing stories of hyper-charismaticism gone wrong.

These stories must be understood in two ways. First, they must be understood as part of the Spirit community. The gathering spaces of Spirit-led worship are the proving grounds for flowing in the Spirit. Mistakes happen here. As a full-time pastor of a Pentecostal church, I am aware that there will always be a risk that someone will experience what they believe is an authentic prompting of the Holy Spirit, only to find they were off target.

27. Archer, *Pentecostal Hermeneutic*, 131.

28. Archer, *Pentecostal Hermeneutic*, 132–33.

I don't have a problem with this risk. I have found that these kinds of instances usually happen when a person is new to the Pentecostal tradition, is trying to find their feet, or is learning to use spiritual gifts or to be led by the Spirit. It's a natural part of spiritual development where the occasional conflation of genuine Spirit prompts becomes intertwined with what was nothing more than a great idea in the moment, but not from the Spirit. The risk is worth the payoff. I'd much rather be the pastor of a Spirit-filled church with occasional messes than be the pastor of a dead church where the Spirit is not moving.

Secondly, the fallout from these kinds of experiences is usually minor and easy to clean up. Sometimes a church will lose a few attenders who could not get past their own unresolved inner struggle with what they experienced. And sometimes the person who made the mistake will leave out of embarrassment. Both of these are easily avoidable through simple conversations.

A similar dynamic is at work in a Pentecostal approach to biblical interpretation. As a movement that is led by Spirit and which embraces divine experience as part of the economy of interpretation, what happens if we're wrong? What happens if subjectivism has gone astray or if experiences have been misinterpreted? These are legitimate concerns. Archer points to a few traits of the Pentecostal community that address this consternation. He notes, for example, the role of community as both a filter and a form within the movement.[29] The focal point here is how the community rises to filter against inappropriate interpretations of Scripture or experiences. A person being healed of a stomach issue aligns with scriptural realities and Pentecostal expectations. Gold dust and angel feathers, on the other hand, which some other hyper-charismatic worship gatherings have claimed to experience, are met with appropriate suspicion.

Archer also notes how claims of Spirit-leading are assessed by Word and community testimonies[30] and that the community provides the orthodox point of view in the interpretation.[31] Keener also emphasizes the need to safeguard. He says, "Nevertheless, as we embrace the new dynamic by the Spirit, we need to keep in mind that the more subjective our guidance, the more it is that our personal revelation needs testing, and the further we move from the objective standard by which it must be tested."[32]

29. Archer, *Pentecostal Hermeneutic*, 157–58.

30. Archer, *Pentecostal Hermeneutic*, 249.

31. Archer, *Pentecostal Hermeneutic*, 130.

32. Keener, *Spirit Hermeneutics*, 118.

As a Spirit-driven movement, our experiences and our interpretations of Scripture will always be threatened by the risk of misinterpretation. With eyes wide open, we embrace the fact that our reality is defined in part by the regions of the ineffable, illogical, and irrational. The community stands guard against faulty interpretations running riot. I think the Johnses describe the role of community in safeguarding interpretation the best: "There is therefore the avoidance of privatized subjectivism on the one hand and totalitarian objectivism on the other."[33]

## CONNECTING THE MOVES

So, what does this all mean for the Pentecostal/Charismatic preacher? Why is it important to have a working knowledge of how Pentecostals interpret Scripture? Pentecostal/Charismatic preachers must grasp Pentecostal hermeneutics to ensure their preaching embodies the Spirit-empowered, transformative essence of the movement rather than mimicking academic or cessationist approaches.

This is important because too many Spirit-filled Bible teachers look to cessationist preachers as models. I've been there and done the same myself. The challenge is that, even though many renowned cessationist preachers have much to offer in terms of presence, delivery, and top-notch research, the overarching flavor of intellectual sophistication is too great a concession to the Spirit's presence and work. What many Spirit-filled preachers don't know is that the homiletical and interpretive frameworks within the Pentecostal/Charismatic movement give the Spirit-filled Bible teacher a leg up.

### Sermon Power and Authenticity

A Pentecostal interpretive framework equips the preacher to interpret Scripture as an active participant in salvation history, yielding sermons alive with God's present power and timeliness. Charismatic phenomena such as speaking in tongues, healings, and prophecies are the norm, not the exception. Without it, exegesis risks becoming more detached spectatorship, producing powerless, information-driven sermons that tickle the intellect rather than ones that demand a response. The Bible-teaching pastor can enjoy high-level exegesis without fear of quenching the anointing.

33. Johns and Bridges-Johns, "Yielding to the Spirit," 116.

## Faithful Witness to the Spirit

Understanding the Spirit-Word-Community triad prevents subjective excess or neglect of Scripture, helping preachers discern the Spirit's guidance in preparation and bridge ancient texts to contemporary outpourings. This matters for credibility. Preaching full-gospel truth with inductive, common-sense methods empowers the Spirit-filled preacher to maintain a healthy respect for the scientific methodologies free from idolization, necessity, or over-prioritization.

### *Spirit*

The emphasis of Spirit reliance, in the context of a Spirit-filled community of believers, puts us in a unique position of hearing from the author of Scripture himself. The fathers of the movement favored inductive observation and Jesus-centric praxis, free from *over*-intellectualism yet not deprived of the higher planes of highly respected exegesis.

The Spirit forms the interpretive core, functioning as guide, illuminator, bridge builder, and Christ-exalter within a Spirit framework for knowledge. Key markers include Spirit-dependent experience and faith-filled Scripture reading. The Spirit breaks into interpreters and demands a transformative response.

### *Word*

Scripture, as inerrant and verbally inspired, stands in the forefront. Read reverently, contextually, christologically, and Pentecostally, from a non-cessationist lens, it reveals God and functions formatively, transformationally, interpretively, and missionally. Experiences refine meaning, but the Scripture itself guards against subjectivity, with the Spirit who inspired it now illuminating its readers.

### *Community*

Interpretation occurs in the interwoven trinity of Spirit-Word-community, in which the believing community provides context, narrative tradition, mutual conditioning, and safeguards. Communal elements like testimonies, worship, and collective testing prevent privatized excess, echoing Acts 15's "It seemed good to the Holy Spirit and to us." This Pentecostal ecclesia ensures exegesis remains participatory, accountable, and missional.

## REFLECTION QUESTIONS

1. How does the "latter rain" motif move interpretation beyond mere historical analysis and into the realm of prophetic fulfillment? Consider how viewing your community as a people of fulfillment changes your sermon's urgency.
2. Explore the concept of "mutual conditioning" between the interpreter and the community. How do your individual charismatic encounters shape the broader church's identity, and conversely, how does the church's ethos shape your private study?
3. How does the "Spirit-Word-Community" triad act as a safeguard against "icy objectivism"? Contrast this communal approach with overly reliant academic methods that might ignore the present-day transformative power of the Holy Spirit.
4. Consider the role of the community as a "crucible" for testing subjective revelations. What practical steps can a local congregation take to assess spiritual manifestations without quenching the genuine moving of the Holy Spirit?
5. Analyze the "narrative tradition" of restorationism within the movement. How does the story of a church restored to its original purity provide a specific framework for what you consider "rational" or "logical" interpretation?

# PART FOUR

## Setting the Model

# 13

# What Is a Pentecostal Expository Sermon?

So now that we've had an opportunity to better understand a Pentecostal preaching foundation and our interpretive framework, we can get down to the heart of the matter. The whole point of this text is to ask the question, "What is a Pentecostal expository sermon?" Or it can be better phrased as "What is an approach to expository preaching that is faithful to Pentecostal homiletical markers and is also faithful to Pentecostal hermeneutical methods of interpretation?" My intent for this chapter is to provide a well-crafted definition of expository preaching that is in full alignment with who we are as a movement. In the following chapter, I will show how it compares with other definitions of well-known cessationist voices within the preaching horizon.

The Pentecostal approach to expository preaching aligns with what has been classically understood as expository preaching. This includes a basic premise that the sermon's main idea and supporting points are derived from the Bible. *The text speaks for itself.* Expository preaching leaves no room for personal agenda, regardless of the occasion, the church's needs, or the times. What this means is that the preacher prepares the expository sermon so that they do not bring to it any notion of the topic or direction beyond what is clearly seen in the text.

Take, for example, the passage of Mic 6:8 (ESV): "He has shown you, O mortal, what is good. And what does the Lord require of you? To act justly and to love mercy and to walk humbly with your God." If one were preparing an expository sermon on this passage, one would quickly see the main idea as the Lord declaring his expectations for those who belong to him. The three main points are acting justly, loving mercy, and walking humbly with God.

This is the historical foundation of expository preaching. The standard, cessationist approach prioritized studying the Bible and exegeting in accordance with sound higher-critical methodologies, preaching what is there, and leaving personal preferences or agenda out of it. The purpose was to expose the Bible in plain terms, making it accessible to the congregation and to provide instruction on how to apply what they have learned to their own lives. This has been the historical approach to expository preaching.

The Pentecostal approach, as you might have already guessed, is different.

## MY DEFINITION OF EXPOSITORY PREACHING

My definition of expository preaching is this:

> Expository preaching is the sermonic proclamation of Scripture whereby the content of the sermon has been derived solely from the text itself, unaffected by outside agenda, for the sole purpose of the kerygmatic exaltation of Jesus Christ, where interpretation of the text is illumined through divine communion of Spirit, Word, and community, in collaboration with methodologies of higher criticisms where appropriate, and delivered in the context of worship, as worship.

This definition fully aligns with the extraordinary Pentecostal hermeneutical methodologies (chapters 9–12) and the unique markers that define our homiletical trajectory (chapters 4–7). My intention over the next several pages is to parse out this definition in the simplest and clearest terms.

### "Sermonic Proclamation of Scripture"

Sermons are a form of public speech distinct from standard public speaking. Most public speaking is propositional, in which the speaker attempts to persuade the audience to accept their propositions. Politicians are a good example of this: they have a point they want to make and are trying to persuade their audience to agree with them. However, sermons are different. Sermons are not propositional, and they are not declared with the intent of persuasion. Sermons are prophetic more than they are persuasive.

If we look at the Old Testament prophets, we find that their speech was intended to proclaim a message from God, whereby, if the listeners did not adhere to it, judgment or discipline would follow. Like the Old Testament's prophetic utterances, sermons share the same prophetic character. They do not contain propositional information with the attempt or intent to persuade. Rather, they are prophetic, as they proclaim truth. A good example is the prophet Jonah, who was called to go preach to the Ninevites. Jonah was called to warn them that judgment was coming unless they repented.

The Ninevites were egregiously evil people. Jonah wanted nothing to do with them. He rejected the notion of God extending his grace to a group of people who had historically mistreated the Jews. So Jonah ran in the opposite direction, and his story of being thrown overboard and swallowed by a great fish is well known. Ultimately, Jonah submitted to God's discipline and carried out the mission to the Ninevites. Jonah's sermon is recorded as one sentence, "Yet forty days, and Nineveh shall be overthrown!" (Jonah 3:4 ESV). Jonah's message was not propositional. It was proclamatory. He proclaimed the message entrusted to him by God. Pentecostal expository sermons are the same.

Sermons, therefore, are unique in their purpose and delivery. They serve as a conduit for divine messages, much like the prophecies of old, emphasizing proclamation over persuasion. The thrust here brings "sermonic proclamation" into focus, in contrast to the more popular notion of expository preaching, that being *teaching*. Many cessationist models of expository preaching are driven by the preacher's commitment to teach the Word of God rather than to proclaim it, resulting in two different worlds of congregational reception.

## "Content of the Sermon Is Derived Solely from the Text Itself"

Here, the Pentecostal definition of expository preaching aligns fully with traditional definitions. Central to this unity is the foundational truth that expository preaching finds its content solely from the text itself. The Bible serves as the starting point, the middle, and the finishing point.

The main idea of the sermon, along with all supporting points, is derived directly from the text.

In expository preaching, the chosen text can vary in length. It can be as short as a single phrase or sentence, or it could encompass a paragraph, an entire chapter, or even a whole book. In some cases, preachers have undertaken the monumental task of preaching through the entire Bible from start to finish. This approach is intentionally systematic and methodological, ensuring that the preacher remains faithful to the intended message of the Scriptures.

Expository preaching emphasizes a thorough and careful examination of the biblical text. The preacher's role is to uncover and explain the meaning inherent in the passage, making it relevant and applicable to the congregation. This method contrasts with topical preaching, where the speaker chooses a theme and selects various Scriptures to support it. Instead, expository preaching remains anchored in the specific text, allowing the Scripture to speak for itself.

By adhering to this method, expository preaching honors the authority and sufficiency of the Bible. It ensures that sermons are rooted in the Word of God, providing a robust and authentic proclamation of biblical truth. This commitment to deriving content solely from the text itself fosters a deeper understanding and appreciation of the Scriptures, encouraging listeners to engage with the Bible in a meaningful and transformative way.

## "Unaffected by Outside Agenda"

This phrase means that the sermon and its content remain free from any external motives the preacher might be tempted to bring to the text. Think of an agenda as a motive that might include personal needs, issues within the congregation demanding attention, current headlines, or even something the Lord has placed on the preacher's heart.

Agenda-driven sermons are perfectly fine in the pulpit. They're called topical sermons (see chapter 3). For example, I have preached several sermons that emerged from the transformative work of the Holy Spirit in my life. The insights I gained during these seasons became valuable material for preaching. The Lord uses such times as prophetic installments of truth, often meant for the congregation. The preacher's ability to worship Jesus during these seasons, and through what was revealed, equips them to lead the congregation into the same worship.

Another occasion when an agenda might influence sermon preparation is the preacher's need for spiritual fulfillment. I have experienced moments when I needed hope, for example. During such times, I had to be proactive in guarding against the temptation to inject the topic of hope into the sermon if the text did not support it. Expository sermons require a commitment from the preacher to resist such temptations and to let the Word of God speak for itself.

This commitment to avoiding external agendas ensures that the sermon remains true to the text. The preacher must suspend personal motives and allow the Scripture to convey its intended message. This approach maintains the integrity of expository preaching, ensuring that the content is derived solely from the biblical text, uninfluenced by personal or external circumstances.

By adhering to this principle, expository preaching honors the purity and authority of Scripture. It allows the Bible to speak on its own terms, free from the preacher's personal influences. This fidelity to the text not only enhances the preacher's credibility but also provides the congregation with an authentic and unadulterated message from God's Word. This discipline is crucial for maintaining the transformative power of expository preaching, enabling it to genuinely impact and guide listeners' lives.

## "Sole Purpose of the Kerygmatic Exaltation of Jesus Christ"

This is an important feature of the definition. The primary function of preaching—I would argue the supreme, unsurpassed, sole purpose of its existence—leaving all other considerations far behind, is the kerygmatic exaltation of Jesus Christ. This purpose is not limited to expository preaching alone but is held to all types of sermons. Immediately, some would argue that this part of the definition leaves little or no room for application, the congregation's learning of doctrine, moral guidance, community building, equipping for outreach, and the like, all of which are part and parcel of standard homiletical function.

To this objection, I would heartily agree! The consolation is found in two areas. First, in the fact that even though such common homiletical features are not the *primary purpose* of Pentecostal preaching, they can still find expression in the sermon, so long as their appearances are supportive in nature, and for the express purpose of worship. The second is that these activities find their greatest fulfillment in the context of discipleship, Bible studies, classes, training, and similar activities, all of which are best delivered in locations other than the sanctuary.

There are several different locations for ministerial communication. For example, it is known that worship takes place in the sanctuary. Teaching occurs in the classrooms. Counseling and pastoral care appointments usually happen in the office. Discipleship is an activity found in homes, coffee shops, and restaurants. Different types of communication take place in different locations.

Locations matter because of the expectations they carry. An Old Testament Jew on their way to the temple would have carried with them the expectation of sacrifice, participation in holy feasts and festivals, prayer and singing, and the giving of tithes and offerings. In the New Testament, Christians would have carried similar expectations for their places of worship, including prayer, singing, participation in the gifts of the Spirit and other charisms, teaching and exhortation, communion, and Scripture readings, all in the context of worship. Worship takes place in the sanctuary.

The classroom is the setting for ministerial communication in learning, training, and preparation. The expectations one carries into the classroom are commensurate with the activities that take place there. For example, most college students these days bring a computer to class to take notes during the lecture. The classroom's expectations differ from those of the worship service.

Location expectations become clearer when one considers the objects of various ministerial communications. In the classroom, where knowledge is transferred, the professor is the subject, and the students are the objects. The students are the focus as they receive knowledge transfer. The same phenomenon occurs in counseling, pastoral care, and discipleship. In each of these, the object is the one receiving the action of the event. The student is the object of knowledge transfer, the parishioner of counseling or pastoral care, and the disciple of discipleship.

However, a drastic change occurs when the location is the sanctuary. As the place of worship, the object is no longer the student, parishioner, or disciple. The Object is Christ. The congregation, along with the preacher, lifts up their hearts, voices, bodies, and spirits as a sacrifice of praise. It is this expectation of worship that is carried into the sanctuary.

The word *kerygmatic* means a proclamation that demands a response. By nature, sermons are kerygmatic speech. However, this does not classify sermons in the same category as typical public speeches that serve as platforms for persuasion. No choice is being formally presented for consideration. The word *kerygmatic* does not lend credence to any choice other than declaring the right choice in the context of worship.

The word *exaltation* means that the name of Jesus is being lifted up in a praiseworthy, worship-filled manner. Preaching exists for the sole purpose of worshiping Jesus. To exalt the name of Jesus Christ means to honor, glorify, and lift up his name in reverence and praise. It involves acknowledging his supreme authority, goodness, and sacrificial love as central to one's faith and life. Exalting Jesus Christ encompasses living according to his teachings, spreading his message of salvation, and recognizing his divine nature as the Son of God. It also involves worshiping him with gratitude and humility, attributing all glory and power to him. Ultimately, exalting the name of Jesus Christ signifies a deep spiritual commitment to magnifying his presence and influence in all aspects of existence.

## "Interpretation of the Text Is Illumined Through Divine Communion of Spirit, Word, and Community"

This part of the definition highlights the Pentecostal movement's interpretive approach. Its inclusion in the definition is essential, as the nature of expository preaching is presupposed by sound exegetical methods. Traditional exegetical methods have been dependent on higher-critical approaches, which leave little-to-no room for the Holy Spirit as the leading voice in the interpretive journey.

The underlying principle acknowledges the Spirit's role as both inspiration and illumination. The Spirit who inspired the writer is the Spirit who illuminates the reader. Pentecostals believe in the verbal inspiration of the Word, which means that the words and phrases that appear in Scripture were divinely inspired by the Spirit during composition. It follows then that the orthodox interpretation of Scripture is dependent upon Spirit illumination.

The apostle Paul knew this. He wrote about the role of the Holy Spirit in interpretation, noting that it is the very Spirit of God who knows the mind of God. He went on to explain that the natural mind cannot comprehend spiritual things because the Spirit gives us understanding and interpretation of spiritual truths (1 Cor 2:11–16).

Pentecostals have a vibrant understanding of Scripture. We agree with the writer of Hebrews that the Word is alive, active, and piercing (Heb 4:12). We agree with Isaiah that the Word of God never returns to him empty (55:11). The Word of God is always accompanied by the presence of God.

Our bibliology carries two distinct implications for our definition of expository preaching. First, Spirit-led exegesis transforms the preacher. The preacher finds that the study of the Word is God studying the preacher. The Word captures the preacher and has its way. These transformative moments of preparation are typically accompanied by tears of joy or repentance. The Word carries the concurrent mission of impartation and conviction. Only the Spirit of God can accomplish this.

Secondly, the Word accomplishes the same task in the delivery of the sermon. The worshiping congregation experiences the same conviction and impartation. The Spirit of God who accompanies his Word is at work. God's Word never returns to him void, which means the presence of God's Spirit always accompanies the proclamation of his word.

Community is always a component of biblical interpretation because the preacher is never divorced from communal context. That is to say that no preacher interacts with the text as a blank canvas, completely free from preconceptions, prejudgments, or bias. Each preacher has been shaped by the communities they have belonged to. The values, beliefs, traditions, practices, etc., of one's community are transmitted to its members.

The impact of this dynamic on the preacher is found in the culture of the Spirit-filled community. The Pentecostal preacher approaches the Word with the embedded beliefs, practices, values, and experiences of a community that sees the Spirit of God as present among them. The evidence of that presence is seen in tongues and other charismatic phenomena, healings, deliverances, and Holy Spirit baptism. This distinctly Pentecostal point of view is carried into the interpretive process.

## "In Collaboration with Methodologies of Higher Criticisms Where Appropriate"

This phrase simply points to the Pentecostal movement's respect for the methods of higher criticism and how those methods should be embraced at the appropriate level when necessary. These methods include historical, literary, and narrative criticisms. There are many other types of higher criticism (see chapter 8), but these three account for the majority of preacher-level access, and the remainder serve more academic purposes.

The word *criticism* means to analyze and evaluate. It does not imply finding fault or being negative; rather, it involves a detailed examination to understand meaning, structure, themes, and cultural significance. Analysis involves breaking down a literary work into its components to understand how it functions. This might involve looking at plot, character, setting, tone, style, and literary devices, where present. Evaluation means assessing the quality, effectiveness, and impact of something to judge its value. For literary considerations, this often means considering its originality, coherence, and emotional or intellectual engagement.

The word *scientific* refers to a methodical and systematic approach that emphasizes empirical evidence, objective analysis, and logical reasoning. This approach often involves components of data collection and observation, hypothesis formulation (developing theories or hypotheses about the Bible's context, meaning, or authorship), testing and analysis (comparing documents with other known texts, using linguistic or stylistic analysis, etc.), replication and peer review (sharing findings with other experts for validation ensuring methods and conclusions are reproducible and withstand scrutiny from the academic community), and logical reasoning.

These scientific approaches of interpretation bring great value to the exegetical journey, but they must be held in the proper context. This involves the preacher acknowledging their usefulness while also recognizing their potential impotency. Jesus highlighted this principle when he scolded the Pharisees for knowing Scripture intellectually but not illuminatively (John 5:39).

A preacher who relies solely upon scientific methodologies is in danger of being intellectually superior but spiritually inferior. They run the risk of holding to a form of godliness but lacking the power therein (2 Tim 3:5). To put it plainly, they are in dire peril of becoming pastorally fraudulent, knowing the Word of God as literature but not knowing the

Word as live, active, piercing, and accompanied by the transformative presence of the Holy Spirit.

## "Delivered in the Context of Worship, as Worship"

Pentecostal preaching takes place in the context of worship, as worship. When we use the term *worship*, we are tempted to think solely of music, but worship is much broader than musical considerations. Several elements make up the Spirit-filled worship experience. These include prayer, Scripture proclamation, fellowship of believers, and singing, water baptism, charismatic phenomena such as tongues, words of wisdom, prophecy, and knowledge, healings and deliverances, communion, and the altar experience.

Preaching is worship. The act takes place in the sanctuary, the location of worship. The words of the sermon function as the exaltation of Jesus Christ. The proclamation is a declaration of praise. The object of the sermon, though the sermon is preached to the congregation, is Jesus Christ.

One of the best illustrations of this dynamic is seen in the worship services of the Orthodox Church, where the priest has their back to the congregation for much of the service. The priest faces the altar as he leads his congregation in worship and serves as mediator between them and God. It is only during the homily that the priest turns briefly to face the congregation.

I know many pastors like to teach on Sunday mornings. Yet one of the challenges with teaching in church services is the *dislocation of its object*. If teaching has as its primary purpose the transference of knowledge from teacher to student, then the student has become the object. When this occurs, the congregation has become the object, not Jesus. There are two challenges with this. First, the congregation should never be the object of a gathering whose sole purpose is the worship of Christ. Second, teaching, as a necessary, nonnegotiable function of the church, belongs in the classroom, not the sanctuary. The classroom is the appropriate place for parishioners to become the object as they participate as students, disciples, candidates for ministerial preparation, and in other roles that lead people to seek learning. In this way, the teaching or learning that materializes during the worship service, as one would expect in an expository sermon, is happily positioned as ancillary.

## REFLECTION QUESTIONS

1. When expository preaching requires deriving content solely from the text, what disciplines or habits might help preachers avoid importing their own assumptions, agendas, or emotional needs into sermon preparation?
2. In your own words, explain how sermon preparation and delivery can become acts of worship. What might change in your preaching if you approached every sermon as a devotion offered to Christ?
3. Why is the kerygmatic exaltation of Jesus Christ the sole and ultimate purpose of Pentecostal preaching, and how does this focus influence what a sermon includes or intentionally leaves out?
4. The chapter notes that different types of ministerial communication belong in different locations. How does understanding the distinction between sanctuary and classroom safeguard preaching from becoming mere instruction?
5. Considering the preacher's call to let Scripture speak for itself, how does humility function as both an interpretive virtue and an act of worship in the task of expository preaching?

# 14

# Definition Comparisons

When we step into the world of preaching, we find a rich tapestry of voices offering guidance on how best to communicate the transformative message of Scripture. This chapter invites you into a conversation with some of the most influential cessationist homiletical thinkers of our time—John MacArthur, Bryan Chapell, John Stott, Haddon Robinson, Tim Keller, and Albert Mohler. These authors have experience, respect, and best-selling books. Each brings insights to the table, shaping the broader landscape of expository preaching. While their approaches are revered and widely taught, they fall short of capturing the heartbeat of Pentecostal preaching, which is why the following comparison matters. For reference, a comprehensive list of the bibliographic entries for all the works cited by these authors can be found in appendix C.

Pentecostal preaching is not merely about delivering information or sound doctrine; it's about creating a living encounter with the risen Christ through the power of the Holy Spirit. It is a vibrant dance between rigorous biblical study and Spirit-led responsiveness, where the sermon becomes a moment of worship, transformation, and altar encounter. The definitions we'll explore here often emphasize the intellectual rigors of exegesis, doctrinal precision, and application, which are essential but incomplete without the dynamic movement of the Spirit. Pentecostal homiletics embraces these foundations but insists on a deeply theological, Christ-centered, and Spirit-empowered method—something that can be missing in many traditional frameworks.

My approach is to engage these voices not in opposition but in dialogue, highlighting where their definitions align with Pentecostal values and where they fall short. For example, while many models focus heavily on application, I argue that the worship context must take precedence, with application flowing naturally, secondarily, *and silently* from the exaltation of Jesus rather than dominating the sermon's purpose. Likewise, terms like *presentation* or *survey*, as used in several of the following definitions, may sound academically safe, but they lack the passionate proclamation and altar-focused outcome that characterize Pentecostal preaching.

This textbook exists to serve and equip you, the preacher, with a sermon construction framework that is faithful to Pentecostal homiletical and hermeneutical traditions. As you read the definitions and critiques from these respected voices, keep in mind the unique Pentecostal emphasis on worship, Spirit empowerment, and altar encounters. This comparison is not about dismissing other traditions but about clarifying what makes Pentecostal preaching distinctively alive and faithful to its calling. With this in mind, let's dive in, not just to learn what others say about expository preaching, but to sharpen our own Pentecostal homiletical identity—one that exalts Jesus, embraces the Spirit, and leads people to the altar, ready for transformation.

## JOHN MACARTHUR

John MacArthur (1939–2025) was a well-known pastor, author, and speaker. He wrote and spoke extensively about preaching, producing numerous articles, books, and videos on the subject. He was a Calvinist, Baptist pastor, widely associated with expository preaching, with an emphasis on sustained, passage-by-passage exposition in which the preacher's task is to explain and apply the meaning of the biblical text as originally intended by God. Drawing from his text *Preaching: How to Preach Biblically*, he writes of expository preaching,

> The message finds its sole source in Scripture. The message is extracted from Scripture through careful exegesis. The message preparation correctly interprets Scripture in its normal sense and context. The message clearly explains the original God-intended meaning of Scripture. The message applies the Scriptural meaning for today.[1]

1. MacArthur and Master's Seminary Faculty, *Preaching*, 10.

MacArthur is correct that expository preaching should have Scripture as its sole source. This means that the sermon's content originates entirely from Scripture, rather than a pre-chosen topic supported by Scripture. This is a crucial distinction between expository preaching and topical preaching. In a topical sermon, the preacher selects a topic beforehand and then searches for scriptural references to support it, which can lead to proof-texting. In contrast, expository preaching involves approaching scripture without a preconceived agenda, allowing the scripture to guide the message.

MacArthur states that the message is extracted from Scripture through careful exegesis. When MacArthur uses the word *exegesis*, he means the tried-and-true, scientific methodologies that provide no formal allowance for Spirit illumination (see chapter 8). The astute Pentecostal interpreter of the Bible would see this as an invitation to boundaries. What's missing from MacArthur's definition is the Spirit's reliance on biblical interpretation, as discussed in chapters 9–12.

Another feature of MacArthur's definition that is challenging to Pentecostal homiletics is his focus on application. The darling of cessationist preaching, application, though a much-needed function of the church, *is mislocated in the worship context.* The Pentecostal movement has accommodated this standard feature of cessationist preaching over the last several decades, but these accommodations come at a cost. Given that application is a function of discipleship, its livelihood belongs in the classroom. When the Pentecostal sermon devolves into a clinic on how to live the Christian life, it sacrifices the altar in the process.

In a different text, *Rediscovering Expository Preaching: Balancing the Science and Art of Biblical Exposition*, MacArthur says,

> Expository preaching is preaching in such a way that the meaning of the Bible passage is presented entirely and exactly as it was intended by God. Expository preaching is the proclamation of the truth of God as mediated through the preacher.[2]

Though MacArthur's focus on presenting the Bible passage "entirely and exactly" as intended by God is on target, his "presentational" structuring warrants attention. The word *presentation* suggests that Scripture is being explained in a propositional manner, with an underlying purpose of appeal. Preaching should not constitute the presentation of

2. MacArthur and Master's Seminary Faculty, *Rediscovering Expository Preaching*, 23–24.

propositions, but should be about the kerygmatic, proclamatory exaltation of Jesus Christ. The preacher proclaims the truth within the context of worshiping Christ, not merely presenting doctrine for consideration. This aligns with the essential nature of preaching as a proclamation rather than a mere presentation.

## BRYAN CHAPELL

Bryan Chapell is a Presbyterian pastor, theologian, and homiletician whose textbook *Christ-Centered Preaching* has become one of the most widely used guides to expository preaching in evangelical seminaries worldwide. He is president emeritus and adjunct professor of practical theology at Covenant Theological Seminary and has served the Presbyterian Church in America in various leadership roles.

Chapell's definition of expository preaching is compelling:

> The main idea of an expository sermon (the topic), the divisions of that idea (the main points), and the development of those divisions (the subpoints) all come from truths the text itself contains. No significant portion of the text is ignored.[3]

Chapell highlights that expositors must remain within the bounds of the text and that the content of the sermon is entirely dependent upon the preacher's exhaustive survey of the text.

There is much to agree with in this definition. Chapell is correct to emphasize that everything should come from the text itself. The preacher approaches the text with no personal agenda, allowing the text to speak for itself. The main idea of the sermon, all the points, and the development of those points all originate from the Bible. This approach is essential and commendable. These are good.

The challenge that exists with Chapelle's definition is the methodology behind the output. Chappelle devotes an entire chapter focusing on the classic scientific methodologies (higher criticisms) that, by nature, force a devaluation of the text as "microscopic specimen" to be analyzed, scrutinized, studied, and mastered in preparation for its delivery. However, in the context of worship, the approach falls short. Again, I'm not trying to nitpick, it's the heart of the approach that gives the Spirit-filled preacher warning.

3. Chapell, *Christ-Centered Preaching*, 118.

When Scripture is treated merely as something to be examined and scrutinized, its presentation to the congregation is devalued to a text *about* Jesus rather than as the living words that facilitate the worship *of* Jesus. What would make his definition more suitable in a Spirit-filled context is an insistence on surveying Scripture with the purpose of worship, which would then require additional moves. Chapell's survey focus is a standard approach for cessationist preachers. Consequently, it misses the point of exaltation.

## JOHN STOTT

John Stott (1921–2011) was a British Evangelical Anglican pastor, theologian, and one of the preeminent expository preachers of the twentieth century. For many years, he served as rector and later rector emeritus of All Souls Church, Langham Place, London, where he modeled text-driven preaching that combined rigorous exegesis with clear, accessible communication. From his classic text *Between Two Worlds*, Stott states that exposition,

> refers to the content of the sermon (biblical truth) rather than its style (a running commentary). To expound scripture is to bring out of the text what is there and expose it to view. The expositor prizes open what appears to be closed, makes plain what is obscure, unravels what is knotted and unfolds what is tightly packed.[4]

Stott's statement that exposition should focus on the biblical truth of the sermon rather than merely provide a running commentary is valid. What's missing from Stott's definition, and throughout the entirety of his text, is the focus of exposition in the context of worship. Expounding upon Scripture is wonderful when done within the context of worship, as worship is the primary purpose of a sermon. When exposition is undertaken for the purpose of learning, the sermon shifts into the realm of education, which belongs in a different setting. His definition would be more consistent with Pentecostal preaching if it used language that positions sermon content as the vehicle for the praise and worship of Christ.

4. Stott, *Between Two Worlds*, 125–26.

## HADDON ROBINSON

Haddon W. Robinson (1931–2017) was an American evangelical pastor, theologian, and homiletician best known for his influential textbook *Biblical Preaching* and his emphasis on the "big idea" in expository sermons. Robinson taught preaching at Dallas Theological Seminary for nineteen years, served as president of Denver Seminary for twelve years, and later held the Harold John Ockenga Distinguished Professor of Preaching chair and directed the doctor of ministry program at Gordon-Conwell Theological Seminary. In his timeless text *Biblical Preaching*, he defines expository preaching as,

> the communication of a biblical concept, derived from and transmitted through a historical, grammatical, and literary study of a passage in its context, which the Holy Spirit first applies to the personality and experience of the preacher and then, through the preacher, applies to the hearers.[5]

Haddon's definition hits in some places and misses in others. His emphasis on communicating biblical concepts is on target, whereas the main points of an expository sermon consist of truths and principles derived from the text itself (which we'll explore more thoroughly in chapter 17). This is the preferred approach for expository preaching, in that the truths and principles of Scripture speak directly to the congregation, rather than relying on interesting facts or details as sermon points. For example, if preaching the story of David and Goliath (1 Samuel), instead of focusing on factual information as sermon points, such as "David was a skilled shepherd," or "Goliath was an intimidating warrior," the expository sermon focuses on truths and principles in the story such as "God uses unlikely servants who trust him rather than conventional resources," or "God's people must interpret intimidating threats in light of God's covenant, not their fears."

Robinson's definition is also unique in its attention to the text's *impact on the preacher*. Hitting close to home for the Pentecostal preacher, Robinson's focus on the Holy Spirit's application of the text to the preacher's personality and experience aligns with Pentecostal distinctives. The Spirit-filled exegete understands that the biblical interpretation is presupposed by the preacher's own interpretation of the Word, by the Word, before the Word. It's only by the preacher's apprehension *by* the Word

5. Robinson, *Biblical Preaching*, 5.

that they are granted comprehension *of* the Word. We'll explore this in greater detail in chapter 20, where we discuss the bidirectional nature of biblical interpretation.

The primary breakaway from Robinson's definition is threefold. First, there is his exclusion of the Holy Spirit and the Spirit-filled community from the interpretive journey. The Pentecostal approach to understanding Scripture is grounded within a triad of Spirit, Word, and community. The same Spirit who inspired the text is the same Spirit who illumines its understanding. The Pentecostal preacher, living within and preaching from a Spirit-filled context, is naturally infused with the *lens-creating values* that characterize their community.

Secondly, Robinson's sole source of interpretation is scientific methodologies, such as historical, grammatical, and literary approaches. As discussed in chapter 8, these higher criticisms are problematic for the Spirit-filled community because of their unapologetic, antagonistic stance toward the Word. And though there is value in the information generated from the methodologies, they must be identified and embraced with collegial respect and healthy caution. Stemming from analysis that bears little-to-no reliance upon the Spirit, the foundation of such approaches delivers truth claims without the safety nets of Spirit objectivity.

Thirdly, Robinson leans on the standard go-to for every cessationist model for expository preaching, application. Application is appropriate in the context of discipleship or training. It is even acceptable to mention application within a sermon as long as the primary focus is on the exaltation and worship of Jesus Christ. However, Pentecostal preaching does not place its focus on Word application; it places its focus on the exaltation of Word himself.

## TIM KELLER

Tim Keller (1950–2023) was an American Presbyterian pastor, Reformed theologian, and Christian apologist. He served as the founding pastor of Redeemer Presbyterian Church (PCA) in Manhattan, where his expository, Christ-centered sermons reached thousands of skeptical and secular New Yorkers and influenced preachers around the world. In Keller's text *Preaching*, Keller defines expository preaching as,

> Expository preaching grounds the message in the text so that all the sermon's points are points in the text, and it majors in the

> text's major ideas. It aligns the interpretation of the text with the doctrinal truths of the rest of the Bible (being sensitive to systematic theology). And it always situates the passage within the Bible's narrative, showing how Christ is the final fulfillment of the text's theme (being sensitive to biblical theology).[6]

Keller's emphasis on expository preaching being rooted in the Bible as the ultimate source aligns with the traditional trajectory of expository preaching. His continued emphasis on sermon points and major ideas derived directly from the text is also orthodox within the tradition. His attention to canonical fidelity is a helpful component of his definition. It's evident that one of Keller's primary concerns was that the sermon faithfully represented the Word and church tradition and that it did not violate the church's accepted theological positions. This feature of his definition is helpful. It invites the preacher to run checks, that is, to make certain there is nothing in their sermon that would be considered heretical.

Of concern in this part of his definition is the temptation for the sermon to have a sole doctrinally driven focus. Even with the obvious importance of doctrine and its dire need for the Christian community, its presence in the sermon should always support the main purpose of the gathering: the worship experience. With such safeguards in place, the teaching of doctrine within the sermon is a welcome inclusion as the name of Christ is lifted up and the people of Christ are being prepared for the altar experience. Without such safeguards in place, Keller's approach can position the sermon more as a tool for teaching and correction, which is a function of discipleship and Bible study, not worship.

What is particularly strong with Keller's definition is his christological emphasis. This feature strongly identifies with the Pentecostal preacher. Christ is the epicenter of all Scripture. The Old Testament points toward Jesus. The New Testament points back to Jesus. When sermons are delivered for the purpose of congregational worship of his name, the very Spirit of Christ is on the move. Jesus told his disciples that when any two or more are gathered in his name, he would be there (Matt 18:20). And even with such praise in hand for Keller's definition, the Pentecostal preacher does not miss how the presence of christological emphases does not guarantee their delivery for the purpose of worship.

6. Keller, *Preaching*, 32.

## ALBERT MOHLER

Albert Mohler is an American Southern Baptist theologian and denominational leader who has served as the ninth president of The Southern Baptist Theological Seminary in Louisville, Kentucky, since 1993. In addition to his presidential role, he has served as pastor and staff minister in several Southern Baptist churches and gained a broad public platform through writing, speaking, and hosting a daily commentary on news and culture from a Christian worldview. His text *He Is Not Silent* defines expository preaching as such:

> Expository preaching is the mode of Christian preaching that takes its central purpose the presentation and application of the text of the Bible. All other issues and concerns are subordinated to the central task of presenting the biblical text.[7]

This definition aligns with the long-held cessationist understanding of expository preaching that emphasizes the primacy of presenting and applying the biblical text. Mohler underscores that the preacher's agenda, topical concerns, or the church's contemporary issues must be subordinated to the central task of delivering the biblical text. This approach ensures that the sermon remains anchored in Scripture, free from external influences or distractions.

However, there are aspects of Mohler's definition that warrant critique. Firstly, his use of the term *presentation* is inherently propositional, implying that the speaker offers propositions for the audience to accept or reject. This is not the essence of a sermon. A sermon is not merely a series of propositions but a dynamic proclamation of God's Word meant to inspire and transform.

Secondly, and not unsurprisingly, Mohler's emphasis on *application* is somewhat misplaced within the context of worship. While application has its place, it is more appropriately situated within discipleship and Bible studies. The primary purpose of preaching is not merely to apply biblical principles but to engage in the kerygmatic, proclamatory exaltation of Jesus Christ. This focus on exaltation is the heart of true worship, aiming to glorify Christ and draw the congregation into a deeper relationship with him.

While Mohler's definition captures the essence of expository preaching's focus on Scripture, his approach to presentation and application

7. Mohler, *He Is Not Silent*, 65.

may detract from the sermon's primary purpose of worship and exaltation. The ultimate goal of preaching should be the kerygmatic proclamation of Christ, elevating him above all other concerns.

## CONCLUSION

As we conclude this chapter, it's clear that engaging with established homiletical voices offers invaluable insight, but Pentecostal preaching calls us to something distinctively alive and Spirit-led. While the respected definitions of MacArthur, Chapell, Stott, Robinson, Keller, and Mohler provide strong academic frameworks, they often center on intellectual rigor, doctrinal precision, and application in ways that don't always capture the vibrant worship and altar encounter that define Pentecostal homiletics.

A Pentecostal model seeks to bridge this gap by embracing the full dynamic of Pentecostal preaching, where Scripture is not just studied but proclaimed with Spirit-empowered passion, where Jesus is not only taught about but worshiped, and where the altar becomes the climactic point of surrender and transformation. This approach challenges us as preachers to move beyond mere presentation or survey of the text and to lean into the kerygmatic, Spirit-empowered proclamation that moves hearts and changes lives.

Pentecostal preaching is a sacred dance between preparation and spontaneity, between study and Spirit, between mind and heart. It invites us to preach not just with our intellects but with our whole being, trusting that the same Spirit who inspired Scripture will illuminate and empower its proclamation today. As you continue your journey in homiletics, may this chapter inspire you to hold fast to the unique Pentecostal calling: to exalt Jesus, to cherish the living Word, and to lead God's people to the altar, where transformation happens in real time.

## A BRIEF OVERVIEW OF A PENTECOSTAL MODEL FOR EXPOSITORY PREACHING

When I set out to craft a Pentecostal model for expository preaching, I realized two important tasks would need to be accomplished. First, the model would have to be faithful to Pentecostal hermeneutical strategies (the unique way we interpret Scripture). And, second, it would have to be faithful to Pentecostal homiletical markers (the features of our preaching unique to the Pentecostal/Charismatic movement). To this end, and with the definition of expository preaching in hand, the following model comes into view.

The model has eight simple steps. Each step will be explained in the following chapters.

## A Pentecostal Model for Expository Preaching

Step 1: Inspiration—Explores the divine inspiration of choosing the passage

Step 2: Preparation—Identifies the processes involved in preparing the sermon

Step 3: Introduction—Explains why the introduction is needed and how to put it together

Step 4: Explanation—Describes the teaching component of each sermon point

Step 5: Implication—Articulates the implications of the truths and principles from step 4

Step 6: Confrontation—Highlights the *offensive* nature of the gospel and how preachers embrace this concept in delivery

Step 7: Invitation—Showcases the opportunity for the congregation to respond to the working of the Holy Spirit

Step 8: Alteration—Illuminates the importance of the altar service during sermon delivery

## REFLECTION QUESTIONS

1. How does the distinction between "presenting" a proposition and "proclaiming" the person of Jesus Christ change your internal posture as you step behind the pulpit to lead a congregation in corporate worship?
2. How do you balance the need for rigorous, "careful exegesis" with the Pentecostal requirement for Spirit-led spontaneity? Can a

sermon be intellectually disciplined while remaining open to "holy chaos"?

3. Evaluate the argument that detailed application belongs in discipleship rather than the worship service. How might shifting "application" to a different setting change the way you structure your actual Sunday morning sermon delivery?
4. Tim Keller emphasizes aligning sermons with systematic theology and the Bible's metanarrative. How can you ensure this doctrinal alignment serves to exalt Jesus rather than merely turning the sermon into a lecture?
5. If the sermon is a "vibrant dance" between rigorous study and Spirit-led responsiveness, which side of that dance do you find more challenging to maintain, and how can you cultivate the other?

# 15

# The Silent Infrastructure Co-Delivering Congregational Interpretation

As we begin discussing the model, we do so by first situating the hermeneutical and homiletical backdrops of Pentecostal preaching in their proper locations. Recall that hermeneutics is defined as the art and science of biblical interpretation. The role of hermeneutics in the act of sermon preparation, specifically in the act of interpreting the meaning of Scripture, was addressed in chapters 9–12. There remains another feature of biblical interpretation that now comes into view, as the preacher delivers their sermon in the act of worship.

This second distinct part focuses on the congregation. This concerns how biblical interpretation functions within the community of believers at the corporate level and how such interpretive moves occur within the context of a worship setting. Adding to this is my assertion regarding the location of congregational interpretation. Does congregational interpretation belong in the sanctuary or the classroom? In other words, is congregational interpretation an act of education and application, or is it an act of worship? If the first, then the task is better suited to the classroom. For the second, the sanctuary. The good news for Bible-teaching pastors in the Pentecostal/Charismatic movement is that there is ample room for biblical interpretation within the context of the corporate worship service, which is the primary topic of this book and the primary function of the teacher in the pulpit.

The model put forth in this text meets the need for solid Bible teaching in our worship services in a way that supports the preaching and interpretive distinctives that make us uniquely Spirit filled. Each step of this model is realized within a collaborative, hermeneutical framework, silently co-delivering understanding of the Word to those who have gathered. Worship stands at the center. Congregational interpretation, therefore, is seated in the act of worship because worship is the sole context through which one can truly understand.

Isaiah's call narrative is a shining example of these dynamics at work (Isa 6). Two life-changing events happened to Isaiah as he worshiped God in the throne room. First, he saw himself in the light of truth and realized the dread of his sinfulness. This is one of the most grace-filled components of a worship service. When the congregation worships, its members see themselves for who they are. The presence of sin in their lives, which may have been otherwise unseen, is now brought clearly into view.

Isaiah's response was expected. The light of truth revealed his condition, and he knew he was a dead man. He declared it as such, "Woe is me!" (6:5). He knew in that moment he was an unclean man dwelling in the midst of unclean people, and as he stood in the presence of a hyper-clean God, he knew this would be his end. This is the profound beauty of conviction that comes when the Word is proclaimed! Too many preachers avoid confrontational moments like this because they fear the offense will drive away their crowds. The opposite is true. There's no truer freedom than seeing oneself in the light of truth, where despair of one's sinfulness is overwhelmed by the hope of God's forgiveness and cleansing.

The underlying hope of conviction is that it is always the forerunner of restoration. As Isaiah saw the truth of his sinfulness, he submitted to the Lord's indictment. God's response was forgiveness and cleansing through the touch of his lips with a burning coal taken from the altar, the very place of sacrifice and atonement. It was declared to Isaiah that he was now free from guilt. Worship stands at the center of interpretation because, in the presence of the Almighty God, one sees clearly the reality of one's circumstances, the reality of the Word, and the reality of one's self.

The second event that happened to Isaiah was the importation of divine destiny and identity. God told him who he was and revealed to him the thrust of his mission. The question rang through the heavens, "Whom shall I send?" Isaiah, now freed from the shackles of his sin and shame and ready to serve, declared, "Send me" (6:8). The next words he heard were his commission to go, followed by the parameters of his mission. God declared Isaiah worthy of serving in the highest capacity. What a statement of identity! Isaiah was also informed of his destiny. He was instructed to proclaim the message given to him.

Worship was the vehicle through which Isaiah saw himself in truth, sought and received forgiveness for sin, received God-given identity being poured into him, and ultimately received his destiny. All of this was accomplished through the Word of God. Isaiah's ability to understand this Word depended on his worship-centered encounter with God. Worship is the driving force behind congregational interpretation.

## THE SILENT INFRASTRUCTURE CO-DELIVERING CONGREGATIONAL INTERPRETATION

This chapter focuses on the silent infrastructure, which is alive, working in tandem with the preacher, and operating behind the scenes to deliver a simultaneous congregational interpretation of the Word. An infrastructure is the hidden but essential framework, like roads, power lines, and internet cables, that quietly carries the life of a city. These are usually long-lasting, costly to build, and essential for everyday functioning, even though people rarely notice them. In our case, the infrastructure metaphor highlights what is underneath, or behind, Pentecostal preaching . . . the patterns, practices, and structures, between Spirit, preacher, and Word, that carry the life of interpretation, even when they think nothing of their presence.

Pentecostal homiletics insists that preaching is not a one-sided transference of facts and information about the Christian life but a deeply communal, Spirit-driven event. The Holy Spirit has not been attending only to the preacher's study or only to the crafted sermon; the Spirit has also been actively at work in the gathered congregation, preparing their hearts to receive and interpret the Word. The same Spirit who initiates, shapes, and sanctifies the preacher's engagement with Scripture likewise prepares, opens, and forms the hearts of the people, so that the preached Word becomes a shared event of divine–human interaction rather than a one-directional transaction of sermon content.

As the congregation gathers for worship, it is the preacher's great delight to guide it through its own interpretive journey. A few moves are silently at work here, different from the model's steps, but working silently in tandem with them. They include preparation, invocation, proclamation, confrontation, and alteration. These five moves constitute a Spirit-led progression in which the preacher guides the congregation to understand the Word.

Preparation names the way the people are readied through prayer, song, silence, and expectation, to attend to God's voice rather than merely to a religious speech. Invocation acknowledges that understanding is not self-generated; the preacher and congregation consciously call upon the Spirit to illumine Scripture and to open their hearts. Proclamation is the clear, faithful explanation of the biblical message, where the text is given central place and where Christ is exalted above every other name. Confrontation follows as the Spirit uses the proclaimed Word to expose assumptions, sins, idols, and wounds, pressing the truth into the lived reality of the hearers. Finally, alteration describes the intended outcome: the congregation, having encountered God in the Word, is invited into concrete repentance, new obedience, and transformed patterns of thought and practice—an ongoing, communal reshaping into the image of Christ.

## Preparation

My contention is that the Word bears witness to the preparatory handiwork of the Spirit, who is performing a parallel readiness within the congregation, in the days and hours leading up to the sermon. The narrative of Lydia in Acts 16 invites us to recognize: "The Lord opened her heart to pay attention to what was said by Paul" (Acts 16:14b ESV). This scene reveals that the Spirit's activity does not begin at the moment of response; it's a work that precedes and enables hearts to hear, receive, and respond to the Word.

The duality of the preparation is evident. The apostle Paul, filled with the Spirit, moved in lockstep with the Spirit's leading during his missionary journeys. All of his words and actions were delivered under the inspiration of the Spirit's guidance. The same Spirit leading Paul, divinely imparting the thrust of his message to Lydia, was at work in Lydia's heart, preparing her to receive his inspired message.

From this, we learn how the Spirit prepares a listener to attend not only to the voice of the preacher but also to the divine address conveyed through that voice. Ezekiel's promise of a new heart and a new spirit demonstrates the same dynamic: "And I will give you a new heart, and a new spirit I will put within you. And I will remove the heart of stone from your flesh and give you a heart of flesh" (36:26 ESV). Describing the Spirit's ongoing work of reshaping the people of God into those who walk in God's statutes, every act of faithful hearing in worship is an outflow of the Spirit's work in preparing the hearts of the congregation.

When James exhorts believers to "receive with meekness the implanted word" (Jas 1:21b ESV), he seems to imply that both impartation and reception are themselves Spirit-enabled acts. Congregational interpretation, then, is the Spirit's work of taking the preached Word and inscribing it upon hearts that the Spirit has already been softening, humbling, and attuning.

This has profound implications for Pentecostal preaching. The sermon is not complete when the notes are finished or the outline settled; its completion occurs in the Spirit's ongoing ministry among the hearers. As the Word is proclaimed, the Spirit who prepared the preacher and shaped the sermon now broods over the congregation, preparing hearts, clarifying meaning, piercing and judging thoughts and attitudes, and summoning obedience. In this sense, interpretation is not merely what scholars do after the fact; it is what the Spirit and the congregation do together in real time as the Word is preached.

The first two steps of the model, Inspiration and Preparation, share the voice of congregational preparation expressed in this infrastructure (see chapters 16–17).

## Invocation

In the sacred space of worship, the invocation stands as a threshold moment—a call to worship that beckons the congregation into the presence of the Holy Spirit, setting the stage for the sermon that is to unfold. This moment is not merely a formality but a vital component of congregational hermeneutics, where the body of believers gathers in anticipation of the Spirit's movement and the proclamation of God's Word.

The invocation is not merely a call to attend but is also a call to preparation. As the congregation enters into this posture of worship, a palpable sense of expectation fills the room. The Holy Spirit, in his omniscience and grace, has been preparing the hearts of the congregants for the very message that the preacher has been entrusted to deliver. The preparation is not a coincidence but a testament to the Spirit's active role in believers' lives, guiding them toward this divine moment of proclamation and the Spirit's continued transformative activity.

The introduction of the sermon, as part of the invocation, is a critical juncture, akin to setting the table for a grand feast. The preacher lays the groundwork for the message that is to be received. The introduction is crafted to engage the senses, creating an atmosphere in which the congregation can almost taste the spiritual feast in the air, a foretaste of the richness to come.

In this setting, the preacher stands as steward of divine mysteries, called to present the Word of God with reverence and humility. The congregation participates in the proclamation of the Word, surrendering and opening themselves to the transformative power of the Word, and trusting that the Spirit will guide them into all truth. In this sacred dance of worship and expectation, the invocation serves as a call to gather and hear the proclamation of God's word. The Holy Spirit, who has already been at work preparing the hearts to receive the Word, is the one who calls. The worship encounter belongs to him and is subject to his agenda and timetable. The third step of the model, Introduction, joins forces with the invocation element of the infrastructure (see chapter 18).

## Proclamation

Proclamation serves a vital function within the interpretive act of the congregation. The best way to discuss this is to examine a few passages of Scripture that address it directly. The first is Heb 4:12 (ESV), "For the Word of God is living and active, sharper than any two-edged sword, piercing to the division of soul and of spirit, of joints and of marrow, and discerning the thoughts and intentions of the heart." The writer of Hebrews reveals the eternal, action-oriented capacity of God's Word as a divine entity. God's Word is forever accompanied by the very presence of God. His words are not static, and neither is his presence. And though the inscripturated Word is of ancient composition, the Ancient of Days is very much a contemporary Composer.

In the context of worship, the Word goes forth into the congregation, accomplishing its task of imparting life and actively holding those who've come to hold it. The Word can search the hearts of every person. As the congregation gathers for worship, the Word examines, reveals, convicts, and invites participants to respond to its mission. The two edges of the sword are truth and grace. The Word speaks truth and calls out sinfulness, while simultaneously making grace, forgiveness, and cleansing available for the restoration of the soul. The congregation stands in the company of Isaiah, saying both, "Woe is me," and "Send me." The congregation stands in agreement with the Word because the Word has been rightly interpreted by the Spirit of God who accompanies its proclamation.

The next verse is Isa 55:11 (ESV), "so shall my Word be that goes out from my mouth; it shall not return to me empty, but it shall accomplish that which I purpose, and shall succeed in the thing for which I sent it." These words of Isaiah were intended to provide comfort to the southern kingdom of Judah during its impending Babylonian captivity. They are delivered in the context of God calling his people back to him, with the promise that his declarations of blessing will become a reality for those who listen and return.

Isaiah declares that the spoken promises of blessings will surely come to pass, just as rain from the heavens brings forth seed for farmers and bread for the hungry. So shall God's Word have its same fulfillment of mission. It will not return to him void. This passage demonstrates to the church the mission of God's Word.

To understand that mission, we draw our attention to 2 Tim 3:16–17 (ESV), "All Scripture is breathed out by God and profitable for teaching, for reproof, for correction, and for training in righteousness, that the man of God may be complete, equipped for every good work." When Paul wrote this to Timothy, he introduced a word that had never been used in Greek before: *theopneustos*, meaning God-breathed. Scripture, as breathed out by God, has the same creative power as God's words in the creation narrative in Genesis.

The creative power of God's Word, according to Paul, functions in several key areas designed to prepare us for good works. Paul identifies God's Words as instructive. It teaches us how to be true followers of God. It is valuable for reproof and correction. Reproof is the act of pointing out a mistake or wrongdoing, and correction is the process of guiding someone to correct that mistake and improve their behavior or actions. Both are important aspects of constructive feedback and personal development. Scripture also serves as the foundation of understanding how to live a righteous life.

But these are not the only functions of Scripture. There are other elements of Scripture that bear witness to God's mission. These include

God's Word being a guide (Ps 119:105), comfort (Ps 119:50), direction (Prov 3:5–6), revelation (2 Tim 3:16), salvation (all of Scripture), renewal of the mind (Ps 119:11), and fellowship with God (John 15:7). God revealed to humanity that his Word accomplishes its purposes. This happens because his Word is always accompanied by his presence.

The presence of God with his Word makes interpretation possible for the congregation. As a hermeneutical move, God's Word is comprehended only to the degree that the congregation is apprehended by God in the context of worship. His Word never returns to him void. It accomplishes its purpose. The fourth step of the model, Explanation, shares voice within this proclamation infrastructure (see chapter 19).

## Confrontation

The next move involves the confrontational component of God's Word. This is evident in Jesus' words to John the Baptist's disciples in Matt 11. To set the scene, John the Baptist is in prison, and he's likely anticipating that he is going to lose his life. Perhaps to satisfy his need for comfort and assurance, he sends his disciples to enquire of Jesus, who is, in fact, the Messiah. Jesus instructed his disciples to return and report on all the charismatic phenomena and miracles occurring in his ministry. He also told them this, "And blessed is the one who is not offended by me" (11:6).

Why the inclusion of beatific blessing for those who are not offended? Most likely to illustrate how the gospel message carries the promises of healing, deliverance, restoration to right relationship with God, peace, joy, and everything else that accompanies the good news, to those who are willing to not only stand in its light of truth but who are also able to *surrender to its exposure of sin.* And so goes the offensive nature of the gospel message. It exposes sin, and people get offended when their sin gets exposed.

Jesus also commented on this in his conversation with Nicodemus. A few verses after John 3:16, Jesus highlighted the confrontational nature of the gospel. He said, "And this is the judgment: the light has come into the world, and people loved the darkness rather than the light because their works were evil. For everyone who does wicked things hates the light and does not come to the light, lest his works should be exposed. But whoever does what is true comes to the light, so that it may be clearly seen that his works have been carried out in God" (3:19–21 ESV).

Confrontation is a dimension of preaching that pastors often avoid, usually out of fear of potentially losing crowds. But the proclamation of God's Word is kerygmatic by nature, which means it demands a response. When God's Word is put forth propositionally, as is often the case, it is stripped of its kerygmatic nature, and the congregation can take it or leave it. This is the nature of sermons delivered outside the context of worship. In reality, these kinds of religious public speeches are better delivered in the classroom than in the sanctuary.

Sermons, by nature, are worship-filled proclamations that lift up and exalt the name of Jesus Christ. This is what differentiates preaching from teaching. The confrontational component of preaching reveals its kerygmatic nature. There is no room for shrugs of mediocrity. The proclamation demands a response. The very fact that offense is possible demonstrates that sin has been seen with clarity. God's Word has accomplished its purpose. It has been clearly seen and understood.

The good news is that those who submit to the convicting light of the Word are those who receive the blessings. As Isaiah shows, the act of interpretation is bidirectional. Isaiah must first be interpreted by God before he understands God's truth. In the same way, Isaiah received forgiveness, cleansing, identity, and destiny. Jesus assured John's disciples that all who were willing to be interpreted first (i.e., those who were offended) would ultimately live in the context of understanding the blessing and living fully within it. The fifth, sixth, and seventh steps of the model: Implication, Confrontation, and Invitation, are couched here (see chapters 20–22).

## Alteration

The final congregational interpretive move is alteration. Interpretation is found in the transformative work that takes place at the altar. For many Pentecostal pastors, the altar serves as the primary focal point of the worship service. This makes perfect sense in accordance with who we are as a people of the Spirit and how the flow of the worship service is leading up to this point.

I have had the privilege of worshiping within several mainline Christian traditions. These include Reformed, Baptist, Anglican, Presbyterian, Catholic, and Orthodox. Each tradition has its focal point for corporate gatherings. For the cessationist traditions, the focal point is the rendering of the Word. For Catholics and the Orthodox, it is the partaking of communion. For Pentecostals, it's the altar service. Catholics and Orthodox view communion sacramentally, meaning they understand the consumption of the elements, in the most literal sense, as the eating and drinking of the body and blood of Jesus Christ. Pentecostals view the altar in a similar sacramental fashion, meaning that we believe the very presence of Christ, through his Spirit, is among us, accomplishing the mission of the Word.

The altar becomes the meeting place of personal and intimate connection with Christ. It is the place of emptying and filling. As the interpretive presence of the Word stirs up divine confrontation, the congregation is invited to come to the altar in obedience. I'm not sure if there exists a more beautiful picture than a person caught up in conviction as they seek the Lord at the altar. As Isaiah has shown us, this dynamic is not something to be avoided by preachers. The tears of contrition are the precursors of forgiveness and cleansing.

The altar is also the place of impartation. I have an altar team that serves our church. It is without question the most important ministry of our church. The members of this team exhibit a high level of sensitivity to the Holy Spirit's guidance. Above their ability to flow in any particular gift is their ability to sense the movement of the Spirit. Those who come down to the altar have words of prophecy, wisdom, and knowledge spoken over them. They also experience divine healing, deliverance, and the breaking of strongholds.

The altar is the place of consummation and culmination of that which the Spirit is inviting the congregation to experience. The invitation is both corporate and personal. The altar becomes the location of transformation. From here, the congregation is sent out as agents of transformation in their own world. The final step of the model, Alteration, is the verbal outworking of this part of the infrastructure (see chapter 23).

Don't worry about keeping track of these as the model is being unfolded in the following chapters. These hermeneutical moves primarily focus on the context of congregational interpretation and will continue to operate in the background as the preacher progresses through the model. Their discussion within the model's overall framework is crucial to addressing the question of the appropriateness of teaching as a function of worship.

## FINAL WORDS

As we draw this chapter to a close, we find ourselves at the nexus of several profound truths. We've explored a unique infrastructure within Pentecostal worship, simultaneously at work with the preacher, delivering congregational interpretation, where each feature works silently, out of sight. It's clear that within the Pentecostal tradition, interpreting the Word isn't just an academic exercise confined to a quiet study; it's a dynamic, communal, and deeply spiritual encounter that takes center stage in our worship. This isn't merely about imparting information; it's about inviting an encounter, much like Isaiah's life-altering moment in the throne room. And let's be honest, who wouldn't want a "throne room" experience every Sunday?

The core message here is that authentic Pentecostal preaching is a powerful, Spirit-anointed act that prioritizes transformation over information. It's about recognizing that the sermon isn't a monologue but a catalyst for divine dialogue, prompting a response that resonates deep within the soul. Ultimately, the expository preaching model I'm about to share with you is designed to ensure that the unique hermeneutical and homiletical markers of our movement find their full and vibrant expression. It's a testament to the belief that when the Word is proclaimed in the power of the Spirit, within a worshipful community, something truly miraculous happens. So, as you continue your journey through this textbook, remember that preaching in the Pentecostal tradition isn't just a job; it's an adventure, a divine dance between heaven and earth, and frankly, a whole lot more exciting than a dry lecture.

## REFLECTION QUESTIONS

1. How does understanding biblical interpretation as both a personal and congregational activity shape your view of what actually happens during a worship service, especially when Scripture is proclaimed with an expectation of spiritual encounter and transformation?
2. In what ways does the confrontational nature of the gospel challenge contemporary preaching practices, particularly in settings where avoiding offense is often prioritized over spiritual honesty, clarity, and transformation?

3. How might recognizing the altar as a sacramental space of encounter, impartation, and transformation influence your understanding of the worship service's flow and the preacher's responsibility during moments of response?
4. How does the idea that interpretation is only fully possible when the congregation is apprehended by God during worship affect your expectations for how Scripture should be engaged and understood corporately?
5. How do the five features of interpretive infrastructure—preparation, invocation, proclamation, confrontation, and alteration—invite you to reconsider the depth, complexity, and spiritual intentionality involved in guiding a congregation toward transformative understanding?

# PART FIVE

## Setting the Preparation

# 16

# Step One: Inspiration

I HAVE PREACHED MORE bad sermons than I like to admit. Occasionally, I get reminded of this as I research old sermon notes. Sometimes I shake my head feeling sorry for how my poor congregation had to endure! The only redeeming factor is knowing that the Spirit of God can use all things for those who love him and who are called to him (Rom 8:28). Thankfully, this means that the Spirit can take a poor sermon and make it good. He can literally change the way people hear it. Thank God!

The single factor that distinguishes a good sermon from a bad sermon is the anointing of the Holy Spirit. When the anointing is present, it matters little whether the preacher is educated, knowledgeable about the Bible, sound in doctrine, or familiar with church history, or how little time was spent in preparation. The opposite is also true. The highest level of education offers no guarantee of good preaching. Nor does the preacher's impressive knowledge base or master craftsmanship guarantee success.

Spirit anointing is also a key factor in determining which passage (or topic) to preach on. The quickest way to a bad sermon is a great idea. I know this firsthand from my too-many-to-count bad sermons. Here's a scenario of how this dynamic works: It's Tuesday morning, and the preacher is wondering what they're going to preach on this Sunday. A video appears in their social media feed about caring for the lost, and suddenly they're struck by a great idea. They spend several hours preparing a sermon, filled with research and insights, excellent illustrations, and perfectly positioned, light-hearted humor, only to find that they're struggling through its delivery.

Does this sound familiar? It may have happened to you a few times already. What's missing? Why the struggle? The answer is simple: no anointing. The truth is worth repeating: *the quickest way to a bad sermon is a great idea.* What the preacher may think is inspiration may only be the curse of a great idea. When my son was a little boy, he had a great idea to wash off some dirt from the backyard patio. He grabbed the hose and started spraying water. Over an hour later, the only thing he accomplished was making huge mud puddles all over the backyard.

Kendra and I couldn't help but laugh. Our son followed through on what he thought was a great idea. However, since he had not been "commissioned" to clean the patio, what he thought was a great idea turned into a great mess. We loved on him and praised him for his efforts (and then got to work cleaning it up!). Preachers make a mess when they preach sermons based on uncommissioned great ideas. Some of these may include wanting to educate their congregation, aligning their sermons with a liturgical calendar, highlighting their own personal convictions or passions, reinforcing of doctrinal foundations, occasional preaching (Mother's Day, Father's Day, etc.), or attempting to win over an individual or group of people (the soldiers at the nearby military base, for example), and many more. All of these are appropriate when commissioned by the Holy Spirit, but they are a disaster when they're nothing more than a great idea from the preacher.

## INSPIRATION—THE STARTING PLACE FOR EVERY SERMON

It is at this point in our journey together that the back world of Pentecostal preaching starts to come together. Every sermon begins with inspiration (divine guidance or influence). This is seen clearly in the original composition of Scripture. Pentecostals believe in the verbal inspiration of Scripture (2 Tim 3:16; 1 Thess 2:13; 2 Pet 1:21). This doctrine holds that every word of the Bible is inspired by God. This means that the words themselves, not just the ideas or concepts, were directly influenced or guided by God. We believe the Scriptures are divine in origin, inerrant, wholly inspired (not partly); that human agency (the author's personality, intellect, and writing style) does not override divine authority and truth; and that the Scriptures are authoritative and trustworthy.

Divine inspiration means the sermon passages or topic in focus are guarded under the guidance and influence of the Holy Spirit. The act is less a choosing and more a following. This means three things for the preacher. First, in accordance with the homiletical identity discussed in chapter 7, the process of inspiration carries prophetic weight and authority. For example, the Old Testament prophets spoke only the words given to them under the divine superintendence of the Holy Spirit (the same is true with New Testament prophets and those who function within the prophetic office and gifts today, 1 Pet 1:11–12). As ambassadors of the almighty God, the words of the prophets were the very words of God, and as such, they carried the same authority. Pentecostal preaching carries a similar dynamic.

Secondly, it means the same dynamics of the original composition of Scripture are present within the delivery of the sermon. What we know to be true about Scripture—that it is alive, active, piercing, and always successful in completing its mission (Heb 4:12, Isa 55:11, and 2 Tim 3:16)—is also true in its proclamation during the sermon. The Spirit who inspired the original composition of the Word is the same Spirit who illuminates interpretation (for both preacher and congregation) and who is present in its proclamation. The preacher need not worry about preaching a bad sermon when on a divine mission to proclaim the message God has sacredly entrusted to them.

Thirdly, sermon inspiration will always align with the agenda of the Spirit's work in congregational preparation. As the Spirit inspires the preacher with Sunday's message, he's also preparing the hearts of the congregation to receive that Word. The Holy Spirit inspired the apostle Peter to proclaim the gospel to gentiles in his vision of the animals on the sheet (Acts 10). At the same time, the Holy Spirit was stirring the heart of Cornelius and his family to receive that message.

Similarly, the apostle Paul received a vision of a man in Macedonia entreating him to come and help them. At the same time, God was preparing the heart of an influential woman named Lydia to receive the message. The Bible says, "The Lord opened her heart to pay attention to what was said by Paul" (Acts 16:14 ESV). Even the two men who had a post-resurrection encounter with Jesus on the road to Emmaus experienced this phenomenon. Luke records them saying, "Did not our hearts burn within us while he talked to us on the road, while he opened to us the Scriptures?" (Luke 24:32 ESV).

There are other stories of the Spirit leading, prompting, and orchestrating encounters between preachers and listeners (Philip and the eunuch, Saul/Paul and Ananias). These narratives present a consistent biblical pattern of the Spirit's preparatory work of the congregation to receive the same inspiration given to the preacher. The Spirit arranges divine appointments and enables spiritual receptivity and spiritual illumination, resulting in transformative encounters with the Word.

## REPORTING FOR DUTY

The phrase *reporting for duty* is used primarily in military settings, where soldiers formally present themselves to their superior officers. When it's time to start prepping for Sunday's sermon, preachers report for duty. Inspiration begins here. In this way, we are more like soldiers awaiting our next command than the explorers searching out our next mission in the pulpit.

This is a posture of wisdom for the preacher. However, the posture entails a struggle that many pastors find difficult to endure. This is the struggle of waiting. The inexperienced preacher often has not yet learned the value of patiently waiting upon the Lord. (It's hard to stand at attention!) There's a lot of grace for this struggle, but it's a lesson that is ultimately forced upon those who stand the test of time in the pulpit. Inspiration is a process of waiting on the Lord through patience, trust, and hope in God's timing and guidance. It means reliance upon God's wisdom and strength, seeking his direction and timing rather than relying solely on one's own understanding or efforts, or worse, great ideas.

I have an assistant who exemplifies this principle. The job description for this assistant is simple: Provide support with whatever I need to carry out my professional responsibilities. Their desk is located nearby for quick access. Much like this assistant, pastors are God's assistants in his church. Each day we report for duty and await our assignments. We provide support for whatever the Lord needs to complete the divine mission. We speak only to that which we have been instructed. We deliver messages, not of our own, but scripted by God and faithfully delivered in accordance with his good pleasure, initiative, and sovereign desire.

## STARTING POINT

The starting point for inspiration is prayer. When my wife, Kendra, and I were dating, I had the pleasure of discovering little things that made her happy. This journey of discovery revealed her love of quality time together and holding hands and her dreams about family and children. With this information in hand, how could I lose? I had access to her heart. I knew what made her happy. I knew her deepest desires. Inspiration is easy when we take the time to hear God's heart. Prayer is like the journey of discovering the little things that make the girl we love happy.

I want to say a few things about prayer because of its importance for inspiration. My comments here are not intended to present prayer in a Pollyanna-like approach. Rather, preacher prayer often starts with gut-wrenching honesty. This is more of a heavy-hearted acknowledgment of one's brokenness and one's need for God. I have found this to be true in my own life. Pastors' prayers often begin with apologies . . . hat in hand, "I'm sorry I blew it again," type of apologies. Accompanied by a request for forgiveness, this is the best starting place for prayer because it centers us in the truth that we still exist within the confines of a sinful nature and that we're constantly in need of a Savior.

Pastors experience a constant barrage of enemy attacks. This truth doesn't need to be sugar-coated. Nor does it need to be sensationalized. Those who stand in the crosshairs of the devil usually begin their prayers with apologies. The devil knows the quickest way to keep a pastor from praying is sin. Isaiah's call narrative exemplifies this kind of prayer (Isa 6). His visionary entrance into the throne room of heaven was met immediately with an awareness of his sinful condition, with the following declaration of his undoneness. Prayer often begins with such confessions because the light of truth reveals the truth of our brokenness. But the light of truth does more than just this. It also reveals identity, mission, and inspiration. Isaiah's mission was clear. For the preacher, the same kind of clarity comes into view when we begin our prayers with this level of honesty. It's not until we come to the Lord in truth that we are able to receive from the Lord the inspiration for next Sunday's sermon.

This moment between the preacher and Jesus is characterized by the most inexplicable peace. As the preacher stands in honesty before the Lord, they are both painfully aware of their shortcomings and, at the same time, bathed in the comforting reminder that they belong to him and that he's doing something in them. Peace comes in these moments of bathing. Truth and grace are the vehicles through which the peace that passes understanding is made available to the preacher. This is the reward of worshiping God in truth. It is also the starting point of prayer.

## THE PROPHETIC LOCATIONS OF INSPIRATION

Inspiration is delivered to the preacher in one of five prophetic locations: the prayer closet, the lamp stand, the pastor's office, the newsstand, and the mirror. The apostle Paul commanded believers to pray without ceasing (1 Thess 5:17). For new believers, the idea of praying without ceasing can feel exhausting. Fortunately, the command does not require constant prayer closet prayer; it requires a mindset of bringing all thoughts to God (2 Cor 10:5), an attitude of communion with God, and an ongoing relationship with Christ throughout the day, rather than limiting prayer to specific times or occasions. Such a mindset is needed to receive divine inspiration. From a posture of praying without ceasing, the preacher can receive their commissioned topic or Scripture passage for next Sunday's sermon.

### The Prayer Closet

The preacher's prayer life is all about moves. The first of these moves is praise. This is always the starting place of prayer for the pastor. The peace found in the intersection of truth and grace gives birth to a fountain of praise within the preacher. But this is not the kind of praise you might be thinking of. For me, this posture is not one of shouting and dancing. Rather, it's about a preacher on their knees, hands lifted up, acknowledging how great and awesome our God is. The "I'm sorry" of truth has been transformed into the "thank you" of praise. Confessions of "you are God, you are sovereign, you are almighty, I belong to you," become the grammar of praise.

There are two types of inspiration that flow from this move. The first is catching a fresh glimpse of God's glory that becomes a fresh burden. These moments are life altering for the preacher. Just like Peter, James, and John experienced the full glory of Jesus on the Mount of Transfiguration (Matt 17, Mark 9, Luke 9) that caused a compulsion within them to tell everyone about it (though Jesus told them not to speak of it until after his resurrection, Matt 17:9, Mark 9:9, Luke 9:36), so the preacher in response of beholding the glory of Jesus is compelled to preach.

The second type of inspiration that emerges from this prayer move is that which flows from God's initiatives. This can be literally any topic, person, passage, or situation about which God wants the pastor to preach. This is a common place of divine inspiration. One example occurred as I was finishing a sabbatical and received a divine download of God's plans for my church over the next few years. My prayer of praise became the means by which a divine deposit was made in my spirit regarding the direction for our church moving forward.

The next of these prayer moves focuses directly on the preacher's needs. This move entails a drastic shift in attention. Some might be tempted to think this is a selfish move, but it's not. The preacher cannot give away that which they do not possess. Prayer for self allows the preacher to seek the Lord for deliverance from all that is sinful and to seek the impartation of all that is holy. Pastors need these moments. Jesus understood this. The Lord's Prayer follows the same path as these first two moves (Matt 6). Prayer begins with declarations of praise followed by one's needs for God's provisions.

These moments become moments of inspiration when the pastor can see themselves in truth. Such a perspective allows insight into what God is doing in and through the preacher in that season of their life. God is always at work in the life of his followers. It is not uncommon for preachers to learn that this is a trustworthy source of inspiration for sermon selection. There are several examples of this in the Bible. The prophet Hosea was instructed by the Lord to marry a prostitute, and the marriage became a living parable of God's relationship with unfaithful Israel. Hosea's life circumstances were directly used to deliver a message of God's enduring love and call to repentance (Hos 1–3). The prophet Jonah is another example. His experience of being swallowed by a great fish after fleeing from God's command to preach to Nineveh became a powerful backdrop for his eventual sermon to the Ninevites about repentance and God's mercy (Jonah 1–4).

There are a few other moves of prayer, all of which flow outward from here. The pastor moves into praying for their spouse, then their children, then outward further to extended family and friends, then to the needs of the church, then to their immediate community, and finally out into the world. The pastor sees themself in the epicenter of all God is doing in their life and all the ways they are being used by God in the process. In each of these moves lies the potential for sermon inspiration.

It is in such moments of prayer that the preacher sees reality through the lenses of truth and receives inspiration for next Sunday's sermon.

## The Lamp Stand

"Thy Word is a lamp unto my feet," wrote King David (Ps 119:105 KJV). For the pastor trying to hear from the Lord about next Sunday's sermon topic or passage, the Bible is a prophetic location of divine inspiration. Shining brightly from every page, nothing is off-limits to the preacher. Life lessons abound in the biblical figures of David, Moses, Esther, and others, as reflected in the numerous stories of the Bible. One summer, the Lord directed me to preach through the stories found in the book of Judges. Little did I know that the story of Gideon would stall out my series with five sermons! The stories of the Bible are excellent sources for divine inspiration.

The parables and teachings of Jesus are also an excellent source of divine inspiration. The moral and spiritual lessons found in Jesus' parables are timeless in both their original composition and their contemporary proclamation. The truths of Jesus' teachings speak with the same force today as when he first uttered them from his own mouth. The Sermon on the Mount, for example, addresses a wide range of topics, including prayer, fasting, forgiveness, and the Beatitudes. The Psalms and poetic/wisdom writings of the Old Testament provide a vast array of themes related to worship, praise, lament, and thanksgiving. They can inspire sermons on how to approach God in various life circumstances. They also provide the language for expressing emotion. The poetic books, such as the Psalms, Proverbs, and Song of Solomon, offer insight into human emotions, wisdom, and love.

The prophetic books of the Old Testament contain messages of judgment and salvation. The writings of prophets such as Isaiah, Jeremiah, and Ezekiel contain messages of hope, repentance, and God's judgment that can be applied to contemporary contexts. These books also contain prophecies about the coming Messiah, such as those in Isa 53, which can inspire sermons about Jesus' life and mission. The Epistles of the New Testament provide practical advice on Christian living and commands. The letters of Paul, Peter, James, John, and Jude provide practical advice for living out the Christian faith, dealing with issues in the church, and understanding doctrinal truths (e.g., Romans, 1 Corinthians, Ephesians). The detailed theological discussions in the Epistles can serve as the basis for sermons on grace, salvation, the Holy Spirit, and related topics.

The Bible is a rich source for themes of righteousness and foundations of doctrinal commitments. It is filled with commands, commissions, and instructions for living a successful life of holiness. The love and service depicted in the stories inspire the preacher. The feasts and festivals explore the significance of God's interaction with the Israelites and the experiences they commemorated. Pastors have the luxury of preaching on the unique ways these pointed to God's present interactions with the Israelites in the days they were prescribed, as well as how they ultimately pointed to Jesus. The book of Revelation and other Old Testament apocalyptic books of Daniel and Ezekiel provide inspiration for sermons on end times, focusing on themes of hope, perseverance, and God's ultimate victory.

## The Pastor's Office

Being a pastor carries the distinct privilege of being at the very center of all that is happening at the local church. This privilege is both a blessing and a curse. My heart is filled when I learn of baby announcements and divine healings. At the same time, pastors bear the full-time burden of caring for their flock during crises. The struggles of church members strike the pastor's heart in a way that no other leadership role can understand. The pastor's office, as the epicenter of communication, is a frequent source of inspiration for next Sunday's sermon.

This is a typical everyday occurrence of the pastor, as guidance for how to lead the local church is sought from the Lord. What's happening in the congregation? Are there unresolved conflicts between members? Is there strife between ministry leaders? Has the church experienced an increase in divorces recently? Is the church being blessed with a wave of new members or the arrival of several new babies? As an organism, the church is always in flux. And here's the important part of this dynamic: The people are always talking about it.

Sometimes the pastor needs to address a situation from the pulpit. Several years ago, we were experiencing a strange wave of abuse toward our church campus from our members and regular attenders. It was an unusual phenomenon that none of us (the church staff and I) could identify the source of. Every week, something new was happening: rocks being put in the fountain, posters being ripped off the walls, bathrooms left in disarray, and all kinds of other curious happenings. The temptation I was enduring was to grab the microphone and let everybody have it! I'm glad I didn't succumb. Instead, I prayed, and the Lord gave me a series on respecting holy ground. As the foundation for the series, I drew on the story of Moses and the burning bush (Exod 3), in which God told Moses to remove his sandals because he was standing on holy ground.

A word of caution is warranted for pastors when addressing an issue from the pulpit. As the sanctuary is the location for worship and as the pulpit is the location for the kerygmatic exaltation and proclamation of Jesus Christ, the sanctuary is not the place for discipline and training, nor is the pulpit the location for problem-solving speeches. The challenge for the pastor in these situations is to address the needs of the church within the context of worship. My sermon series on respecting holy ground was framed to glorify God, recognizing that he has created special places for worship and that the physical location of worship is just as important as the worship of Jesus that takes place in our hearts.

## The Newsstand

Karl Barth is famously quoted as instructing pastors to "take your Bible and take your newspaper, and read them both. But interpret newspapers from your Bible."[1] His quote emphasized the importance of viewing and understanding current events and the world around us through the lens of biblical teachings and Christian faith. The quotation encourages pastors to stay informed about current events while remaining deeply rooted in their faith and in their understanding of the Bible. It also suggests that the Bible should serve as the primary framework through which Christians interpret and understand contemporary events, thereby applying biblical principles, values, and teachings to make sense of these issues.

Preachers are invited to be diligently aware of current events garnering the headlines. The principle is simple: If everyone is talking about it, the pastor should preach about it. This principle is especially true when the current event is somewhat controversial. Congregants want to know what their pastor thinks about it. A well-known example of this appears in the Harry Potter series of books from the early 2000s. The Christian community was divided over whether the series should be embraced or avoided by Christian readers. Many pastors recognized this need and preached sermons about the matter.

1. *Time Magazine*, "Barth in Retirement," para. 5.

The newsstand is a site of sermon inspiration because it reflects the pastor's commitment to staying attuned to issues that command the congregation's attention, whether or not they appear in the headlines. There may be events that do not make the headlines, such as the need for a traffic light near the church due to a high frequency of accidents there. This is an occasion when something may be occurring that is affecting the congregation but is not making headlines.

The pastor's posturing when considering the headlines is one of prayer. This satisfies Barth's emphasis on interpreting current events through Scripture. Here are some prayerful approaches to interpreting the headlines through Scripture:

1. Relating Headlines to Biblical Themes. Example: A headline about a natural disaster can be related to themes of God's sovereignty, human suffering, and hope in times of crisis. Biblical Reference: Preach on Ps 46:1 to offer comfort and encouragement.
2. Addressing Moral and Ethical Issues. Example: Headlines about social justice movements can inspire sermons on biblical justice, mercy, and righteousness. Biblical Reference: Use Mic 6:8 to challenge the congregation to seek justice and mercy.
3. Encouraging Compassion and Action. Example: News about humanitarian crises or refugee situations can be used to inspire sermons on compassion and helping those in need. Biblical Reference: Preach on Matt 25:35–40, where Jesus talks about feeding the hungry, welcoming strangers, and clothing the naked, to motivate the congregation to take action.
4. Discussing Modern Challenges. Example: Headlines about technological advancements (like artificial intelligence, bioethics) can be used to discuss how Christians should navigate these challenges. Biblical Reference: Explore themes from Prov 3:5–6 to emphasize trusting God's wisdom in modern dilemmas.
5. Highlighting Stories of Hope and Redemption. Example: Headlines about acts of heroism, kindness, or personal transformation can inspire sermons on God's redemption and the power of grace. Biblical Reference: Use the story of the prodigal son (Luke 15:11–32) to illustrate themes of forgiveness and redemption and relate it to modern narratives of transformation.

6. Responding to Political and Social Turmoil. Example: Headlines about political unrest or social divisions can inspire sermons on peace, reconciliation, and the Christian's role in society. Biblical Reference: Preach on Eph 4:3 to encourage unity and reconciliation.
7. Teaching on Wealth and Stewardship. Example: Economic news or headlines about financial crises can inspire sermons on biblical principles of stewardship, generosity, and trust in God's provision. Biblical Reference: Use 1 Tim 6:17–19 to teach about the proper attitude toward wealth and the importance of generosity and storing up treasures in heaven.
8. Exploring Issues of Identity and Purpose. Example: Headlines about cultural shifts, identity politics, or debates on human dignity can inspire sermons on the biblical view of human identity and purpose. Biblical Reference: Preach on Gen 1:27 to affirm the inherent dignity and worth of every person.
9. Offering Perspective on Fear and Uncertainty. Example: Headlines about global crises, pandemics, or threats can be used to address fear, anxiety, and the assurance of God's presence. Biblical Reference: Use Phil 4:6–7 to offer peace and reassurance.
10. Promoting Peace and Peacemaking. Example: Headlines about conflicts or wars can inspire sermons on peace and the Christian call to be peacemakers. Biblical Reference: Use Matt 5:9 to encourage the congregation to pursue peace and reconciliation.

## Mirror

Most changes in the local church begin with its pastor. God instructed Hosea to marry a prostitute, have children with her, and name the children Jezreel, No Mercy, and Not My People, all intrinsically connected to Israel's sins. He was also instructed to go after the prostitute, redeem her, and restore her. Hosea's prophetic message from the Lord to the Israelites declared their guilt for prostituting themselves out to other nations and the spiritual children being born out of their unfaithfulness.

Hosea had to first live the experience that God was communicating to the nation of Israel. This is a common occurrence for the Spirit-filled preacher, in which changes that take place in the local church often first occur in the preacher. The phenomenon is the most underappreciated gift of God's grace. The preacher's lived experiences become the bedrock of authority and empowerment in their preaching. The preacher has lived it. They've gone through the journey with the Lord.

The preacher's own life, as seen in moments of divine reflection, becomes a rich source of sermon inspiration. Questions asked by the preacher in such contemplation include, "What is God doing in me? How is he inviting me to be changed and grace upon grace, season upon season?" Every lesson learned in the valley of the shadows of death becomes fodder for sermon inspiration. Spirit-filled preachers have learned not to run from trials, tribulations, and persecution, but to learn from them. What God is doing is often a precursor of God's intentions for their church. So the mirror is a very important place for sermon inspiration.

## CONCLUSION

As we've explored the process of receiving inspiration, we've discovered the importance of beginning with the foundational step of prayer. This is not just any prayer, but a series of moves that open us up to the presence and direction of God. Through praise, confession, and intercession, we've learned that moments of divine inspiration are birthed from a posture of humility and openness to God's timing and guidance.

Several key locations for inspiration have been identified: the prayer closet, where personal encounters with God's glory and specific directions for sermons are found; the lamp stand (the Bible), a rich source of biblical stories, teachings, and prophecies; the pastor's office, offering insights into the needs and issues of the congregation; the newsstand, where current events are interpreted through a biblical lens to provide relevant and timely sermon topics; and the mirror, where God's dealings with the pastor often serve as precursors to his plans for the congregation.

As we close this chapter, we're reminded of the importance of viewing our role as preachers akin to soldiers reporting for duty. We stand ready to receive and faithfully deliver the messages entrusted to us by God. This calls for deep humility, patience, and openness to God's timing and guidance. By relying on divine inspiration rather than our own great ideas, we can ensure that our sermons are not only effective but also life-changing for our congregations.

Ultimately, inspiration has much to do with the Holy Spirit's anointing. When the Spirit of God is present, our educational level, knowledge of the Bible, or time spent in preparation matter little. The Holy Spirit can take a poor sermon and make it good, can change the way people hear it, and can use all things for those who love him and are called to him. This is the power of divine inspiration, and it is our privilege to be instruments of this transformative work.

## REFLECTION QUESTIONS

1. How would you describe the difference between a sermon born from a "great idea" you generated yourself and one that comes from being divinely commissioned by the Holy Spirit? Share a personal example if possible.
2. Consider the five prophetic locations of inspiration (prayer closet, lamp stand/Bible, pastor's office, newsstand, mirror). Which of these locations has been the most frequent or fruitful source of sermon ideas in your own experience so far, and why?
3. How can beholding God's glory in the prayer closet produce a compelling burden to preach? Describe how such a moment of awe and praise might naturally lead to a specific sermon topic or passage.
4. When current events or congregational struggles appear in the newsstand or pastor's office, how can a preacher ensure that addressing them from the pulpit remains worship-centered rather than turning into discipline or problem solving?
5. The mirror location suggests that what God is doing in the preacher's own life often foreshadows what he wants to do in the congregation. Reflect on a personal trial, growth area, or season that could become the foundation for a future sermon.

## APPLICATION ACTIVITIES

1. Prayer Closet Praise and Burden Exercise—Set aside 20–30 minutes in a quiet, private place (your literal prayer closet or equivalent). Start with 10 minutes of praise focused only on God's attributes (no requests). Then ask: "Lord, what fresh glimpse of your glory do you want me to proclaim?" Journal what burden or topic rises. If nothing comes, simply thank him for the time and stop.

2. Lamp Stand Bible Scan with Prayer—Choose one book of the Bible (e.g., Psalms, one of the Gospels, or a short Epistle). Read three to five chapters slowly while praying, "Holy Spirit, show me what you want to say right now." Mark any verse, story, or theme that stirs your heart unusually. Write a brief paragraph explaining why it felt "lit up" to you.

3. Pastor's Office Observation Log—Over the next week, intentionally listen in your current ministry context (church service, small group, campus fellowship, family, or workplace). Note three to five situations, needs, joys, or tensions people are experiencing. For each one, pray: "Lord, is this something you want proclaimed from the pulpit?" Journal your impressions without forcing an answer.

4. Newsstand Headline Prayer Assignment—Select two to three major news headlines or trending topics from the past week (print or digital). For each, pray: "Lord, what does your Word say about this?" Write a short response connecting the headline to at least one biblical passage or principle. End by answering: Would I feel commissioned to preach on this? Why or why not?

5. Mirror Location Personal Reflection—Spend 30 minutes in prayer asking: "Lord, what are you currently doing in my own life this season—growth, trial, conviction, or grace?" Write a 300–400 word description of one specific area God is working on in you. Then answer: How might this personal journey become the seed for a future sermon to your congregation?

# 17

# Step Two: Preparation

SERMON PREPARATION FOLLOWS FOUR simple phases: adoration, observation, interrogation, and interpretation. These phases, infused by the Holy Spirit, provide the preacher with a constant supply of growth, transformation, and the elation that comes from divine illumination. For the Pentecostal/Charismatic preacher, the task of homiletical development is not a chore; it's a joy. The following phases are quick in description, manageable, and accessible, and they begin with a few preliminary steps.

## PRELIMINARY STEPS

### Print Out the Passage

This is simple. The task of sermon preparation begins with printing out the passage. The passage is best positioned on a page that leaves ample space for freehand notations. Specifically, the text should be centered on the page, with a minimum of two-inch margins on the left and right sides. In addition, the line spacing should be set to at least double spacing. This layout centers the text in the middle of the page, leaving room in the margins and between the lines for circling, underlining, double-underlining, squares, connecting arrows, and any other scrawls, scratches, or doodle symbols the preacher wants to employ during their time of observation.

Your page should look like this:

## Create a Space of Intimacy

There's an intimacy between the preacher and the Word that deserves special attention and consideration. At the risk of sounding awkward, this intimacy is not to be taken lightly. It's the preacher's responsibility to create a distraction-free, private space. Intimacy does not necessitate an absence of people. It necessitates an absence of *familiar* people. That is, a preacher can enjoy quality, alone time in many places, and even in the most crowded of circumstances, so long as everyone is unfamiliar. Here, the preacher can write without interruption for long periods. Some practical considerations would include access for bio-breaks, internet, a table and chair, and electrical outlets. Some of my favorite places are libraries, hospitals, coffee shops, monasteries (yes, I visit these often), and food courts. Wherever it is, the preacher can create a carefully crafted and guarded space for the holy hushes and divine whispers that emanate from the Spirit during sermon preparation.

## Pray

Pentecostal sermon preparation carries with it the expectation of Holy Spirit inspiration and personal transformation during the preacher's study time. This does not need to be a surprise. There's a distinct difference in sermon preparation for the Pentecostal minister who believes the Word is alive and active. Therefore, study time is not an academic exercise; rather, it is a personal encounter with the very Spirit who inspired the Word's original composition. This time of preparatory prayer brings into focus several key distinctives from Pentecostal homiletical and hermeneutical markers that protect the preacher.

### *Expectation*

Spirit-filled preachers pray with a different kind of expectation than our cessationist brothers and sisters. We don't pray out of duty because the Bible prescribes it (even though that is important). We pray with an expectation that the Holy Spirit will illuminate our understanding of the Word and deliver God's will for the life-altering message for the congregation. Prayer is a nonnegotiable for sermon preparation because it aligns the preacher's mind with the will of God.

### *Spirit-Interpretation*

The expectation of Spirit-interpretation becomes bedrock to this time of prayer. This is one of the more celebrated features of Pentecostal hermeneutics. Sermon preparation is not an intellectual endeavor; it's revelation from the very Spirit who wrote it. I have a leader in my church who recently told me he plays the trumpet. I have known this man for four years. I was surprised at the revelation. I was thrilled at the discovery as he mentioned his interest in joining the worship team. The presence of prayer in sermon construction is like these kinds of moments. The same Spirit who inspired the passage is the same Spirit who illuminates its meaning to the preacher. Sometimes we can have familiarity with a passage for years, only to be surprised by a new and deeper revelation of its meaning.

Sermon preparation is not merely a process of cerebral exegesis or historical-critical analysis of the passage. There are many cessationist preachers who can prepare a sermon without ever praying or acknowledging their need for Spirit illumination. How do I know this? I've done it! And I'm not proud of it. There have been occasions, due primarily to poor time management, when I harvested an old sermon and repackaged it for delivery. Not surprisingly, these sermons are at risk of falling flat. They've felt more like a college lecture than a Spirit-fueled delivery of the Word of God.

There are many atheists who impress with their knowledge of Scripture and can even articulate Christian theological distinctives better than many pastors (online debate videos bear this out). Answer this question: True or false, pastors don't need the Holy Spirit to create a sermon. Answer: True, but not for Pentecostal preachers. The same Spirit who inspired the writer is the same Spirit who illuminates the preacher's understanding. Pentecostal Sermon preparation is characterized by life-altering encounters with the Spirit. By the time the congregation hears the message, it will have been the *second* time that sermon has been preached, with the first being to the preacher.

### *Sanctity of the Word*

Prayers of gratitude for being called into the service of the King are appropriate here. Here, the preacher is reminded, joyfully, of the character of the Word of God. The preacher delights in the task whereby they are honored and privileged to sit with and hold God's Word as a treasure. The nature of Scripture as eternal, authoritative, alive, and active takes the preacher's breath away. The nature of the Word gives cause for exaltation. The Spirit's verbal inspiration of the Word locks in its authority and reliability. The christological focus of the Word, in its entirety, glorifies the name of Jesus on every page.

The creative power of God's Word reminds the preacher that no task is too big for God to complete. The foundational axiom that the Word is the baseline of reality and moral prescription intensifies its power to lead the sermon preparation process. And the fact that the Word is the power of God unto salvation allows the preacher to trust in its efficacy to transform the congregation. The preacher ought not even think about bringing their torch to the pulpit; the One who baptizes with fire is capable enough.

### *Function of the Word*

Next on the prayer checklist is the prayer of gratitude for the Word's formative and transformative nature. Have you ever prayed this way, in which you thank God for the power of his Word? The Word is the forming agent of Christ within the preacher and believers, and it is the beacon of truth that scatters false conceptions about God. Scripture is the prime interpretive agent for reality and for the preacher. Scripture interprets the preacher, the congregation, and the casual reader and creates moments of divine self-reflection. The preacher celebrates the Word's voice in missional preparation. As the church goes out, Scripture equips believers for the church's universal mission, providing teachings, examples, and inspiration. And Scripture is the standard-setter, serving as the benchmark for orthodox beliefs and practices, safeguarding against unorthodox subjectivism.

### *Holy Spirit Submission*

The joy of preaching is discovered afresh every time the preacher sets out to prepare Sunday's sermon. The final preliminary component directing the process of sermon preparation is the glad-hearted commitment to allow the Holy Spirit to guide the preacher through the four moves outlined in the next few paragraphs. As Guide, the Spirit leads the preacher through the preparatory process. He points the way. The Spirit helps the preacher hold in tension the Word's past activity with the Spirit's present activity in the congregation. Since the Spirit leads the preacher, the Spirit is also confronting the preacher. It should not be a surprise that the kerygmatic, confrontational nature of the Word would be so directed to the preacher as they submit to its mission. The Spirit shapes the preacher as the preacher shapes the sermon.

When set within these prayer-fueled guardrails, the task of sermon preparation transforms the chore of preaching into the joy of preaching. Once the preacher has set the guidelines, they are ready to begin the four phases of sermon preparation: adoration, observation, interrogation, and interpretation.

## FIRST PHASE: ADORATION

### Meditation and Multiple Readings

I have learned over the years that the best starting place for preparation is intentional, silent, and contemplative adoration. Think of the groom, caught up in the moment, as he watches his bride-to-be walking down the aisle. Or the father as he watches his daughter charm the room at a social gathering. The Holy Spirit creates within the preacher similar moments of unashamed reverence and awe for the text, causing the preacher to flush with adoration. This is a feature of Pentecostal homiletics to be proudly celebrated. It's an expected activity of the Spirit.

Such adoration is the direct result of the Spirit's work of Christ exaltation. The preacher, to their great delight, gets caught up in this exaltation. These moments are expected during sermon preparation. Jesus declared in advance that his Spirit would cause his followers to testify about him (John 15:26). The Spirit exalts the name of Jesus. These Spirit-infused moments of adoration draw the preacher deeper into the living Word . . . the Word that is alive and active and promises never to return to God void.

The posture is easy to adopt and comes quickly for those willing to make it a regular practice. This move involves sitting with the text and reading it through several times. The process begins slowly, just as if the preacher has unearthed a precious jewel, slowly drinking in every facet as he sits in awe of his discovery. The Word is turned in the light to catch every possible reflection of its brilliance. This move is not about the preacher's comprehension *of* the Word. It is about the preacher's apprehension *by* the Word.

This is a time of multiple readings and meditation. It is also a time marked by deliberate readings with measurable stops at every turn. Regardless of passage length, intentionality is a key component here. *This is not the time for gathering observations, studying, or exegetical analysis.* Any kind of formal or systematic approach to text analysis is unwelcome here. Adoration is not a time for learning, analysis, or exploration. I understand the temptation to go there. It's too easy to see a glint of sparkle and start digging deeper, triggering a full-on study-driven pursuit. At the risk of sounding awkward, adoration is a time of homiletical courtship between preacher and Word. It's an indispensable time of intimacy and aloneness with the Word for the preacher to be captured by the wonderment of its brilliance.

Often, the multiple readings are not actual readings at all, but rather a holy, silent sitting with the text. The move here is to let the text take one's breath away. Being overwhelmed is not out of the question. The preachers who are willing to sacrifice their time are rewarded. The Spirit who inspired the original composition of the Word illuminates it in a whole new light. The move of adoration re-establishes a proper alignment between the preacher and the Word. For pastors too often taken by the busyness of ministry, these moments of adoration are the reset into the posture needed for the task at hand. The ultimate goal of adoration is to be blown away by the beauty of the passage the Lord has called the preacher to preach.

## SECOND PHASE: OBSERVATION

The second phase involves collecting observations. With pencil and paper in hand, the preacher starts jotting down facts, features, anomalies, details, questions, and anything else that comes into view. I still remember my graduate course on inductive Bible study with great fondness. As one called to the office of the teacher (Eph 4:11), this course was a life changer. The preacher in me came alive during this course. It was my formal welcome into the world of biblical interpretation.

For every pastor involved in pulpit ministry, developing the skill of observation is nonnegotiable. The investment through the learning curve is well worth it. My wife, Kendra, is a great example of this kind of venture. I have watched her work a classroom full of first-graders, thinking to myself, "If I were in charge of this classroom, these kids would have me tied and gagged on the floor, taken my wallet, and released the hamster out of its cage." Not her. She works the room like a master. Her time of learning how to manage a classroom (coupled with some amazing natural talent) was a big investment on her part. Several virtues accompany the investment. These include the strengthening of one's will, the fortitude of persistence, the staying power of patience, and intuitive attention to detail. These virtues bless the preacher in all facets of life.

### Rules for Spirit-Filled Observation

#### *Secure the Area*

A few simple rules guide the observation gathering process. The first rule is to secure the area. Think like the detective securing a crime scene. Securing the area prevents contamination of evidence. This means removing unauthorized individuals, establishing a protective perimeter, and ensuring the scene can be processed safely. For the preacher, securing the area is equivalent to creating an intimate space for gathering observations. The same kind of care the preacher applied during the adoration move is now applied here. This can literally be the same place or a different place. I give myself permission to work on my sermon anywhere I want. It's not uncommon for me to put a do-not-disturb sign on my office door, take my dog to a dog park, pause while on hikes, or do many of the other things mentioned earlier. I do not limit myself to staying in one area the whole time, either. By the time my sermon preparation is complete, I will often have been in several different locations. The primary goal of securing the area is to *prevent interruptions*.

### *No Contamination*

Good observations are gathered free from contamination. Carelessness is not allowed. Detectives understand the importance of wearing gloves, for example, when conducting their investigations. This prevents the transfer of fingerprints and DNA, avoids cross-contamination, and maintains the chain of custody. For the preacher, the gloves are the guardrails that protect them from seeing what isn't there or mishandling what is.

For example, a few days ago, a friend of mine heard a loud bang outside his house. Fearing it may have been the discharge of a weapon, he called the police. The next day, he found a bullet casing on the ground. He picked it up and called his friend, who happened to be a police officer, for advice. His friend asked, "So, you picked up the bullet casing and you have it with you?" "Yes," he said. "Well, you're now the prime suspect. Your fingerprints are all over it." They both had a good laugh, and my friend felt embarrassed. He had contaminated the evidence. He allowed something from himself (the oils in his fingertips) to taint the evidence. Had he been more careful, the casing he had gathered might have had value.

The only oil the preacher wants while gathering observations is the Spirit's. A preacher's oil consists of attitudes, beliefs, values, and positions that do not align with Scripture. Oftentimes, these exist without the preacher's awareness. However, seasoned preachers know about this dynamic. The "gloves" worn by the preacher are a simple acknowledgment of their oils. What this looks like, practically, is the preacher's recognition and owning of their own brokenness and sensitivities. If the preacher still struggles with people pleasing, for example, their awareness of it needs to be present during preparation to avoid forcing the message into something pleasing, rather than allowing the Word to speak for itself.

### *No Tampering with Evidence*

As much as the absence of gloves can contaminate evidence, an agenda can inflict far greater harm. Expository preaching does not allow the preacher to carry preconceived agendas into the task of observation-gathering. The preacher doesn't have a say in what the Word has already said. They don't have a say in what the Lord is currently saying to their congregation. When the preacher has an agenda in hand, there is no possible means for the text to speak for itself. Instead, the preacher has forced their agenda onto the text.

The practice of a preacher imposing an agenda on the text is called *eisegesis*. It occurs when a preacher interprets a text by reading their own ideas or biases into it, rather than seeking the original meaning. It's essentially imposing personal interpretations onto the text, leading to subjective understanding rather than objective observation. Here's an example of this dynamic. An American preacher who feels particularly patriotic may be tempted to read a sense of nationalism or patriotism into Gal 5:1 (ESV): "For freedom Christ has set us free; stand firm therefore, and do not submit again to a yoke of slavery." Such a preacher might see the word *freedom* and be tempted to deliver a sermon about American freedom using this passage as their anchor. Such eisegesis would miss the text's original meaning, which clearly points to the Jewish Christians who were experiencing the freedom of being in right relationship with God, without the Old Testament mandate of law-adherence, and to not surrender that precious freedom and return to old-covenant shackles.

No greater violation of trust can occur than when the preacher pretends to speak for God but, in reality, speaks for themself. Old Testament penalties were stiff against false prophets. The New Testament also delivers strong warnings against false teachers. The preacher should avoid, at all costs, manipulating observations to fit a narrative they are trying to force into the text.

### *No Interpretation Allowed*

If you're like me, this rule will require the utmost discipline. Teachers get excited when observations seem to point toward a certain interpretation, only to discover they were wrong. The temptation to move into interpretation is a constant battle for the seasoned observation gatherer. It takes discipline and practice to resist the temptation. The time for interpretation is coming, but we must be patient. For now, the preacher must suspend interpretive temptations until all the evidence has been gathered so that a comprehensive exegetical analysis of the passage can take place in the next move, Interrogation.

A classic example of rushing into interpretation appears in 1 Cor 10:13 (ESV): "No temptation has overtaken you that is not common to man. God is faithful, and he will not let you be tempted beyond your ability, but with the temptation he will also provide the way of escape, that you may be able to endure it." From this passage, many people have heard sermons proclaiming, "God will never give you more than you can handle," which is not true. Closer observation of this passage reveals a different sentiment: that God never allows *temptations* beyond what we can endure. This is a classic example of premature interpretation. When in doubt, a good question to ask is: "Is my observation clearly defensible by the words of the passage, only?" If not, then you may have slipped into interpretation mode, which needs to wait until the fourth phase of the preparation step.

## Securing the Mind

The task of preaching is both a profound privilege and a sacred responsibility. At its core lies the preacher's relationship with Scripture, which demands more than mere analysis or exposition—it requires a posture of humility, faithfulness, and deep reverence for the Word of God. Securing the mind, submitting to Scripture's transformative truth, and approaching it with a sanctified, Spirit-led mindset are mandatory postures when gathering observations. By embracing these principles, preachers can more fully honor the divine message entrusted to them and faithfully guide their congregations in understanding and living out God's Word.

### *Reverence*

The practice of preaching necessitates a deep sense of reverence. This reverence arises from the understanding that the preacher is engaging with the sacred writings, the Holy Spirit–inspired revelation of God. Crucially, this reverence is rooted in humility, a conscious awareness of God's sovereignty and the preacher's role as a humble servant. This approach also demands a suspension of doubt, a commitment to study the Word with careful attention to context, and a pursuit of its truth.

### *Faithful Reading*

In the context of observation-gathering, the rule of faithful reading is a transformative practice involving a profound submission of the preacher's life to the authority and truth of Scripture. This submission means allowing the Bible to shape one's understanding of God, oneself, and the world. As the preacher engages with Scripture, its story begins to weave itself into the fabric of their own life story. The preacher's life becomes a reflection of the biblical narrative, demonstrating the gospel's power in their own transformed heart. This personal immersion in Scripture is crucial because it ensures that preaching flows from a deeply rooted understanding of God's Word and fosters a mindset firmly grounded in its truths. The preacher is not just presenting external data; they are sharing a message that has shaped them from the inside out, making their preaching authentic and impactful.

### *Sanctified Reading*

A sanctified reading of the text involves approaching the Word missionally, faithfully, and christologically, all while anticipating its eschatological fulfillment. This holistic approach encourages the preacher to move beyond mere proof-texting, fostering a posture of openness to hearing the Spirit speak through the Scriptures. By reading in this way, the preacher remains attentive to the broader narrative and the transformative power of the Word, allowing it to shape both the message and the ministry in alignment with God's redemptive purposes.

## LET THE OBSERVATIONS BEGIN

Once the area is secured and the right observational mindset is established, the process of harvesting observations can begin. Keen observations are easier than one thinks. There's a famous story about a post-graduate student, Samuel Scudder, who was placed under the tutelage of the renowned Swiss zoologist and professor, Louis Agassiz. Trying to teach Scudder how to perform scientific analysis, Agassiz gave Scudder a fish and told him to study it and make observations. As the story goes, Scudder reported having seen all that could be seen in ten minutes.

Hours passed before Agassiz returned. After delivering his findings, Scudder was told he had missed the most obvious observation and to keep looking. The remainder of the day was similarly consumed, with Scudder frustratingly trying to observe what had been missed, all while faithfully recording his notes. The next day, the process repeated. The next day after that, the same again. Through the frustrations, however, a new realization began to dawn on Scudder. He was seeing details in this small fish no one had ever seen. Before long, another fish would be added for comparisons. At the end of several months, Scudder's workspace included several other fish as a database of new, never-before-known facts emerged. Ultimately, Scudder made original contributions to knowledge, and his life was changed in the process.[1]

I perform a similar exercise with my hermeneutics students when I open a box of plastic forks and distribute one to each student. I give them one minute to record as many observations as possible about the fork. After completing their findings in the class discussion, they are told to repeat the exercise, but this time without including any observations that had already been shared with the class. A new round of shared findings ensues, and the process is repeated a few more times. Each time I do this, the students are amazed by their ability to see what they had not seen in their introductory observations. Bible teachers are born in moments like this.

## Shapes and Sizes

Observations of the text come in all shapes and sizes. If you have not already done so, take a class in inductive Bible study or purchase one of the excellent texts available in this area. Observations are found in words, phrases, relationships, truths/axioms, principles, and theological or doctrinal statements. Here are some common categories to be taken into consideration:

- Nouns and verbs: These are the most common observation fodder. I usually start here. Nouns identify the *who* or *what* in a text—they denote people, places, things, concepts, or events. Observing nouns helps you determine the subjects, objects, and key ideas in a passage, which is foundational for understanding the central message

1. Taylor, "Agassiz and the Fish."

or theme. Verbs indicate the action or state of being in the text. They show what the key subjects are doing or experiencing or what is happening to them. Focusing on verbs lets you track how events progress, how characters or subjects interact, and how the narrative or argument develops.

- Repetition of words and phrases: Example: The story of David and Bathsheba, spanning fifty-one verses through 2 Sam 11–12, mentions Bathsheba's name only three times in comparison to Uriah, her husband's name, which is mentioned, directly or indirectly, twenty-three times. When the author repeats words and phrases, the preacher should take note.
- Lists/Sequence: Word ordering is important, especially in Greek. Example: Spiritual gifts listed in Rom 12 and 1 Cor 12.
- Quantities: Any amount, specific or symbolic, large or indefinite. Example: Revelation 5:11 depicts an indefinite number of angels: "Then I looked, and I heard around the throne and the living creatures and the elders the voice of many angels, numbering myriads of myriads and thousands of thousands" (ESV).
- Position: Details of location and proximity in space. Example: John 13:23 positions the apostle John leaning back into Jesus' chest during the Last Supper narrative: "One of his disciples, whom Jesus loved, was reclining at the table at Jesus' side" (ESV).
- Cause and effect: Action with a following result. Example: Galatians 6:7 (ESV), "Do not be deceived: God is not mocked, for whatever one sows, that will he also reap."
- Value: Refers to the importance, usefulness, or benefit. Example: Proverbs 16:16 (ESV), "How much better to get wisdom than gold! To get understanding is to be chosen rather than silver."
- Authority: The right to control or direct. Example: Psalm 115:3 (ESV), "Our God is in the heavens; he does all that he pleases."
- Problem/Solution: A method or answer for addressing a challenge. Example: Philippians 4:6 (ESV), "Do not be anxious about anything, but in everything by prayer and supplication with thanksgiving let your requests be made known to God."
- Principle: A fundamental standard for Christian living. Example: Colossians 2:6–7 (ESV), "Therefore, as you received Christ Jesus the

Lord, so walk in him, rooted and built up in him and established in the faith, just as you were taught, abounding in thanksgiving."

- Truths: Biblical truths are absolute realities as revealed by God in Scripture.

Many other categories exist. For a more comprehensive discussion of these categories, several textbooks on inductive Bible study can be consulted.[2]

## Making Your Observations

### *Markings*

Observations employ various kinds of markings according to the preacher's preference. These include underlining, circling, squares or rectangles, arrows, question marks, stars, exclamation points, highlighting, clouds, letters or numbers for lists, and many others. Marginal notations are equally varied. Many include lists, truths, principles, noted theological insights or doctrinal positions, and process notations. The preacher is free to use whatever markups and notations make sense to them.

Over the years, I have fallen into a somewhat repetitive pattern for my markups. Important words get circled. Supportive words or phrases are underlined or double-underlined if super important. Major ideas get clouded (a circle made with a curlicue line). Marginal notations usually end up in groupings. For example, if I see a list emerging, I record it off to the side. Use your imagination. Make it your own.

### *Method to the Madness*

Observations are usually, at best, only somewhat orderly. Cleanliness is not a concern when gathering observations. Your paper will undoubtedly appear a little chaotic to an unskilled observer. I have used the same somewhat chaotic-looking method for over twenty years while preparing thousands of sermons and teachings, and no one has ever asked to see my observation marks. I remember the comical orderliness I tried to maintain in my early years of learning to make observations. My

2. See Bauer and Traina, *Inductive Bible Study*; Fuhr and Köstenberger, *Inductive Bible Study*; and Leigh, *Direct Bible Discovery*, for example.

lines would be almost perfectly straight. My double underlines would be evenly spaced. It didn't take long for me to abandon such silliness. The important part of observations is *gathering them*, not worrying about orderliness. Be free.

Pencils and erasers are preferred over pens and highlighters. I make substantive erasures on every page of observations, without exception. I have discovered that erasing a mistake is a huge time-saver compared to utilizing pens and highlighters. I learned early in my observation journey how costly it is to throw away a page because it was nearly unreadable with all the scratch-outs, x-outs, and ink smudges. Mechanical pencils and block erasers are the preacher's best friends during observations.

Observations begin at the beginning of the passage. The preacher works through the first sentence, carefully poring over words and phrases, looking for anything that catches their attention. Trained observers have a working knowledge that allows them to identify certain kinds of relationships more quickly, such as those listed above. At the beginning, identifying verbs and nouns is always a good place to start. These are low-hanging fruit and usually deliver immediate insights.

Trigger words are usually easy to identify. These include words such as faith, mercy, sin, and forgiveness. These are the kinds of words and phrases that make up the jargon of the Christian faith. These need to be immediately harvested when spotted. If the preacher catches the word *grace*, for example, in Paul's writings, there's a good chance that word will make an appearance in their sermon.

The most treasured of observations are those that identify, or when put together, make up truths and principles. These are particularly easy to observe. First John 4:4 is a great example of this, "Little children, you are from God and have overcome them, for he who is in you is greater than he who is in the world" (ESV). The truth is clear: The Spirit of Christ in a believer is stronger than the spirit of the devil who is in the world. This makes for good preaching. These kinds of truths and principles make up the heart of expository preaching.

Themes are excellent observations. Themes are often discerned rather than directly observed. For example, in Jesus' instructions to the seventy-two being sent out to nearby villages, he gave several commands. Behind all the commands was a theme of trusting in God while serving God's work. A keen observer will pick up on themes and notate them.

Structure is also relatively easy to harvest during observations. For example, I was teaching on Romans not long ago. Romans 6:11 contains a command that was easy to spot: "consider yourselves dead to sin and alive to God in Christ Jesus" (ESV). Immediately following this, the apostle Paul goes on to identify four rapid-fire implications from such obedience in verses 12–14, which include not letting sin reign in the body, not presenting one's body parts to unrighteousness, presenting oneself to God as a living sacrifice, and presenting one's body parts to God as instruments of righteousness. It wasn't glaringly obvious at first, but sure enough, the structure appeared in a very short time. The observation went on to become a solid teaching point.

Questions are also excellent discoveries. I've never had a sermon or teaching where my observations didn't prompt questions. My typical process for handling questions is simple. Whenever an observation creates a question, I circle the word or phrase that triggered it, then I shoot a quick line from it to the margin, connecting to a circled question mark. This serves as a note to myself for later research. The temptation in this moment is to stop observing and chase down the answer to the question. Don't do this. I have fallen for this temptation too many times. Wait for the appropriate time, which comes next during the interrogation phase (exegesis). Answering the questions comes later. For now, let them be safely identified and tucked away for later research. Research is not a part of the observation-gathering process. Your disciplined self-control safeguards your time and the sanctity of the observation gathering.

As the preacher continues to harvest their observations, their paper fills with markups and marginal notes that often spill onto the back as well.

Finally, observations shouldn't be rushed. I allow myself as much time as necessary to complete the task. For shorter passages, the process can take as little as a few hours. For longer ones, several hours will probably be needed. The process should not be rushed. Those who don't dash through are usually handsomely rewarded.

## THIRD PHASE: INTERROGATION

The third major move, interrogation, is of utmost importance. The word *interrogation* here is not the same kind of experience in which a detective questions a suspect in a locked room. But it's not far off! Interrogation refers to the systematic process of asking questions about a text to uncover its meaning and implications. It moves beyond observation to a deeper engagement where the preacher can challenge and probe the text, considering different perspectives and explanations. The move delivers an understanding of the text in its original, intended meaning.

The homiletical word for interrogation is *exegesis*. The word carries a connotation of explanation or interpretation. It's a Greek compound word from *ex*, a Greek preposition meaning *out of* or *from*, and *hegeisthai*, a Greek verb meaning *to lead* or *to guide*. Therefore, exegesis literally means *leading out* or *guiding out*. This third phase of interrogation is the exegetical analysis of the text. Proper exegesis is the foundation of faithful expository preaching and teaching. Clean exegesis is the orthodox handling of God's Word, approved of in 2 Tim 2:15 (ESV): "Do your best to present yourself to God as one approved, a worker who has no need to be ashamed, rightly handling the Word of truth." Bible teachers carry a scripturally founded mandate to be serious, responsible handlers of God's Word. Let's go over a brief rundown of the interrogation process.

## Several Translations

The process of interrogation is a Spirit-led endeavor. It's a mandate driven by several key distinctives. Typically, a good place to start the interrogation process is to examine the passage in other translations. Different translations employ various approaches, ranging from literal word-for-word (formal equivalence) to thought-for-thought (dynamic equivalence) to paraphrase. By comparing different translations, the preacher gains a multifaceted perspective on the passage's original meaning and potential nuances.

Each Bible translation is the product of years of scholarly work and interpretation, reflecting the translators' collective perspectives and expertise. By consulting multiple translations, the preacher is essentially engaging with the text through the lens of different scholars, potentially gaining a broader and more insightful perspective, especially when dealing with doctrinal or complex theological concepts.

Comparing translations isn't a passive exercise; it encourages active engagement with the text, prompting questions, seeking answers, and exploring potential areas of differing interpretation. This active study approach deepens the preacher's connection to the Bible and can lead to further research in the original languages or to consulting resources such as Bible dictionaries and commentaries to understand the reasoning behind translation choices.

A good example of this is Phil 2:6. The ESV reads: "who, though he was in the form of God, did not count equality with God a thing to be grasped." Compare this with the King James Version, "who, being in the form of God, thought it not robbery to be equal with God." The King James Version engages forceful language that portrays Christ's equality with God as something he did not steal, as if to say it wasn't rightfully his for all eternity. The softening language used in the English Standard Version somewhat loses the forceful affirmation of Christ's divinity found in the King James Version.

## Reading in Context

Reading the Bible in context means understanding a passage's words and ideas within the context of its surrounding verses, chapters, and the Bible's overarching story. It also involves considering the text's historical, cultural, and literary background. This helps the preacher to avoid misinterpretations, see the big picture, and gain a deeper understanding. This is the posture of honoring the original audience's assumptions of reception and the original authorial intent.

Understanding context helps uncover the original author's intended communication to their audience. It provides insight into the author's purpose, audience, and the cultural setting. Ignoring context will impose personal ideas onto the text, rather than letting the text speak for itself. For example, reading Jer 29:11 without considering its address to the Israelites in Babylonian exile could lead to misapplying it as a promise of prosperity rather than as a message of hope and restoration for a specific group facing hardship.

Taking verses or phrases out of context can lead to misunderstandings and misapplication of biblical principles. For instance, extracting verses about judging others without the broader context of righteous judgment could lead to the conclusion that all criticism is forbidden. Context helps discern the proper application of Scripture, ensuring the accurate handling of the Word of truth, as Paul encourages in 2 Tim 2:15.

The Bible is not a collection of disconnected verses but a story of God's redemption woven throughout its books and genres. Understanding the historical and literary context of a passage helps us see its contribution to the larger narrative, how it connects with other parts of Scripture, and what it reveals about God's plan and character. Considering the overall context helps appreciate nuances and connections that might be missed when focusing solely on individual verses. For instance, understanding the Old Testament sacrificial system helps appreciate the significance of Jesus as the ultimate sacrifice in the New Testament.

## Genres

The genres of Scripture (discussed in chapter 11) include Law, narrative, wisdom literature, poetry, prophecy, Gospel, Epistle, and apocalyptic. Each genre has its own set of interpretive tools. For example, interpreting Old Testament poetry requires a unique set of tools that can handle and process Hebrew parallelism. This is different from interpreting the New Testament Epistles, which draw on knowledge of ancient letter writing and Paul's distinctive features. Just like a detective would handle a robbery differently from how he would process a missing person's report, so the preacher will make observations differently depending on the genre of their passage.

## Higher Criticisms

The Pentecostal movement has historically struggled to find a working relationship with the academic, method-driven, systemic, or higher-critical approaches to sermon preparation. The struggle is not without warrant. Our movement's hesitation evolved from an overarching mantra: "We have the Holy Spirit, and he's all we need." It's hard to argue against this, and I won't! I believe, along with my Pentecostal forefathers, that the Spirit is more than enough. No doubt about it. However, I also agree that respect for higher criticisms has value and that their voice in the interpretive journey should not be silenced but rather handled with care.

The higher criticisms, for example, provide insights into Scripture that would otherwise not be attainable through surface readings. A good example of this is found in the Bible's apocalyptic literature. Any Pentecostal preacher can read the books of Revelation, Daniel, Ezekiel, and other apocalyptic biblical writings and gain helpful, faith-filled insights, even deliver quality sermons from them.

However, a more solid understanding of this genre depends on insights from higher criticism, where the preacher has access to the legends that explain the symbolic and figurative imagery that would otherwise be unavailable through straightforward readings. The preacher would also have access to many features of the original historical contexts from which the genre derives, as well as to other extrabiblical books that aid interpretation. A good example of this appears in numerical compositions throughout the Bible, particularly in the apocalyptic genre. There is significance to the numbers three, seven, ten, twelve, forty, seventy, one hundred forty-four, one thousand, and others in the Bible. Quick access to the fruit of higher criticisms provides the meaning behind these numbers as they are used both literally and figuratively throughout the Bible.

The higher criticisms, as discussed in chapter 8, include historical, redaction, narrative, textual, literary, source, form, and reader-responsive. Pentecostal preachers do well when they have a basic understanding of these criticisms, know their structure and contours, and can use them when appropriate.

As scientific approaches to studying the holy writings of Christianity deliver scientifically based interpretations, and even though the results produced by such efforts are not dependent upon the safeguarding of Spirit illumination, *it doesn't mean they're not true*. And it certainly does not mean that they're not useful. What it *does* mean is that their presence is welcome in the interpretive journey, provided they are taken at face value. Two of the more friendly higher criticisms that often find expression in the interrogation process and are relatively standard in the course of biblically faithful interrogation are the historical and literary analyses, which will be discussed here in general terms.

## Historical Analysis

### *Five Ws*

Interrogation begins with the full-press examination of the who, what, when, where, and how/why questions, otherwise known as the historical-critical analysis. Establishing the author and the date is first priority. If the author of the text is not immediately observable in the selected passages, then research needs to be conducted to determine this. This should take no more than a few moments with the various tools available for the process. These tools include Bible dictionaries, Greek and Hebrew dictionaries, commentaries, lexicons, journal articles, monographs, concordances, textbooks, and other online resources. The date of composition is next. The date of composition is important because it helps the preacher understand the time in which the passages take place. The historical context includes religious, social, political, and other cultural factors that may have shaped the author's intentions or the audience's needs.

### *Purpose*

The next question addresses the purpose of the book in which the text appears. Again, this step should take very little time if the preacher has access to the right tools. If you're a purist and if you have the time, conducting your own research is the preferred approach here. But if you're like most busy pastors, commentaries provide a good source for discovering this kind of information. It's good to reference several commentaries to ensure they all follow a similar trajectory. Of course, the best kind of commentaries are those authored by Pentecostal scholars.

### *Outline Position*

Once the author's purpose for writing the book is identified, the next step is to position the text within the book's overall flow and structure. Book outlines are also readily available in commentaries and other online resources.[3] The outline provides deeper insight into the author's mind and the Spirit's inspiration. This is a crucial component of exegesis.

The text needs to be understood only in the context of its connection to the verses immediately preceding and following it, along with the remaining content before and after the passages, and within the chapter, section, and overall outline of the book. For example, in Rom 8:28, the apostle Paul says, "And we know that for those who love God all things work together for good, for those who are called according to his purpose" (ESV). Before the preacher rushes off to write a sermon about God's providential goodness, they should consider how this passage fits into the book's overall flow to ensure the sermon is properly aligned.

In this case, the preacher would discover that Rom 8:28 is part of Paul's comments about the Spirit-led life, where Paul was writing about the contrast of living a life in the flesh versus living a life in the Spirit.

3. Have a preference for commentaries written by established Spirit-filled scholars, published by reputable publishers. Commentaries by non–Spirit-filled scholars are widely available and are useful. The caution with these is to know that the content of these commentaries has been derived through scientific interpretive methodologies (see ch. 8) that do not include, or allow for, any role of the Holy Spirit in the interpretive journey.

The preacher would also discover that this passage serves as a segue into Paul's discussion of God's calling of the nation of Israel. And, finally, they would discover that God's providential ability to use all things for good is part of the theological goodness that comes with the gospel message. The discovery of these attributes changes the trajectory of the sermon preparation from uninformed to enlightened.

The historical analysis also identifies the passage's intended audience. With the identification comes also the circumstances in which the audience found themselves. The book of James, for example, identifies its audience as "the twelve tribes in the dispersion." The preacher immediately recognizes that the audience is suffering persecution and will likely need encouragement.

### *Sitz im Leben*

*Sitz im Leben*, a German term meaning "setting in life," is a crucial concept for understanding the social, political, religious, and economic conditions that shaped a text's original audience and, consequently, the interpretation of the passage itself. It underscores the fundamental truth that the Bible was not composed in an isolated intellectual void. Rather, every facet of the biblical narrative was meticulously crafted with a specific purpose in mind and directed toward a particular audience, whose unique circumstances heavily influenced the text's meaning and reception. Therefore, a thorough understanding of the socio-historical context in which each segment of the Bible originated is essential for nuanced, accurate exegesis, allowing readers to bridge the gap between ancient contexts and contemporary understanding.

## Literary Analysis

The next step in the interrogation process is to analyze the text using a literary grid. This method focuses on the text's literary features and how they contribute to its overall meaning. The starting point for this step is identifying the text's genre. One crucial aspect of studying any text, particularly in fields like biblical exegesis, involves crafting a passage outline. The primary objective of such an outline is to diligently identify the inherent organizational structure woven into the text by the author. This process involves recognizing the natural divisions and transitions the author intentionally employed to guide the reader through the material, ultimately revealing how the text's ideas are systematically presented and interconnected.

Furthermore, this detailed structural analysis goes beyond simply mapping the flow of ideas; it encourages the interpreter to discern and appreciate any literary devices the author may have intentionally incorporated. By recognizing these rhetorical strategies, a preacher or interpreter can gain a richer understanding of how the author sought to convey nuanced meaning, emphasize points, or evoke specific emotional responses in their original audience. Some common examples of these literary devices are listed below. Understanding these devices is vital to moving beyond a superficial reading and truly grasping the depth and intention behind the sacred texts.

- Metaphor and Simile: Figurative language that compares one thing to another.
- Imagery: Use of vivid language to create mental pictures.
- Parallelism: Two or more lines that correspond in meaning or structure.
- Chiasm: A literary structure where elements are arranged in an ABBA pattern.
- Inclusio: Using the same or similar words or phrases at the beginning and end of a section.
- Hyperbole: Exaggeration used for emphasis.
- Irony: Use of words to convey a meaning that is the opposite of its literal meaning.
- Personification: Giving human qualities to non-human things.
- Literary Markers: Words or phrases used by the author to convey meaning. For example, Mark's Gospel uses the word *immediately* to signal the end of one scene and the beginning of the next.

A literary analysis also includes an examination of the narrative arc within the overall context of the passage. The goal of this portion is to determine if the passage has an exposition, rising action, climax, falling action, or resolution. The preacher seeks to determine how the narrative builds suspense or conveys a message.

Character development and setting analysis are key questions to ask here. Who are the main characters in the passage? What are their traits, motivations, and relationships? How do they change or develop over the course of the passage? Where and when does the passage take place? How does the setting contribute to the meaning or mood of the passage?

The literary analysis ends with an examination of themes. What are the central ideas or themes of the passage? What message is the author trying to convey? All of this information is recorded in preparation for the last step of the sermon preparation. The ultimate goal of the interrogation step is to conduct a thorough critical analysis of the components of the text.

## FOURTH PHASE: INTERPRETATION

Much analysis has been completed by the time we arrive at the fourth and final phase. If the preacher has been disciplined, the temptation to move into interpretation has been successfully allayed. As we approach this final phase, the interpretive waiting has ended, and the preacher can now turn to the most important task of asking, "What does all this mean?" At this point, all the reference materials have been returned to their shelves. Scientific methodologies (if employed) have been tucked away. The bright lights of interrogation have been replaced with the soft lights of contemplation and the seeking of meaning. And as the preacher is left with their notes, the Spirit and the rich heritage of their faith community now join the conversation.

It's time to put it all together. As discussed in chapters 9–12, the Pentecostal model of biblical interpretation involves three distinct and interrelated components: Word (now including your study notes on the Word), Spirit, and Community. Thus far in the interpretive journey, the preacher has handled the Word in a manner that is faithful to Pentecostal distinctives. Additionally, the Holy Spirit has already been at work in the journey as a guide, protector, exalter of Christ, and faithful comforter and companion in understanding. However, there is still work to be done with the preacher's community, and the work of the Spirit is not yet complete.

## Spirit

### *Spirit as Bridge Builder*

As a bridge builder, the Holy Spirit connects the preacher's horizon to the text's horizon. The span between is created by differences in culture, language, location, time, customs, practices, etc. The Spirit is he who resolves the gap yet keeps both horizons fully intact. The work of the Spirit here is completed in the preacher's quiet moments of sanctified reflection and prayer.

The question here is, "Can the preacher exercise enough patience to hear the Spirit's revelation?" This is key. As I write this paragraph, I am currently sitting in a monastery deep in the Arizona deserts. I've come here on a writing retreat. The nuns are delightful and accommodating. The priests are always eager to engage in theological discussions. An interesting connection between this question and the Catholic worship experience caught my attention. As I find the awe and reverence of the Catholic Mass to be spiritually therapeutic, and I say this with the deepest amount of respect, I am particularly moved by the gaps of silence that often occur. The intimacy of these moments is powerful. Though I'm here not as a member of the Catholic Church, I'm also not here as a simple spectator. I'm here to worship, which I can easily do in such settings. And though these moments of silence last only a minute or two, I'm always amazed at where the Spirit leads me as I sit in quiet reflection.

How long can the preacher sit in quiet reflection with the Spirit and with the text? These are crucial moments in biblical interpretation. In the stillness of the silence and in the darkness of unknowing, the light of universal truths, axioms, and principles begins to break through. And there it is, just like that, the Spirit delivers insights into a passage they may have read a hundred times previously yet never seen before this moment. Practically speaking, this is where the sermon outline begins to take shape.

These are the moments that best define the joy of preaching. And if the illumination were not enough, the preacher receives the added joy of being personally apprehended in the process. This light of revelation brings about two powerful, life-changing, and transformative events. The first is the acknowledgment of one's unworthiness to be on the receiving end of such a moment, which is met with immediate gratitude. The second is the divine purpose in its delivery. Revelation is always given in the context of purpose. For the preacher, one moment of sanctified reflection becomes the enlightenment to their own identity, purpose, and destiny.

Recently, I delivered a sermon in which I proclaimed that humanity was created in the image of God. As I sat in reflection with this truth, it occurred to me how many years I had wasted chasing a false image of myself. These years were both before *and after* I was saved. Even as a minister, I wasted several years trying to be a preacher God had never intended me to be. I was crushed under the conviction I was experiencing in the moment. I wept as I cried out to God to forgive my errant ways. And yet at the same time, I was somehow inexplicably taken by a cleansing kind of hope as a vision of myself—of who God *intended* me to be—came into view.

As clearly as I saw my fraudulent ways, I was also filled with the hope of the truth of who God created me to be. Truth and grace always go hand in hand like this. This is what the writer of Hebrews meant when he said Scripture (revelation) was a double-edged sword. In the same thrust of the sword comes the truth of sin and the grace of redemption. Moments like this are part and parcel of the interpretive journey of sermon preparation. And for the Spirit-filled preacher, they deliver a constant supply of grace and truth. The work of the Spirit gives us cause for rejoicing.

### *Spirit as Shaper*

As the shaper of the preacher's understanding, the Holy Spirit causes the preacher to see Scripture in the light of orthodoxy. During this time of sacred reflection, the Holy Spirit opens the mind of the preacher to understand Scripture, much as Christ did for his disciples after the resurrection (Luke 24:45). The Spirit brings conviction and clarity, helping the preacher discern how the biblical message speaks to the present needs and situations of the congregation. This includes the boldness to address sin, the wisdom to offer hope, and the compassion to encourage faith and repentance. The task in all of this is for the preacher to create, as an indispensable component of preparation, the dedicated place and time for prayerful reflection.

## Community

### *The Preacher's Community of Believers*

Where does the preacher's Spirit-filled community come into play in the act of interpretation? The answer to this begins with a reminder to the preacher of their identification within the Pentecostal community, at large. The Pentecostal preacher is part of a tradition that identifies itself with the primitive church in Acts. It's a full-gospel community that believes in the continued ministry of the Holy Spirit, including Spirit baptism, supernatural manifestations, and charismatic phenomena, which are regular parts of the worship gathering. It is a community with a strong sense of eschatological fervency.

The Pentecostal community is revivalistic, restorationist, and evangelical. Infused with charismatic expectation, scriptural and spiritual supernaturalism is the norm. It is here, in the midst of this community, that the Pentecostal preacher finds themselves *anchored and mutually conditioned*. When the Pentecostal preacher knows this, believes it to be true, and identifies themselves within these dynamics, the question arises, "What kind of interpretation of Scripture would one *expect* to see come out of a preacher immersed within this movement?" As the preacher settles into the interpretive flow of the Spirit, the process is energized by such reminders of community identity.

Here, the preacher's community sets the tone and the parameters of interpretation. Take, for example, the sermons and speeches of Dr. Martin Luther King Jr. One need not be surprised to learn that the faith community from which he hailed was fiercely dedicated to social justice and racial equality. Naturally, his sermons and speeches would reflect the kind of biblical interpretation one would expect from his community.

The Pentecostal preacher has been shaped by their Pentecostal community. They have been formed by the Spirit through charisms, healings, miracles, and testimonies. If the preacher were being true to who they were, wouldn't they expect that their interpretation would be coming from a posture of such authenticity? If the preacher is Pentecostal, the sermon will be shaped by Pentecostal values.

The preacher is also invited to pray in tongues over their notes during this time of prayerful reflection. Praying in tongues is a near-guarantee that their interpretation is on the right track. The apostle Paul said it like this in Romans, "Likewise the Spirit helps us in our weakness. For we do not know what to pray for as we ought, but the Spirit himself intercedes for us with groanings too deep for words. And he who searches hearts knows what is the mind of the Spirit, because the Spirit intercedes for the saints according to the will of God" (8:26–27 ESV). The Spirit knows the will of God for the sermon. Praying in tongues allows the preacher's mind to be open to the guiding of the Spirit.

Praying in tongues ensures alignment with God's will while also providing personal edification for the preacher, strengthening their inner spirit and deepening their intimacy with God. As 1 Cor 14:4 states, "The one who speaks in a tongue builds up himself" (ESV). This spiritual strengthening is crucial for a preacher facing ministry demands, enabling them to minister effectively and with greater spiritual authority.

### *The Acts Community of Believers*

Another insightful interpretive question is, "How would the church in Acts respond to the sermon developing from these notes?"

I am particularly fond of this question as it emphasizes the practical implication of biblical principles to contemporary church contexts, ensuring the message resonates with the spirit and actions of the early church described in Scripture. The early Christians were known for their boldness, unity, love, and unwavering faith amid persecution. Therefore, considering their likely reactions can guide the preacher toward crafting a sermon that is both doctrinally sound and deeply relevant to the spiritual lives of believers.

It prompts reflection on whether the developing sermon would inspire the same passion for spreading the gospel, foster a vibrant sense of community and fellowship, and encourage resilience in the face of adversity, as seen in the lives of the apostles and early believers. Ultimately, this line of questioning helps the preacher to move beyond theoretical interpretations and engage with the living Spirit of the Word, ensuring the sermon is not merely informative but transformative, as it addresses the needs and challenges of a Spirit-led congregation.

## FINAL TASK: ASSEMBLING THE NOTES

By now, the preacher has spent much time in the Word and in the Spirit and has come to fully appreciate their Pentecostal communal identity.

They've blushed as they've sat in adoration of the text. They've carefully made their observations. They've interrogated the text. They've entered into a prayerful, Spirit-dependent time of asking, "What does this all mean?" and "Lord, what is your message to the church through this?" A divine sense of where the sermon is going is fully in bloom. And now it's time to put everything together.

## Assess the Observations

The first step in putting it all together is to assess the previously harvested observations. These will be extensive, representing a wealth of findings during the gathering process. The task requires a focused session of deliberate contemplation as you examine the printout of recorded insights, scribbles, squares, circles, interconnecting lines and arrows, and marginal notes. Many of the observations, though insightful and helpful, will not make it into the sermon notes. Instead, because of the investment made during the observation gathering process, these details become part of the preacher's knowledge base. They stay there forever. This is the fruit of interrogation. This base continues to grow throughout the preacher's life. Before long, it becomes a foundation on which the preacher can confidently stand, delivering a constant supply of biblical, doctrinal, and theological knowledge at their disposal.

As we have already observed in chapters 3 and 13, the content of the expository sermon is wholly dependent upon the text. Unlike topical sermons, where the main point and supporting points of the sermon are determined by the preacher in advance, the expository sermon is at the mercy of only that which exists in the selected passage. The content of the sermon, therefore, is unknown until the preacher begins preparing. The assessment of the observations reveals the sermon's teaching points. They're already there in the preacher's observation notes.

## Identify the Primary Features

Typically, by now, many of the more salient observations have already begun to rise off the page. These rising primary features are the fruit of discernment. This is the Holy Spirit at work, guiding and revealing to the preacher the teaching points, the direction, and the overall flow of the sermon. The same Spirit who inspired the writer is now illuminating the preacher, all occurring in alignment with the Spirit's agenda for the congregation. What was originally entrusted to the ancient composer is now finding an entrusted refrain with the Spirit-filled preacher.

By the time the congregation hears this sermon, it will be the *second* time the sermon has been preached. The first time the sermon is preached is here and now. The Holy Spirit is preaching now. The preacher, who in this moment is the congregation, experiences their own apprehension by the Word. There's no getting around this dynamic. The words of Heb 4:12 come to life, that the Word is alive and active. The words of Isa 55:11 follow behind, that the Word of God never returns to him void. The light of truth, now being personally directed to the preacher by the Holy Spirit, often penetrates the preacher, bringing both the crushing weight of conviction and the brilliance of divine impartation. I often find myself in a posture of tearful repentance while preparing sermons, and I'm thankful for the power of the Word.

## Now It's Time to Create Your Outline

The primary features of the sermon need to be identified and ordered. This is typically a simple positioning that places the primary features in the order in which they will appear in the sermon. Usually, the ordering follows the flow of the passage, but this is not always the case. Some occasions warrant an unconventional ordering that starts with a primary feature that appeared later in the passage due to its systematic building throughout the passage or because the preacher discerns the appropriateness of the order. One time this happened to me was when I was giving a sermon on 1 John 5:6–12. Even though verse 6, the first verse in the passage, contained a phrase about the water and blood, I ultimately preached on this phrase as the *second* primary feature of the sermon, after I had preached on the importance of testimony first. I moved that feature of the sermon to the second position because the word *testimony* appeared eight times throughout the passage, in all its variances, so I felt it should be the leading feature of the sermon.

## Primacy of Truths and Principles as Sermon Points

### *Truths*

At the heart of every Pentecostal expository sermon lies the crucial focus of truths and principles. *These make up the main points of the sermon.* Truths and principles emerge during the observation, interrogation, and interpretation phases of the Preparation step. They constitute the foundational realities, guiding doctrines, and self-evident statements that describe and prescribe the Christian faith and practice. Each has a distinct nuance, but both serve as anchors for theological understanding and ethical living. Together, truths and principles provide the dynamic framework for the sermon outline. Truths establish theological foundations, while principles provide practical pathways for Christian living.

Biblical truths are absolute realities as revealed by God in Scripture. For example, "Jesus is the only name under heaven by which one can be saved" (taken from Acts 4:12) is an absolute truth. "All have sinned and fallen short of the glory of God" (taken from Rom 3:23) is another example. Biblical truths stand as the revealed will, character, and works of God. Truth is unchanging and coherent and emanates from the nature and purposes of God. Both Old and New Testaments ground truth in the character of God, the Son, and the Holy Spirit, as well as in the Word of God, which is described as *truth* (see 2 Tim 3:16–17; John 17:17).

Truths are characterized by the verb *to be*. This means they are expressed in the form of declarative statements about God, Jesus, Spirit, kingdom, the demonic realm, or what it means to be human. They are rooted in reality and in terms of being: "Jesus *is* the only name" (Acts 4:12), "All *are* sinners" (Rom 3:23), "God *is* love" (1 John 4:8), and "The Lord *is* my Shepherd" (Ps 23; my emphases). These truths are absolute, objective, and unchanging statements of what is, rather than merely what should be or might be.

Truths are descriptive, reflecting God's attributes—his unchangeable character and perfect righteousness—and serve as foundational ontological truths rather than merely moral ideals or laws. They are the self-expression of God and are a product of the very nature and being of God. The use of *to be* asserts reality rather than just commands or conditional promises. The focus on being ensures that biblical truths speak to what objectively is, not what is subjectively preferred or constructed.

Truths function as a formative dynamic in the economy of sanctification. They invite the hearer to position themselves under their illuminative light and to see themselves as who they truly are. The experience is never void of the double-edged nature of God's Word that pierces, cuts, divides, and judges (Heb 4:12). God's Word never returns to God unsuccessful (Isa 55:11). Such moments, when not rejected by the hearer, deliver *trans*formative grace that radically reorients the hearer and forms within them the Christian passions, virtues, and values.

Truths constitute the spiritual vertebrae of Christian posture. The practical outworkings of biblical truths into the lives of Christ followers are born in moments of sermonic implication (more on this in chapter 20). The preacher, upon finishing their teaching about a particular truth, circles back to the truth in hand and asks the question, "What are the implications of this truth in our lives?" These usually take the form of conditional clauses. For example, "If it's true that Jesus is the only name under heaven by which one can be saved, then what does that mean about how we're still trying to earn God's favor by doing good works?" In Pentecostal sermons, truths are applied ontologically, not vocationally.

Biblical truths are identified by several distinct criteria that ensure their validity, reliability, and relevance for faith and life. These truths go beyond subjective interpretation and are rooted in the character and revelation of God. Criteria for identifying biblical truths include:

- Testamental Continuity: Biblical truths must align with the clear teachings of Scripture, across both Testaments.
- Rooted in Divine Revelation: All truths emanate from God's special divine revelation contained in the Word. This is affirmed by passages like "All Scripture is God-breathed and is useful for instruction" (taken from 2 Tim 3:16). The truthfulness of the Bible is tied to its divine inspiration, inerrancy, and authority.
- Exaltation of Jesus Christ: Biblical truths direct attention and glory to God, especially as revealed through Jesus Christ (John 14:6).
- Timelessness: Though some passages are culturally and historically anchored to social phenomena ("Greet one another with a holy kiss," Rom 16:16 ESV), biblical truths speak to eternal realities and remain relevant across all generations.
- Spirit Confirmation: Genuine biblical truth is confirmed in the lives of believers by the convicting and illuminating work of the Holy Spirit (John 16:13).

Ask: "Does this reveal a distinct feature or characteristic about God, Christ, the Holy Spirit, the Word, the kingdom of God, the demonic realm, or what it means to be human?" If yes, and if it meets the criteria above, then it is a truth.

### *Examples of Truths*

Note the following examples of truths. Also, note how cleanly and simply they come into view:

Psalm 51:10 (ESV): "Create in me a clean heart, O God, and renew a right spirit within me."

- Truth: God is in the business of creating new hearts.
- Truth: God is the one who creates cleanliness out of dirtiness.
- Truth: God is a spirit-renewer.

First Samuel 2:2 (ESV): "There is none holy like the Lord: for there is none besides you; there is no rock like our God."

- Truth: God alone is holy.
- Truth: God has no equals or rivals.
- Truth: God is a solid rock of strength.

Ephesians 4:17 (ESV): "Now this I say and testify in the Lord, that you must no longer walk as the Gentiles do, in the futility of their minds."

- Truth: Christ is truth ("testify in the Lord").
- Truth: The walk of God is opposite to the walk of the world.
- Truth: The walk of Christ is a walk of sound thinking.

I pray the simplicity of truth-harvesting does not escape you. It really is just that simple to identify the main points of a sermon. Assembling the proper wording may present challenges, but that's just a matter of practice. For as long as the preacher has the truth in hand, the Spirit will assist in observing, preparing, and structuring it.

### *Principles*

Principles carry a different function in the Word. Biblical principles are fundamental doctrines or rules derived from the teachings and commandments of Scripture. These principles guide believers' beliefs and conduct in their daily lives. They are often distilled from specific passages or stories and provide frameworks for moral decisions, spiritual growth, and interpretation of life's circumstances. Classic examples include the Ten Commandments (Exod 20:1–17) and Jesus' summing up of the law into two principles: "Love the Lord your God," and "Love your neighbor as yourself."

Principles shape values, decisions, and actions over time. This means that principles gradually influence, and often transform, the way individuals think, what they prioritize, and how they behave in daily life. They serve as foundational convictions and standards, becoming personalized and internalized within the believer's value system. They define what is important, admirable, or right. These values shape real-world choices. For example, the principle of loving your neighbor as yourself forms the value, and then the outworking actions, of compassion, generosity, care, consideration, etc., of others.

As principles take root into habits, they find expression within daily activities, attitudes, and behaviors. They are like seeds that, once sown in the heart, over time, yield a harvest of values, wise decisions, and righteous actions. This results in life patterns that reflect godly character, align with Scripture, and bear fruit in all facets of personal, family, community, and professional life. The transformative work of principles is ongoing and dynamic. The more biblical principles are absorbed, the more they guide Christian behavior.

Like truths, principles transcend historically and culturally specific groundings. Their value is universal and timeless, providing consistent functionality across all situations. Their voice is internal and motivational, rather than external and regulatory. For example, integrity, as a principle of Christian living, guides behavior from the inside rather than requiring codification or external enforcement. In this way, principles act as bridges between absolute realities and practical conduct.

Principles are prescriptive in nature. That is, they carry an expectation of responsive obedience. It also means that, for every preached principle, there is a corresponding command. The grammar of principles is indicative. For example, "Jesus goes to the places nobody wants to go" (from the story of the Samaritan woman at the well, John 4). However, the implication is never divorced from unspoken imperatives. The preacher seizes this dynamic by asking the congregation, "If it's true that Jesus goes to the places nobody wants to go, then what does that mean about the places in your heart where you're not allowing him to enter?" The prescription for the congregation is to allow Jesus into the dark, unwanted places of their hearts.

Principles need to be harvested. They are found in the fields of biblical imperatives and underlying narrative details. Every biblical command is the product of a biblical principle. This means every time the preacher spots a command in the Bible, there exists an underlying principle. For example, Jesus' command to forgive others (Lord's Prayer, Matt 6) is fueled by the principle that Christians must forgive when wronged. Paul's admonishment to pray without ceasing (1 Thess 5:17) is grounded by the principle "Prayer is a constant posture of every believer."

Other principles are implied and tucked away in stories, parables, teachings, and other parts of Scripture. These can be seen in scenes such as Moses' sandal removal in the burning bush story of Exod 3. Though not explicitly stated, the implied principle is "Sacred meeting spaces with God are to be treated with reverence and respect." Or, when Mordecai tells Esther, "And who knows whether you have not come to the kingdom for such a time as this?" (Esth 4:14 ESV), the implied principle is "One's position in life fulfills a purpose in God's plan."

The prescriptive nature of principles constitutes a performative dynamic within the economy of Christian good deeds. They fund the believer's moral currency, which in turn is expended in Christian behavior, beliefs, and attitudes. The presence of biblical principles is measured by Christian performance. James addressed this in his epistle when he stated, "So also faith by itself, if it does not have works, is dead" (2:17 ESV). The works about which James speaks are the practical outworkings of the principles that have populated the Christian heart.

Where biblical truths are the spiritual vertebrae of Christian posture, biblical principles serve as the spiritual traffic control system for Christian pattern. Principles guide the believer through the complexities of life by providing tested, reliable pathways that reflect God's intentions. They provide practical guidance for Christian daily living, functioning as spiritual traffic lights that dictate the direction and flow of a believer's life. Obediently responding to the directives of biblical principles enables believers to pattern their lives after Christ.

Biblical principles can be identified using several key criteria. Such principles are not limited by historical or cultural context; they reveal the universal and timeless nature of God's unchanging character and expectations for all people across all generations. Criteria for identifying biblical principles include:

- Universality: The prescriptive value of the principle does not waver across times, places, peoples, or cultures and is not restricted to the original audience or particular historical circumstances.
- Rooted in God's Character: Principles are grounded in the nature and character of God. For example, God's righteousness, holiness, and justness provide the basis for a Christian theology of forgiveness.
- Scriptural Consistency: The principle is affirmed throughout Scripture.
- No Cultural Grounding: The principle transcends specific cultural practices, rituals, or ceremonial laws tied to ancient Israel or first-century settings. For instance, the Pauline admonition to greet with holy kisses is not timeless, while the call to corporate worship is.
- All-Inclusive Relevance: The principle holds practical utility and guidance for all believers of any demographic.

Ask: "What general guide for godly living does this passage make available beyond its immediate context?"

Utilizing the same passages as above, note the following examples of principles. Also note the ease of their accessibility:

Psalm 51:10 (ESV): "Create in me a clean heart, O God, and renew a right spirit within me."

- Principle: Prayer is always the starting place for God to clean a dirty heart.
- Principle: The only hope for a dirty heart is God.
- Principle: God knows how to scrub a heart clean.
- Principle: Spirit renewal is something only God can do.

First Samuel 2:2 (ESV): "There is none holy like the Lord: for there is none besides you; there is no rock like our God."

- Principle: God's holiness demands a holy response.

- Principle: God makes no room for idols in our lives.
- Principle: A sure foundation is found only in God.

Ephesians 4:17 (ESV): "Now this I say and testify in the Lord, that you must no longer walk as the Gentiles do, in the futility of their minds."

- Principle: Truth is found only in Christ.
- Principle: The Christian walk should not look like a worldly walk.
- Principle: The Christian mindset is free from foolish thinking.

Truths and principles can be summed up in the following chart:

| | Truths | Principles |
|---|---|---|
| Grammatical Identity | Descriptive/Indicative | Prescriptive/Imperative |
| Function | Formative | Performative |
| Inform Christian | Posture | Pattern |

## ILLUSTRATIONS

Illustrations are necessary in sermons because they help make abstract truths concrete, clarify complex concepts, capture attention, and assist congregants in self-positioning under the light of the Word. Jesus himself set the standard by regularly using illustrations and parables, showing how images and stories from everyday life illuminate spiritual truth and engage the audience more deeply.

Illustrations function as *spotlights*, illuminating otherwise difficult or abstract ideas, enabling congregations to see and understand them more clearly. A compelling illustration draws the listeners' interest, making the sermon point more lively. This fosters congregational acceptance, so the message can take root deeply in their lives and avoid becoming dry or forgettable.

Concrete stories and vivid word pictures highlight truths and principles through colorful incidents or images. Illustrations can also stir emotions and move listeners toward divine self-examination and desire for altar participation, not just intellectual assent. Illustrations bridge the gap between biblical times and the congregation's contemporary life, showing how scriptural truths and principles relate to listeners' real-time circumstances. They offer examples that guide listeners in shining the light of biblical principles on their need for Jesus Christ. There are three types of illustrations: stories, citations, and statistics. A good rule of thumb is to have one illustration for each sermon point.

## Stories

Stories as sermon illustrations are vital tools that bring biblical truths to life, making them real and contemporary for congregations. A good story goes beyond mere explanation. It engages the heart, mind, and emotions in a way that pure theological exposition often cannot, bridging Scripture and modern experience. It invites listeners to follow the story's trajectory of crescendos and crashes as its conflict escalates and its resolution is reached.

The story of Erika Kirk's moving eulogy during the 2025 memorial service for Charlie Kirk, a Christian conservative political activist and influencer in the United States, who was assassinated for his outspokenness in favor of Christian ethics and virtue, provides an excellent example of a Christian response to persecution. I attended Charlie Kirk's memorial and was particularly moved by Erika's expression of forgiveness to the shooter, which proved to be the highlight of her speech. Stories like this can illustrate sermon points on forgiveness, hope, trials and tribulations, and more.

Stories are narrative illustrations with a clear beginning, middle, and end. People love stories. They effectively capture the congregation's attention, engaging their emotional and cognitive imaginations. Jesus himself set the model through his own parables—simple stories with profound spiritual meanings—that connected deeply with the crowds' everyday lives and experiences. Following the example of Christ, pastors use stories to paint pictures that help the congregation see themselves in the light of the truth or principle being explained, thereby assisting the congregation in altar preparation.

Stories stoke emotions that facts alone cannot ignite. Pentecostal preachers need not fear stirring emotional engagement in the congregation. The Bible contains evocative literature, as evidenced by the wisdom literature of Job, the Psalms, Proverbs, the Song of Solomon, Ecclesiastes, and many other passages throughout Scripture. It's not uncommon for these writers, under the divine inspiration of the Holy Spirit, to include much evocative language—such as similes, metaphors, vivid imagery, and personification—to convey deep emotions, spiritual truths, and memorable scenes. This kind of language appears in the Bible on purpose. God intended it to be there. Evocative language pulls readers into the narrative, stirring up awe, sorrow, anger, hope, or conviction.

Many cessationist preachers go to great lengths to avoid what they might define as emotionally manipulative preaching, which they feel is dangerous within the Pentecostal movement. The argument can be made, however, that if emotional engagement with the congregation is wrong, then God was wrong to employ it in Scripture. If God speaks in evocative language, *on purpose*, then the Pentecostal preacher need not apologize for speaking it as well. The only caveat is the caution against purposeful manipulation, which is exactly what cessationist preachers are right to criticize. Such tactics are weak, unnecessary, and immature, and they nearly guarantee the rapid departure of the Spirit's anointing when employed. The emotional connection of stories encourages listeners to internalize and respond to the Holy Spirit's call during sermon delivery.

Sources of stories for sermons include:

- Personal Experience: Sharing personal stories adds authenticity and helps build trust between the preacher and the congregation.
- Biblical Narratives: The Bible is rich in stories and parables, which remain timeless and priceless in their usefulness and value.
- Everyday Life: Observing people, current events, history, and culture offers a vast reservoir of stories that connect contemporary life to biblical truth.
- History and Biography: Stories of faith from history or modern Christians can inspire and model Christian living.
- Creative Use of Media and AI Tools: Pastors can leverage technology and contemporary resources to find fresh, relevant illustrations.
- Object Lessons: The preacher brings actual objects to aid in visualization.
- Testimonies: People other than the preacher share stories of personal, life-altering experiences with God.

Effective storytelling techniques need to have a clear structure of delivery. That is, stories should have a defined beginning, rising action, climax, and resolution that clearly tie back to the sermon point. Preachers do well when they employ vivid details, utilizing sensory and descriptive language, painting pictures that engage listeners' imaginations. Stories should be authentic and simple. They should feel genuine and be easy to follow without unnecessary complexity or length. The preacher's posture during storytelling should be appropriate, with a clear vocal tone, a natural pace, and effective body language, to enhance the story's impact. Avoid reading word for word to maintain naturalness.

## Statistics

By definition, statistics count or measure phenomena—such as population sizes, belief trends, or behaviors—and present them as numerical data. When used well, statistics help illustrate how groups of people's actions or beliefs align or diverge from what God calls us to in Scripture. By adding these to truths and principles, pastors can use statistics to make abstract moral or spiritual concepts concrete. This can engage the congregation by providing factual evidence that prompts reflection and a deeper understanding of biblical teachings applied to modern life.

Statistics highlighting the correlation between teen suicide and the rise of social media, for example, communicate the clear challenge many teens face. For a preacher delivering a sermon on hope, statistics like these bring the absence of hope among teenagers clearly into view.

Statistics are valuable tools for sermon illustrations because they add layers of credibility and relevance to the message. Using well-researched and accurate statistics helps the congregation understand the complexity of contemporary issues related to the biblical themes being taught. Statistics provide context that bridges ancient biblical truths with present-day realities, making the sermon more relatable and impactful. Functioning like parables, they represent broader truths or societal conditions that help listeners grasp the significance of the sermon point in concrete terms.

For example, a pastor might cite a trustworthy survey on how many people experience loneliness in contemporary society in a sermon point on community and fellowship. This data piques interest and frames the sermon topic in a contextual way, helping listeners grasp the relevance of Scripture in their lives. Statistics are typically brief and are often complementing stories or analogies. They enhance credibility because they are grounded in research or authoritative sources and can counter misconceptions.

Statistics can engage the audience by presenting factual, numerical evidence that supports the sermon's point. Good statistics can prompt listeners to reflect on their own beliefs and behaviors in light of Scripture. They can make abstract or theological concepts more tangible by providing real-world examples or trends, such as demographic patterns or social behaviors, that align or contrast with biblical teachings. When integrated skillfully, they perform their function without overshadowing the sermon point.

Statistics must be utilized responsibly, ensuring they are accurate, verifiable, and relevant. Misusing or relying on misleading statistics can undermine the preacher's credibility and distract from the sermon's flow.

## Citations

A citation is the precise repetition of another person's spoken or written words, quoted to provide authority, insight, illustration, or emphasis for the sermon point. In homiletics, citations refer specifically to carefully selected words from notable figures, scripture, literature, or tradition, purposefully inserted to clarify, reinforce, or enliven the preacher's message. "Nothing short of God can satisfy your soul" is an oft-quoted statement by John Wesley in Pentecostal sermons.[4]

Well-chosen citations often clarify sermon points with more precision than lengthy expositions. Preachers rely on citations to express ideas with beauty, impact, depth, and force that their own words may not fully capture. By painting with words, citations help to illuminate concepts in a fresh light. Emily Dickinson once penned, "Hope is the thing with feathers that perches in the soul."[5]

Quoting well-known, reputable theologians, scholars, or other preachers adds credibility to the sermon and connects the congregation with a broader tradition of faith. When congregants hear trusted names being cited, it fosters confidence in the preacher's ability as a reader and one who is well adept to research. The dynamic carries a balanced tone of humility as the pastor demonstrates openness to the learning and sharing of communal wisdom.

Citations come in like the hot sun, burning off the morning fog. They're punchy. They strike with force. They cut through unclarity.

4. Wesley, "Means of Grace" 5.4.

5. Dickinson, "Hope Is the Thing."

Quotes that are pithy, poignant, or artistically crafted make light work of the preacher's task of congregational interpretation. One line from a well-known person can sum up five minutes' worth of sermonic teaching. The practicality of citations does not go unnoticed. Famous quotes embed biblical truth within narratives of real people in real-life situations, making them practical and relatable. Listeners are invited into a dialogue, not just a monologue, inspired by voices other than the preacher's own. They invite hearers to inhabit the message, providing additional points of entry into the hearts of the congregants.

## PUTTING IT ALL TOGETHER

Putting this all together, the preacher's notes prepare them to move methodically through the passage during delivery. With all the preparatory activities now complete, the sermon outline can be put together. The process is simple in principle. The sermon's main points consist of truths or principles, with substantive content ready for explanation and, as a good rule of thumb, at least one illustration used for each. Note the following example of sermon points from Lam 3:22, paying careful attention to the following elements:

- Main sermon points are made up of either a truth or a principle and are derived solely from the text.
- Notes contain substantive explanation content.
- There is at least one illustration for each main sermon point.

Passage: Lam 3:22 (ESV): "The steadfast love of the Lord never ceases; his mercies never come to an end."

Sermon Point #1: God Is the God of Steadfast Love (Note how this is a truth. It can now be followed by substantive explanation content.)

- Worldly love definition
    - "God's love stands in contrast to worldly love."
    - Worldly love is finicky . . .
        - Often dependent upon emotions—the person *feels* in love
        - Happiness driven: Absence of conflict (unrealistic)
        - Self-directed: "I'm in love because they make me happy."

- Worldly love falls short
  - Illustrate cheap love: Examples from modern culture are celebrities or other famous people . . . citing some who have had several marriages (be lighthearted here)
  - Even "committed" love fails: Story of a family whose love fell apart after a tragedy
- What is godly love?
  - Hebrew word for *love* in this verse: *checed*, often translated as *lovingkindness*: Means favor, manifested in good works, mercy, covenantal (all of these words can be briefly attended to)
  - Transitive nature of God's love: God's love always takes a direct object. It is never abstract. God loves justice and righteousness, for example. God loves humanity. God loves you.
- God's love is a steadfast love
  - Worldly love is disposable—People "fall out of love" and then move on . . . explain
  - God's love never ceases
    - Hebrew word for *steadfast*: *tamam*, means (with the included negation) ceased, to be finished, consumed
    - Ps 136:1 (ESV): "Give thanks to the Lord, for he is good, for his steadfast love endures forever."
    - Ps 11:5 (ESV): "For the Lord is good; his steadfast love endures forever, and his faithfulness to all generations."
    - Illustration: King David's sin with Bathsheba did not disqualify him from being loved by God.
  - God's love is unshakable: It cannot be removed in the midst of our storms, seasons of doubt and uncertainty, or even being angry at God.

Sermon Point #2: God Is the Source of Steadfast Love

- Many people search for love in all the wrong places
  - Illustration: Country song, "Looking for Love" by Johnny Lee
  - Wrong places to look for love: Romantic relationships, material possessions, career success, money and wealth, social media

influence, addictions, entertainment, etc. (Each of these words can be briefly commented upon.)

- Many suffer the consequences of never finding true love (sadness, loneliness, depression, lowered self-worth, etc.)
- Illustration: Statistics on depression and/or anxiety

- Hebrew word for the "Lord" (*Yahweh*): Means eternal, self-existent, covenantal, the proper name of the God of Israel
  - Tied to Old Testament sworn promises
  - Connected with several compound names such as Yahweh-Jireh (The Lord will provide), Yahweh-Rapha (The Lord heals), Yahweh-Shalom (The Lord is peace), etc.
  - The Ten Commandments prohibit taking his name in vain: Speaks to the holiness, reverence, and awe due to the Creator of the universe
- If God is the source of his love, then that means his love is holy, just, righteous, and perfect
  - God's love is the only love that satisfies the longing of humanity
  - The depravity of the human condition cries out for it
  - God created us to need, long, and pine for it
- Illustration: How does one get access to God's steadfast love? John Wesley's Means of Grace: Worship, Scripture, prayer, fellowship, and others

Sermon Point #3: God's Mercies Never Come to an End

- Hebrew word for *mercy*: *racham*, means compassion, by extension from the womb, tender love . . . implies a kind of womb-like tenderness that is extended to acts of mercy
- God's love for Israel, and by extension, God's love for you, is characterized as the kind of compassionate love that extends from a mother to her infant in the womb.
  - Selfless
  - Spiritually natural: In the same way that biology drives a mother's prenatal care so that it happens naturally, without requiring

the mother's will, God's nature delivers compassionate love to his people.

- Reflection of God's nature: God's mercy flows from God's nature . . . briefly make a few comments about God's attributes of love, holiness, justice, righteousness, etc., and include mercy.

- Biblical understanding of mercy: The kind of treatment given by God that provides what has not been earned or deserved (salvation) and withholds that which has been earned or deserved (judgment).
  - Compassion: *Racham* is often translated into English as *compassion*
  - Ps 51:1 (ESV): "Have mercy on me, O God, according to your steadfast love; according to your abundant mercy blot out my transgressions."
  - Isa 49:15 (ESV): "Can a woman forget her nursing child, that she should have no compassion on the son of her womb? Even these may forget, yet I will not forget you."
- Parallelism:
  - Briefly describe the synonymous parallelism employed with Hebrew poetry (how the concept delivered in the first line is paralleled with a similar concept in the second line).
  - Show how the author (King Solomon) was demonstrating that the eternal nature of God's steadfast lovingkindness is reinforced, clarified, and pressed more deeply into the hearer's minds and hearts.
  - By drawing in the statement about mercy, Solomon brings the central idea more clearly into view from two different angles.
  - God's mercies never end in the same way that God's steadfast love never ceases.

Sermon Point #4: God's Love Is Covenantal

- God's favor-filled, covenantal, compassionate, womb-like, tender, steadfast love never ceases
- Covenant definition: A solemn, binding relationship of mutual commitment, established by oath, pledge, promises, and obligations

- Between God and people (Noah, Abraham, Jacob, David) or between humans (Jacob and Laban)
- Different from contract:

| | Contract | Covenant |
|---|---|---|
| Core Difference | Legal/Transactional Performance | Relational Faithfulness |
| Commitment | Mutual benefit | Promise |
| Failure | Other party can terminate | Continued faithfulness |
| Duration | Limited | Eternal |

God's love for you is not (talk about each one of these):

- Transactional
- Performance driven (based on works)
- Expecting something in return
- Open to termination
- Limited

## REFLECTION QUESTIONS

1. During the adoration move, the text emphasizes being overwhelmed by the beauty of the passage rather than analyzing it right away. Describe a time when you allowed yourself to simply sit in awe of Scripture. How did that moment of divine apprehension change your perspective?
2. Why is it essential to gather observations before moving into any form of interpretation? Share an example from your own Bible reading when rushing to interpret a passage caused you to miss or misrepresent its meaning and how careful observation might have helped.
3. The chapter warns strongly against eisegesis and contaminating observations with personal agendas. How can you recognize when your own biases, cultural assumptions, or preconceived ideas are influencing how you read a biblical text, and what practical steps can help you maintain objectivity?

4. Consider the discipline required to resist interpretation during the observation phase. What makes this discipline challenging for you personally, and how might practicing patience in this area strengthen both your character and your ability to preach faithfully?
5. Reflect on the role of the Holy Spirit as both bridge builder and shaper during the interpretation phase. Describe a moment in your preparation or devotional life when waiting in quiet reflection led to fresh revelation or personal transformation—what made that encounter possible?

## APPLICATION ACTIVITIES

1. Adoration Meditation Exercise—Print out a single paragraph or short pericope (e.g., John 15:1–8) with wide margins and double spacing. Spend 20–30 minutes in silent, contemplative adoration. Create your own sacred study space, and read it slowly multiple times, pause to let the text "take your breath away," and resist any urge to analyze or note details. Write a 200–300 word reflection describing any moments of awe, Christ exaltation, or emotional response you experienced, and explain how this posture resets your approach to Scripture.
2. Observation Harvest on a Familiar Text—Print a well-known passage (e.g., Ps 23 or Phil 4:4–9) in the recommended format. Spend 45–60 minutes gathering observations only—no interpretation allowed. Use markings (circles, underlines, arrows, question marks) and marginal notes to record nouns/verbs, repetitions, lists, cause/effect, principles, themes, etc. Submit your marked-up page (or photo) and a separate list of at least 15 specific observations you discovered.
3. Basic Historical Interrogation Drill—Pick a passage from an Epistle (e.g., Eph 4:1–6). Using only a study Bible, online Bible dictionary, or free commentary resources, quickly answer the five Ws: Who wrote it? When? To whom? What was the historical/*Sitz im Leben* context? What was the book's purpose? Where does this passage fit in the book's outline? Summarize your findings in a one-page report, explaining how this context shapes your initial reading.

4. Spirit-Led Reflection Time—After completing observations and basic interrogation on your passage, set aside 30–45 minutes of quiet, undisturbed time (ideally in your sacred space). Pray in the Spirit (tongues if practiced), then sit in silence with your notes. Journal any fresh insights, truths, or principles that "rose off the page," personal convictions, or sense of the Spirit shaping your understanding. Reflect on how this moment felt like the sermon was being "preached" to you first.

5. Truths and Principles Distillation—From your full work on the passage, identify two to three clear biblical truths (absolute realities using "to be" statements about God, Christ, humanity, etc.) and two to three biblical principles (prescriptive guides for living that transcend culture). For each, write a brief explanation of why it meets the chapter's criteria (e.g., testamental continuity, Spirit confirmation, universality). End with a short personal application: how one truth and one principle challenge or encourage you right now in your life.

# PART SIX

## Setting the Delivery

# 18

# Step Three: Introduction

For many contemporary church services, the sermon introduction transitions worship from song to Word. If you're like me, the introduction can be one of the most challenging parts of the sermon to write. Bible teachers have a tendency to want to jump directly into the meat of the message and blow past all the fluffy segues and cute storytelling transitions. However, over the years, I have learned the importance of all these sermon components, especially the introduction. In classical homiletical concerns, the introduction satisfies several transitional criteria. However, for the Pentecostal preacher, the introduction serves additional, crucial purposes.

In a classical sense, introductions are intended to present the sermon's main idea to the congregation and invite listeners to lean in as the preacher transitions into the sermon. The introduction presents to the congregation why they're here, what this message is all about, and the heart of the sermon. It carries the function of establishing the need of the sermon content and speaking to the question, "Why are we even talking about this topic? Why should I care? What is the relevance of this for my life?" The introduction gets this in the air on both a corporate and a personal level.

The introduction also creates anticipation and captures attention. Skilled orators, especially those skilled in the art of rhetoric, capitalize on the sermon introduction to create anticipation. As they create the need, they talk about the solution, saying comments like, "Church, when it comes to knowing how to pray when you're in crisis, I've got the perfect answer this morning. You're not going to want to miss this."

## READING OF SCRIPTURE

Several key elements go into a good introduction. Of particular importance is a reading of a Scripture passage that is anchoring the sermon. This can appear at any point during the introduction. Some preachers like to begin with the passage. Others wait until the end. There's no right or wrong approach. The preacher may place the Scripture reading wherever it makes the most sense.

The reading of the Scripture passage should be delivered with clarity, emphasis, and liveliness. The preacher doesn't need to be afraid to read dialogue lines with the flair and passion one would expect to hear in a scene played on stage. Allowing the vigor of the apostle Paul's writing to find expression in their readings makes the Word come alive for the congregation. Romans 7:24 is a great example of this. You can almost hear Paul shouting with frustration, "Wretched man that I am! Who will deliver me from this body of death?" (ESV). The balance is found in the preacher's ability to bring life to the reading of the Word without being overly theatrical and, therefore, distracting.

## STORIES, STATISTICS, CITATIONS, AND QUESTIONS

Good introductions are further anchored by a specially curated illustration. Illustrations serve as bridges that connect listeners' experiences to the truth being preached, making the message both engaging and memorable. They're an effective tool for the preacher to capture attention and clarify complex ideas. Illustrations capture attention immediately. They enrapture congregational engagement.

Introductory illustrations include stories, citations, statistics, or a question to aid in the transition into the body of the sermon. Stories include any narrative, fictional or true, that demonstrates the main idea of the sermon in concentrated form. For example, in a sermon I preached on the importance of a Christian worldview, my introduction referenced the story of Lawrence Sperry, a twenty-four-year-old American aviator who invented the world's first aircraft autopilot. His technology allowed airplanes to maintain a straight, level course hands-free, freeing pilots from constant manual corrections and reducing fatigue on long flights. His display was one of bravado and courage, with him and his co-pilot standing on the wings of the plane as it flew by the fully amazed crowd.[1] I ended the story with the comment, "Everyone has a preprogrammed autopilot working behind the scenes that keeps them on course. It's called a worldview. Is your autopilot preprogrammed from a Christian worldview?"

Statistics are quite effective for sermon introductions, as well. Statistics are drawn from the preacher's research during sermon preparation. They are particularly resourceful at establishing within the congregation an awareness of a problem that typically strikes home and needs immediate resolution. Sharing statistics has the uncanny ability to create a sense of urgency. They communicate, "Here's the situation. Here's the reality of its damaging effect. Now what does the Bible provide as the solution?"

I once preached a topical sermon about dealing with depression and anxiety. I conducted research during the sermon preparation stage to better understand the scope of these mental illnesses in American society. I was dismayed by the prevalence of these conditions, which are widespread across all generations in American society. Some of these statistics were cited in the introduction to this sermon to underscore the urgency of the situation. Typically, the introduction contains only a sampling of statistics, leaving the full expression for the sermon itself.

Citations carry tremendous weight in the sermon introduction. Citations include quotes from well-known individuals that highlight the sermon's main idea. For example, a sermon on charity could include a famous quote by Mother Teresa, "It's not how much we give but how much love we put into giving,"[2] or one from Anne Frank, "No one ever becomes poor from giving."[3] Referencing a quote from a household name creates a social connection between the listener and the sermon. The immediacy of name recognition strikes a chord of familiarity that resonates positively. For a sermon on courage, one could quote the illustrious John Wesley's famous quote, "Give me one hundred preachers who fear nothing but sin and desire nothing but God, and I care not a straw whether they be clergymen or laymen, such alone will shake the gates of hell and set up the kingdom of heaven upon earth."[4]

1. Scheck, "Lawrence Sperry."
2. Mother Teresa, "Mother Teresa's Quotes."
3. Frank, *Works of Anne Frank*, 10.
4. Wesley, *Letters*, 6:272.

Citations lend credibility to the sermon's direction. If John Wesley finds the topic congruent, the sermon has instant credibility. The curiosity and interest sparked by the quote act as a hook, drawing people in to what happens next. Listeners lean in when they hear the voice of someone they already admire speaking about the topic. Undoubtedly, one of the strongest elements of the introduction is the well-crafted question. "If God is so powerful, loving, and all-knowing, then why is there so much evil and suffering in the world?" Questions capture the congregation's attention and invite them to participate in the sermon. Questions transform the congregation from passive recipient to active participant.

These moments of engagement are ordinarily accompanied by personal connections made by the congregation. The question "Have you ever been hurt by someone you trusted implicitly?" quickly resurrects personal memories of past or present hurts. The preacher now has the gift of undivided attention. Adding to this gift is the anticipation of the preacher's response. The seasoned preacher discerns this phenomenon and suspends the anticipation *in the air* as they segue into delivering the sermon. The answer is unresolved in the moment, but the promise of resolution unfolds as the sermon progresses.

## WHAT TO AVOID IN SERMON INTRODUCTIONS

There are a few things preachers should avoid in their introductions. The first is the lengthy introduction. We've all heard introductions that run twenty-plus minutes. When the congregation discovers that *that* was just the introduction, they're tempted to zone out or walk out. Preachers serve their congregations well when they keep their introductions at approximately 10–12 percent of their allotted time. For example, if a typical sermon runs forty minutes, the sermon introduction should be four to five minutes.

### Apologies

Secondly, the preacher should avoid apologies in their introduction. As a rule, apologies are never welcome, *at any point*, in the sermon, but particularly so in the introduction. Apologies, contrary to what one might expect, do not engender compassion from the congregation. They have the opposite effect. They solicit the congregation to tune out, begging them to not take the preacher seriously. Consider the associate pastor who was informed only minutes before the start of Sunday service that the lead pastor wasn't coming and that he had to preach. Imagine the response of the congregation when the associate pastor says, "Good morning, church! Unfortunately, our lead pastor was unable to be here today, so you're stuck with me. I'm not good at last-minute preaching when I haven't prepared, but I'm going to give this my best shot. I'm nervous. I'm praying this goes okay. Cross your fingers. Here we go." This poor guy has little chance at success. More so, not only has he given the congregation permission to tune out, but he's also nearly guaranteed them to do so.

Note well that even in the absence of direct apologetic language such as "I'm sorry" or "I apologize," as in the case above, the *posture* of apology says it all. The presence of defeat guarantees the absence of victory. If the preacher's presence is one of a soft-spoken, uncertain voice, looking down while speaking, the shrugs of embarrassment, shoulders forward, and the searching pleas of "Amens?" at the end of statements, then they've lost them. Apologies discredit the preacher and devalue the Word.

I once heard a preacher apologize for his sermon, comparing it to the Sermon on the Mount. He said, "My sermon is woefully inadequate." This was a huge apology, which was an equally huge mistake. The apology made it difficult to stay focused on the sermon. The congregation appeared to have tuned him out before he ever got started. The preacher should avoid projecting nervousness or lack of confidence—not just for themselves, but for the sake of the Word being delivered.

On the other hand, the presence of direct apologetic language, when delivered from a posture of confidence, has no detrimental effect on the congregation. Imagine our associate pastor friend from above starting his introduction with "Good morning, church! Today's your lucky day! Our lead pastor was unable to be here, so I'm sorry to inform you, but you get to shout like you just won the lottery because today you get me! Open your Bibles to . . ."

I once heard Dr. Tim Hill, general overseer for the Church of God (Cleveland, Tennessee), who was guest preaching at a local church, begin his sermon with "I always feel in these revival weeks, after all the great speakers you've had, and I know them all well, I always feel like the mule at the Kentucky Derby for some reason." His comment was a self-deprecating compliment to the other speakers, flowing from his confidence as a seasoned preacher. He wasn't serious. And it wasn't an apology for not measuring up.

The takeaway here is that posture matters more than words. A good rule of thumb is to always provide an explanation when one is needed, but never apologize. Explain, but don't apologize. For example, if a preacher has a strained voice because he was at a youth rally all weekend, his congregation will wonder why. The preacher can't leave that question unanswered. A simple explanation will suffice. "Good morning, church! Many of you can hear the strain in my voice. That's the evidence that our youth know how to praise the Lord! I've been up at the youth rally this weekend, and let me tell you, our youth know how to bring the praise during games and worship! I couldn't be prouder to have strained my voice! Open your Bibles to . . ."

## Over-Promising

Pastors should be cautious about overpromising in their sermon introductions, as it can erode the trust and credibility vital to effective preaching. When a pastor promises transformative outcomes or insights that the sermon ultimately does not deliver, the congregation may feel misled or disappointed. This breach of trust can create skepticism and disengagement, affecting how listeners receive future messages. Maintaining honest and realistic expectations helps preserve the pastor's integrity and the congregation's trust in both the message and messenger.

Over-promising can also overwhelm or confuse the congregation, particularly at the very start when their attention is most vulnerable. A sermon introduction that packs in too many guarantees or sensational statements risks losing the listeners' focus before the core message has been unpacked. Instead of building anticipation, it can cause frustration or distraction. Furthermore, if promises are made that stray from the biblical text or spiritual realities, it can diminish the authority of Scripture and expose the congregation to false hopes or misunderstandings.

The best approach is to craft sermon introductions that engage attention honestly and thoughtfully, connecting emotionally without exaggeration. Introductions should clearly preview the sermon's main theme or question and set a tone consistent with the message's content. By offering an accurate and compelling forecast grounded in Scripture, pastors invite listeners to journey attentively into the Word. This honest foundation fosters deeper engagement, lasting impact, and a strong connection between the preacher's call and the congregation's spiritual growth. Thus, avoiding over-promising ensures the sermon introduction honors both God's truth and the listeners' trust.

### Theological Overkill

Theological overkill is another area to avoid. Too many words and too many concepts weigh down the introduction. The weight is confusing. This is often a temptation for a new or inexperienced preacher trying to impress. When it comes to higher theological concepts and language, the introduction is served well when these are postponed for later appearance in the sermon, and even then, with the appearance of flavoring more so than the main dish.

Avoiding theological overkill in sermon introductions is crucial because the introduction sets the tone and prepares the congregation for the message. Overwhelming listeners with complex theology or multiple theological ideas too early can confuse and disengage them, particularly those who are new to the faith or unfamiliar with detailed doctrinal concepts. By keeping the introduction clear and focused, pastors help the audience follow the sermon's flow more easily and stay engaged throughout the message.

A well-crafted introduction connects the theological truth to the listeners' real-life experiences, creating tension or posing a question that the sermon will answer. This connection invites the congregation into the message. The introduction is not the place for exhaustive theological exposition but rather a strategic moment to provide a single, clear theme that guides the sermon. This approach establishes a road map for the sermon, allowing the message's fuller theological richness to unfold gradually in the body and conclusion, enhancing clarity and impact without overwhelming the audience prematurely. In this way, pastors ensure their sermons are accessible, engaging, and spiritually nourishing from start to finish.

## FROM A PENTECOSTAL POINT OF VIEW

In most cessationist church services, there's a distinct separation between song and sermon. When someone is asked, "What kind of worship do you have at your church?" the question is automatically interpreted to mean "What's the music style of your church?" The sermon typically is not understood in the context of worship. The sermon is the teaching part of the service.

## Congregational Objectification

The introduction safeguards against congregational objectification. In most cessationist church services, the sermon functions as a *lesson*, in which the preacher has prepared their notes and the congregation is ready to learn. The challenge with this kind of emphasis on preaching is the objectification of the congregation. A standard pedagogical principle holds that teachers (the subject) are the ones with the content, and students (the object) are the recipients of the content. Teaching is the transactional transference of knowledge from subject to object. For our cessationist brothers and sisters (whom we love and appreciate!), the sermon has transformed the house of worship into a lecture hall. Class is in session. The pastor has become the teacher. The congregation has become the students.

In Pentecostal worship, the congregation is not the object—we're here for him! Jesus is the object. Though the congregation might learn during the sermon (hopefully so!), that's not the reason for the gathering. A good introduction ushers the congregation from worshiping through song into worshiping through proclamation. The preacher knows this. They're committed to keep the focus on Jesus, not the congregation.

## Preserving the Tone of Worship

The introduction is the critical first moments for preserving the worshipful tone. For many churchgoers, when the pastor begins preaching, the congregation settles into a posture of passive receptivity. The Pentecostal introduction maintains the atmosphere of active participation. As far as the pastor is concerned, the worship has hardly just begun. I have learned over the years to include specific language that invites the congregation to stay put in their worship posture. "Stay with me as we continue to worship through the proclamation of the Word." "How many of you know that the preached Word is a crucial component of worship?" "Isn't it good to know that the Word gives cause to erupt in worship?"

The introduction is a good place for micro-teachings on the definition of worship. Many people think that worship is over when the singing has concluded. This is incorrect. Worship continues as the Word is preached. "As we continue to worship." "Let's exalt the name of Jesus through this preaching." "Please take your seats and get ready to worship with me." "We are not done worshiping yet, but just beginning." "Let's not only receive the word, but worship through it." These are things the preacher can say. Let the congregation know—the transition from singing to sermon is not a transition out of worship. It's a segue into the worship through the proclamation of the Word.

Let's look at two traditional sermon introductions, one cessationist and one Pentecostal, and see what we can learn. One preacher opened his expository sermon: "If you have your Bibles, open up with me to John chapter eight." That's a classic way to set the tone for an expository message—invite people into the text. And then, "I hope you take notes. I want you to walk away with something." Now, that's a posture of knowledge transfer, classic among our cessationist brothers and sisters. "I hope you'll learn something good" is the essence.

However, in the Pentecostal setting, the preservation and continuation of the worship atmosphere is the task at hand, not the objectification of the congregation. The preacher seeks to invite the congregation to exalt the name of Christ—"Lean in to what God is saying. Let's receive together. Let the Spirit speak." That's a different approach. This is the heart of teaching as worship in the Pentecostal expository sermon. We are not here simply to teach but to worship. The introduction is the preacher's invitation for the congregation to join in worship—a worship that happens in the Word received and proclaimed as God intends.

## Stoking the Embers of Faith

The introduction to a Pentecostal expository sermon sets the tone, posture, and expectations for worship and for hearing from God. The preacher's job is to help facilitate that sense of readiness, to call people not just to learn, but to worship, to experience, to enter in. One of the key functions of the Pentecostal sermon introduction, then, is an intentional, hermeneutical function that stokes the embers of faith as a receptive response to the Spirit's movement in worship through the proclamation of the Word.

Faith is the essential channel through which the power of the Holy Spirit is released in the lives of listeners, and Scripture robustly affirms this dynamic. Jesus himself emphasized the importance of faith when he healed the paralytic, saying, "According to your faith be it done to you" (Matt 9:29 NIV). This demonstrates that faith is not merely mental assent but an active receptivity to God's power. Again, Jesus saw the faith of the paralytic's friends who lowered him through the roof (Mark 2:1–12).

Sermon introductions thus play a critical role in awakening and engaging the congregation's faith, setting the spiritual atmosphere for the Holy Spirit's transformative work. In Acts 14, Paul healed a man lame from birth after observing that "he had faith to be made well" (8–10). This episode beautifully illustrates how faith can be seen as an active trust that unlocks divine power. Paul's writings also emphasize that the Spirit's power enriches preaching when it aligns with faith rather than human wisdom (1 Cor 2:4–5). As such, sermon introductions must call the congregation into a posture of faith, rather than a posture of learning, fostering openness and expectancy for the Holy Spirit's movement.

The Holy Spirit is always ready to move, but faith in the listener is the gateway. Therefore, the introduction is more than a mere opening; it is a spiritual invitation to activate faith, making it a pivotal moment for the Spirit to enliven the Word preached and bring transformation to the hearts of all who hear. This understanding elevates the sermon introduction from a routine start to a powerful, faith-engaging moment in worship.

The sermon introduction is not the setup for transferring knowledge. School is *not* in session. The congregation has gathered in the presence of God to worship, to be known and interpreted by God, and to respond. The introduction is not just a prelude or a perfunctory one; it is the open door, the invitation. As preachers, we protect and cultivate the atmosphere with every word we say, every story we tell, every choice we make, from our posture to our tone, and especially in how we handle the unexpected.

The preacher is invited to avoid those things that pull away from the Word God has given you. Don't let apologizing, over-explaining, or lack of preparation rob you or your congregation of what the Spirit wants to do. Maintain that posture of confidence—not in yourself, but in the One who has sent you. Always bring the congregation into participation; invite them to lean in, to anticipate, to expect. That's teaching as worship, and that's the heart of the Pentecostal expository sermon.

## The Base Structure of the Introduction

Taking these components into consideration, sermon introductions should contain the following base elements:

- Continuation of Worship Comment: "As we continue to worship this morning, open your Bibles to . . . ," thereby avoiding congregational objectification and preserving the tone of worship.
- Reading of Scripture: In a placement that makes best sense for the trajectory of your introduction, read through the Bible passage being expounded upon, making sure to inform the congregation of the translation you're reading.
- Illustration: Include a story, citation, statistic, or question.
- Comment Inviting Expectancy and the Activation of Faith: "Lean in to what the Spirit has to say to you this morning."

## REFLECTION QUESTIONS

1. How would you explain to a friend why a strong sermon introduction is essential, especially in a Pentecostal context where the goal is worship rather than simply transferring information?
2. Why do you think reading the Scripture passage with appropriate energy and emphasis matters so much during the introduction, and how can a preacher balance liveliness with avoiding excessive theatricality?
3. Consider the dangers of apologizing or projecting uncertainty in a sermon introduction. How might such a posture unintentionally affect the congregation's ability to receive the preached Word with confidence?
4. In your own words, explain how the Pentecostal sermon introduction serves to protect against "congregational objectification" and instead maintains the congregation as active participants in worship.
5. How does intentionally "stoking the embers of faith" during the introduction prepare the congregation for the Holy Spirit's movement, and why is this dimension particularly important in Pentecostal preaching?

## APPLICATION ACTIVITIES

1. Practice Vivid Scripture Reading—Consider Rom 7:24–25. Record yourself reading it aloud three times: once flatly, once with dramatic emphasis on Paul's frustration and hope, and once balanced to avoid theatrical excess. Submit the best recording (or transcript with notes on tone/pauses) and explain how this delivery makes the Word "come alive" for listeners. Write a 250-word reflection on how this exercise helped.
2. Build a Question-Based Introduction—Write a complete 300–400 word introduction for a sermon on forgiveness (e.g., Matt 18:21–35) that begins with two to three provocative, personal questions like "Have you ever been deeply hurt by someone you trusted?" Build anticipation by hinting at the biblical answer without revealing it fully, then include language that stokes faith for Spirit-led transformation.
3. Create a Statistic-Driven Opener—Research two to three current, credible statistics on a common struggle (e.g., depression, loneliness, or prayerlessness). Write a four-minute introduction for a topical sermon on that topic, using the stats to establish urgency, then transition to Scripture and a promise of hope. Note how this avoids over-promising while creating corporate and personal relevance.
4. Incorporate a Powerful Citation—Select a well-known quote (e.g., from John Wesley, Mother Teresa, or a modern figure) that aligns with a sermon theme like courage or generosity. Write an introduction that uses the quote as the hook, explains its connection to the main idea, and invites the congregation to continue in worship as they hear God's Word on the topic.
5. Draft a Worship-Continuation Introduction—Compose a 400-word introduction for any expository sermon text that explicitly preserves the worship atmosphere. Include at least three phrases (e.g., "Let's continue to worship through the preached Word"; "We're not done exalting Jesus yet") to prevent congregational objectification and stoke the embers of faith for Holy Spirit movement.

# 19

# Step Four: Explanation

THE NEXT STEP OF this model focuses on the heart of expository preaching, the teaching. This step differs from most expository preaching models. The purpose of explanation, for example, is *not* couched in terms of learning. Instead, the Spirit-filled purpose of explanation is *worship*. That is to say, the question in the midst of sermonic teaching is not a question of learning and application, "how do we learn and apply this truth to our lives?" (which is a question of discipleship). Rather, the question is "What are the *implications* of this truth in our lives?" (a question of divine self-reflection—the natural reaction of the missional aspect of the Word—in anticipation of response). The response to the question of implication is the heart and fuel of the Pentecostal altar experience.

For the Spirit-filled, Bible-teaching pastor, this is the step that delivers the greatest joy! The step of explanation encompasses the teaching moments when the truths entrusted to the preacher, illuminated by the Holy Spirit during preparation, are made accessible to the congregation. At this point in the sermon, the preacher has been inspired by the Spirit, they've prepared and assembled their notes through the four steps of adoration, observation, interrogation, and interpretation, they've given the introduction, and now it's time to start preaching through the sermon's points. Proclaiming the Word is a distinct privilege for which any preacher called into pulpit ministry should rejoice. As the preacher stands to deliver the Word, the congregation is brought into the light of interpretation.

## THE TEACHER'S PRIVILEGE

The preacher's task in explanation is to cast the truths and principles into illuminative light so the congregation can observe the truth for themselves. The anointed preacher moves through truths and principles, while lighting, illuminating, inviting, and leading toward transformation. There are moments in a preacher's life when the sheer gravity of their calling sinks in—not as a burden, but as a profound joy and privilege. It's easy, for example, in the midst of sermon preparation or the routine of pastoral ministry, to lose sight of just how extraordinary it is to be used by God to preach his Word. For every pastoral pause, even just for a moment—right before they step into the pulpit or rise from their study—they begin to appreciate the wonder of this vocation.

Pulpit pastors know this truth; preaching is not just a task, nor a weekly obligation. It is, at its very core, a sacred exchange. Here's the humbling truth: the God who made the heavens and earth, who spoke life into being, chooses to speak through preachers. The truth is worthy of a second take. The preacher is not simply a communicator; they are, for that moment, the vessel through whom eternal truths are being interpreted for a specific people, in a specific moment.

This is the bidirectional nature of preaching that revs up the preacher's soul. God isn't only interpreting the congregation through his Word; he is also interpreting the preacher. When the preacher spends hours poring over the Scriptures, wrestling with meaning and implication, they find that the text does not leave them unchanged. God uses his Word to shape, to form, to transform the one who will speak it. Then, in the mysterious moment of preaching, God uses the preacher to interpret his Word for others, inviting the congregation into encounter.

To stand before their people, Bible in hand, is to experience the fullness of this privilege. The preacher does well in never losing sight of this truth. Preachers are called, not by accident, nor by the will of man, but by the gentle, purposeful choosing of God, to be a channel through which his Spirit moves. Every time they open their mouths to proclaim, to encourage, to exhort, they are participating in God's ongoing work of revelation.

Preachers fully apprehended by this privilege are the ones most joyfully fulfilled. It is a great honor to be used by God for this holy purpose: to help others see, to help others hear, to partner with the Spirit as the Word is interpreted in the hearts of those present. There is nothing quite like it. To preach is to be caught up in something grander than oneself—to be used, for a fleeting moment, as part of God's dialogue with his people. The truth of this becomes volcanic delight in the life of the preacher.

## THE TEACHER'S POSTURE

### Simplicity

I've learned over the years that the best sermons are the ones with the fewest words. Anointed simplicity is the prophetic task at hand (faithfully delivering the message God has laid upon the heart) and one that finds peace in the simple, unmolested delivery of God's Word. Conditioned Pentecostal preachers know this truth. They've already discovered Paul's testimony in Rom 1:16, "For I am not ashamed of the gospel, for it is the power of God for salvation to everyone who believes, to the Jew first and also to the Greek" (ESV). Power-filled preaching is not a product of energy, enthusiasm, volume, or elaborate gesture, even though these manifestations are welcome in a passionate delivery of the Word. The power is in the Word itself, not the preacher.

Simplicity always makes way for clarity. Sermons free from the over-clogging of videos, over-reliance on humor, heavy-handed research citations, or overbearing storytelling carry the greatest weight of impact. The clear view of truth is at risk of getting lost in the mess of such accessories. And, if the truths and principles of the Word get lost in translation, then the congregation is at risk of interpretation failure.

### Notes

Preachers do well when they trust in their notes. It's not uncommon for the pastor's wife to playfully tease from the front row, "Stick to your notes, honey!" followed by the laughter of the congregation. These wives know their husbands. Some preachers tend to chase down unplanned stories, anecdotes, or "inspirational promptings." These place the congregation in danger if they're unable to follow the rabbit trail, which is not uncommon for such story-chasing pastors. Too much clutter or chatter undermines the simplicity and clarity of the delivery. Accessories (and illustrations) should always be kept to a minimum and should enhance clarity, not detract from it. The same goes for extemporaneous storytelling.

Sermon notes should reflect the pastor's needs and the demands of the occasion. The needs of a pastor are often in a state of flux. Some days, the pastor's readiness requires very few notes. On other days, the pastor may need extensive notes. Easy days require easy notes, typically a one-page outline with a few illustrations ready to go. More difficult days may require several pages of a carefully crafted hierarchical outline.

Some pastors utilize manuscripts for their notes. A manuscript is the preacher's original, fully prepared written text of the sermon, carefully crafted prior to delivery. It contains the entire sermon, word for word, and is intended to be read aloud exactly as written. These are particularly helpful for newer preachers or for occasions that call for a heightened sense of formality (such as weddings and funerals). Experienced preachers tend to stay away from manuscripts because the word-for-word delivery proves to be too constricting.

Outlines are the standard go-to for sermon notes and are exceptionally useful for expository sermons. Main points, subpoints, and further divisions are easily identified within the outline structure. Many seasoned pastors use their own outline templates for sermon notes. These are the product of years of sermon preparation, melded with their unique approach to content organization. Their notes become a snapshot of their brain's wiring.

A good rule of thumb for new preachers is to start with handwritten notes (the same applies to any preacher seeking to revamp their notes strategy). Handwritten notes are better because they force a synchronization between mind and hand. It's a good rhythm for sermon preparation. Not only that, but handwritten notes impart a solid memory of the content, reducing dependence on notes. Many classroom teachers are familiar with the old trick of allowing students to bring in one flashcard of notes for an upcoming test. Students spend hours preparing their legally allowed miniature cheat sheet with the tiniest pencil strokes, cramming in as much content as possible. But the joke was on them! The hours needed to prepare their cheat sheet are usually greater than what it would normally have taken them to study. Handwritten notes are the beginner preacher's best friend.

## Staying in the Flow

As much as note-preparedness is key to simplicity and clarity of delivery, the preacher's ability to stay in the flow of the Holy Spirit is even more crucial. This ability is foundational to Pentecostal homiletics and is not just a theological ideal but an experiential necessity for authentic, Spirit-empowered preaching that transforms lives. Pentecostal homiletics recognizes that the Holy Spirit is actively involved before, during, and after the sermon, guiding the preacher's words during delivery and preparing the congregation's hearts in the lead-up to delivery, empowering the message to pierce hearts.

The apostle Paul's preaching focused not on human rhetoric but on "demonstration of the Spirit and power" (1 Cor 2:4), underscoring the necessity of the Spirit's empowerment to the preacher's effectiveness. The Holy Spirit enables preaching not merely as a skilled oratorical exercise but as a spiritual encounter that brings about real change, and it depends on the preacher's ability to stay in the flow of the Spirit.

During preaching, the flow of the Holy Spirit gives guidance for immediate adjustments—introducing fresh insights, replacing illustrations, or emphasizing certain Scripture spontaneously. This Spirit-led flexibility contrasts with rigid, formulaic sermons and invites the preacher to be a living instrument in God's hand. The Spirit also works in the congregation, creating an environment conducive to receiving the Word (Eph 2:21–22; 1 Cor 12:13). Pentecostal homiletics, therefore, sees preaching as a dynamic interaction among the preacher, the Spirit, and the community, where discernment of the Spirit's movement is critical to the sermon's impact.

Theologically, Pentecostal preaching embraces a view of the Spirit that is both personal and powerful, abiding in the preacher and flowing out to the listeners as rivers of living water (John 7:38–39). The Spirit's presence is not momentary but continuous, creating an inseparable partnership with the preacher. This experiential theology encourages preachers to expect and depend on the Spirit's ongoing guidance and renewal throughout the sermon.

Staying in the flow of the Holy Spirit while preaching means cultivating a Spirit-filled life, engaging in Spirit-led preparation, and remaining open and responsive to the Spirit's leadership in the moment of delivery. This allows the sermon to transcend human ability and become a transformative encounter with God's presence and power, fulfilling the

Pentecostal vision of preaching as Spirit-empowered proclamation that changes hearts and communities.

## Faithful Delivery

Pentecostal preaching is prophetic preaching. The Old Testament prophets spoke only what was delivered to them. They were chosen by God because of their faithfulness to the task. They died long before their actual deaths. Prophets were divinely appointed to speak God's words, not their own opinions. Their messages were characterized by phrases like "Thus says the Lord" to distinguish divine inspiration from personal initiative. The authority of their words was derived solely from God's command and revelation.

Pentecostal pastors preach only that which is given to them through divine inspiration (as discussed in chapter 16). Once received, the preacher is free to prepare and to deliver the sermon with full confidence, understanding the clarity of the task. The preacher's sermon preparation has imparted to them a Spirit-fueled interpretation of the Word. This process, as discussed in chapter 17, often includes the preacher's own interpretation *by the Word*, a transformative experience normative to Pentecostal sermon preparation, that takes place in conjunction with their own interpretation *of the Word*. The preacher, having fully experienced the Word and being fully charged with the authority of the encounter, now has the privilege of faithfully delivering that which they have received.

## THE TEACHER'S METHOD

The concept of explanation is best understood in terms of accessibility, meaning the pearls of Scripture, those truths and principles that can seem elusive or intimidating, must be brought within congregational reach. Preachers highlight the key words and core phrases. They take the hard, abstract concepts and, in the illuminative power of the Spirit, make them accessible. They set the biblical passage in its proper context: historically, scripturally, literarily, pastorally.

The preacher tackles confusing issues as they set the logic and the flow of the passage, so it makes sense to real, living, everyday people. If Jesus is called our great high priest, preachers explain what that means, why it is unique, how it compares to other priests in the biblical narrative, and why it ought to matter to the one sitting in the pew, the seat, or the tent.

Hard concepts, under the anointing of the Holy Spirit, are brought into view through the preacher's highlighting, clarifying, and words that shine light in the hard-to-understand places. Preachers have the joy-filled task of being used by the Spirit for the congregation's divine acquisition of textual comprehension. The preacher is giving the church the tools to see themselves in the mirror of the text. The Word is the light, and the preacher's job in this step of explanation is to hold the mirror up, in the light of truth, and to let the revelation, the newness, and the correction of the Word do its work.

## Methodical

Expository preaching is characterized by a methodical handling of the Word. The expository sermon, by nature, examines only small portions of Scripture at a time. This stands in stark contrast to other types of sermons, such as topical sermons that draw on multiple passages as they address various aspects of a particular topic, narrative sermons that examine full stories in the Bible, and textual sermons that begin as expository but allow for expanded commentary from the preacher. Expository sermons are limited to one pericope at a time. A pericope is a self-contained section or unit of biblical text that conveys a coherent thought, narrative, or teaching. The word comes from the Greek term *perikope*, meaning *a cutting out or section*, and refers to a passage that stands on its own within the larger context from which it appears. Attempts to treat larger sections of Scripture in a single sermon are not practical in an expository approach.

The task of expository preaching invites the preacher to begin at the beginning of the pericope and to take the congregation on a journey through the passage(s), intentionally treating every word, phrase, and concept along the way. Expository sermons feel like a sermonized Bible study. The passages are treated with respect, like a field, ready for harvesting, line upon line, gathering all the harvest to be distributed to the congregation.

## Word for Word, Phrase for Phrase, Concept for Concept

The Word is treated with careful, deliberate examination. No word, phrase, or concept is left unexplored. The preacher's observations from the Preparation step (see chapter 17) have identified every substantive occurrence. Micah 6:8, for example, lends itself to clean expository handling. "He has told you, O man, what is good; and what does the Lord require of you but to do justice, and to love kindness, and to walk humbly with your God?" (ESV). The observations from this verse would probably include special attention to the words "he," "you," "man," "what is good," "what does the Lord require of you," "do justice," "love kindness," "walk humbly," and "with your God."

The expository sermon based on this verse would focus on these words, phrases, and concepts. Some would garner more attention than others. For example, in a typical three-point sermon approach, Mic 6:8 is relatively simple. The preacher would focus on what it means to "do justice," "love kindness," and "walk humbly." This would make a handsome sermon. The other words and phrases could be handled in the introduction or in supportive, lead-up subpoints. At the conclusion of expository sermons, the congregation should leave with a solid understanding of the passage(s). In a distinctly Pentecostal worship setting, the experience should be part sermonized Bible study and part transformative encounter with the Spirit.

## SUMMARY

The Explanation step is the favorite among Spirit-filled Bible-teaching pastors. When properly prepared, the pastor methodically works through the passage(s), teaching and explaining the biblical truths and principles. Each one is handled in turn. One by one, the pastor journeys through the verse(s). There's an ease of movement for both the pastor and the congregation. Illustrations assist the pastor and provide aid in congregational interpretation. The preaching comes off as clean and accessible without sacrificing depth and insight.

## REFLECTION QUESTIONS

1. How does viewing the purpose of explanation as leading to worship rather than mere learning change the way you would approach teaching a biblical truth in a sermon? Reflect on a specific passage and describe the shift in focus this perspective creates for both preacher and congregation.
2. Why do you think simplicity and clarity are described as essential postures for anointed preaching? Consider how overusing illustrations, humor, or media might hinder rather than help the congregation encounter the transforming power of Scripture.
3. What does it mean practically for a preacher to "stay in the flow" of the Holy Spirit during sermon delivery? Share an example from your own life or observation when openness to spontaneous Spirit-led adjustments enhanced the impact of the message.
4. Distinguish between biblical truths and biblical principles as presented in the chapter. Provide an example of each from a single passage and explain how presenting them together builds a foundation for both belief and obedient living in listeners.
5. Why are illustrations, especially stories, so powerful in helping congregations see themselves in the light of Scripture? Reflect on a personal or biblical story you might use to illustrate a truth or principle, and explain how it could prepare hearts for an altar response.

## APPLICATION ACTIVITIES

1. Prepare Handwritten Notes for One Point—Print out Jer 1:4–5 in the format described in chapter 17. Identify one main point (truth or principle). Create handwritten sermon notes for that single point only (no typing). Include the Scripture, key words/phrases, one brief explanation, one illustration, and the worship implication. Deliver this one point aloud to a mirror or phone recording as practice.
2. Identify Truths vs. Principles in a Passage—Choose a short pericope (6–12 verses) you have not preached before. List at least three clear biblical truths (declarative "to be" statements about God, humanity,

or reality) and three biblical principles (prescriptive guidance for living) from the passage. Write one sentence for each explaining how it leads to worship rather than just application.

3. Craft One Powerful Story Illustration—Find or create one personal, biblical, or contemporary story (200–250 words) that illustrates a truth or principle from your current sermon passage. Structure it with clear beginning, conflict, climax, and resolution. End with one sentence that ties the story directly back to divine self-reflection and surrender at the altar.
4. Responsibly Use a Statistic—Choose one contemporary issue related to your passage (e.g., loneliness, anxiety, forgiveness, generosity). Locate one accurate, verifiable statistic from a credible source (Barna, Pew, etc.). Write a 150-word explanation of how the statistic makes the biblical truth or principle more concrete and urgent, then show how it invites worshipful response.
5. Select and Integrate a Strong Citation—Find one short, powerful quotation (from a theologian, hymn, historical figure, poet, or well-known preacher) that beautifully captures a truth or principle from your passage. Write a 200-word section showing how you would introduce the quote, deliver it, and immediately connect it to the Scripture so it illuminates rather than distracts.

20

# Step Five: Implication

God's Word is never divorced from its mission. The Word, as a live agent, sword, lamp, and mirror, shines as a beacon during the Explanation step. In the Spirit-filled context, the nature of the expository sermon takes on a whole new life. Yes, God uses the preacher to release this light into the sanctuary, but the mission of that light is to reveal the congregation's need for Jesus. As the light radiates into the congregation, they see themselves within its truth-filled illumination. Without fail, they realize their need for their Savior. It invites the congregation to participate in the mission of the Word. The Implication step is a nonnegotiable, all-important, necessary hermeneutical shift into congregational interpretation. *This hermeneutical pivot is the single most critical moment in every sermon point.* This is the moment in which sermonic teaching carries the light of truth out of the shallows of intellectualism into the real, happening-right-now depths of human existentialism.

The Implication step ushers the congregation immediately into the *consequences* of the truth or principle being preached. The ushering transports the congregation into a posture of divine self-reflection. This is where Pentecostal worship comes truly alive. Implication becomes the launching pad for inner transformation. For example, if the preacher has taught that Jesus is our ever-present, all-knowing high priest, then the Implication step asks the questions, "If Christ is omniscient, then what does that mean about what I'm trying to hide from him, my secret struggles, my weaknesses? Am I allowing him to lead me?" The heart of the Implication asks, "If God's Word is true, then what truth does it reveal about me?" The truths and principles, when expounded upon during the Explanation step, are now pressing upon the hearts of the hearers.

Rather than allowing preaching to focus on battering people with knowledge or simply on stirring emotions, Pentecostal expository preaching embraces an interweaving of both teaching and worship. Explanation, though indispensable in the act of Pentecostal expository preaching, is not the star of the show. Actually, the act of teaching plays second fiddle. It serves as the caddie for the professional golfer, or the sous chef in the kitchen, or the sheepdog to the Shepherd. It serves at the leisure and at the service of the Spirit. Where the Explanation step has shone the light, set the context, and clarified meaning, it has done so in the preemptive service of the personalization of the Word that takes place through the Implication step.

The Implication step is a pivot away from the sacred cow of application (respectfully addressed in chapter 24). Application, which has been dangerously accommodated from cessationist models of preaching, plays a leading role in the theater of discipleship. Ironically, however, application actually has a counterproductive effect in the context of worship. When a congregant begins to focus on applying a principle or truth in their life, they have moved from a posture of worship to a posture of learning and real-life application. Such a posture is great in the context of discipleship! But it works against the preacher in worship. Though the believer's accommodation of spiritual truths into practical application in their lives is a crucial function of the church, its presence in the Sunday morning worship service is dislocated and better placed in the classroom as a function of discipleship.

## CONGREGATIONAL INTERPRETATION

The Implication step is central to everything Pentecostal preachers do in the pulpit. The focus of the Implication step is congregational interpretation. The heartbeat of Pentecostal preaching, congregational interpretation, is why Pentecostal preachers are not just storytellers but worship facilitators. The local church pastor fulfills many functions of shepherding their flock, but on Sunday mornings, they are more sheepdog than shepherd. The preacher's task in the worship gathering is to draw the congregation into the Shepherd's penetrating gaze.

Congregational interpretation carries a bidirectional focus. The first focus addresses the congregation's task of interpreting the Word.

The second is the Word's mission of interpreting the congregation. The co-interpretation takes place within a delicate perichoresis that can only be facilitated by the Spirit. *Perichoresis* is a term typically used to describe the relational nature of each member of the Trinity within the Godhead and how each member of the Godhead is intricately and simultaneously interwoven with the others, so that each is a unique individual yet inseparable from the others.

The word *perichoresis* is perfectly suited to explaining the mysterious, twofold purpose of congregational interpretation. The divine interplay of the congregation's interpretation of the Word is presupposed by the Word's simultaneous, interweaving, interpretive work of the congregation. The proclamation of the Word in the Explanation step is the Word on mission to pierce, judge, discern, and draw all men unto Christ (Heb 4:12, Isa 55:11, Rom 1:18). The light of truth shines brightly in this moment. As the congregation steps into an understanding of the Word, they cannot escape its light shining into every nook and cranny of their own lives, illuminating the inescapable reality of their need for Jesus.

The light of truth becomes a double-edged sword (Heb 4:12) that, in the same moment, delivers life-saving, grace-filled truths of deliverance on the one hand, while exposing sin on the other. The exposing is a well-worn pattern throughout Scripture. Moses, in his divine encounter at the burning bush, though he received his call and destiny for ministry, hid his face from God, sensing his unworthiness in the holy presence. Job, after God's speeches from the whirlwind, proclaimed he despised himself and repented. Ezekiel, in his inaugural vision, saw the brilliance of God's glory and fell to the ground, overwhelmed by the revelation. Peter, when Jesus miraculously filled the nets, fell prostrate and implored Jesus to leave him because of his sinfulness. John, in the book of Revelation, turned to see the glorified Christ, whose face shone like the sun, and promptly fell at his feet as though dead, undone by the overwhelming vision of divine glory. Paul, surrounded by a heavenly light, fell to the ground, blinded and trembling, in his encounter with the risen Christ.

Isaiah's vision of the throne room carries the same phenomena (Isa 6). Upon encountering the splendor of God's glory, Isaiah was immediately apprehended by the inescapable and piercing nature of God's glory. This was it for him. This was the moment he died long before his actual death. He said in so many words, "I'm dead. I'm lost. I'm unclean." This was followed by two extraordinary events. First, in the moment of Isaiah's sacrifice of his own life, an angel brought a coal from the altar to touch his lips. This signified Isaiah's forgiveness and cleansing of his sin. Second, Isaiah received his commission from the Lord. Isaiah's ability to interpret God's Word (his commission) was presupposed by his being interpreted by the Word. The transforming embers of forgiveness and cleansing were made possible only through Isaiah's divine apprehension by the Word, and the ultimate sacrifice of his sinful ways unto the Lord, which in turn enabled him to comprehend the message of God's mission for his life.

What does this mean when the congregation is confronted by the living Word? It means the preacher's obligation of Word proclamation (Explanation) is in the service of the congregation's apprehension by the Word (Implication) in order to facilitate their comprehension of the Word. It means the nature of expository preaching takes on an entirely different composition in Pentecostal homiletics. The preacher exposes the Word. The Word exposes the congregation. The congregation's interpretation of the Word is presupposed by their own interpretation by the Word.

This feature of Pentecostal homiletics deserves the highest of accolades and distinction. What a privilege to be God's chosen agents participating in the delicate perichoretic interchange between worship and teaching, between imparting information and inviting transformation. The teaching of the Word is not an intellectually driven endeavor as an end in itself. No, it's a means to a greater end, functioning within a real encounter with the Spirit of Christ, and having the Word inscribed upon their hearts.

Congregational interpretation is not passive. Its aim is *not* for people to sit and say, "Good sermon, Pastor." Congregational interpretation is active engagement with the Word, grappling, reflecting, wrestling, receiving, and responding. The preacher, in the act of explaining, necessarily objectifies the congregation for a moment, that is to say, as they become the focus of the teaching, but the celebration of Pentecostal expository preaching is that the congregation doesn't stay in this place of objectification. This can feel like a contradiction. How does one preach in such a way as to lead people to worship, while also expecting them to reason, to process, to interpret? That is the unique posture of Pentecostal expository preaching, in which teaching takes place as worship. The preacher's task is not to produce theologians so much as to lead the congregation in the corporate worship of Jesus Christ, for their Spirit transformation into a biblically literate, Spirit-filled, and ready-for-action people of God. Congregational objectification is brief, transient, and in the service of their worship participation.

As soon as the light shines through the Explanation step, "Here is what the Word is saying! Here's what God is showing us!" the congregation is quickly illuminated within its penetrating beam. And just like that, the congregation finds itself caught up in a moment of holy shock and awe. In the same juncture of beholding the glory, brilliance, and awe of Christ in the Word, they cannot escape the confrontation of their own need for him. The moment ushers the congregation out of the cold winds of intellectualism and into the warming embers of sacrifice. They are not just passive recipients but active worshipers. Information becomes encounter.

In the Explanation step, the preacher intentionally sets the passage in context for the hearers. They're highlighting, clarifying, and identifying the central truths not as academic points, but as living realities meant to be incarnated within the congregation. In the Implication step, they're asking, "What does this passage actually mean for one's relationship with Christ? What implications does it have for who they are?" "If it's true that God is love, then what does that say about me and the kind of love I'm receiving from God and giving to others?" The preacher expects the congregation not only to hear but also to be interpreted by the Word, each in their own context. This is not passive listening. The kerygmatic nature of Pentecostal preaching demands an active, interpretive response.

When the preacher stands at that pulpit, their role is not to impress with theological acumen or to deliver a lecture fit for a seminary classroom. Their role is to serve the congregation in its own bidirectional interpretation. The preacher's explanation sets the table, but they must eat the meal. The preacher brings the light, but it is the Spirit who gives sight. *The goal is interpretation that leads to worship.* The Implication step asks, What does this truth, freshly revealed, mean to the congregation? In what ways does this truth or principle open doors for divine self-reflection? Where does the Spirit want to confront? To invite?

When preaching Jesus as the high priest, for example, the task in the explanation phase is to situate that reality so that the congregation sees not merely a biblical title but the living person of Christ, relevant to their struggles, temptations, and needs. The preacher might say, "Jesus as high priest is not a distant sacerdotal figurehead. This is the One who gets us, who sympathizes with our weaknesses." At that moment, the preacher is shining the light, but the expectation is for the congregation to receive it, comprehend it, and allow it to search their hearts.

The Implication step is the intersection at which Pentecostal expository preaching departs from other homiletical traditions. While some may stop at cognitive comprehension, Pentecostal preaching pushes hard for interpretation that leads to response. Congregational interpretation is one of the unique Pentecostal contributions in the wider conversation of homiletics. Born of Spirit-filled Explanation, sermonic teaching always leads to the exaltation of Jesus Christ.

## IMPLICATION IN ACTION

Implication materializes through simple questions from the preacher that facilitate the transition from learning to worship. These typically take one of two forms: either a simple *check-in* on the truth or principle of the sermon point or an *if/then clause* question. The check-in is a direct, personal question about how the sermon point has impacted their own lives. For example, when the preacher asks, "If it's true that being in Christ changes your point of view, then how Christlike is your point of view?" they create a simple yet powerful self-check that invites honest evaluation. This question encourages the listener to consider where they stand spiritually in the light of the truth, fostering personal accountability and opening the door for transformation.

By framing the question as a personal check, it becomes a reflective posture in which each person measures their life against God's word in an engaging and accessible way. This also allows the preacher to connect the timeless biblical principle directly to the congregation's immediate life context. Thus, the check-in question is a crucial bridge from biblical exposition to lived inner reality, encouraging each congregant to move from a posture of being over the text, in the context of learning, to a posture of submission under the text, in a posture of worship. It emphasizes that the gospel is not just truth to know but truth that knows us.

An if/then clause is a type of expression that conveys a condition and a consequence. It consists of two parts: the *if* clause (or condition), which states the conditions that must be met, and the *then* clause (or main clause), which describes the result or outcome that depends on the condition. The clause sets up a condition and a dependent result, establishing a move of personalization of the Word into the hearts of the congregants. For example, in the sentence "If you heat the water to 100 degrees Celsius, then it will boil," the *if* clause states the condition (heating the water) and the *then* clause states the consequence (it will boil). "If it rains, then we will stay inside" has an *if* clause stating the condition (raining outside) and a *then* clause stating the consequence (staying inside). You get the point. This works whether the *then* word is explicit or implicit. "If I were rich, I would travel the world" has an *if* clause stating the condition (I'm rich) and a *then* clause, here stated without the word, stating the consequence (travel the world).

If/then clauses are anchored to the truth or principle of the sermon point in hand. For example, if the preacher is teaching through the sermon point "Jesus is the Way" from John 14:6, after they have concluded their teaching on how Jesus is the way, their if/then clause might sound like:

- *If* clause (condition): If Jesus is the way . . .
- *Then* clause (consequence): Then what does that mean about all the ways we're searching for life outside of him?

Or, if the preacher is working through the sermon point entitled "God is sovereign," their if/then clause might sound like:

- *If* clause: If it's true that God is sovereign . . .
- *Then* clause: Then what does that mean about how we're not submitting to his authority in our lives?

## FORMULATING IF/THEN QUESTIONS

The method by which a preacher identifies the kinds of if/then questions to be used during the Implication step is surprisingly accessible. Since each sermon point is grounded in a truth or principle, the starting point is for the preacher to identify that truth or principle and ask two questions. The first question identifies *reasons* why a person's life may not be fully aligned with the truth or principles. For example, if a pastor is preaching on the sermon point "The Christian Life Is Characterized by the Pursuit of Righteousness" (Prov 21:21), the preacher might ask why a person might not be pursuing a righteous life. These reasons might include:

- Not fully identifying as a Christian (struggling to be an all-in Christian)
- Too many worries or distractions cloud their ability to exercise faith
- Too much sin in their life

With these in hand, it's easy for the preacher to assemble several potential Implication questions to include in the sermon.

The second question identifies the *features* that ought to be in a person's life if the truth or principle were in their life to the fullest. Here, the preacher might ask, "What kinds of spiritual benefits would be in the life of a person who *was* pursuing righteousness?" Such a list might include:

- Peace that passes understanding
- Unshakable self-confidence
- Genuine care for others
- Being fully immersed into a vibrant Christian community

Similar to the above, these become options the preacher can choose to include in their sermon notes.

The next step involves contextualizing the findings from these two questions. The principle being brought forth during the Explanation step now needs some teeth to pierce through the veneer of intellectualism and into the realm of implication. It's time to get personal. Going back to our lists established from the two questions above, the Implication step might sound like:

- Not fully identifying as a Christian (struggling to be an all-in Christian):
  - If it's true that the Christian life is characterized by the pursuit of righteousness, then what does that mean about how very few of our coworkers know we're believers?
- Too many worries or distractions cloud their ability to exercise faith:
  - If it's true that the Christian life is characterized by the pursuit of righteousness, then what does that mean about our stubborn insistence on focusing on our problems?
- Too much sin in their life:
  - If it's true that the Christian life is characterized by the pursuit of righteousness, then what does that mean about the double life many of us are living as Christians?

For the second question, the Implication step might sound like:

- Peace that passes understanding:
    - If it's true that the Christian life is characterized by the pursuit of righteousness, then what would our lives look like if peace were fully activated?
- Unshakable self-confidence:
    - If it's true that the Christian life is characterized by the pursuit of righteousness, then what would our lives look like if they were marked by an unshakable confidence?
- Genuine care for others:
    - If it's true that the Christian life is characterized by the pursuit of righteousness, then what would our lives look like if they were marked by a genuine care for others?
- Being fully immersed into a vibrant Christian community:
    - If it's true that the Christian life is characterized by the pursuit of righteousness, then what would our lives look like if they were marked by our full immersion into a vibrant Christian community?

Once these are identified, the preacher has a few options. One, they can harvest all of them into their notes and then isolate one or more in the moment of delivery. Or, they can prayerfully isolate one or more during sermon preparation and include them in their notes. Either way, they're in the flow. The first option allows them to choose according to the flow of the Spirit in the sermon; the second is anchored in the Spirit's flow during preparation.

Some general rules that guide the formulation of the Implication step include:

1. They are anchored to the sermon point at hand (truth or principle).
2. They are personally, lovingly, authoritatively invasive.
3. They ask one of two kinds of questions: check-in or if/then.
4. They are best delivered in first-person plural (we, us, our).

## DIVINE SELF-REFLECTION: PRACTICAL OUTWORKING OF IMPLICATION

The practical outworking of the Implication step is evident in the way it ushers the congregation into a posture of divine self-reflection. This pivotal move by the preacher shifts their function from divine proclaimer to divine doorman, escorting the congregation into the throne room of encounter. Once inside, they cannot escape the ever-penetrating mission of God's Word.

There's an appealing connection between this dynamic and the Jewish understanding of prayer. Rabbi Alan Lew, in his text *This Is Real and You Are Completely Unprepared*, highlights how the infinitive of the Hebrew word *to pray* is in a *reflexive form*, "denoting action that one performs on oneself."[1] Lew positions prayer in the context of being in the very presence of God, where in such a posture of divine, irresistible reflection, one sees oneself "through God's unblinking gaze."[2] In this way, being in the presence of God illuminates the true nature of the inner self. The heightened self-awareness is not without a demand for response.

The kerygmatic nature of the Word is at work here. Once held by the listener, the demand for response is inescapable. Since the mission of the Word does not return to God void, and since the hearer is now held within the interpretive gaze of God's Word, they have no choice but to acquiesce. The listener is being interpreted. If their aim was to measure God's Word, they now find God measuring them. In the presence of God, the question "What are the personal implications of this truth in my life?" is met with one of two simple and clear responses: Yes or no. The yes carries the hearer deeper into the transformation journey of salvation and becomes the currency of the altar. The no, further away.

The danger of misinterpretation is mitigated in the context of worship. Rather than being an act of subjective interpretation, the divine self-reflection here is the ontological appropriation of the objective truth of God's Word. Any notion of subjectification is at the mercy of the mission of the Word, not something that arises out of individual imaginations.

1. Lew, *This Is Real*, 66.
2. Lew, *This Is Real*, 67.

## CONGREGATIONAL PREPARATION

The Word of God, in the hands of a Spirit-filled, inspired preacher, will always be on time. This confidence is without controversy. If the Spirit was the source of divine inspiration in the preacher's choosing the passage for the expository sermon, then the Spirit is also the source of divine preparation of the congregation's reception of that passage. As the Spirit guides the preacher in preparing the sermon, he also prepares the congregation's hearts for reception.

This dynamic is visible in Scripture. The apostle Paul received a vision to come to Macedonia (Acts 16). Led by the Holy Spirit, Paul set out to obey with confidence, knowing that if the Spirit was guiding him, the Spirit was also preparing hearts in anticipation of his coming. Three cities received churches in response to the Spirit's preparation: Philippi, Thessalonica, and Berea. In Philippi, the first convert was Lydia. The Bible says, "The Lord opened her heart to pay attention to what was said by Paul" (Luke 16:14 ESV). If the Spirit has inspired the preacher, the Spirit is *also* concurrently preparing the hearts of the congregation.

Paul's first letter to the church in Corinth highlights this phenomenon even further. In the apostle's discussion of the wisdom of the Spirit, he teaches that the things of the Spirit are indiscernible without the Spirit because they are spiritually discerned. The things of the Spirit of God are not accepted by those whom the Spirit has not given understanding. Paul reminds the believers in Corinth that believers have the mind of Christ, which is what enables them to understand the things of the Spirit (1 Cor 2:6–16).

Jesus, in one of his post-resurrection appearances to his disciples, opened their minds to understand the Scriptures (Luke 24:45), indicating that it is the work of the Spirit of Christ to open minds and prepare them to receive the Word. In his opening prayer for Solomon's Temple, King David asked the Lord to direct the hearts of the people toward him (1 Chr 29:18), revealing that it is the work of the Lord that prepares, protects, and reorients them toward God.

John the Baptist's ministry is also characterized by this Spirit phenomenon. It was prophesied of John that his ministry would make straight the paths for the coming of the Lord. It was also prophesied that he would be filled with the Holy Spirit. Matthew's Gospel reports that many in Israel were coming to him and being baptized in keeping with the fruit of repentance. This was a fulfillment of the Spirit's work, preparing the hearts of the Israelites for responding favorably to John's ministry. This also fulfills the Malachi prophecy of Elijah's return to turn the hearts of fathers to children and children to fathers (Mal 4:5–6).

The Spirit's dual work in both preacher and congregation forms the bedrock of effective, timely preaching. As the Spirit inspires and directs the preacher's selection and preparation of the Word, the Spirit simultaneously prepares the congregation's hearts to receive that Word with openness and readiness. This inseparable dynamic ensures that the proclamation of Scripture is not merely a human endeavor but a divine encounter, in which transformation flows from the Spirit's illumination and power, and in which the preacher's proclamation is right on time.

Spirit-filled expository preaching is fundamentally a shared spiritual journey in which the preacher is a prophetic vessel, filled and led by the Spirit, while the congregation's receptivity is cultivated by the same Spirit. This truth calls preachers to rely wholly on the Spirit's guidance in every stage of sermon preparation and delivery, confident that the Spirit is simultaneously at work in the listeners. Such an awareness elevates preaching beyond technique to the realm of divine partnership, where God's Word accomplishes its redemptive purpose in his perfect timing.

## FINAL WORDS

The Implication step is a unique contribution in Pentecostal expository preaching. It is the pivotal moment when the preacher moves from explanation to intimate, Spirit-facilitated congregational interpretation, a divine interplay where the Word not only reveals truth but also personally convicts and empowers worship. This hermeneutical move shifts the congregation from passive listeners to active participants who engage deeply with the Word, allowing it to penetrate their hearts and draw them into authentic worship and self-reflection. It is here that Pentecostal preaching distinguishes itself by intertwining teaching with worship, making the sermon's truth not just a message to be heard intellectually but a living reality to be embraced existentially.

Moreover, the implication step serves as the gateway to transformation, where the Word's mission to judge and redeem meets the congregation's openness to be interpreted and changed by that Word. By framing the implication step as a Spirit-led, loving, and authoritative invitation to self-examination and response, the preacher facilitates a perichoretic dance involving the preacher, the Word, the Spirit, and the congregation.

This dynamic keeps the focus not on the preacher's eloquence but on the Spirit's work to bring the truth of Christ alive in worship. Ultimately, the preacher's faithful explanation leads to the congregation's worshipful response to proclamation, not merely intellectual assent but dynamic participation in the mission of the Word.

The invitation for Pentecostal preachers is to embrace their role as divine doorkeepers, guiding the congregation beyond mere understanding into the life-changing encounter with Jesus at the heart of the Word, where teaching becomes worship and worship becomes transformation. This delicate balance, undergirded by Spirit empowerment, ensures that preaching remains a living, active force that bridges Scripture's eternal truths with the real needs and longings of the congregation's hearts. Pentecostal homiletics, through the Implication step, moves the Word off the page and into the very fabric of the worshiping community's life and mission.

Using if/then questions bring the freshly explained truth into direct, Spirit-led contact with the hearts of the people. Here's how to make this happen in your sermon notes. Each of the following steps take the expositor deeper into congregational interpretation, where the Word not only reveals who God is but also lovingly exposes the congregation in relation to that truth, inviting worship, surrender, and transformation in real time.

## STEPS FOR CREATING IMPLICATION QUESTIONS

### Step 1: Anchor Your If/Then Clause Questions to the Sermon Point at Hand

Important: Implication points do not exist outside of the truth or principle at hand in the current sermon point. Circle back to the exact truth you have just explained (e.g., "Jesus is our compassionate high priest"). Start here. This keeps the implication from drifting into generality. The preacher's *if* always begins with the biblical principle at hand (see examples below).

### Step 2: Ask Two Diagnostic Questions

Before writing the Implication, ask:

1. Why might people's lives *not* be in alignment with this truth or principle (identifying specific obstacles)?

2. What would their lives look like if this truth or principle were operating fully (vision seeding)?

Answering these two questions supplies the raw material for your if/then clauses.

## Step 3: Formulate If/Then Clauses (or a Simple Check-In)

Craft the Implication using the truth or principle and your diagnostic answers.

Structure: If (truth or principle), then (implication/consequence question).

Examples:

- If Jesus truly sees everything about us, then what are we still trying to hide from him?
- If God is sovereign, then what does that mean about our need to control everything ourselves?

This pattern converts explanation into encounter—it invites interpretation and introspection.

## Step 4: Keep It Personally, Lovingly Invasive

- Speak with pastoral compassion, not condemnation.
- Use language that tenderly confronts: "What does this mean about the way we . . ." rather than "You need to . . ."
- Tone: Use first-person plural (we, us, our) to include yourself with the congregation.

See yourself as the divine doorkeeper ushering people into God's presence for self-reflection.

## Step 5: Discern Delivery Options

You can prepare several Implication clauses and decide in the moment which to use.

- Option A: Spirit-led preparation. Pray through which implication to use during the Preparation step. Include in sermon notes.
- Option B: Spirit-led spontaneity. Prepare multiple implications to include in your notes but select one or two based on real-time prompting during delivery.

Both are Spirit-dependent; the difference is timing of discernment (in prep vs. in pulpit).

## EXAMPLES OF IMPLICATION

In each of the following examples, a Bible passage will be listed, followed by the model's steps. Starting with the Explanation step, a potential Implication step will be identified.

Passage: Eph 1:7 (ESV): "In him we have redemption through his blood, the forgiveness of our trespasses, according to the riches of his grace."

- Explanation: We have redemption through the blood of Jesus.
- Implication: If we have redemption through the blood of Jesus, then what does that mean about how we're still trying to earn God's grace through works?

Passage: Jonah 2:1–2 (ESV): "Then Jonah prayed to the Lord his God from the belly of the fish, saying, 'I called out to the Lord, out of my distress, and he answered me.'"

- Explanation: God answers prayers of distress.
- Implication: If God answers prayers of distress, then what does that say about our struggles with trusting him?

Passage: Rev 3:15–16 (ESV): "'I know your works: you are neither cold nor hot. Would that you were either cold or hot! So, because you are lukewarm, and neither hot nor cold, I will spit you out of my mouth.'"

- Explanation: Jesus knows everything (he is omniscient).
- Implication: If Jesus knows everything, then what does that mean about the secret struggles we're trying to hide from him?

## REFLECTION QUESTIONS

1. How would incorporating the Implication step change the way you currently listen to or prepare sermons, especially in moving from intellectual understanding to a posture of active worship and personal encounter with the living Word?
2. In what ways do you see the concept of congregational interpretation as a bidirectional process—where we interpret the Word and the Word simultaneously interprets us—playing out in your own spiritual life or church experience?
3. Why do you think a sharp distinction exists between implication (leading to worship and encounter) and application (geared toward discipleship)? How might confusing these two affect the atmosphere of a Sunday worship service?
4. How does understanding the preacher's role as a "divine doorkeeper" or "sheepdog" rather than the primary shepherd challenge your view of what makes preaching effective and Spirit-led in a Pentecostal context?
5. Reflecting on the Spirit's dual work of inspiring the preacher and preparing the congregation's hearts, how can reliance on this divine partnership influence your confidence and approach when stepping into the pulpit to proclaim God's Word?

## APPLICATION ACTIVITIES

1. Personal Scripture Implication Exercise—Choose one short passage you read in your daily devotions this week (three to five verses). Write out a clear one-sentence explanation of the main truth or principle. Then craft three different if/then implication questions that would help you personally move from understanding the truth to allowing it to search your heart. Journal your honest reflections in response to each question (300–400 words total).
2. Diagnostic Questions Drill—Select any well-known biblical truth (e.g., "God is faithful," "Christ is our peace," "The Spirit empowers witness"). Answer the two diagnostic questions: (1) Why might

believers' lives not fully align with this truth? List four to five specific reasons. (2) What would a life look like if this truth operated fully? List four to five characteristics. Then turn at least three items from each list into personalized if/then implication questions.

3. Group Discussion Preparation—Prepare to lead a five to seven minute discussion in your small group or with two or three friends. Choose one biblical truth (e.g., "God is sovereign"). Write a brief explanation (two sentences), then prepare three implication questions (at least two if/then, one check-in). Deliver the explanation and questions to your group, then journal what you observed about their engagement and any visible shift toward worship or reflection.
4. Compare and Contrast Analysis—Find an online sermon transcript or video (5–10 minutes long) that ends with traditional application points. Listen/read carefully, then rewrite the final two to three minutes using only implication-style questions (if/then and/or check-in) instead of application statements. Submit both the original ending and your rewritten version, along with a paragraph explaining the difference in tone and expected congregational response.
5. Spirit-Led Spontaneity Practice—Prepare three different implication questions for the same sermon point/truth (e.g., "We are redeemed by Christ's blood"). Practice delivering the explanation out loud, then immediately follow with one of the three questions—choose spontaneously as you feel led (simulate the moment). Record the practice session, then listen back and journal which question felt most Spirit-prompted and why.

# 21

# Step Six: Confrontation

Most people don't like confrontation. They either don't like discovering that their words or their actions have caused harm somewhere, or they don't like having to confront others who have done so to them. What happens when the Lord confronts one of his followers? Such is the nature of the good news. Jesus told John the Baptist's disciples that blessings come to those who are not offended by the gospel message (Matt 11:6). The gospel is offensive. It is confrontational. When preachers seek to preach unoffensive messages, they deliver messages stripped of power and purpose. What person would not intervene upon seeing their friend headed down a road of destruction? How much more do the words of Christ intervene for those who are similarly inclined? Jesus loves enough to confront.

What a tremendous privilege it is for a person to be called into the ministry of preaching! God uses the preacher to deliver difficult messages that are both delicate and powerful. They're the ones who are called to confront the people of God. It's God's message; it's the preacher's words. The Word comes in to confront sin, attitudes, and excuses with prophetic clarity.

The next step of the model focuses on the preacher's authoritative and loving confrontation of the congregation. Confrontation is when the Word pricks the hearts and exposes the gap between God's truth and reality. If the Implication step invites the congregation to ask, "What does this truth or principle reveal about me and my relationship with God?" then Confrontation continues the enquiry into "What am I going to do about it?" In the Confrontation step, the Word serves as a mirror, revealing the congregation's need for repentance and transformation.

Here again, the kerygmatic nature of Scripture comes into view. As the Spirit begins to move through the proclamation of the Word, the mission of the Word sets out to pierce, judge, and interpret the congregation. The Confrontation step comes next to usher the congregation into the sacred space of preparing for the altar. More than a proposition under consideration, the Confrontation step further facilitates an immediate response to the Word's piercing and searching nature. A few simple phrases are used during these moments to continue congregational preparation for the worship that takes place at the altar.

Many have been confronted by the Word in a way that created a distinct compulsion for the altar. In those moments, the Holy Spirit revealed to them something requiring urgent attention, prompting immediate repentance. And when they made their way to the front of the church, offering that sacrifice of surrender, the coals of forgiveness and cleansing began to remove shame, deliver from strongholds, and impart the loving, transformative grace into the hearts of believers. It is a powerful moment of grace and renewal.

Pentecostal preachers never have to apologize for confronting God's people. The rod of comfort wounds to bring about healing. The Psalmist says, "Even though I walk through the valley of the shadow of death, I will fear no evil, for you are with me; your rod and your staff, they comfort me" (Ps 23:4 ESV). Why does the presence of the rod and staff bring comfort? Because the rod, an instrument of discipline, is also an instrument of protection. The rod is a short, solid, club-like stick used by shepherds as a tool of authority. It is typically shorter and heavier than the staff and sturdy enough to be used as a weapon against predators and to reprimand the sheep. In biblical imagery, the rod conveys the shepherd's strength, defense, and right to rule and discipline, assuring the sheep that they are guarded and accounted for. A shepherd's staff is a long, slender stick, often about five to six feet in length, usually made of wood, and sometimes featuring a curved or hooked end. This curved end is used to gently guide and manage sheep, such as pulling straying sheep back to the flock, rescuing them from precarious places like thickets or crevices, or lifting newborn lambs to their mothers to prevent rejection. It represents gentle guidance and rescue.

Confrontation is the Holy Spirit's rod and staff of comfort to the congregation. Where the Implication step has already begun the process of conviction, Confrontation brings them to the point of decision. As the Implication step reveals the congregation's need for Jesus, Confrontation asks, What will you do now that you're aware of this need? The encounter is full of grace. It's not manipulation on the part of the preacher; it's truth. The rod of comfort wounds to bring healing.

## SCRIPTURAL WITNESS OF CONFRONTATION

The Bible contains numerous accounts of the gospel's confrontational nature. A few are listed below. What they all have in common is the demonstration of how truths and principles exist not to simply inform the reader of what it means to be a Christian, but how their nature is to pierce, penetrate, and reveal one's need for Christ.

### David and Nathan (2 Samuel 11–12)

The Bible states that David was a man after God's own heart (1 Sam 13:14). However, David was not perfect. His most famous sin occurred on a day when he was in the wrong place, wrong time, and wrong frame of mind; not unsurprisingly, he committed the worst kind of offense. As he spotted Bathsheba and as his mind filled with lust, he summoned her and, upon discovering her pregnancy, had her husband, Uriah, killed to cover up his sin.

The Lord sent the prophet Nathan to confront King David. When he arrived, he told King David a fictional story about two men in a certain city: one rich, with many animals; the other poor, with only one ewe lamb that had become a pet to the poor man. Upon the arrival of the rich man's guest, instead of preparing a feast with an animal from among his own flocks, the rich man stole and prepared the poor man's lamb. The Bible says David's anger burned within him as he demanded the rich man's death and the poor man's fourfold repayment. Nathan responded to David, "You're the man!" God used Nathan to confront King David about his sin.

### John the Baptist and the Pharisees (Matthew 3)

As John the Baptist preached and baptized, the Lord was at work preparing the hearts of the Israelites for a response. This was in fulfillment of the prophecies spoken of by John and in the Spirit's work of congregational preparation. The Spirit's work was wide-ranging. Many Israelites were coming to the Jordan River to be baptized in response to John's Spirit-led, fearless, and uncompromising calls for repentance. As a group of Pharisees and Sadducees came out to observe, John confronted them. Out of his deep devotion and in the boldness of the Holy Spirit, he cast them directly into the ever-gazing light of truth. "You sons of the great serpent! Who warned you to flee the coming judgment? Repent! Your Abrahamic blood does not deliver you" (taken from Matt 3:7–12). God used John the Baptist as a voice of confrontation.

## Jesus and the Religious Leaders

Matthew records Jesus' seven-fold, woe-filled confrontation of the scribes and Pharisees. In the midst of large crowds, Jesus zeroed in on their self-righteousness and publicly declared God's indictments against them. Their blinded, attention-seeking, and hypocritical ways were not impervious to the truth-revealing Word made flesh. In the Bible, the word *woe* frequently appears in prophetic contexts in which God or Jesus pronounces judgment on individuals or groups for their evil actions, hypocrisy, or rebellion. Confrontation is an expected component of Spirit-filled preaching (Matt 23).

## Paul and the Galatians

One need not be surprised to learn of Paul's confrontational comments. His letters are filled with such a tone. In his epistle to the believers in Galatia, Paul pressed in with a posture that could only come from the Holy Spirit. "You foolish Galatians! Who has bewitched you?" (Gal 3:1 NIV). The apostle Paul was upset that the believers had so quickly abandoned the gospel of grace he preached, turning instead to legalistic observance of the Mosaic law. No one knows if his frustrations with the Galatian community was ever resolved, but what is known is that Spirit-inspired confrontation is a norm for the Spirit-filled preacher.

## Peter's First Sermon

Peter's first post-Pentecost sermon shines a most spectacular light upon the Confrontation step. Acts reveals the drastic, transformative nature of Peter's Spirit baptism, producing a courageous man on a mission. The Peter portrayed in the Gospels was rash, quick to speak, and slow to understand. However, the Peter who preached on those Jerusalem streets was someone altogether different. As the crowds taunted the believers as having had too much wine, Peter rose in defense. As he raised his voice, he quickly dismissed the false accusation of drunkenness and identified the outpouring as the fulfillment of the Joel prophecy (Joel 2).

What came next was unexpected but not surprising. Peter wasn't done. He began the account of Christ's suffering, crucifixion, and resurrection. Quoting King David, he reminded the crowd of the Messiah's prophetic resurrection and of how Christ's resurrection fulfilled that prophecy. Peter finished with one of the clearest examples of Confrontation when he said, "Let all the house of Israel therefore know for certain that God has made him both Lord and Christ, this Jesus *whom you crucified*" (Acts 2:36 ESV, emphasis mine).

Peter's sermon also reveals the astonishing results of the confrontation. Instead of laughing off the fisherman's appeal, the crowds fell under conviction and were desperate to resolve their need for Christ. Out of their mouths was heralded the phrase every preacher longs to hear when preaching, "Now when they heard this they were cut to the heart, and said to Peter and the rest of the apostles, 'Brothers, what shall we do?'" (Acts 2:37 ESV). The church baptized three thousand people for Peter's first sermon! The Word of truth became the rod of comfort. This is what Spirit confrontation looks like in the hands of a Spirit-filled preacher.

In the hands of the anointed preacher, the Confrontation step comes off without a hitch. Only the Holy Spirit can do this. Only the Holy Spirit can make this kind of statement. When preachers attempt the Confrontation step outside of the anointing, they actually *do* run the risk of offending the congregation. Confrontation can only be delivered in the context of the anointed grace. Truth and grace, simultaneously coexisting together in this step, are both sides of the double-edged sword of the Word. In the same thrust of the blade, one side cuts with the truth, the other comforts with grace (Heb 4:12).

One of the most breathtaking features of the anointing is that preachers don't have to worry about its presence if they're preaching an inspired message. If the Spirit has inspired the preacher, the Spirit has been preparing the hearts of the congregation. The anointing will be there. The Preparation step has led to the preacher's own undoing by the truths and principles of the text. They've already been interpreted by the Spirit, who gave them the interpretation of the text. Now it's the congregation's turn. When the preacher knows this and believes the Holy Spirit has already been preparing hearts, they know that, when it's time for the Confrontation step, the move will be a rod of comfort to the congregation. It may be painful, but it will immediately bring significant relief.

## FEATURES OF CONFRONTATION

### Confrontation Is a Product of God's Love

Confrontation flows out of the love of God for his people. The Bible says that God disciplines those whom he loves (Prov 3:11–12; Heb 12:6). The mere fact that God could easily wield a hand of destruction against sin but instead chooses to intervene is evidence of his gracious and patient love for humanity. The loving act of confrontation does not subside once a person gets saved. The love continues, without ceasing, as long as the recipient is on this side of eternity.

Confrontation is an act of God's love because it serves as a means through which God lovingly corrects, guides, and restores his people. Confrontation is not about condemnation or punishment for its own sake but about lovingly addressing sin, error, or harmful behavior to bring about repentance and reconciliation. This is rooted in God's desire for the well-being and holiness of his people. Confrontation, then, is a tangible expression of that loving discipline.

### Confrontation Flows Out of Pastoral Authority

The Spirit-filled pastor is gifted with a threefold authority: first, rooted in God's call; second, energized by the Spirit; and third, grounded in the experiential fluency born of the interpretative journey. The preacher's call is a sure foundation of authority. Caught in the updraft of prophetic ambassadorship for the kingdom of God, the preacher serves at the leisure of the Spirit's messages to the church. Sermon content is not a product of religious imagination or pastoral agenda; it's a clear, unambiguous message from God himself, entrusted to his servant for faithful delivery. With such a mission in hand, the preacher approaches the microphone, not accompanied by authority, but immersed in authority.

Spirit anointing is integral to the preacher's call. Anointing is referred to as a baptism because of its immersive nature. The anointing is not so much a kingdom credential, conferred upon the preacher, as if to be carried like a badge. Rather, the anointing is like a kingdom commandeering, in the appropriation of the preacher, as if they have been carried off for official service. The apostle Paul's conversion story illustrates the point (Acts 9). With the authority of the religious leaders having been conferred upon him and with official letters serving as his credentials, Paul made his way toward Damascus to arrest Christians. When confronted by Jesus on the road, however, Paul discovered the possessive nature of the anointing. Having been sequestered for kingdom work, Paul no longer carried letters of authority; he was being carried by the Letter itself. The preacher does not possess the anointing as much as the anointing possesses them. The preacher's authority is the anointing, in which they are immersed.

The third layer of authority is found in the interpretive process of sermon preparation. More than the task of intellectual comprehension of the text, the preacher's sermon preparation is a journey of their own interpretive encounters with the Word himself. More than standing over the text in a posture of analysis, the preacher yields to the text's authority, submitting to its measurements, poking, prodding, and piercing. It's only in the context of being interpreted by the Word first that the preacher can hope to have an interpretation of the Word.

If a minister is preaching the story of Paul's conversion (Acts 9), one of their sermon points might focus on Ananias's hesitation to obey the Holy Spirit's instructions to lay hands on Paul in order for him to regain his sight. Ananias had a legitimate concern based on Paul's reputation and having knowledge of Paul's mission in the area to persecute Christians. The sermon point might be titled "Obedience Requires Faith." As the preacher prepares this point, they will not escape the Spirit's searching gaze into their own lives, asking, "What instructions have you received that you are too fearful to fulfill?"

The preacher's own experience with the principle thus deposits deep conviction, which becomes the mortar of authority in the foundation of their own lives and in the delivery of the point to the congregation. The interpretive journey is now one of experience, not simple intellectualism.

The encounter has transported their teaching out of the dull drum of pharisaical philosophy and into the penetrating call of godly authority.

## Confrontation Is Invasive and Personal

Sermons are intended to touch people's lives in personal ways because they constitute a grammar for addressing sin, wayward behavior, and harmful attitudes that affect a person's soul. The mission of the Word extends beyond surface issues and a discipleship-driven agenda to the core areas of one's identity, values, and spiritual well-being. This kind of confrontation can feel intrusive because it directly challenges hearts and consciences, often eliciting strong emotional responses. Though such moments can elicit pain, they are intended not to harm but to bring restoration and spiritual growth.

Sermonic confrontation is often experienced as invasive because it involves entering into personal and sometimes hidden areas of a person's life where sin and dysfunction may be present. Unlike casual correction, pastoral confrontation addresses matters of the soul and moral conduct, requiring careful yet direct engagement that may disrupt a person's comfort or defenses. It situates the sermon in the context of worshipful altar preparation rather than in instruction for Christian living (a function of discipleship).

With the church functioning as a genuine Christian community, Confrontation is inevitably personal. It addresses the individual in their unique identity and relationships within the church body. This personal nature requires sensitivity and respect that only the Holy Spirit can provide, as it can affect not only actions but also relationships and reputations. The goal of Confrontation is altar preparation, which means addressing the person's innermost spiritual condition with tender yet unmitigated authority.

Effective pastoral confrontation respects the congregation while being forthright about truths and principles. Its invasive nature demands compassion, so it is not perceived as an attack or abuse. The balancing of grace and truth is key here, in prioritizing conviction over condemnation. This balance underscores the pastoral responsibility to love deeply even when disclosing hard truths that affect a person's soul and standing in the community.

## The Productive Nature of Confrontation

The concept of productivity implies fertility and fruitfulness. When a person's land is identified as productive, it means the land produces large amounts of goods, crops, or other commodities. God's love is a productive kind of love, meaning when his love makes contact with its object, it gives rise to the virtues that characterize the Christian life. Divine productivity, though measurable in word and deed, is ontologically oriented. That is, its purpose is transformational, even though its outcomes are vocational. The production draws out the best in identity, more so than in doing.

The productive nature of Confrontation is anchored in God's love. It's not about getting things done, but in pulling out the best of God's creative intentions for the individual. Sometimes I ask, "If I bumped into you in heaven, say ten thousand years from now, what kind of person would I meet?" The question invites the listener to envision themselves in the true nature and fullness of who God created them to be. King David had this truth within his grasp. He declared the wonder of God knitting together each person in their mother's womb (Ps 139). The productive feature of the Confrontation brings God's authorial intent for the believer clearly into view.

God sees his original design in each person. Confrontation presses in to allow the believer to see the same. This dynamic can be observed, for example, among music producers, who are skilled at eliciting the finest expression of talent from musicians and singers during the recording process. It's not uncommon for producers to discern ability that extends beyond the ability that the artist thinks they are capable of. The resulting clash of the extraction can be painful. The artist says, "I can't do what you're asking me to do." It's not until the producer prevails upon them, with the resulting surrender and effort of the artist, that the artist discovers what the producer had seen all along. Good producers are unthwarted by tears of frustration. Good preachers, though compassionate to the pain, are the same.

## The Compulsive Character of Confrontation

The kerygmatic nature of the Gospel always elicits a response. For those willing to yield, the response becomes the currency of the altar. Confrontation is inseparable from compulsion. The Spirit-filled preacher knows this truth. They don't manipulate it, but they also don't hesitate. Confrontation is a necessary and loving component of worship-filled preaching. The preacher who denies their congregation confrontation is like the doctor who informs a patient of dangerous symptoms (Implication) but refuses to give a diagnosis (Confrontation).

Most people, upon delivery of a health diagnosis, are immediately eager to discover two crucial pieces of information: One, what is the prognosis, and two, what is the pathway of treatment? When it comes to matters of the Spirit, the prognosis is always the best possible: total healing and permanent eradication of symptoms (forgiveness and cleansing) are possible. And the pathway of treatment is equally joyful, immediate, and free: a short walk down to the altar. It's time for sacrifice. Something sinful needs to die. They are ready to go. All that is needed is the invitation.

For those not quite ready, the response leads to rejection and a retreat back into the shadows. Not many people like the light shining into the dark pockets of their inner resistance. Jesus described this dynamic to Nicodemus, explaining that some people prefer darkness to light because their works are evil (John 3:19–20). The offense is too great. The comfort and familiarity of the darkness give them a strange and fraudulent source of life, from which they are unwilling to depart. On the other hand, for those now antsy for the invitation to the altar, life awaits on the other side of the sacrifice. For those walking away, further darkness. The great hope for those walking away is knowing how brightly the faintest of light shines in the darkness. The darker it is, the easier it is to see Jesus.

## THE STRUCTURE OF CONFRONTATION

### Spirit Dependency

True Confrontation is impossible without deep dependence on the Spirit. The preacher's authority and effectiveness do not originate in personal charisma or eloquence but from the Spirit's anointing. The preacher who has not first been confronted by the Word in the Spirit can hardly expect to deliver a message that transforms hearts. It is the Spirit who prepares both preacher and congregation. When the moment of Confrontation arrives, it is the Spirit who empowers the preacher to speak in a manner that is both piercing and compassionate. Only by relying on the Spirit can Confrontation avoid becoming manipulative or harsh.

## Tone and Delivery

Tone and delivery of Confrontation are crucial to its effectiveness. Confrontation does not require volume or bravado to be impactful. When rooted in the Spirit's anointing, Confrontation should have a balance of authority with compassion. At times, the words must pierce and provoke self-examination, yet they should always be seasoned with love. Many of the most effective moments of Confrontation come with a gentle urgency, not harshness—and though passion is often a component of Confrontation, a preacher's voice need not be raised to reach the heart.

Compassionate delivery is the tender meeting place of trust and openness, allowing the congregation to receive hard truths without defensiveness. The authority to confront stems not from personal charisma or bravado, but from a deep sense of care for the people and alignment with God's truth. Ultimately, it is the Spirit that guides tone and delivery, ensuring that Confrontation leads to conviction, healing, and spiritual growth rather than shame or alienation.

## The Interrogative Framework

Effective Confrontation thrives on clear structure and practical execution. Confrontation is most effective when delivered as a question rather than a statement. Probing questions invite the congregation to continue in their posture of divine self-reflection, now borne by the Implication step. The Confrontation step further deepens the divine self-reflection, challenging the congregation with the question, "What am I going to do about it?"

The shaping of these questions is best structured through the five Ws—who, what, when, where, and why/how. *Who* identifies the individuals or groups involved, clarifying key stakeholders or actors, who are working against, preventing, or causing friction, to a person's ability to live in accordance with the truth or principle at hand. *What* defines the subject or action, revealing the core issue or event that has become a barrier to obedience. *When* and *where* establish the timing and location, situating the sinful in a specific context. Lastly, *why* explores the reasons or causes behind the sin, while *how* often explains the process or method by which something occurs. Together, the interrogative framework clears away any fog of indecision and leads the congregant to the doorway of resolute action.

## The Implication Connection

The Confrontation step in preaching is never isolated but directly connected to and grounded in the prior Implication step. What the congregation has come to see and acknowledge about itself in the Implication moment now constitutes the essential content of Confrontation. This process brings deep self-revelation from the divine text into clear focus, placing it on the heart's table for open engagement. The preacher's role at this point is to carefully lift what has been exposed and move it into a direct, purposeful confrontation, engaging the congregation with a truth that requires a spiritual response.

For example, if a principle or truth is like an arm, then the Implication step might reveal a fracture in the arm's humerus through an X-ray. The preacher, acting as a divine physician, confronts the congregation with what needs to happen next: "This fracture needs to be healed. You need a cast." In ministry terms, this means identifying the spiritual fracture or sin that hinders growth or health and calling for the necessary corrective or redemptive action. The Confrontation is thus anchored in what has already been understood and personalized, making it both invasive in its demand for honest reflection and personal in its direct address to the individual's soul and spiritual condition.

## First-Person Plural

Using first-person plural language in confrontational preaching is essential because it places the preacher within the call for change, preventing a disconnect between the preacher and the congregation. Using *we* instead of *you* acknowledges the shared need for transformation and demonstrates humility, making the confrontation less accusatory and more inviting. This inclusive language fosters a sense of shared sojourning, showing that the preacher is not above the people but alongside them in the struggle to live out God's truth. By sharing in the indictment, the preacher models vulnerability and accountability, which deepens trust and openness in the congregation.

Moreover, first-person plural language helps soften the inevitable tension inherent in Confrontation, transforming it into a pastoral act rather than an authoritarian declaration. It communicates that the challenge is communal and that growth requires mutual responsibility. This approach avoids creating an adversarial, legalistic atmosphere in which congregants may feel condemned. Instead, it embodies the biblical pattern of loving correction within the body of Christ, where everyone, including the leader, participates in the journey toward holiness. Consequently, Confrontation delivered with *we* language becomes a collective call to repentance and renewal, enhancing both the preacher's credibility and the congregation's engagement with the message. This dynamic connection is vital for effective spiritual formation through preaching.

## CREATING THE CONFRONTATION STEP IN YOUR NOTES

The Confrontation step follows from the Implication step. Here's a step-by-step guide that delivers a clear, reproducible method. This approach assumes that the preacher has already completed the Explanation and Implication steps and is now ready to guide the congregation toward a Spirit-led decision.

### Step 1: Confrontation Is Always Connected to the Implication Step

Confrontation arises directly from what the congregation has just realized during the Implication step. Here's what this looks like:

- Identify the core principle or truth previously uncovered (e.g., God calls his people to reconcile broken relationships).
- Turn that realization into a decision point, something that requires action.
- Implication asks: What does this truth reveal about my relationship with God?
- Confrontation asks: Now that I see it—what will I do about it?

Confrontation builds on revelation during the Explanation step.

### Step 2: Shape the Confrontation Using Questions

Instead of making accusatory statements, craft probing, Spirit-led questions that elicit reflection and compel decision. Use the five Ws to design these:

- Who is affected by this truth or failing to live it out?
- What specific sin, behavior, or attitude is being challenged?
- When does this truth or principle tend to occur in our lives or community rhythms?
- Where does this misalignment show up—in our homes, work, relationships, or worship?
- Why do we resist change in this area? How might obedience look today?

These questions move the congregation from vague conviction to concrete awareness and readiness for repentance.

## Step 3: Include a Direct, Straightforward Confrontation

Every Confrontation should culminate in a clear opportunity for the listener to respond.

- Express it naturally: What (or who, where, why, when, or how) is the Spirit asking us to surrender right now?
- Invite specific actions: repentance, reconciliation, prayer, confession, or service.
- Guide the congregation toward the altar moment.

The goal is not emotional manipulation but Spirit-born compulsion leading to surrender.

## Step 4: Balance Truth and Grace in Tone and Delivery

The tone of Confrontation must carry both authority and compassion.

- Speak firmly but tenderly, as one who loves deeply.
- Use first-person plural language (*we* vs. *you*).
- Allow moments of silence after asking confrontational questions to let the Word work in hearts.

This balance helps the message be a wound for healing, not harm, mirroring Ps 23's rod-and-staff comfort.

## EXAMPLES OF CONFRONTATION

Picking up from examples in the last chapter, note the following examples of Confrontation.

Passage: Eph 1:7 (ESV): "In him we have redemption through his blood, the forgiveness of our trespasses, according to the riches of his grace."

- Explanation: We have redemption through the blood of Jesus (followed by substantive teaching).
- Implication: If we have redemption through the blood of Jesus, then what does that mean about how we're still trying to earn God's grace through works?
- Confrontation: Why do we seem to waste so much time in our lives before we surrender to God's grace and receive his forgiveness?

Passage: Jonah 2:1–2 (ESV): "Then Jonah prayed to the Lord his God from the belly of the fish, saying, 'I called out to the Lord, out of my distress, and he answered me.'"

- Explanation: God answers prayers of distress (followed by substantive teaching).
- Implication: If God answers prayers of distress, then what does that say about our struggles with trusting him?
- Confrontation: What will it take for us to finally fully place our trust in Christ?

Passage: Rev 3:15–16 (ESV): "'I know your works: you are neither cold nor hot. Would that you were either cold or hot! So, because you are lukewarm, and neither hot nor cold, I will spit you out of my mouth.'"

- Explanation: Jesus is omniscient (followed by substantive teaching).
- Implication: If Jesus is omniscient, then what does that mean about the secret struggles we're trying to hide from him?
- Confrontation: Are we ready to stop running from Jesus' desire to help us with our secret struggle?

## REFLECTION QUESTIONS

1. Recall a time when a biblical truth or sermon strongly confronted something in your own life. What made that moment painful, and how did the combination of truth and grace eventually bring healing or change?
2. The chapter presents Confrontation as an expression of God's love rather than condemnation. How does viewing difficult messages this way change the way you respond when you sense the Holy Spirit challenging your attitudes or behaviors?
3. Why do you think many people are instinctively uncomfortable with personal confrontation encounters, even when they come from a place of genuine love? How might recognizing this resistance help you become more open to the Spirit's work in your own heart? How might this assist you in serving a congregation with confrontational sermons?
4. Reflect on the statement that effective confrontation depends entirely on the anointing of the Holy Spirit. What practices in your personal life and preparation help you stay dependent on the Spirit rather than your own strength or cleverness?
5. When have you experienced a sermon or Scripture passage that moved you quickly from conviction to a desire to respond at the altar? What made that moment of compulsion feel like grace rather than manipulation?

## APPLICATION ACTIVITIES

1. Rod and Staff Prayer Exercise—Read Ps 23 slowly three times, focusing on the phrase "your rod and your staff, they comfort me." Then pray aloud for 10 minutes, specifically asking the Lord to use his "rod of comfort" to confront one area of your life where you are resisting change (e.g., unforgiveness, secret sin, pride). Write down what the Spirit brings to mind and share that insight with a trusted Christian friend within the next three days.

2. Rewrite a Confrontational Moment—Think of a time when someone lovingly confronted you about sin or a wrong attitude (parent, pastor, friend). Write a one-page reflection describing how you initially felt, how grace was (or wasn't) present, and what the outcome was. Then rewrite the confrontation using first-person plural language (*we* instead of *you*) as the chapter teaches. Notice how the tone changes, and apply that insight the next time you need to speak truth to someone.
3. Five Ws Confrontation Practice—Select one biblical principle you've recently learned (e.g., forgiveness, honesty, generosity). Using the five Ws (who, what, when, where, why/how), write six probing questions that move from implication to confrontation for your own life. Example: "Why do we keep waiting until Sunday morning to confess the anger we felt all week?" Keep these questions in your prayer time for the next week and note any new conviction or action steps.
4. Scriptural Confrontation Rewrite—Choose one of the biblical confrontation stories from the chapter (Nathan and David, John the Baptist, Peter at Pentecost, or Jesus and the Pharisees). Rewrite the confrontational statement(s) in modern language as if the preacher were speaking directly to your congregation today. Make sure the rewrite keeps both truth and grace in balance. Share your rewritten version with one other person and ask for their honest feedback.
5. Productive Love Reflection and Action—Answer the chapter's heaven question in writing: "If I bumped into you in heaven ten thousand years from now, what kind of person would I meet?" Then identify one current attitude, habit, or sin that is keeping you from becoming more like that future, redeemed version of yourself. Write one practical, Spirit-dependent step you will take this week to allow God's productive love to confront and change that area. Begin the step before the next class.

# 22

# Step Seven: Invitation

Every Pentecostal expository sermon point ultimately leads to an invitation. While exposition establishes truth, implication reveals our need for Christ, confrontation challenges rebellion, and invitation opens the door for encounter. The Invitation step flows from the preacher's posture of Spirit partnership, issuing a sacred summons to congregants to respond to God's revealed Word. In these moments, preaching has moved far beyond the transfer-of-information mode and has become a transformative encounter in which divine truth intersects with human will.

Miles away from rhetoric, the Invitation step is the healing salve to theological conviction. The Spirit who inspired the text is now activating the hearts of listeners. The preacher's task here is not to coerce or control, but to continue curating a holy space for the congregation's response to the mission of the Word. Invitation, then, is not manipulation. It is a gesture of grace that respects both the dignity and the desire of the congregation. Ultimately, the invitation reminds both the preacher and the congregation that every sermon ushers them toward a transformative encounter with Christ.

## SATISFACTION OF CONGREGATIONAL DESIRE

As the preacher moves through the Explanation step, they arrive at the all-important place of response. The Word, alive, active, and on mission, has examined the heart of the congregation, and they are ready for action. Just as Isaiah felt the sting of his own sinfulness (Isa 6), so the congregation feels the weight of its own. The Spirit's gracious stirrings of conviction and correction have created a longing for healing. The desire for resolution is inescapable. Truths and principles have shone their interpretive light into the hearts of every listener. The work of the Spirit has created a hunger for the healing encounter of Jesus.

But more than a superficial response, a person's spiritual response to the probing nature of the Word carries eternal consequences. Once the need for Christ has been exposed, it creates conviction that demands a response. Free of the need for flashy emotion, this ontological throbbing persists until the desire is satisfied. Awareness of one's core separation from God through sin (Rom 6:23) delivers a permanent desire that only Christ's redemption can quiet. Superficial responses, warned against in Isa 29:13 and Jesus' rebukes of hypocritical worship, fade without heart transformation, but genuine Spirit-led conviction leads to lasting repentance and life.

The most gracious component of this model for expository preaching is found in the Invitation step, when the preacher invites the congregation to respond to the Word's convicting nature. They're ready for healing. Peter's sermon after the Pentecost event illustrates the point. After Peter's pointed teaching about Christ, and after his confrontation of their culpability in his murder, the crowd, in response to seeing themselves in the light of truth, cried out, "Brothers, what shall we do?" (Acts 2:37 ESV). The invitation came swiftly from Peter, "Repent and be baptized every one of you in the name of Jesus Christ for the forgiveness of your sins, and you will receive the gift of the Holy Spirit" (Acts 2:38 ESV).

## PREPARATION FOR SACRIFICE

The Invitation step is a crucial component for congregational preparation for sacrifice. The Old Testament sacrificial system was given so that a holy God could dwell among a sinful people, graciously providing a God-ordained way for Israel to draw near to him, receive forgiveness, and live as his covenant people. It addressed both the problem of sin and the positive call to worship, gratitude, and fellowship with God.

At the most basic level, the Old Testament altar sacrifices answered the question, "How can a holy God live among a sinful people without destroying them?" Through sacrifice, God provided an appointed means for Israel to draw near to him without being consumed by his holiness, with the altar functioning as the meeting point between God and his people. Many sacrifices were offered directly for sin, guilt, and impurity, so that the people of the sanctuary could be cleansed (Lev 1–7). Sacrifices also expressed positive devotion, deepening the bond between God and the Israelites as an expression of love, loyalty, and joy in the covenant relationship.

In contrast to cessationist preaching, where the congregation has been trained to focus on the takeaways of sermonic application, Pentecostal expository preaching has the opposite effect, serving to aid the congregation in giving. The Invitation step invites the participant to bring their sacrifice to the altar. Often, the sacrifice is whatever is keeping the congregant from aligning with the truth or principle at hand. For example, if the sermon point is honesty, after explaining the virtue of honesty and as the preacher pivots to the Implication step, they might ask the congregation why we're not being honest with ourselves about our relationship with Jesus. The Confrontation step might ask how much longer they will avoid truly seeing themselves in the light of truth. And, the Invitation step would invite them to sacrifice their procrastination and start living in the truth.

Other times, the sacrifice is one of praise or thanksgiving. This has happened to me on several occasions when gratitude for God's grace, intervention, protection, or one of many other reasons to be thankful overwhelms my heart and puts me in a posture of overflow. In such moments, my presence in the altar is one of extreme gratitude. For example, with the same sermon point on honesty above, some congregants may feel thankful for how God has moved in their lives when they have been honest with him in the past. For them, their offering at the altar is one of joy.

## CALL FOR IMMEDIATE, DECISIVE RESPONSE TO CONFRONTATION

One of the more appealing features of the Invitation step is its utility for expediency. The Invitation step serves as a direct follow-up to the Confrontation step. It is precise and immediate. This is not a *tomorrow event* for the congregation. This is not God doing something great in your life, *and it's right around the corner*, kind of phenomenon. The Invitation step is happening right now. Today is the day. This moment is the moment.

For those who have been around the Pentecostal movement for a while, it's common to hear the kind of hope-driven pronouncements of "God's preparing you for something great in your life" or "Your season of harvest is right around the corner." To be honest with you, I've grown weary of these kinds of proclamations. I learned that the best kind of hope is found in what God is doing right now. Here's a truth that will change the life of every Spirit-filled preacher: Every altar encounter is immediately transformative. There's no need to advocate tomorrow's hope when today's encounter vaporizes its need.

## SPECIFIC

Some invitations are a request to act, participate, or go somewhere or do something. Being optional in nature, invitations can be accepted or rejected. Some are simple; others more formal. Some are provocative and alluring, such as an invitation to go to Hawaii. Others are more official, being carried along in the spirit of a summons more so than opportunity. All share similar features of specificity, providing details needed for an affirmative response.

The Invitation step's specificity flows naturally from the preceding Implication and Confrontation steps. For example, if the sermon point is focusing on having a posture of humility, the Implication, Confrontation, and Invitation steps might be:

Implication: If it's true that a culture of Christianity is one that embraces a posture of humility, then what does that mean about the presence of self-reliance that continually works against us?

Confrontation: Why do we waste so much time spinning our wheels in the mud of pride?

Invitation: Today is the day when all the spinning comes to an end. What's one, specific area of your life where you have not yet come to Christ for help? Let go your pride-filled self-reliance and start trusting in Christ in all things.

A good Invitation feels more like a hand extended than a finger pointed. It is warm, hopeful, and clear. As preachers, we are not pressuring people; we are shepherding them toward the next faithful step. The Spirit is the true closer of the sermon, but we cooperate with him by giving people concrete ways to respond to what they've just heard. In this way, the Invitation becomes a moment of grace, in which hearers are gently but firmly led to turn from self and toward Christ in a fresh act of trust and obedience.

## CALL TO SAY YES

The Invitation step is a call to action. It's a call to say yes. More than a proposition, there's only one answer when the Spirit of the Lord is telling us to do something. The fact that God's plans are always for our good (Rom 8:28) makes our response in the affirmative all the easier. "Yes, Lord," is the only response. As truths and principles cut through the hard exteriors of the human heart, and as they seek out, isolate, and corner pockets of darkness that are working against us, the Word beckons us to surrender them to Jesus.

The good news here is that God has created humanity in his image and deposited within each person a spirit that longs to be with him (Eccl 3:11; Pss 42:1–2; 63:1; 84:2; Isa 26:9). A person's spirit *wants* to say yes to the penetrating invitation of God's Word. The invitation helps them do so. Even the hearts of unbelievers experience this dynamic. It's why, when I was lost and in need of redemption, my mother made a simple appeal I could not refuse. She said, "You don't have to quit running around (sinning) and quit all your bad habits . . . can you just come to church on Sundays?" She knew the power of the Word. She knew if I were in reach of the mission of the Word that I would soon surrender to my heart's longing for reconciliation with the One who created me. She was right.

The invitation gives permission for the human desire to say yes. Since humanity is made in God's image (Gen 1:26) and our ontological desire is for reconciliation, we have no excuse for rejecting the invitation. Romans 1:19–20 declares that God's invisible attributes are discernible throughout all creation, leaving unbelievers without excuse as their consciences bear witness to the truth of God's existence, even with continued suppression. The story of the rich young ruler (Mark 10) illustrates the main character's desire for Christ, yet he left sad, having rejected the call to leave everything to follow him. The story of the two on the road to Emmaus also bears witness. The two, after having traveled a long distance while in discourse with the living Word himself, declared to one another, "Did not our hearts burn within us while he talked to us on the road, while he opened to us the Scriptures?" (Luke 24:25 ESV). The Word sets hearts ablaze. The Invitation step gives every congregant permission to say yes to the burning desire within them to make their way to the altar.

## ACTIVE SURRENDER AND HEART COMMITMENT

The Invitation step is a simple move in which the preacher invites the congregation to make a commitment in their hearts. A commitment is being seared into the flesh of their heart that will soon find full ratification in the sacrifice of the altar. For every person who says yes to the invitation, there is an accompanying surrender of their resistance against the ongoing work and wooing of the Spirit in their lives. For many in the congregation, the location of surrender is in the very place the Spirit had been preparing their hearts in anticipation of the preacher's inspired Word.

The act of surrender is one of release, relief, and reconciliation. It's not uncommon for such moments to be infused with emotion. This doesn't need to be a surprise to anyone. Broken heartstrings, now mended, are often the fountainhead of emotional release. Sometimes people don't realize their disconnection with God until their brokenness comes into view in the presence of the preached Word. What had been lying dormant now comes to life and needs action. The Invitation step permits and compels them to surrender.

Not every sermon point will resonate with everyone in the congregation in the same way. For many preachers, they're going to connect on all cylinders. The sermon will be strong, and connections will be made to every sermon point. In some cases, with some people, the connection may be limited to one or two points of the sermon. Either way, by the time the preacher arrives at the altar portion of the service, every person has some kind of offering ready for sacrifice at the altar. Whether they come to the front of the church or stay in their seats, the invitation has been accepted, and they have something to offer.

Practically speaking, it's important for the preacher to know that the Invitation step takes place with *every main point of the sermon*. This doesn't need to be a surprise. If every main sermon point is based on a truth or a principle, then the need for invitation is obvious. As the Word, alive and active, and on mission to seek, pierce, divide, and judge, has its way in the congregation, listeners cannot escape the kerygmatic nature of the Word's demand for a response. Divine self-reflection always cries out for an invitation to respond.

## EXECUTIONER OF INTENT

There's an old maxim that says "the road to hell is paved with good intentions." Jesus uttered something similar when he said, "The gate is wide and the way is easy that leads to destruction" (Matt 7:13–14 ESV). Everyone's got good intentions, but most remain unrealized. High on such lists is the intention to get right with God, kick a bad habit, or start living a righteous life. Intentions usually fail because *there's always tomorrow.* Many fail to recognize that the absence of follow-through is not a neutral shrug or a simple delay of action; it's rebellion. Desire for a better life, even when fueled with the resolve of future immediacy, becomes the asphalt of a one-way road that leads to destruction. Intention needs action.

The Invitation step is the preacher's best friend. The preacher never needs to be apprehensive. The Invitation step is where intention meets expediency, and intent is handed over to the executioners. With the desire to take action already being fully activated, the invitation to respond to the cleansing blood of Christ, or to receive the impartation of his divine grace, is the most gracious divine executioner of good intention. There's no room for good intentions in the act of worship. There's no need for it. The notion of "Yes, I'm looking forward to making this a reality in my life soon" dies at the threshold of invitation. The time for action is now.

## EXPECTATION OF OBEDIENCE

The Invitation step is a time of response. As the Word prepares the congregation for the altar, it carries with it an expectation of obedience to the Spirit's call. The pastor's role is to lovingly and authoritatively assist the congregation in taking action in obedience. At the heart of the step is a simple yes or no from each person in the congregation. Not every sermon point will connect with everyone. Some will find that their lives are already aligned with the truth or principle of the sermon point at hand. The response in situations like this is one of gratitude for God's transformative work already at work in their lives. Others may say they're not ready for the sacrifice. Either way, the Word has accomplished its mission. Even for those who are not ready, the Word has sown a desire that will be continually watered by the Spirit.

As the pastor moves through the sermon, point by point, these responses are collected in the worshiper's heart. They're ready to bring these to the altar. They're ready to do something about it. Like Isaiah's realization of his need for grace (Isa 6), the congregation needs the burning coal of the altar brought to their lips. The Word has spoken with expectation.

## NOT RUSHED

The Invitation step also attends to the preacher's commitment to the moment. Even though the Invitation step is interrelated with the Implication and Confrontation steps and does not need belaboring, it is not rushed through to save time or to anticipate reaching the next sermon point. Time saved in such contexts is time lost. Sermons that move through the Explanation step of one sermon point only to move directly into the Explanation step of the next sermon point are at risk of losing the worship-centered purpose of the gathering. Sermons that function as such remain stuck in the lower realms of intellectual stimulation. They are in danger of leaving the congregation with information about Jesus but denying the opportunity of encounter with Jesus. That's like the food server telling you what's on the menu but not letting you order.

Cadence is the appropriate concept under consideration here. For many people, the confrontational nature of the Word demands major concessions from listeners. Since these kinds of concessions are never surrendered out of the believer's surplus, the response is truly sacrificial. Take, for example, the invitation referenced above for a sermon point addressing the Christian posture of humility, "Today is the day when a life-altering decision can be made. What's one specific area of your life where you have not yet come to Christ for help? Let go of your pride-filled self-reliance and start trusting in Christ in all things." For most listeners responding to this Invitation step, the Spirit has led them to a situation in their lives in which they have not submitted to Christ. The concession being asked is equal to Peter's first step out of the boat. The reality of the moment is thick. And even though the clarity is crisp, the moment need not be rushed. The preacher's cadence allows the rhythm of the sermon to proceed, but not without the appropriate pacing needed for proper inner response from the congregation. This is not manipulation. This is good preaching. The preacher pauses, letting the invitation hang in the air, even for just a moment or two, before moving on to the next sermon point. That's all it takes, a moment or two.

## IMPERATIVE LANGUAGE OF FINALITY

Up to this point in the model, the Implication and Confrontation steps have used questions in their delivery. The Invitation step moves away from this approach and embraces imperative language that conveys finality. The Invitation step functions more as a summons than an opportunity. As such, its delivery is authoritative and immediate. It is vital that the congregation respond affirmatively to the Confrontation in the room. The exhortation from the preacher is not a simple "What's your response?" It's a gentle statement that delivers authoritative command.

The Invitation is not a high-pressure moment. It's when the preacher's love for the people and the Spirit's work in the Word converge. The tone should be compassionate in its urgency, but never persuasive. The preacher stands here not as a salesman closing a deal but as an authoritative sheepdog ushering the flock toward the safety of its shepherd. The imperative nature of this step does not negate grace; rather, it embodies it. When the preacher says, "come," "believe," or "surrender," these words are not detached demands; they are extensions of divine mercy spoken with human affection.

The tone of finality within the Invitation step is the outworking of a crucial theological dynamic. The congregant's decision to surrender to the mission of the Word means that some kind of thought, attitude, behavior, or activity is coming to an end. Something is dying. The language of finality helps the believer come to terms with the end of what has been leading them down a path of destruction. Words such as *stop*, *turn*, *lay down*, and *put off* carry the weight of this finality. They recognize that grace not only invites us to something new but also compels us to turn from something old. The Invitation step becomes the sacred space where death to sin, self, or misplaced devotion is realized before God.

Yet this language of ending must always carry within it the hope of resurrection. The tone may bear finality, but its heart is filled with hope. The preacher's summons to *put off* makes room for the joy of *putting on* the new life in Christ. Every invitation to die is, in truth, an invitation to live more fully. So, when the preacher speaks words of finality, they must be seasoned with promise, the assurance that God never calls something to die unless he intends to raise something better in its place. Finality, then, is not despairing closure but the beginning of redemption's reordering work.

## PUTTING IT ALL TOGETHER

Every sermon point carries within it a call to action. The preacher's role is not to coerce but to curate, guiding the congregation gently yet decisively toward obedience. The language of the Invitation must sound both compassionate and final, urging immediate response without manipulation. In this holy convergence of urgency and tenderness, people prepare themselves to lay down what must die so that new life may arise. When faithfully executed, the Invitation transforms preaching from proclamation into participation, ensuring every sermon ends not with information about God but with renewed intimacy with him.

The Invitation step is crafted during the Preparation step. It is thought out and planned in advance through prayerful consideration of the Holy Spirit's direction in the sermon. The Invitation step is presupposed by the direction taken in the Implication and Confrontation steps, adding to the flow already taking shape. Below is a simple process a pastor can follow to formulate it from any expositional sermon.

### Step 1: Stay in the Flow

Get locked in to the flow already established in the Implication and Confrontation steps immediately preceding.

### Step 2: Discern the Specific Sacrifice

Ask what must be laid down to be in alignment with the truth or principle (sin, pride, procrastination, self-reliance, etc.). Also, identify the positive sacrifices of praise, gratitude, fresh obedience, etc.

### Step 3: Write a Concrete, Present-Tense Invitation

Your invitation should be:

- Imperative: Use command-driven, hope-filled language of immediacy that is specific to the direction and flow of the moment (e.g., Let go of your pride-filled self-reliance and trust in Christ today). Make it immediate (today, this moment), not someday.

- Final: Let your words carry both finality (stop, turn, lay down) and promise (so that you may walk in freedom/joy/new life).

### Step 4: Guard the Tone

Speak as an authoritative shepherd, not a salesperson. Be warm, earnest, and clear, without manipulation or shaming.

- Speak with hope, not condemnation.
- Tone: Use second-person plural (*you*) as you lead the congregation into healing.

## EXAMPLES OF INVITATION

Borrowing from the examples in the last two chapters, note the following Invitation step examples:

Passage: Eph 1:7 (ESV): "In him we have redemption through his blood, the forgiveness of our trespasses, according to the riches of his grace."

- Explanation: We have redemption through the blood of Jesus (followed by substantive teaching).
- Implication: If we have redemption through the blood of Jesus, then what does that mean about how we're still trying to earn God's grace through works?
- Confrontation: Why do we seem to waste so much time in our lives before we surrender to God's grace and receive his forgiveness?
- Invitation: This is your moment of freedom. Jesus' love for you is already finished. Lay down your need to impress him and step in to his acceptance of you.

Passage: Jonah 2:1–2 (ESV): "Then Jonah prayed to the Lord his God from the belly of the fish, saying, 'I called out to the Lord, out of my distress, and he answered me.'"

- Explanation: God answers prayers of distress (followed by substantive teaching).

- Implication: If God answers prayers of distress, then what does that say about our struggles with trusting him?
- Confrontation: What is it going to take for us to finally start placing our trust fully in Christ?
- Invitation: Today is the day to cast aside fears and apprehensions. Start trusting Jesus.

Passage: Rev 3:15–16 (ESV): "'I know your works: you are neither cold nor hot. Would that you were either cold or hot! So, because you are lukewarm, and neither hot nor cold, I will spit you out of my mouth.'"

- Explanation: Jesus is omniscient (followed by substantive teaching).
- Implication: If Jesus is omniscient, then what does that mean about the secret struggles we're trying to hide from him?
- Confrontation: How much longer are we going to reject Jesus' desire to help us with our secret struggle?
- Invitation: Your Deliverer stands at your door, knocking. Quit pretending you're not home. Open the door and give your struggle to Jesus.

## REFLECTION QUESTIONS

1. How would you describe the difference between viewing the Invitation as a moment of manipulation versus a genuine act of ministry that honors both human freedom and the Spirit's initiative?
2. Explain how the Invitation prepares the congregation for sacrifice rather than simply for intellectual application. How might this shift change the way you experience an altar call?
3. If it's true that every sermon point should include its own invitation, why do you think addressing response at each main point, rather than only at the end, might be spiritually significant?
4. Reflect on the idea that the Invitation gives permission for the human spirit to say "yes" to God. In what areas of your own life have you sensed this inner desire to respond positively?

5. Why is the posture of the preacher during the Invitation described as that of a shepherd rather than a salesperson? How might adopting this posture affect the way people respond to the call?

## APPLICATION ACTIVITIES

1. Crafting a Redemption-Focused Invitation—Craft a specific invitation for a sermon point on forgiveness based on Matt 6:14–15. Ensure it uses imperative language with finality and hope, addressing the immediate surrender of grudges. Write it out and explain how it flows from an Implication and Confrontation step.
2. Delivering an Invitation on Humility with Proper Cadence—Develop an invitation for a sermon on humility from Phil 2:3–4. Make it concrete, present-tense, and shepherd-like in tone. Practice delivering it aloud, pausing for cadence, and reflect on how it encourages active surrender without rushing.
3. Self-Recording and Reviewing Invitation Delivery—Record yourself giving a short sermon point on trust from Prov 3:5–6, including Implication, Confrontation, and Invitation. Review the recording to ensure the Invitation isn't rushed and allows space for inner response.
4. Adapting a Non-Pentecostal Application into a True Invitation—Examine a non-Pentecostal sermon and adapt one of its application points into a full Invitation step. Make it specific, imperative, and transformative, highlighting the shift from information to encounter.
5. Building a Complete Sermon Outline with Integrated Invitations—Prepare a complete sermon outline with three points from Rom 12:1–2, ensuring each includes an invitation that curates space for the Spirit's work. Practice the transitions to maintain expectant openness without coercion.

# 23

# Step Eight: Alteration

PENTECOSTAL PREACHING HAS LONG emphasized the altar portion of the worship service. The model for Pentecostal expository preaching discussed in this book does not deviate from this central emphasis of Pentecostal worship. As the model has demonstrated, the Implication, Confrontation, and Invitation steps ultimately prepare the congregation for the altar service. When referencing *the altar*, we're not bringing into view a piece of wood or a strip of carpet at the front of a sanctuary. We're talking about a consecrated margin where heaven and earth intersect. It is in this liminal space in which the cry of the heart is met with the comfort of the Spirit. In a very real and profoundly mysterious sense, the altar is the worship gathering's high-water mark.

Pentecostal worship, by its very nature, welcomes spontaneous, experiential, and demonstrative expressions often experienced in the altar service. It's not uncommon for altar services to move beyond the realm of orderly sophistication. Tears, shouts, groans, trembling, falling, prophetic utterances, and manifestations of demonic oppression are not hypothetical for us; they are part of the lived reality of Spirit-filled worship encounter.

In Old Testament liturgy, the altar was a place of sacrifice. As people approached the altar, they did so with purpose in their hearts. Obedience to the law was an expression of faith (Rom 3–4). Adherents arrived at the encounter, bringing with them the currency of the altar, the sacrifice. These would include animals, grain, wine, and thanksgiving. Pentecostal expository preaching leads the congregation to this moment of sacrifice.

The pastor's sermon helps the congregation discover and prepare the abundance of their own currency for the altar. My concern for orthodox altar theology is deeply pastoral. I am not interested in turning the altar into a tightly scripted factory line, nor in romanticizing it as a free-for-all of spiritual theatrics. I am interested in helping Spirit-filled pastors and leaders steward this sacred space with theological clarity, spiritual sensitivity, and practical wisdom. My conviction is simple: if we learn to pastor well at the altar, the fruit of our preaching will deepen, our people will be better formed, and our churches will be safer, healthier places for the Spirit to move in power.

## THE ALTAR AS CULMINATING MOMENT

The altar is the culminating moment of invitation, becoming action. Throughout the sermon, the preacher has not been merely informing minds; they have been leading people toward an encounter with God. The shepherdly guidance is a summons to concrete obedience. The altar is the place where the congregation has been brought to meet their Savior. In many ways, everything in the sermon points to this moment. The preacher has opened the text, clarified its meaning, drawn out its implications, and allowed the Word to confront the congregation. But confrontation without a space to respond is mean. It freezes people, suspending them in desire, without allowing culmination. It would be quite unloving for the preacher to leave the sheep hungry, once they've seen the Shepherd and his provision, and not usher them into his presence.

This is more than symbolic. The simple act of standing, walking the aisle, and positioning oneself at the altar is where confession finds expression in the Pentecostal movement. This is a good thing. The walk down to the altar is a confession of "God has known me, and I am responding." The obedience breaks open layers of resistance, some of which are perhaps decades old. In my own pastoral experience, I have witnessed countless people who seemed largely unmoved during the sermon finally begin to break when they crossed the invisible threshold into the altar space.

For this reason, the altar ought not to be treated as periphery or as the part of the service that makes the Spirit-filled Bible teacher nervous (me, for many years). It is the point at which the Invitation steps embedded in the sermon are allowed to find fruition in actual actions before God. The more intentionally we preach toward this culminating moment, and the more carefully we pastor within it, the more our preaching bears lasting fruit.

## SACRED, PERSONAL RESPONSE

Because of this, the altar must be understood as a sacred moment of personal response to the Word's mission. By this point in the service, the congregation is no longer simply listening to the preacher; they are standing before the Lord with the Word pressing on their own hearts and histories. The altar, in this sense, personalizes everything that has just been proclaimed. What happens at the altar is unique to every person who responds to the call. Some kneel quietly, others weep openly, some stand with hands raised, others sit in silence at the front, and others jump and shout in exaltation of deliverance. But the essential dynamic is the same; they are answering the call of the Spirit. It is one thing to nod in agreement from the safety of a pew; it is something else entirely to step forward in view of others and say, "This Word has found me. I need to meet God on this."

Never to be rushed through, pastors should not trivialize the altar portion of the service by using it as a space for announcements or chit-chat from the platform. Nor should we assume that everyone at the altar must be visibly emotional for it to be real. Some of the deepest work God does in people happens beneath the surface, in quiet, almost imperceptible exchanges between the Spirit and the human heart.

Our task as pastors is to fiercely protect this moment as sacred and holy. That means giving it time. It means curating an atmosphere that embraces honest responses, no matter the colorfulness or the quietness of the manifestations. It also means training our congregations to see the altar not as a place of shame (where everyone will know I have a problem), but as a place of honor (I am taking God seriously enough to respond). When that shift happens, the altar ceases to be a place reserved only for the desperate and becomes the normal, healthy place where believers regularly do business with God.

## CALL FOR PARTICIPATION

The altar is fundamentally a call for participation in the mission of the Word and the work of the Spirit. The call extends beyond the person's immediate needs and carries missional and congregational implications. When the Word is rightly proclaimed and the Spirit is actively moving, the natural and necessary next step is participation. The altar is the primary space where that participation finds its fullest expression. From the very beginning of the service, the Word is on mission. The Spirit is pressing that Word into minds, consciences, and hearts. By the time we reach the altar, the question is no longer "Did you understand the sermon?" but "Are you ready to surrender to that which the Spirit is beckoning in your life?" The invitation to participate in the altar is therefore not just an invitation to receive help; it is an invitation for the hearer to join the action of God in their own lives and, by extension, in the life of the church.

This participation has multiple layers. First, the person who responds to the altar call is participating in the mission of the Word by allowing it to take effect in them. The congregation does not exist as passive recipients of religious cerebralism; they are active responders to a divine summons. To step out of a row, walk forward, and stand or kneel at the altar is to say, "I am aligning myself with what the Spirit has said today. I am surrendering to his work."

Second, as people respond, the altar becomes a place where the Spirit recruits and commissions for broader participation. Many calls to ministry, evangelism, reconciliation, and sacrificial service are sealed at the altar. A young man senses the Spirit calling him to pastoral work through the preached Word; his walk to the front is the first public act of obedience to that call. A woman hears the Word confronting her bitterness; her movement to the altar is her agreement to become, by grace, an agent of forgiveness and peace. In each case, they are not merely receiving prayer; they are entering into God's outward mission in their families, workplaces, neighborhoods, and beyond.

Third, the altar invites the wider congregation to participate not only as responders but also as co-laborers with the Word and the Spirit. A trained altar team is not there to *work the altar* while everyone else watches; they are there as representatives of the body, embodying the truth that the Spirit distributes gifts to all. When a mature believer lays a hand on a shoulder, offers a Spirit-led prayer, or stands silently in intercession, they are participating in the same mission that the preached Word initiated. They become, in that moment, instruments through whom the Spirit applies the Word to another person's life.

Even those who remain in their seats are not exempt from being called to serve those who have come forward. When they worship, when they stretch out a hand in faith toward the altar, when they quietly intercede for those who have come forward, they, too, are taking up their share in the work. The entire congregation becomes a missional community under the authority of the proclaimed Word and the guidance of the Holy Spirit.

A good altar theology exposes and corrects any temptation toward consumer Christianity. It refuses to allow the congregation to remain as passive spectators or consumers. Instead, it insists that everyone present is being summoned into participation—first in their own transformation, and then in the Spirit's mission to the world. The call to the altar is, at its core, a call to join the ongoing work of the Word and the Spirit in and through the people of God.

## THE *KENOSIS* AND *THEOSIS* OF THE ALTAR

Theologically, the altar enacts the bilateral movements of *kenosis* and *theosis*. The term *kenosis*, drawn from Phil 2, speaks of self-emptying. At the altar, people come to pour out pride, pretension, self-righteousness, secret sin, and illusions of control. It is where they acknowledge that they cannot save, sanctify, or heal themselves. As they empty their hands of such sacrifices, they are better able take hold of Christ more fully.

*Theosis* speaks of participation in the life of God, being conformed to the image of Christ, and sharing in the divine nature by grace. At the altar, participation is not in the abstract. The Spirit meets people there, not simply to comfort them in their current condition, but to draw them into a deeper likeness to Jesus. As much as the altar is a place to deepen our relationship with Christ, it is also the location where divine grace is imparted. God's grace is the substance and the essence of transformation. The person who rises from the altar is, in very real ways, not the same as the one who came down.

When we understand altar ministry through this lens, our posture changes. We do not treat the altar as a place for mere emotional catharsis, nor as a mechanical fix-it station where people get quick solutions to complex lives. Instead, we see it as a focal point in the ongoing process of sanctification, where believers are repeatedly invited into this rhythm of emptying and filling, dying and rising, surrendering and being renewed.

This also means that our language at the altar should be theologically rich. We are not just saying, "Come get a blessing," but "Come lay down your life. Come die. Come receive the life of Christ in a deeper way."

## NOT EMOTIONALISM

Because the altar is often emotionally charged, we must say clearly that it is not a place for emotional manipulation when emotion becomes the goal and the measure of spiritual authenticity. In this paradigm, the louder you shout, the more you cry, the more dramatic your fall, the more anointed the moment is perceived to be. That is a dangerous distortion. When antagonists toward the Pentecostal/Charismatic movement rise to cry foul against such manipulation, they're right. When pastors embrace such manipulation, they do so at peril to themselves, their congregation, and the Pentecostal/Charismatic movement. What's worse, the foul is particularly egregious, given that the manipulation is unnecessary. The Spirit does not need this kind of illicit help.

Emotionalism is not embraced for its own sake but for the sake of responding to the sanctifying work of the Shepherd. The sinful woman at Jesus' feet illustrates the point (Luke 7). Her tears and her hair became the water and the towel for Christ's foot washing. The Pharisee's disgust at the display reflects the common cessationist response today. Jesus' embrace of the woman's emotion-laden act is our model. Her great love response flowed from her great forgiveness.

The presence of emotion is not the problem; God created us as emotional beings, and the Spirit frequently touches the emotions. Scripture, divinely inspired by the Holy Spirit, is full of emotively provocative language (see the Wisdom writings, the prophets, the writings of Paul, and many others). The problem arises when we begin to equate emotion with the Spirit's work or, worse, when we begin to manufacture emotion to simulate the Spirit's work. In altar ministry, this temptation can be subtle. A certain song, played in a certain way, with certain lights and certain language, can easily be used to push people toward a predetermined emotional outcome. It doesn't need to be this way.

As pastors, we must resist this temptation. We should absolutely use music, testimony, and exhortation to support what the Spirit is doing! We should help in every way we can. Background music, dim lighting, and the pastor's passionate appeal are wonderful in the service of the moment. But we must refuse to cross the line into manipulation. Our responsibility is to invite and to steward, not to coerce. The safest way to do this is to keep our eyes on the fruit of repentance, obedience, reconciliation, enduring freedom, deepened love for Christ and his church. These are the markers of genuine spiritual work, not how many people fell or how loudly they cried.

In practice, this means we sometimes must let a service end more quietly than our flesh might prefer. It means we do not push someone to go deeper simply to make the altar look more intense. It means we affirm the work of God in the person who stands still and remains silently at their seat, just as readily as in the one who is visibly overwhelmed. Emotional responses will come and go, and we bless God when they are real. But we anchor our assessment of the altar in transformation and order, not in theatrics.

## SACRED, TIMELESS ENCOUNTER WHERE HEAVEN MEETS EARTH

The altar is best described as a sacred, timeless encounter where heaven meets earth. In these moments, something happens that refuses to fit neatly into our normal categories of time and space. People will later say things like, "I don't know how long I was there," or "It felt like the whole room faded away and it was just God and me." This kind of language is the testimony of stepping into a genuine experience, however briefly, into the liminal intersection of realms. Scripture itself gives us such images: Jacob's ladder, Isaiah in the temple, John caught up "in the Spirit on the Lord's day" (Rev 1), and others. While our weekly altar calls are not identical to those visions, they do participate in the same framework: God chooses to meet his people in particular moments and places with particular intensity. The altar, in a Pentecostal service, is one of those sites.

This sense of sacred encounter has practical implications. It means we're careful with platform banter. It means we are careful about what we allow to happen physically in that space—no casual wandering, no joking, no side conversations. It means we cultivate an awareness among our people that when we move into the altar, we are entering a different kind of moment, one that demands reverence even when it is loud and celebratory.

At the same time, recognizing the altar as a place where heaven meets earth should humble us as pastors. We receive no credit for that which takes place there. We're in the service of our King. We are the sheepdogs bringing the flock to the Shepherd. Our authority in that space is real but stewarded. Our presence is one of deep gratitude and deep fear of the Lord, aware that we are ministering in the mysterious space of the finite and the temporal.

## PLACE OF SACRIFICE, CONFESSION, AND TRANSFORMATION

On the ground, the altar functions as a place of sacrifice, confession, and transformation. People come carrying all sorts of burdens—hidden addictions, broken relationships, gnawing anxieties, long-standing bitterness, patterns of disobedience. The invitation of the altar is to bring those things into the light and lay them down. Sacrifice, in this context, is not about earning God's favor; it is about relinquishing whatever stands in the way of obedience and intimacy. A person may come forward to surrender an ungodly relationship, to renounce a pattern of deceit, to yield a calling they have been resisting. These decisions, when made honestly at the altar, often become turning points that mark the rest of their lives.

Confession is closely tied to this. In many cases, the altar is the first place someone has ever spoken openly about a particular sin or wound. I have watched the faces of men and women as they finally say, sometimes in a whisper, "I am addicted to pornography," or "I have been unfaithful," or "I cannot forgive what was done to me." That act of acknowledgment, in the presence of God and a trustworthy pastor or altar worker, breaks the stranglehold of secrecy. For some, the immediate upshot is instant healing and deliverance. For many others, it opens the door to real healing; for others, it sets in motion a season of migration into the higher plane of spiritual existence to which the Spirit is calling.

Transformation and sanctification are the long-term fruits of these sacrificial and confessional moments. Not every transformation is dramatic or instant. Sometimes the change is gradual, unfolding over months and years. But again and again, I have seen that pivotal decisions are often made at the altar. A young person decides to answer a call to ministry. A couple chooses to fight for their marriage rather than give up. A believer bound by shame chooses to step into accountability and grace. The altar becomes, in retrospect, the point at which a life's trajectory was altered.

## PLACE OF SURRENDER AND COVENANT

The altar is also a place of surrender and covenant. Not everyone who comes forward is in crisis. Many are simply responding to the steady, sanctifying work of the Spirit. In my own congregation, a striking number of young adults regularly come to the altar during worship or preaching, not because there has been a particularly sensational appeal, but because they have learned to treat that space as the natural place to renew their surrender.

What is witnessed week after week are young men and women kneeling, often with heads bowed, sometimes with tears, sometimes in quiet stillness. I do not always know what they are saying to the Lord; often, I do not ask. I simply sense that they are laying something down or taking something up in response to God's dealings in their hearts. That rhythm of recurrent surrender is one of the healthiest signs in a church.

Covenant language helps name what is happening in moments such as these. At the altar, people are not just asking for help; they are pledging themselves afresh to God's purposes. "Lord, I give you this relationship. I give you my future. I will go where you send. I will release this offense." These are covenantal statements, even if they are not framed in formal liturgy. The Spirit uses the intensity of the moment to etch those commitments deeply into the heart.

As pastors, we can assist this process through how we pray and preach. We can frame the altar as a place not only for crisis response but also for covenant renewal. We can remind the congregation that God often seals his dealings with us in specific, remembered places. Years later, many will say, "It was at the altar in that service that I made this decision." Attending to that reality helps us steward the altar, not as a mere problem-solving station, but as a covenant-forging space in the life of the church.

## EXPECTATION OF DIVINE MANIFESTATION

Given all this, preachers should come to the altar with an expectation of divine manifestation. If God is truly meeting his people there, we should not be surprised when that encounter has visible and tangible effects. The book of Acts and the history of revival testify that when the Spirit moves, bodies and emotions are often involved. In a Pentecostal/Charismatic context, that may include tears, trembling, people being slain in the Spirit, speaking in tongues, prophetic words, deep sighs of relief, visible joy, deliverance from demonic oppression, and physical healings. These are not foreign to us; they are part of our spiritual family story. We should therefore make room for them, both the quiet and the dramatic, without embarrassment.

At the same time, this kind of expectation must be accompanied by discernment. Since not everything that happens at the altar is inherently spiritual in a healthy sense, pastors need the kind of altar-realm fluency that empowers them to intervene when necessary. Some reactions are purely emotional. Some are learned behaviors. Some may be fleshly attempts to gain attention. In a few cases, manifestations may be so disruptive as to put the anointing at risk. Our role as pastors and altar workers is to, as best we can, by Scripture, by the Spirit, and by wisdom, distinguish what is actually taking place and provide whatever assistance is needed when situations dictate it.

Such discernment requires calmness. When something unusual happens, our tone and posture from the platform will either settle the room or inflame it. If we respond with measured authority, neither panicked nor sensationalizing, we teach our people that we both honor and pastor manifestations. We acknowledge God's real work; we protect the congregation from confusion or fear; and we quietly correct what is unhelpful or unhealthy. In this way, the altar remains a place of genuine divine encounter rather than a stage for uncontrolled spectacle.

## BREAKING THE POWER OF SHAME AND SECRECY

One of the more potent functions of the altar is that it breaks the power of shame and secrecy. Shame, the primary by-product of sin, is the collateral damage from sin's presence. Shame causes a person to avoid God, avoid themselves, and avoid others. It's a fundamental lie from the devil that communicates unworthiness to receive love. It's an unavoidable, standard message of condemnation that is never divorced from sin. It affects every person touched by sin, on both sides of perpetrator and victim alike. This includes church members, leaders, and even pastors in training. Shame lives and thrives in the secret, underground, hidden pockets of our identity.

The altar is a respite-driven place where years-long conspiracies of silent shame are shattered. I have watched young women stand before a congregation and testify that God delivered them from pornography during a retreat. I have listened to young men at the altar confess that they are still struggling, but that they are choosing to step into the light and seek help. I have had pastors-in-formation sit with me after an altar time and, often with tears, finally admit that this has been their hidden battle.

In those moments, my response as a pastor and leader is crucial. If I react with shock, condemnation, or immediate disqualification, I reinforce the very shame that has kept them bound. Instead, my posturing communicates, "You are not alone. Let me walk through this with you. This conversation stays between us, unless there is some necessary exception. You are not automatically disqualified from ministry because you are in a battle, but you must be honest and accountable." I also make it clear that if they ever fall in ways that injure others or cross moral boundaries, they must tell me so we can respond appropriately. I'm not bragging here. These moments are turning points in the lives of up-and-coming pastors. They reflect the deliverance of shame and secrecy made available at the altar.

When this kind of grace-filled accountability is anchored at the altar, people begin to learn that the front of the church is not a place where they are exposed to humiliation, but a place where vulnerability seeks healing. The secrecy loses its hold; shame begins to dissipate; genuine repentance becomes possible. Over time, this shifts a church's spiritual culture. The altar becomes known not just as a place of power, but as a place of safe, honest deliverance.

## LOCATION OF THE ALTAR

As we move into the more practical aspects of the Alteration step, there are a few key details we need to consider. First, the Alteration step is more effective in time than in space. That is to say, the alteration that takes place is more a matter of moment than location. The alteration of the encounter is not dependent upon proximity to the zone, though it is enhanced by it. Jesus' healing of the centurion's servant is a prime example of this (Matt 8, Luke 7). The centurion knew Jesus could heal his servant with just a word. A personal visit from Christ to his location was not necessary. Only his Word was needed. In addition to this, the faith of which Christ spoke so glowingly to those around him was not emanating from the sick servant but from the centurion. The point is that Jesus does not need a prescribed physical meeting place for divine encounters. He needs only the faith of the one seeking the encounter, even if it's on behalf of someone else. The implication of this is that the entire sanctuary becomes the venue of divine encounter (not just the section in front of the pulpit).

Secondly, there is something to be said about taking the faith-filled move down to the altar space. The journey holds significant theological weight, effecting a physical drawing near to God (Jas 4:8). It symbolizes the surrender of the human will to God's will. It signifies cleansing and purification, marking a new beginning away from the old and into the new. It encapsulates the physical manifestation of obedience. It mirrors biblical altars as sites of sacrifice and covenant (e.g., Noah, Abraham), now fulfilled in living sacrifice and Spirit-baptism.

Coming forward is confessional. This dynamic is measured not only salvifically but also within the economy of sanctification. It makes the statement to the believing community, to God, to the world, to Satan, and to self, that the believer has been seen and known by God, and their journey to the altar is a confession of agreement. Some come down to give their life to Christ for the first time. Others are called to move their faith deeper with Christ. Others for an area where they need God to move in their life. All in confessional agreement, "You are justified in your words and blameless in your judgment" (so says David, Ps 51:4b).

The journey down to the altar also fosters a time of communal prayer, intercession, and faith. The laying on of hands among believers deepens a sense of togetherness within the body, becoming a shared evoking of the fires of faith. Practically speaking, there's more faith, actualized faith, in the altar. Many benefit from the communal expression of faith. Like the paralytic lowered through the roof, there's power in the faith of our friends.

The altar, then, is both encompassing of the sanctuary and targeted. It is the sacred convergence of time, faith, and presence where the Spirit meets humanity—sometimes at the front of the sanctuary, and sometimes in the individuality and solitude of the pew. Whether the feet move forward or remain still, the heart's movement is what matters most. Yet, when worshipers do step forward, they set in motion a visible confession of faith. The pastor's task is not merely to prompt people to come forward, but to prompt them to be active in their obedient response. In this way, the altar's location is less a measured distance from the platform and more a holy intersection of divine initiative and human response.

## PASTORAL PRESENCE: CADENCE, TEAM, AND MUSIC

All of this requires intentional pastoral presence at the altar. We cannot delegate the altar entirely to others or treat it as the after-service while we mentally clock out. The way we carry ourselves in that space teaches our people, explicitly and implicitly, how to understand what is happening. First, we must learn to discern the cadence of the moment. Some altar times are marked by exuberant celebration—shouts of praise, dancing, joy breaking out across the room. In those moments, our leadership will reflect our ability to read the room in how the Spirit is moving. At other times, the atmosphere is thick and introspective, heavy with conviction or grief. There, in lockstep with the Spirit's movement, our presence remains in flow. In either case, we are asking, "What is the Spirit doing right now, and how do I join him rather than working against him?"

Pentecostal/Charismatic preachers serve their congregation well with a trained altar team. No pastor can personally pray, counsel, and discern for every person at the altar in a growing church. It is incumbent upon us to identify and equip spiritually mature, teachable, humble, and discerning men and women. We train them in basic ministry skills—how to ask good questions, how to pray briefly and clearly, how to maintain appropriate boundaries, and how to involve us quickly when a situation is beyond their scope. We also coach them on practical matters: where to stand, how to avoid crowding, how to handle physical manifestations safely and modestly.

In addition, the church needs permission to be a healthy, multi-participatory body of believers, called to pray for one another and to exercise their spiritual gifts. The woman who offers a word of encouragement to the elderly woman on the other side of the church needs permission to faithfully deliver it during the altar time of the service. The man with a word of correction to the young adult in danger of destruction needs freedom to deliver such a word with love and grace.

The church in Corinth was overly exuberant in fulfilling these expectations, to the point that they needed help from the apostle Paul. As Paul wrote in 1 Cor 12–14, there is a requisite order that accompanies the worship service's communal charismatic phenomena. The altar becomes the appropriate space and time for participation in such charismatic expressions.

Pentecostal worship, at its best, is not a spectator sport. We are not staging a religious performance in front of the sanctuary, with spectators looking on. The New Testament picture, for example, in a city like Corinth, is that of a community gathered, with many members contributing: a word, a psalm, a prophecy, a tongue, an interpretation, an encouragement.

In the same spirit, the altar is one of the primary spaces where the body is invited to function as a body. Yes, the pastor issues the call, and yes, pastoral oversight remains crucial, but the point is not that one or two especially gifted individuals carry out all the spiritual heavy lifting. Instead, we invite the people of God to step into their own roles, coming forward for prayer, laying hands on one another when appropriately trained and authorized, interceding quietly from their seats, or standing with someone who should not stand alone. When messes occur, as they are expected in the context of a Spirit-filled church, especially with newer believers practicing their gifts, we clean them up. It's as simple as that! It's better to have a Spirit-enlivened church with occasional messes than to have a dead church with hypocritical perfection.

This has significant implications for how we structure altar ministry. If we consistently model altar times in which only the anointed are allowed to minister while everyone else remains passive, we unintentionally disciple our churches into a clergy-centered model of ministry. Conversely, when we form a healthy altar team and encourage congregational charismatic participation by allowing mature believers to come alongside others, and when we visibly honor the contributions of various gifts in that space, we teach our people that the Spirit's power is not confined to one or two individuals.

The call for participation, therefore, operates on several levels. It calls sinners to repentance, believers to deeper surrender, the wounded to healing, and the gifted to active service. In all of this, the altar becomes not just a line at the front of the sanctuary but a laboratory of participation, where the people of God learn, in real time, how to respond to the presence and voice of the Spirit.

Music is not a magic switch, but it can either support or distract from what God is doing. A worship team that knows how to follow the Spirit will shape its song choices, volume, and intensity to match the moment. Sometimes, a simple, quiet chorus repeated softly is what is needed. At other times, a strong declaration of praise helps faith rise in the room. What we must avoid is using music to manipulate emotion; instead, we use it as a safety net in which people can respond freely to the Spirit.

When pastoral presence, a healthy altar team, and wise musical leadership come together, the altar becomes a well-stewarded environment. It is neither chaotic nor sterile. It is a place where God's people can encounter him deeply, safely, and repeatedly, and where the preached Word finds its most powerful and lasting expression in the lives of the congregation.

## PUTTING IT ALL TOGETHER

This chapter began with a simple conviction: The altar is not an optional add-on to Pentecostal worship. It is the place where the preached Word, the presence of the Spirit, and the response of God's people converge in a uniquely potent way. To neglect the altar, or to mishandle it, is to squander fertile ground for transformation in the life of your church.

With the altar service being a time and place of sacrifice and confession, believers freely bring their sins, idols, fears, and wounds before the Lord. It is there that patterns of disobedience are called out, that hidden struggles come into the light, and that people choose—often with trembling—to die to self so that Christ might live more fully in them. Closely tied to this is the altar as a place of transformation, surrender, and covenant, where the *needle* of a person's spiritual life often moves the most. In those moments of kneeling, weeping, or quiet stillness, the Spirit forges bonds of intimacy and commitment that a sermon alone cannot produce.

The Pentecostal/Charismatic movement need not be ashamed of the characteristic, occasional messiness or disorderliness of the Spirit-filled worship gathering. In a movement that welcomes spiritual gifts and manifestations, the altar service embraces such visible responses: tears, shouts, falling, tongues, prophecy, and at times, even demonic exorcisms. Rather than fear these things or pursue them as ends in themselves, we noted the expediency of ordered openness. The Spirit is not the author of confusion, and yet he is not domesticated by our preferences. Our role as pastors is to make room for his work while providing wise, Scripture-shaped boundaries.

The pastor's language during the altar service is crucial, needing to flow more from posture than from script. The pastor's posture during the Alteration step is faithful steward, leading the congregation to the Shepherd. I've come to embrace a posture that exudes the following dynamics:

- The Spirit has been moving.
- The Word has probed, confronted, and invited.
- The congregation has a response.
- The altar is ready.

When these principles are embedded in the pastor's posture, the wording can flow in the moment. I often say something like, "As we move into our closing moments together, I know the Spirit has been moving on your heart this morning. I know the Word has been meddling, confronting, and inviting you. I also know that each one of you has something to say in response. As our musicians come forward, and as we move into this last song, let me ask you, what do you need to say to Jesus this morning? Some of you need to make the journey down to the altar. Don't miss your opportunity. Our altar is open, and our altar team is ready to pray with you."

The altar is the place where the Spirit often does his deepest work in the lives of God's people. Our calling as Pentecostal pastors is not merely to preach powerful sermons, but to shepherd faithfully in the moments that follow—to listen, to discern, to protect, to guide, and to participate with reverence in what God is doing. When we treat the altar with that kind of intentionality, we honor the Spirit, we bless the people, and we allow the Word we have preached to achieve its full, transforming purpose.

## REFLECTION QUESTIONS

1. How would you explain to someone unfamiliar with Pentecostal worship why the physical act of walking to the altar carries deep theological and confessional significance, even when God can meet people anywhere?
2. In what ways does viewing the altar as a place of both *kenosis* (self-emptying) and *theosis* (participation in divine life) change the way you understand your own potential responses during an altar call?
3. Reflect on a time when shame or secrecy kept you from honest response to God. How might a well-shepherded altar space help break that power, and what pastoral attitudes would make it feel safe?
4. The chapter presents the altar as the culmination of the preached Word rather than an optional ending. Why do you think leaving people in confrontation without a response space could be unloving?

5. How does the chapter's vision of the entire congregation participating in the altar ministry, whether by coming forward, praying from seats, or ministering to others, challenge consumer Christianity and call you into active mission?

## APPLICATION ACTIVITIES

1. Observing and Reflecting on a Live Altar Call—Attend a Pentecostal worship service and observe the altar call portion. Write a 500-word reflection on how the pastor shepherded the moment, noting elements of discernment, order, and participation, and suggest one improvement based on the chapter's principles.
2. Crafting a Theologically Rich Altar Invitation—Draft a sample altar invitation script for a sermon you've prepared or heard recently. Ensure it incorporates language of sacrifice, confession, and surrender, while emphasizing the altar as a space for covenant renewal rather than just crisis response.
3. Interviewing an Experienced Altar Minister—Identify and interview a mature believer in your church about their experiences ministering at the altar. Ask about qualities like boldness, restraint, and wisdom, then summarize in a one-page report how this aligns with forming an effective altar team.
4. Personal Journaling: *Kenosis* and *Theosis* at the Altar—Reflect on a personal altar experience or observe one in a service. Journal about how it embodied *kenosis* (self-emptying) and *theosis* (participation in divine life), and describe how this could deepen your own spiritual rhythms.
5. Creating Integrity Guidelines for Altar Ministry—Create a set of guidelines for physical touch and gender boundaries during altar ministry. Base it on the chapter's emphasis on integrity, and share it with a ministry leader for feedback, documenting their response.

# 24

# Application: The Tipping of a Sacred Cow

What follows is delivered with the utmost respect to our movement and to our cessationist brothers and sisters abroad. I wrote this chapter out of my deep-seated concern about an accommodation that has been made over the last several decades within the Pentecostal/Charismatic movement. The accommodation has not come without concessions. In light of this concern, I offer the following critique.

In most cessationist preaching models, application has become the gold-standard darling of every sermon. Following Paul's epistolic model of *doctrine and duty*, or *creed and conduct*, most preaching models embrace a similar, unchallenged model of *teaching followed by application*. If the sermon does not conclude with application, so we are told, it has somehow failed the congregation. The "Seven Steps to Being a Good Neighbor" must follow the teaching of the good Samaritan parable. "Five Standards for Honesty in the Workplace" should accompany the sermon on Zacchaeus's encounter with Jesus and his subsequent insistence on being honest about his fraudulent dealings with the community (Luke 19:1–10). The preacher's task is to deliver clear steps, concrete tools, and practical takeaways that people can *apply* on Monday morning.

Over time, this accommodation has solidified into a near-idolatrous sacred cow. In this chapter, the cow is examined. My proposition is not that obedience is optional or that practicality is unimportant. My proposition is that the sermon, as an act of worship, has been quietly miscast as a Christian skills workshop lecture. To recover a more faithful Pentecostal homiletic, application must be tipped from the pulpit. In its place, as elaborated throughout this text, the category of implication emerges as a healthier, more theologically honest preaching move.

## HOW APPLICATION BECAME A SACRED COW

The rise of application language is not difficult to trace. As preaching increasingly absorbed assumptions from classroom pedagogy and popular communication theory, sermons were framed as vehicles for information and instruction. Within that frame, the *so what* of the text naturally became *Now here is how you apply this.* Lists proliferated: five steps to stronger faith, four practices for better marriages, seven habits for financial freedom. The sermon's success was measured by its perceived usefulness and practicality in equipping believers to live the successful Christian life. In many circles, this emphasis hardened into a nonnegotiable expectation. The never-questioned and never-challenged assumption underlying all of this was that the primary purpose of preaching is to teach people what to do rather than to invite them to transformative encounters with Christ.

Within a Pentecostal framework, that assumption is problematic. The sermon is not a lecture inserted into the middle of a service; it is a function of the worship event. The Word is alive, on mission, and present not merely to inform but to confront, comfort, and transform. When the application becomes the unquestioned endpoint of preaching, it quietly redefines the nature of the sermon itself.

## WHY APPLICATION FEELS SO NATURAL (AND WHY THAT'S A PROBLEM)

The pull toward application is understandable. Congregants live complex lives and hunger for guidance. Preachers, out of pastoral concern, want to be as helpful and concrete as possible. Application promises to bridge the gap between text and life in a way that feels tangible. "Here is the passage; here are three things you can do this week." Everyone leaves with a sense that something practical has happened.

The difficulty is not that the action is unwelcome. Scripture consistently presses toward obedience. The difficulty is that the sermon's horizon narrows to a how-to manual, which is better suited to a discipleship framework. The pulpit becomes a distribution center for spiritual *life hacks*, and the text is pressed into the mold of whatever how-to structure the preacher favors that week. The Word suffers devaluation through its transmutation into utility, being treated like raw material for lists.

This is especially true in cessationist traditions that already treat the sermon as primarily instructional or equipping. In the example of a cessationist preacher who invites their congregation to take good notes and writes the sermon title at the top of the Sunday morning bulletin, the people have been explicitly gathered as students. As learners, not worshipers, the sermon's logic is to learn the content, write down these points, and then apply them. There is much to commend in careful teaching, but when this paradigm is imported uncritically into worship, something crucial has been lost.

## APPLICATION AS DISCIPLESHIP, NOT WORSHIP

The first step in tipping the sacred cow is to relocate application to its proper location outside the sanctuary. Respectfully, I am not contending that application is in some way heretical; in fact, the opposite is true. Application is a necessary, nonnegotiable, indispensable, valuable function of the church! What I am maintaining is that application is simply miscast when it is made the climax of what is supposed to be the worship gathering. In form and function, application belongs under the category of discipleship.

When we think about the spaces of discipleship, e.g., the classroom, the midweek study (even if it's in the sanctuary), the mentoring group, coffee shop, family room, etc., school truly is in session. There, the teacher's role is indeed to equip students: to teach them, to help them build a prayer rule, to walk through a budget, to model conflict resolution, to practice spiritual disciplines. In those contexts, saying "Here are seven practices" is not only appropriate but also the championed setting for such pedagogy.

The sanctuary, however, is not a classroom in disguise. The sanctuary is the location in which the people of God assemble to worship, to exalt Christ, to participate in the proclamation of the living Word, and to respond to the call of the Spirit's summons to the altar. In that space of divine encounter, the preacher is not a life coach distributing tools; the preacher is a herald, a witness, a servant of the Word. The sermon is not primarily about learning the Word but about being known and interpreted by the Word, apprehended by the Word, and transformed by our response to its invitation. It is on the other side of such encounters that the congregant can see clearly to comprehend the Word. Application, in the detailed, step-by-step sense, is not the central work of that moment.

## THE OBJECTIFICATION OF WORD AND CONGREGATION

One under-explored problem with application rhetoric is its tendency to objectify both the text and the congregation. When preachers stand to *apply* the Word, it is easy to speak as if the text were an instrument in hand and the congregation a set of problems to be solved. The aim is to use the Bible effectively on them.

In classroom teaching, this objectifying necessity is somewhat inherent; teaching requires students, and students are treated as receptive minds to be formed. Content from the teacher is passed on to the students. The students are the object. It's transactional. The risk in the sanctuary is that the same posture is imported into worship. The congregation becomes the primary object of the preacher's attention, the sermon becomes a strategy for improving them, and the Word is at risk of devaluation to utility.

Pentecostal homiletics insists on a different orientation. In the sanctuary, Jesus is our object of attention, not the congregation. School is not in session. The congregation is not gathered to learn about Jesus as much as to worship him. Learning may well occur, but it is subsumed within doxology. The Word is not a tool to be wielded at people but a loving, living Word on mission that interrogates the preacher and people alike. Application language, when unexamined, tends to reverse these dynamics, placing the preacher in the position of one who manages the Word and maneuvers the people.

## WHAT WE LOSE WHEN WE PREACH FOR APPLICATION

When application is treated as the necessary climax of every sermon, several losses accumulate. First, awe is diminished. If the ultimate goal of the sermon is to produce an actionable list, then the preacher is under pressure to move quickly past encounter and into management. The Word, that would otherwise evoke wonder and awe, is forced to yield to *three tidy takeaways.*

Second, the sense that God himself is addressing his people evaporates. Rather than standing under the Word as a people being interpreted, the congregation is positioned as recipients of the preacher's pseudo-ambassadorial advice. The Word stops reading us and becomes something we are supposed to *use.*

Third, in a Spirit-filled setting, the altar gets lost in takeaway. Instead of serving as a place of encounter, repentance, and commissioning, where one might experience the simultaneous weight and joy of Isaiah's "Woe is me" and "Here am I" (Isa 6), the thrust of response is abandoned to checklists of tomorrow's good living. Encounter is sacrificed to the successful execution of the list rather than the ongoing work of divine metamorphosis in worship.

## INTRODUCING IMPLICATION: A BETTER HOMILETICAL MOVE

If application is not the healthiest preaching category, what should take its place? The best Spirit-filled alternative, as presented in this model, is *implication.* Implication shifts the fundamental question. Instead of "What are three things you must do this week?" the Implication step asks, "If this text is true, what must be true about us?" The center of gravity remains the Word and how the congregation is being seen in its light. The preacher is not fashioning the Word into a how-to list; they are holding up a mirror for the congregation to see itself in truth.

This move does not eviscerate the text into a handful of prescriptions. On the contrary, it respects the breadth of the Word's reach. A single principle, such as "God is near to the brokenhearted," has countless implications for individuals, families, churches, and systems. The preacher does not, and cannot, name them all. Implication, therefore, is fundamentally humble. It acknowledges the preacher's limited vantage point and the Spirit's unlimited creativity.

## THE IF-THEN CLAUSE AND DIVINE SELF-REFLECTION

In practice, implication is often framed as an if/then clause: "If this is so, then what?" (See chapter 20). This structure is simple enough to be written directly in sermon notes. After identifying the truth or principle in the text, the preacher crafts questions that invite self-examination. "If the Lord is my shepherd, then why do I trust other voices more than his?" Or, "If we are called the light of the world, then where have we grown comfortable in the shadows?"

These questions usher the congregation into *divine self-reflection.* The Word that interpreted the preacher in the Preparation step, often leaving the preacher wrecked, convicted, and then strengthened, now turns to interpret the people in proclamation (Explanation, Implication, Confrontation, and Invitation). The Implication moment becomes the place where men and women stand in the light of a principle and measure themselves against it. The congregation is not hurried past conviction into homework. Instead, they are given space to respond inwardly, and then an invitation to respond bodily at the altar.

## IMPLICATION IN A SPIRIT-FILLED, PENTECOSTAL FRAMEWORK

Implication is not merely a stylistic preference; it is deeply rooted in Pentecostal theology of the Spirit and the Word. In Pentecostal hermeneutics, interpretation is a communion of Spirit, Word, and community. The preacher does not approach the text with purely *scientific* tools, though historical and grammatical work certainly has a voice; the preacher approaches as one who expects the Spirit to shape Word understanding in light of a Spirit-filled community's expectations.

It need not be a surprise that the same Spirit who inspired the original text, and who illuminates the text in the study, is active in the sanctuary during proclamation. When the preacher proclaims, "God is a God of the brokenhearted," that truth enters the spiritual atmosphere and begins to work on people, pressing them toward a response. Every point in the sermon is a fresh opportunity for such Spirit-driven transformation.

For the Pentecostal preacher to accommodate application is to deny the congregation the Spirit's transformative activity. Implication, by contrast, honors the Spirit's agenda. It names the necessary implications of the Word and then asks, "What does this mean about you, for you?" trusting the Spirit to customize that work in each heart.

## CURATING THE SANCTUARY: SCHOOL IS NOT IN SESSION

If I may be direct, the sanctuary is not a classroom, and worship is not school. Preachers, therefore, do well to avoid application language that triggers the student mode. One simple practice is to refrain from projecting sermon outlines, numbered lists, and subpoints on screens during Sunday worship. Those tools are invaluable in classroom contexts; however, in the sanctuary, they subtly invite people to sit back, take notes, and treat the sermon as information to be mastered. I decided many years ago that, even though the teacher in me desperately wanted the congregation to have fill-in-the-blank outlines and shnazzy screen graphics to illustrate sermon point headings, including such might tempt people to go into student mode. I opted instead for the simplicity of my attempt to curate a genuine worship gathering, with the sole focus on the worship and exaltation of Jesus Christ. I quit using them.

Language matters. When preachers make a concerted effort to transform their congregation into a worshiping one, it gradually internalizes a different posture. Congregants are trained to lean in, not merely to learn, but to participate. They are reminded that receiving the Word is itself an act of worship, not a separate component that accompanies worship through song (as the sermon is more often than not interpreted). The typical bifurcation of worship and Word need not be the norm. This protects both the preacher and the people from slipping into a teacher–student paradigm in which the goal is mastery of content and the inevitable next step is application.

## WHERE APPLICATION BELONGS AND WHERE IT DOESN'T

None of this denies the need for concrete practice! The church must form disciples whose lives are patterned after Christ in the most practical arenas: money, sexuality, speech, work, and relationships. The point is not to banish application from the life of the church, but to restore it to its proper home.

That home is discipleship. Classes, small groups, workshops, and mentoring processes are designed for exactly this kind of work of the church. There, preachers become teachers; they can bring whiteboards, handouts, and frameworks. Participants rightly receive objectified attention as students. It is entirely appropriate in those settings to say, "Here are four practices that may help you forgive," or "Let us map out together what a daily prayer rhythm might look like," or "Write these down in your handouts or notebooks."

When those same moves occupy the center of the sermon, however, the categories are confused. Tool-training invades the holy encounter. The weight room is brought out to the playing field. The kitchen is brought out to the dining room. The result is that worship is at risk and, ironically, discipleship is weakened, because people come to expect a weekly list from the pulpit rather than owning their call to seek deeper instruction in discipleship settings. A healthier pattern is to preach implication in worship and then point to spaces where practical outworking can be explored. "If this Word has stirred something in you, join the group, the class, the process where we will walk out what this looks like in detail."

## PASTORAL COURAGE: *ACTUALLY* TIPPING THE SACRED COW

Tipping the sacred cow of application will not happen accidentally. If application has worked itself into your preaching as a standard component, fear not. Tipping the cow requires intentionality and courage, but it's a simple commitment. Follow this model. Embrace the exhilaration of being a Spirit-filled preacher. Own your tradition. It's possible for you to be a proud, confident, competent, authority-filled, Spirit-filled Bible teacher, fully ensconced in what it means to be a Pentecostal homiletician and exegete. Don't be afraid of feeling exposed without the safety net of application. Decades of training and expectation do not evaporate overnight. Some congregants may respond with curiosity or pushback. Accustomed to sermons that end with numbered lists, they may initially complain that preaching has grown less practical. If such comments materialize, you have all the proof you need to move away from application in your sermons. Love them and lean into them. Encourage them to find the practicality they're seeking in the classrooms, Bible studies, and small groups being offered at your church.

Narrate your change. Explain, patiently and repeatedly, why the sermon is moving from "Here is what you all must do this week," to "If this is true, what does it mean for you?" Rejoice in the fact, and declare with passion, that the sermon is part of worship. And that even though learning happens within that worship, it is not the primary goal, and that discipleship spaces exist for detailed practical work.

Practically, this will mean writing implication questions into sermons, leaving room for silence, inviting responses at the altar, and resisting the urge to resolve everything with one more list. Over time, your congregation will embrace the shift. They will feel the weight of the Word in new ways. Altars will become places of genuine encounter. And you, having tipped the sacred cow, will rediscover the joy and freedom of proclaiming, not merely prescribing.

## REFLECTION QUESTIONS

1. How has the expectation of receiving "practical takeaways" every Sunday shaped your own posture during worship? In what ways have you noticed yourself slipping into a student mindset rather than a worshiper mindset while the Word is proclaimed?
2. Imagine a sermon that ends with an open-ended implication question instead of concrete steps. How comfortable or uncomfortable would you feel leaving the service without a clear "to-do" list, and what does that reaction reveal about your view of preaching?
3. Reflect on the idea that the living Word should interpret and confront us rather than being treated mainly as raw material for our personal improvement. Where in your own life do you tend to use Scripture more as a tool than as a divine address?
4. In what specific ways might relocating detailed application to discipleship settings (small groups, classes, mentoring) actually strengthen both worship in the sanctuary and practical growth in your Christian life?
5. How does the shift from application to implication honor the agency and creativity of the Holy Spirit in the lives of hearers? In what areas of your own heart do you need to trust the Spirit's customized work rather than relying on prepackaged instructions?

# 25

# Final Words

## TEACHING AS WORSHIP: RETURNING THE WORD TO THE ALTAR

GOOD PREACHING STILL LOOKS like what it looked like at the beginning of this book. It comes from a space of authenticity, vulnerability, and invisibility. No model, no method, no hermeneutical precision—no matter how faithful—can compensate for the absence of these postures. They are not techniques to be learned; they are dispositions to be embraced. Without them, the preacher becomes the event, the sermon becomes a performance, and worship quietly slips out the side door.

A Pentecostal approach to expository preaching that is faithful to both the Word of God and the Spirit of God is possible. But beneath that argument is a deeper conviction: that preaching itself, when rightly ordered, is an act of worship. It is not merely worship-adjacent. It is not preparation for worship. It is worship, an offering brought to the altar through the proclamation of Scripture, empowered by the Spirit, and oriented toward the exaltation of Jesus Christ.

## AUTHENTICITY REVISITED

Authenticity remains the starting gate. Preachers do not manufacture it; they steward it. God has made each preacher a certain way for a reason, and that design includes personality, intellect, temperament, experience, and calling. Pentecostal preaching does not ask the preacher to erase these things, nor does it invite the preacher to showcase them. Authenticity allows the preacher to stand fully present without standing fully exposed.

Congregations are discerning. They know when a preacher is posturing, performing, or borrowing a voice that is not their own. When authenticity is absent, trust erodes. When trust erodes, worship fractures. But when authenticity is present, the congregation leans in—not toward the preacher, but toward the exaltation of Christ being proclaimed.

Expository preaching, particularly within a Pentecostal framework, demands authenticity because the preacher cannot hide behind clever topics or emotional momentum. The text governs. The Word leads. And the preacher submits. This submission is not a weakness; it is a strength. It signals that the preacher stands under the authority of Scripture rather than over it.

## VULNERABILITY AND POWER

Vulnerability remains the great risk of the pulpit. It is also its great power. No preacher wants their limitations, struggles, or insufficiencies on display. And yet, Scripture insists that power is perfected in weakness. The Spirit does not bypass vulnerability; he inhabits it.

In Pentecostal expository preaching, vulnerability does not mean oversharing, nor does it mean turning the sermon inward. Rather, it means allowing the text to confront the preacher before it confronts the congregation. It means preaching as one who is still being taught, still being healed, still being formed by the Word.

This posture creates a sacred solidarity between preacher and people. The congregation does not merely receive the sermon; they participate in it. They pray through it. They endure sound doctrine together. They respond together. In this space, teaching ceases to be a lecture and becomes a shared act of worship.

## INVISIBILITY AND GLORY

Invisibility remains the quiet virtue that guards the pulpit. All eyes may be on the preacher, but the preacher must not become the point. The temptation toward visibility—toward self-preservation or self-exaltation—is always present. The antidote is a settled conviction that Jesus is the reason people come to church.

The invisible preacher is not forgotten; they are fulfilled. Like the master of ceremonies, they guide the moment without becoming the moment. They announce, interpret, and invite—but they do not replace the event. And the event, in the gathered church, is the worship of Jesus Christ.

Expository preaching practiced as worship insists on this invisibility. The text is foregrounded. Christ is exalted. The Spirit is trusted to work beyond the preacher's voice, notes, and timing. Ironically, it is here—when the preacher disappears—that the sermon carries the greatest weight.

## THE TEACHER RETURNED TO THE PULPIT

Throughout this book, we have traced the absence of the *didaskalos* from Pentecostal pulpits and the cost of that absence. Biblical illiteracy, doctrinal fragility, and shallow formation do not arise in a vacuum. They emerge where the teaching office has been neglected or misunderstood.

The recovery of the teacher in the pulpit is not a rejection of Pentecostal identity; it is a return to it. The Spirit who empowers proclamation also illuminates Scripture. The same Spirit who heals bodies heals minds. The *didaskalos*, empowered by the Holy Spirit, stands in the pulpit not to replace the evangelist or the pastor but to complete the fivefold witness Christ gave to his church.

When teachers preach expositionally as worship, the congregation is not merely informed—they are formed. The Word does not remain abstract; it becomes embodied. Doctrine is not endured as a burden but received as a gift that brings healing, stability, and maturity.

## THE SERMON AS SACRED MOMENT

The Pentecostal expository sermon is not a static transfer of information. It is a Spirit-led event. From passage selection to the altar, the preacher listens, submits, prepares, and responds. Preparation does not quench the Spirit; it creates space for him to move with clarity and power.

Teaching as worship insists that the sermon has a direction, a rhythm, and a telos. It moves toward Christ. It invites response. It expects transformation. The congregation is not the object of the sermon; Jesus is. The congregation is the witness, the participant, and the respondent.

## A FINAL WORD TO THE PRACTITIONER

If this book has offered anything of value, I pray it is not a technique to master but a posture to embrace. Pentecostal expository preaching requires patience, humility, discipline, and trust. It calls the preacher to lifelong learning, deep submission to Scripture, and unwavering dependence on the Holy Spirit. This path will not always be celebrated. It will not always be easy. But it is faithful.

My prayer for this book remains what it was at the beginning: that it would arrive to you out of my own authenticity, vulnerability, and invisibility. This work is not offered to make me shine. It is offered as a testimony to what I believe God is inviting the Pentecostal church to recover.

Teaching as worship is not a novelty. It was already there. It belongs at the altar. And when the Word is returned to its rightful place—exalted, proclaimed, and trusted—the Spirit will do what he has always done: bring life, healing, conviction, and glory to Jesus Christ.

May our pulpits once again be places where the Word is taught, Christ is worshiped, and the Spirit is free to move.

# Appendix A

## Pentecostal Preaching Books

### Books Referenced in Chapters 5–7

Charles T. Crabtree, *Pentecostal Preaching: Empowering Your Pulpit with the Holy Spirit* (Springfield, MO: Gospel Publishing House, 2003). Charles T. Crabtree is a pastor in the Assemblies of God denomination. He has served in executive leadership within his denomination. He has also served in leadership of several strategic missional institutions with the Assemblies of God.

Guy P. Duffield Jr., *Pentecostal Preaching* (New York: Vantage, 1957). Duffield is an Assemblies of God pastor and lecturer. His publication from 1956 is the oldest existing publication on Pentecostal preaching. The publication is a collection of lectures given at the L.I.F.E. Bible College Alumni Association.

Ray H. Hughes, *Pentecostal Preaching* (Cleveland, TN: Pathway, 1981). Ray Hughes was a Church of God pastor and evangelist. He served the Church of God denomination at various executive levels. His publication *Pentecostal Preaching*, published in 1981, came twenty-four years after Duffield's. The Pentecostal movement was in full-swing mode, and his work represents a somewhat more developed understanding of the task at hand.

John A. Lombard, *Speaking for God: A Refresher Study of Preaching Principles* (Cleveland, TN: Pathway, 1995). John Lombard has long held the distinguished title of the "go-to" guy for homiletics within the Church of God. Highly respected, Dr. Lombard is an author, professor, and leader.

Lee Roy Martin, ed., *Towards a Pentecostal Theology of Preaching* (Cleveland, TN: CPT, 2015). This publication is a collection of articles written by well-respected Pentecostal scholars related to the formulation of a Pentecostal theology of preaching.

F. J. May, *A Church of Faith, Love, and Hope: Expository Sermon Outlines from 1st and 2nd Thessalonians and Colossians* (Cleveland, TN: Self-published, 1991). For decades, F. J. May was the premier expository preacher within the Church of God (Cleveland, TN). He has a long homiletical history as a pastor and professor.

Aldwin Ragoonath, *Preach the Word: A Pentecostal Approach* (Winnipeg: Agape Teaching Ministry of Canada, 2004). Aldwin Ragoonath is a trained homiletician with special interest in Pentecostal preaching. His publication was written to assist Pentecostal preachers in becoming better at their craft.

Mark L. Williams and Lee Roy Martin, eds., *Spirit-Filled Preaching in the 21st Century* (Cleveland, TN: Pathway, 2013). This publication is a collection of essays written by many of the well-respected homileticians and leaders in the Church of God upon invitation from editors Mark Williams and Lee Roy Martin.

* For copies of my footnoted research of these texts, along with their specific contributions to this book, please see Jeff McAffee, *A Formulation and Evaluation of a Pentecostal Model for Expository Preaching* (Lusaka, Zambia: Koinonia Africa, 2022).

# Appendix B

## Significant Texts in Pentecostal Hermeneutics

### An Annotated Bibliography

Kenneth J. Archer, *A Pentecostal Hermeneutic: Spirit, Scripture and Community* (Cleveland, TN: CPT, 2009). Ken Archer (PhD, University of St. Andrews) offers the most detailed and comprehensive analysis of Pentecostal hermeneutics available at the time. He traces the historical development of early Pentecostal interpretive practices, rooted in the movement's "paramodern" ethos, its fivefold/Full Gospel narrative, and experiential spirituality, while critiquing the later adoption of modernistic historical-critical methods by Pentecostal scholars. Archer proposes a contemporary Pentecostal hermeneutic centered on a dynamic tridactic (three-way) interrelationality for biblical interpretation involving the Holy Spirit, Scripture, and the Pentecostal community.

Chris E. W. Green, *Sanctifying Interpretation: Vocation, Holiness, and Scripture* (Cleveland, TN: CPT, 2015). Green (PhD, Bangor University, Wales; DMin, Oral Roberts University) argues that Scripture is rightly understood not only through methodological precision but through a life being formed by the sanctifying work of the Holy Spirit. Interpretation, in this vision, is inseparable from discipleship, ecclesial practices, and the moral transformation of the interpreter. Drawing deeply from Wesleyan-Holiness theology, Pentecostal spirituality, and theological hermeneutics, Green challenges modern assumptions that prioritize detached objectivity. Instead, he contends that holiness—understood as participation in God's life and mission—shapes how Scripture is read, heard, and obeyed.

Jackie Johns and Cheryl Bridges-Johns, "Yielding to the Spirit: A Pentecostal Approach to Group Bible Study," *Journal of Pentecostal Theology* 1 (1992), 109–34. Jackie Johns (PhD, Southern Baptist Theological Seminary) is an experienced Pentecostal theologian and educator whose scholarship is rooted in practical theology, Bible study pedagogy, and theological interpretation within communal and Spirit-led contexts. Cheryl Bridges-Johns (PhD, Southern Baptist Theological Seminary) is a well established academic and ecumenical leader whose scholarship bridges Pentecostal identity, rigorous theological reflection, and communal interpretive practice. Her impact extends within both Pentecostal studies and broader theological conversations. This article traces four distinctive steps for Spirit-led Bible study: "Sharing Our Testimony," "Searching the Scriptures," "Yielding to the Spirit," and "Responding to the Call." This seminal work provides the foundation for robust and methodological searching of the Scriptures with, and through, Spirit-guidance, and with the ultimate goal of the participant's transformation through responding to the immediate call of the Spirit through the Word.

Craig S. Keener, *Spirit Hermeneutics: Reading Scripture in Light of Pentecost* (Grand Rapids: Eerdmans, 2016). In this text, Keener (PhD, Duke University) offers a robust and carefully argued account of how the Holy Spirit functions in the interpretation of Scripture. Arguing that responsible exegesis and Spirit-led reading belong together, Keener draws on biblical theology, early church history, global Christianity, and contemporary scholarship. Of particular value is Keener's insistence that the Spirit does not replace historical-grammatical interpretation but works through it—illuminating, applying, and sometimes challenging readers as Scripture is read in community. This work is especially helpful for preachers and pastors who seek to honor both the academic study of Scripture and the lived, Spirit-empowered experience of the believing community.

Rickie D. Moore, "A Pentecostal Approach to Scripture," in *Pentecostal Hermeneutics: A Reader*, ed. Lee Roy Martin (Leiden: Brill, 2013), 11–14. In this article, Moore (PhD, Vanderbilt) traces the theological instincts that have historically shaped Pentecostal engagement with Scripture, particularly its expectation that God continues to speak and act through the Word. Scripture is understood not merely as a source of doctrinal propositions but as a means of divine encounter that invites faith, obedience, and participation in God's ongoing work. Moore highlights the central Pentecostal conviction that Scripture is best read within a posture of expectant openness—what he describes as a readiness to encounter the same God who acted in the biblical narrative.

John Christopher Thomas, "Women, Pentecostals and the Bible: An Experiment in Pentecostal Hermeneutics," *Journal of Pentecostal Theology* 5 (1994), 41–56. In this influential article, John Christopher Thomas (PhD, University of Sheffield) offers an insightful approach in Pentecostal hermeneutics by examining how Pentecostal spirituality and experience shape the interpretation of biblical texts related to women in ministry. Rather than beginning with abstract method alone, Thomas situates interpretation within the lived faith, worship practices, and historical experiences of Pentecostal communities, especially their long-standing affirmation of women's participation in ministry. He argues that Pentecostal readings of Scripture emerge from a dynamic interaction between the biblical text, the Spirit's ongoing activity, and the community's discernment.

Amos Yong, *Spirit-Word-Community: Theological Hermeneutics in Trinitarian Perspective* (Eugene, OR: Wipf & Stock, 2006). In this text, Yong (PhD, Boston University) integrates pneumatology, metaphysics, epistemology, and Trinitarian theology to reshape hermeneutics for the twenty-first century, making it a significant constructive contribution to Pentecostal and broader theological interpretation. The book was recognized by the Society for Pentecostal Studies (Book of the Year) and has been subject to ongoing scholarly engagement, including interpretive reviews in academic journals. The book proposes that interpretation is not a solitary intellectual exercise but a relational and imaginative process involving interpretive subjects, the horizons of interpreters, the biblical and ecclesial traditions, and the surrounding world. Yong develops his concept of the "pneumatological imagination"—the Spirit-enabled cognitive and affective capacity of interpreters—as key to discerning truth and engaging Scripture faithfully in a post-foundationalist context.

## OTHER SIGNIFICANT TEXTS NOT RESOURCED IN THIS TEXT

Archer, Kenneth J., and L. William Oliverio Jr., eds. *Constructive Pneumatological Hermeneutics in Pentecostal Christianity*. New York: Palgrave Macmillan, 2016.

Grey, Jacquelyn. *Three's a Crowd: Pentecostalism, Hermeneutics, and the Old Testament*. Eugene, OR: Pickwick, 2011.

Martin, Lee Roy, ed. *Pentecostal Hermeneutics: A Reader*. Leiden: Brill, 2013.

Oliverio, L. William, Jr. *Pentecostal Hermeneutics in the Late Modern World: Essays on the Condition of Our Interpretation*. Eugene, OR: Pickwick, 2022.

———. *Theological Hermeneutics in the Classical Pentecostal Tradition: A Typological Account*. Leiden: Brill, 2012.

Philemon, Leulseged. *Pneumatic Hermeneutics: The Role of the Holy Spirit in the Theological Interpretation of Scripture*. Cleveland, TN: CPT, 2019.

Spawn, Kevin L., and Archie T. Wright, eds. *Spirit and Scripture: Exploring a Pneumatic Hermeneutic*. New York: T&T Clark, 2011.

Yong, Amos. *The Hermeneutical Spirit: Theological Interpretation and Scriptural Imagination for the 21st Century*. Eugene, OR: Cascade, 2017.

# Appendix C

## Expository Preaching Books

### Textbooks Composed from a Cessationist Perspective, Referenced in Chapter 14

Chapell, Bryan. *Christ-Centered Preaching: Redeeming the Expository Sermon*. Grand Rapids: Baker Academic, 2005.

Keller, Tim. *Preaching: Communicating Faith in an Age of Skepticism*. London: Penguin, 2016.

MacArthur, John. *Preaching: How to Preach Biblically*. Nashville: Thomas Nelson, 2005.

Mohler, Albert. *He Is Not Silent: Preaching in a Postmodern World*. Chicago: Moody, 2008.

Robinson, Haddon. *Biblical Preaching: The Development and Delivery of Expository Messages*. Grand Rapids: Baker Academic.

Stott, John. *Between Two Worlds: The Challenge of Preaching Today*. Grand Rapids: Eerdmans, 1982.

# Appendix D

## For the Professors

First, thank you for considering this text for your homiletics course. The content of this text is intentionally comprehensive. Please use or do not use any portions as you see fit.

Each chapter ends with Reflection Questions that can be used as homework. Please contact me if you would like a list of salient points to look for in students' answers. Additionally, the chapters that address the model's steps are accompanied by Application Activities. These are designed to provide students with specific, actionable, measurable activities to put the chapter's principles into practice. These are also good for homework.

Admittedly, some parts of the text may be a stretch for some undergraduate students and, as such, can be left out of consideration for your course. This, again, was by design. My aim in the text was to make it fully accessible to undergraduate students and lay pastors alike, with just enough invitation to higher-level thinking and processing to create a taste, desire, and hunger for further deepening their homiletical foundation. These would include chapters discussing Pentecostal hermeneutics (chapters 8–12 and 15).

Required readings for an eight-module course can be divided utilizing the recommendations below. I have found over the years that it is best to immediately introduce students to the model to complete the instruction with sufficient time for class sermon presentations. The required readings follow a twofold structure: the first, Exploring the Model; and the second, Exploring the Pentecostal Distinctives.

## REQUIRED READINGS RECOMMENDATION

Module One

- Exploring the Model
    - Step One: Inspiration (Chapter 16)
- Exploring the Pentecostal Distinctives
    - The Need for This Book (Chapter 1)
    - Reclaiming the Office of Teacher in the Pentecostal Pulpit (Chapter 2)

Module Two

- Exploring the Model
    - Step Two: Preparation (Chapter 17)
- Exploring the Pentecostal Distinctives
    - Different Types of Sermons (Chapter 3)
    - What Is a Pentecostal Expository Sermon? (Chapter 13)
    - Definition Comparisons (Chapter 14)

Module Three

- Exploring the Model
    - Step Three: Introduction (Chapter 18)
- Exploring the Pentecostal Distinctives
    - The Minister's Call (Chapter 4)
    - Purpose of Pentecostal Preaching (Chapter 5)

Module Four

- Exploring the Model
    - Step Four: Explanation (Chapter 19)
- Exploring the Pentecostal Distinctives
    - Method Behind the Pentecostal Approach (Chapter 6)
    - Identity of the Pentecostal Sermon (Chapter 7)

Module Five

- Exploring the Model
    - Step Five: Implication (Chapter 20)
    - Application: The Tipping of a Sacred Cow (Chapter 24)
- Exploring the Pentecostal Distinctives
    - The Scientific Approaches (Chapter 8)
    - The Spirit-Filled Approach (Chapter 9)

Module Six

- Exploring the Model
    - Step Six: Confrontation (Chapter 21)
- Exploring the Pentecostal Distinctives
    - Spirit Dependency (Chapter 10)
    - Word on Mission (Chapter 11)
    - Communal Conditioning (Chapter 12)

Module Seven

- Exploring the Model
    - Step Seven: Invitation (Chapter 22)
    - Step Eight: Alteration (Chapter 23)
- Exploring the Pentecostal Distinctives
    - The Silent Infrastructure Co-Delivering Congregational Interpretation (Chapter 15)

Module Eight

- In-Class Sermon Presentations

## RUBRIC INFORMATION

Using your own scales or point values, the following criteria can be plugged into any rubric-generator or form:

| Step | Descriptor |
|---|---|
| Inspiration | Sermon passage/topic clearly received through discernment and spiritual sensitivity; reflects Pentecostal openness to prophetic "locations" (prayer closet, Lamp Stand, pastor's office, newsstand, and mirror). |
| Preparation | Sermon demonstrates solid commitment to the four sermon preparation steps of adoration, observation, interrogation, and interpretation. |
| Introduction | Introduction intentionally bridges the posture of worship from song to Word. Connectors utilized (story, citation, statistics, questions). Kept congregation engaged and in a posture of worship. |
| Explanation | Key concepts, words, and principles are explained accessibly; proclamation is clear, contextualized, and relevant to the congregation. Illustrations: Use of personal, historical, contemporary, or biblical illustrations; illustrations illuminate rather than distract from the Word. |
| Implication | Sermon draws out personal and congregational implications of the text; encourages divine self-reflection and application. Uses if/then clause. |
| Confrontation | The Word confronts sin, attitudes, and excuses with prophetic clarity; preacher exercises pastoral authority with grace and truth. Uses five Ws (who, what, when, where, why or how). |
| Invitation | Immediate call to action. Uses imperative language to invite congregation into decisive commitment. |
| Alteration | Clear, Spirit-led call to response and transformation; altar moment is sacred, is participatory, and expects divine manifestation. |

For any questions, comments, and access to other resources, please visit mcaffeeresources.com or contact me at jeff.mcaffee@mcaffeeresources.com.

# Bibliography


Achtemeier, Paul J., ed. *Harper's Bible Dictionary*. San Francisco: Harper and Row, 1985.

Anderson, Robert M. *Vision of the Disinherited: The Making of American Pentecostalism*. New York: Oxford University Press, 1979.

Aquinas, Thomas. *Summa Theologica*. Christian Classics Ethereal Library. https://www.ccel.org/ccel/a/aquinas/summa/cache/summa.pdf.

Archer, Kenneth J. *A Pentecostal Hermeneutic: Spirit, Scripture and Community*. Cleveland: CPT, 2009.

Augustine. *City of God*. In *Nicene and Post-Nicene Fathers, First Series, Vol. 2*, edited by Philip Schaff; translated by Marcus Dods. Buffalo, NY: Christian Literature, 1887. https://www.newadvent.org/fathers/120108.htm.

———. *On Christian Doctrine*. In *Nicene and Post-Nicene Fathers, First Series, Vol. 2*, translated by James Shaw. Buffalo, NY: Christian Literature, 1887. Rev. and ed. for New Advent by Kevin Knight. https://www.newadvent.org/fathers/12024.htm.

Bauer, David R., and Robert A. Traina. *Inductive Bible Study: A Comprehensive Guide to the Practice of Hermeneutics*. Grand Rapids: Baker Academic, 2014.

Calvin, John. *Commentary on Galatians and Ephesians*. Grand Rapids: Christian Classics Ethereal Library, n.d. https://ccel.org/ccel/c/calvin/calcom41/cache/calcom41.pdf.

———. *The Institutes of the Christian Religion*. Translated by Henry Beveridge. Grand Rapids: Christian Classics Ethereal Library, 1845. https://ccel.org/ccel/c/calvin/institutes/cache/institutes.pdf.

Catholic Church. "Code of Canon Law: Book III, The Teaching Function of the Church." https://www.vatican.va/archive/cod-iuris-canonici/eng/documents/cic_lib3-cann747-755_en.html.

Chapell, Bryan. *Christ-Centered Preaching: Redeeming the Expository Sermon*. Grand Rapids: Baker Academic, 2005.

Cox, Harvey. *Fire from Heaven: The Rise of Pentecostal Spirituality and the Reshaping of Religion in the Twenty-First Century*. Reading, MA: Addison Wesley, 1995.

Dickinson, Emily. "Hope Is the Thing with Feathers (254)." Poets.org. https://poets.org/poem/hope-thing-feathers-254.

Easton, Matthew George, ed. *Easton's Bible Dictionary*. 3rd ed. New York: Scriptura, 2015.

Edwards, Jonathan. *A Treatise on Religious Affections*. Monergism. https://www.monergism.com/thethreshold/sdg/edwards/A%20Treatise%20on%20Religious%20Affecti%20-%20Jonathan%20Edwards.pdf.

———. *The Works of President Edwards, in Four Volumes with Valuable Additions and a Copious General Index, and a Complete Index of Scripture Texts*. Vol. 3. New York: Robert Carter and Brothers, 1879.

Frank, Anne. *The Works of Anne Frank*. Garden City, NY: Doubleday, 1959.

Fuhr, Richard Alan, and Andreas J. Köstenberger. *Inductive Bible Study: Observation, Interpretation, and Application Through the Lenses of History, Literature, and Theology*. Nashville: B&H Academic, 2016.

Fulks, Jeffrey, et al. *State of the Bible USA 2022: Research from the American Bible Society*. Philadelphia: American Bible Society, 2022. https://1s712.americanbible.org/state-of-the-bible/stateofthebible/State_of_the_bible-2022.pdf.

———, et al. *State of the Bible USA 2025: Research from the American Bible Society*. Philadelphia: American Bible Society, 2025. https://www.americanbible.org/wp-content/uploads/2025/04/SOTB-2025-04-Final.pdf.

Gear, Spencer D. "Where Are the Expositors in Pentecostal-Charismatic Churches?" *Truth Challenge* (blog), Dec. 25, 2013. https://www.truthchallenge.one/blog/2013/12/25/where-are-the-expositors-in-pentecostal-charismatic-churches/.

Gee, Donald. *The Ministry Gifts of Christ*. Springfield, MO: Gospel Publishing House, 1930.

Green, Chris E. W. *Sanctifying Interpretation: Vocation, Holiness, and Scripture*. Cleveland, TN: CPT, 2015.

Hall, Steve. *The Uniqueness and Danger of Ministry: A Soul Health Manual for the Minister and Their Family*. Eugene, OR: Wipf & Stock, 2025.

Heidegger, Johann Heinrich. *The Office of the Doctor*. Translated by Steven Dilday. Central, SC: From Reformation to Reformation Translations, 2016.

Johns, Jackie, and Cheryl Bridges-Johns. "Yielding to the Spirit: A Pentecostal Approach to Group Bible Study." *Journal of Pentecostal Theology* 1 (1992) 109–34.

Johnson, Todd M. "Protestants Around the World." Gordon-Conwell Theological Seminary, July 22, 2020. https://www.gordonconwell.edu/blog/protestants-around-the-world/.

Johnston, Chris. "Muhammad Ali's Best Quotes: Float Like a Butterfly, Sting Like a Bee." *The Guardian*, June 4, 2016. https://www.theguardian.com/sport/2016/jun/04/muhammad-ali-greatest-quotes-sting-butterfly-louisville-lip.

Keener, Craig S. *Spirit Hermeneutics: Reading in Light of Pentecost*. Grand Rapids: Eerdmans, 2016.

Keller, Tim. *Preaching: Communicating Faith in an Age of Skepticism*. London: Penguin, 2016.

Klein, William W., et al. *Introduction to Biblical Interpretation*. Rev. and exp. ed. Nashville: Thomas Nelson, 2004.

Kosmin, Barry A., and Ariela Keysar. *Religion in a Free Market: Religious and Non-Religious Americans, Who, What, Why, Where*. Ithaca, NY: Paramount Market, 2006.

Land, Stephen J. *Pentecostal Spirituality: A Passion for the Kingdom*. Cleveland, TN: CPT, 2010.

Leigh, Ronald W. *Direct Bible Discovery*. Nashville: Lifeway Christian Resources, 1982.

Lew, Alan. *This Is Real and You Are Completely Unprepared: The Days of Awe as a Journey of Transformation*. New York: Back Bay, 2003.

Lightfoot, J. B., trans. *The Martyrdom of Polycarp*. http://www.earlychristianwritings.com/text/martyrdompolycarp-lightfoot.html.

———. *The Shepherd of Hermas*. http://www.earlychristianwritings.com/text/shepherd.html.

Luther, Martin. "An Open Letter to the Christian Nobility: Proposals for Reform, Part 3." In *Works of Martin Luther: With Introductions and Notes, Vol. 2*, translated by C. M. Jacobs. Philadelphia: Holman, 1915. http://www.projectwittenberg.org/pub/resources/text/wittenberg/luther/web/nblty-07.html.

MacArthur, John, and The Master's Seminary Faculty. *Preaching: How to Preach Biblically*. Nashville: Thomas Nelson, 2005.

———. *Rediscovering Expository Preaching: Balancing the Science and Art of Biblical Exposition*. Nashville: W Publishing, 1992.

Magruder, Jeff C. "Why Pentecostals Don't Preach Expository Sermons." *Enrichment*, Spring 2010. https://enrichmentjournal.ag.org/Issues/2010/Spring-2010/Why-Pentecostals-Dont-Preach-Expository-Sermons.

Martin, Lee Roy. "Fire in the Bones: Pentecostal Prophetic Preaching." In *Towards a Pentecostal Theology of Preaching*, edited by Lee Roy Martin, 34–63. Cleveland, TN: CPT, 2015.

McAffee, Jeff. *A Formulation and Evaluation of a Pentecostal Model for Expository Preaching*. Lusaka, Zambia: Koinonia Africa, 2021.

Mohler, R. Albert, Jr. *He Is Not Silent: Preaching in a Postmodern World*. Chicago: Moody, 2008.

Moore, Rickie D. "A Pentecostal Approach to Scripture." In *Pentecostal Hermeneutics: A Reader*, edited by Lee Roy Martin, 11–14. Leiden: Brill, 2013.

Mother Teresa. "Mother Teresa's Quotes—On the Family Life." Mother Teresa Center of the Missionaries of Charity. https://www.motherteresa.org/mother-teresa/quotes.

Murphy, Caryle. "The Most and Least Educated Religious Groups." Pew Research Center, Nov. 4, 2016. URL no longer available.

Osborne, Grant R. *The Hermeneutical Spiral: A Comprehensive Introduction to Biblical Interpretation*. Rev. and exp. ed. Downers Grove, IL: IVP Academic, 2006.

Osmer, Richard Robert. *A Teachable Spirit: Recovering the Teaching Office in the Church*. Louisville: Westminster/John Knox, 1990.

Our Catholic Faith. "Canon Law: The Teaching Office of the Church." https://ourcatholicfaith.org/canon-law-the-teaching-office-of-the-church/.

Perrin, Norman. *What Is Redaction Criticism?* Eugene, OR: Wipf & Stock, 2002.

Pew Research Center. "Global Christianity—A Report on the Size and Distribution of the World's Christian Population." Dec. 19, 2011. https://www.pewresearch.org/religion/2011/12/19/global-christianity-exec/.

Piper, John. *Expository Exultation: Christian Preaching as Worship*. Wheaton, IL: Crossway, 2018.

Powell, Mark Allan. *What Is Narrative Criticism?* Minneapolis: Fortress, 1991.

Richards, Lawrence O. *The Expository Dictionary of Bible Words*. Grand Rapids: Zondervan, 1985.

Roberts, Alexander, and James Donaldson, trans. *The Didache*. http://www.earlychristianwritings.com/text/didache-roberts.html.

Robinson, Haddon. *Biblical Preaching: The Development and Delivery of Expository Messages*. Grand Rapids: Baker Academic, 2025.

Scheck, William. "Lawrence Sperry: Genius on Autopilot." HistoryNet, Nov. 15, 2017. https://historynet.com/lawrence-sperry-autopilot-inventor-and-aviation-innovator/.

Sharp, Granville, et al. *Remarks on the Uses of the Definitive Article in the Greek Text of the New Testament: Containing Many New Proofs of the Divinity of Christ, from Passages Which Are Wrongly Translated in the Common English Version*. London, 1803. https://archive.org/details/remarksonusesofdoosharrich/page/2/mode/2up.

Smietana, Bob. "LifeWay Research: Americans Are Fond of the Bible, Don't Actually Read It." Lifeway, Apr. 25, 2017. https://lifewayresearch.com/2017/04/25/lifeway-research-americans-are-fond-of-the-bible-dont-actually-read-it/.

Smith, William. *Smith's Bible Dictionary*. Revised by F. N. Peloubet and M. A. Peloubet. Peabody, MA: Hendrickson, 2018.

Stetzer, Ed. "The Epidemic of Bible Illiteracy in Our Churches: How Small Groups Can Change the Statistics." *Christianity Today*, June 1, 2015.

Stott, John. *Between Two Worlds: The Challenge of Preaching Today*. Grand Rapids: Eerdmans, 1982.

Strong, James. *Strong's Exhaustive Concordance of the Bible: Updated Edition*. Peabody, MA: Hendrickson, 2007.

Taylor, Justin. "Agassiz and the Fish." The Gospel Coalition, Nov. 16, 2009. https://www.thegospelcoalition.org/blogs/justin-taylor/agassiz-and-the-fish/.

Thayer, Joseph Henry. *Thayer's Greek-English Lexicon of the New Testament: Coded with Strong's Concordance Numbers*. Peabody, MA: Hendrickson, 2019.

Thomas, John Christopher. "Women, Pentecostals and the Bible: An Experiment in Pentecostal Hermeneutics." *Journal of Pentecostal Theology* 5 (1994) 41–56.

Thomas, Robert L., ed. *New American Standard Exhaustive Concordance of the Bible: Hebrew-Aramaic and Greek Dictionaries*. Nashville: Holman Bible, 1981.

*Time Magazine*. "Barth in Retirement." May 31, 1963. https://time.com/archive/6831843/barth-in-retirement/.

Timmerman, Daniel. *Heinrich Bullinger on Prophecy and the Prophetic Office (1523–1538)*. Göttingen: V & R Academic, 2015.

Vine, W. E. *Vine's Expository Dictionary of Old and New Testament Words*. Edited by Merrill F. Unger and William White Jr. Nashville: Thomas Nelson, 1985.

Verbrugge, Verlyn D., ed. *The NIV Theological Dictionary of New Testament Words: An Abridgment of New International Dictionary of New Testament Theology*. Grand Rapids: Zondervan, 2000.

Wesley, John. *Explanatory Notes upon the New Testament: Ephesians*. London, 1767.

———. *The Letters of the Rev. John Wesley, A.M.* Edited by John Telford. 8 vols. London: Epworth, 1931.

———. "Notes on St Paul's Epistle to the Ephesians." Wesley Center Online. https://wesley.nnu.edu/john-wesley/john-wesleys-notes-on-the-bible/notes-on-st-pauls-epistle-to-the-ephesians/#Chapter+IV.

———."The Sermons of John Wesley—Sermon 15: The Means of Grace." Wesley Center Online. https://wesley.nnu.edu/john-wesley/the-sermons-of-john-wesley-1872-edition/sermon-16-the-means-of-grace/.

———."The Sermons of John Wesley—Sermon 115: The Ministerial Office." Wesley Center Online. http://wesley.nnu.edu/john-wesley/the-sermons-of-john-wesley-1872-edition/sermon-115-the-ministerial-office/.

———. *The Works of John Wesley*. Vol. 29, *Letters V (1774–1781)*. Edited by Randy L. Maddox. Nashville: Abingdon, 2023.

Wikipedia. "Educational Attainment in the United States." https://en.wikipedia.org/wiki/Educational_attainment_in_the_United_States#cite_ref-PewResearch_41-0.

Yong, Amos. *Spirit-Word-Community: Theological Hermeneutics in Trinitarian Perspective*. Eugene, OR: Wipf & Stock, 2002.

Youngblood, Ronald F., et al., eds. *Nelson's New Illustrated Bible Dictionary: An Authoritative One-Volume Reference Work on the Bible, with Full-Color Illustrations*. Nashville: Thomas Nelson, 1995.

Zodhiates, Spiros, ed. *The Complete Word Study New Testament: With Parallel Greek*. Chattanooga, TN: AMG Publishers, 1992.

www.ingramcontent.com/pod-product-compliance
Lightning Source LLC
LaVergne TN
LVHW020522100826
845148LV00010B/1306

*9781666779561*